CANADIAN POLITICAL PARTIES

This is Volume 13 in a series of studies commissioned as part of the research program of the Royal Commission on Electoral Reform and Party Financing

CANADIAN
POLITICAL
PARTIES
LEADERS,
CANDIDATES AND
ORGANIZATION

~

Herman Bakvis
Editor

Volume 13 of the Research Studies

ROYAL COMMISSION ON ELECTORAL REFORM
AND PARTY FINANCING
AND CANADA COMMUNICATION GROUP –
PUBLISHING, SUPPLY AND SERVICES CANADA

DUNDURN PRESS
TORONTO AND OXFORD

© Minister of Supply and Services Canada, 1991
Printed and bound in Canada
ISBN 1-55002-109-5
ISSN 1188-2743
Catalogue No. Z1-1989/2-41-13E

Published by Dundurn Press Limited in cooperation with the Royal
Commission on Electoral Reform and Party Financing and Canada
Communication Group – Publishing, Supply and Services Canada.

Canadian Cataloguing in Publication Data

Main entry under title:
Canadian political parties

(Research studies ; 13)
Issued also in French under title: Les Partis politiques au Canada.
ISBN 1-55002-109-5

1. Political parties – Canada. I. Bakvis, Herman, 1948–   . II. Canada.
Royal Commission on Electoral Reform and Party Financing. III. Series:
Research studies (Canada. Royal Commission on Electoral Reform and Party
Financing) ; 13.

JL195.C35 1991   324.271   C91-090525-8

#29.95

Dundurn Press Limited
2181 Queen Street East
Suite 301
Toronto, Canada
M4E 1E5

Dundurn Distribution
73 Lime Walk
Headington
Oxford, England
OX3 7AD

CONTENTS

FIGURES

TABLES

2. ATTITUDES OF LIBERAL CONVENTION DELEGATES TOWARD PROPOSALS FOR REFORM OF THE PROCESS OF LEADERSHIP SELECTION

3. CANDIDATE NOMINATION IN CANADA'S NATIONAL POLITICAL PARTIES

4. PARTIES AND PARTY GOVERNMENT IN ADVANCED DEMOCRACIES

6. THE NEW DEMOCRATS, ORGANIZED LABOUR AND THE PROSPECTS OF ELECTORAL REFORM

FOREWORD

THE ROYAL COMMISSION on Electoral Reform and Party Financing was established in November 1989. Our mandate was to inquire into and report on the appropriate principles and process that should govern the election of members of the House of Commons and the financing of political parties and candidates' campaigns. To conduct such a comprehensive examination of Canada's electoral system, we held extensive public consultations and developed a research program designed to ensure that our recommendations would be guided by an independent foundation of empirical inquiry and analysis.

The Commission's in-depth review of the electoral system was the first of its kind in Canada's history of electoral democracy. It was dictated largely by the major constitutional, social and technological changes of the past several decades, which have transformed Canadian society, and their concomitant influence on Canadians' expectations of the political process itself. In particular, the adoption in 1982 of the *Canadian Charter of Rights and Freedoms* has heightened Canadians' awareness of their democratic and political rights and of the way they are served by the electoral system.

The importance of electoral reform cannot be overemphasized. As the Commission's work proceeded, Canadians became increasingly preoccupied with constitutional issues that have the potential to change the nature of Confederation. No matter what their beliefs or political allegiances in this continuing debate, Canadians agree that constitutional change must be achieved in the context of fair and democratic processes. We cannot complacently assume that our current electoral process will always meet this standard or that it leaves no room for improvement. Parliament and the national government must be seen as legitimate; electoral reform can both enhance the stature of national political institutions and reinforce their ability to define the future of our country in ways that command Canadians' respect and confidence and promote the national interest.

In carrying out our mandate, we remained mindful of the importance of protecting our democratic heritage, while at the same time balancing it against the emerging values that are injecting a new dynamic into the electoral system. If our system is to reflect the realities of Canadian political life, then reform requires more than mere tinkering with electoral laws and practices.

Our broad mandate challenged us to explore a full range of options. We commissioned more than 100 research studies, to be published in a 23-volume collection. In the belief that our electoral laws must measure up to the very best contemporary practice, we examined election-related laws and processes in all of our provinces and territories and studied comparable legislation and processes in established democracies around the world. This unprecedented array of empirical study and expert opinion made a vital contribution to our deliberations. We made every effort to ensure that the research was both intellectually rigorous and of practical value. All studies were subjected to peer review, and many of the authors discussed their preliminary findings with members of the political and academic communities at national symposiums on major aspects of the electoral system.

The Commission placed the research program under the able and inspired direction of Dr. Peter Aucoin, Professor of Political Science and Public Administration at Dalhousie University. We are confident that the efforts of Dr. Aucoin, together with those of the research coordinators and scholars whose work appears in this and other volumes, will continue to be of value to historians, political scientists, parliamentarians and policy makers, as well as to thoughtful Canadians and the international community.

Along with the other Commissioners, I extend my sincere gratitude to the entire Commission staff for their dedication and commitment. I also wish to thank the many people who participated in our symposiums for their valuable contributions, as well as the members of the research and practitioners' advisory groups whose counsel significantly aided our undertaking.

Pierre Lortie
Chairman

INTRODUCTION

THE ROYAL COMMISSION'S research program constituted a comprehensive and detailed examination of the Canadian electoral process. The scope of the research, undertaken to assist Commissioners in their deliberations, was dictated by the broad mandate given to the Commission.

The objective of the research program was to provide Commissioners with a full account of the factors that have shaped our electoral democracy. This dictated, first and foremost, a focus on federal electoral law, but our inquiries also extended to the Canadian constitution, including the institutions of parliamentary government, the practices of political parties, the mass media and nonpartisan political organizations, as well as the decision-making role of the courts with respect to the constitutional rights of citizens. Throughout, our research sought to introduce a historical perspective in order to place the contemporary experience within the Canadian political tradition.

We recognized that neither our consideration of the factors shaping Canadian electoral democracy nor our assessment of reform proposals would be as complete as necessary if we failed to examine the experiences of Canadian provinces and territories and of other democracies. Our research program thus emphasized comparative dimensions in relation to the major subjects of inquiry.

Our research program involved, in addition to the work of the Commission's research coordinators, analysts and support staff, over 200 specialists from 28 universities in Canada, from the private sector and, in a number of cases, from abroad. Specialists in political science constituted the majority of our researchers, but specialists in law, economics, management, computer sciences, ethics, sociology and communications, among other disciplines, were also involved.

In addition to the preparation of research studies for the Commission, our research program included a series of research seminars, symposiums and workshops. These meetings brought together the Commissioners, researchers, representatives from the political parties, media personnel and others with practical experience in political parties, electoral politics and public affairs. These meetings provided not only a forum for discussion of the various subjects of the Commission's mandate, but also an opportunity for our research to be assessed by those with an intimate knowledge of the world of political practice.

These public reviews of our research were complemented by internal and external assessments of each research report by persons qualified in the area; such assessments were completed prior to our decision to publish any study in the series of research volumes.

The Research Branch of the Commission was divided into several areas, with the individual research projects in each area assigned to the research coordinators as follows:

F. Leslie Seidle	Political Party and Election Finance
Herman Bakvis	Political Parties
Kathy Megyery	Women, Ethno-Cultural Groups and Youth
David Small	Redistribution; Electoral Boundaries; Voter Registration
Janet Hiebert	Party Ethics
Michael Cassidy	Democratic Rights; Election Administration
Robert A. Milen	Aboriginal Electoral Participation and Representation
Frederick J. Fletcher	Mass Media and Broadcasting in Elections
David Mac Donald (Assistant Research Coordinator)	Direct Democracy

These coordinators identified appropriate specialists to undertake research, managed the projects and prepared them for publication. They also organized the seminars, symposiums and workshops in their research areas and were responsible for preparing presentations and briefings to help the Commission in its deliberations and decision making. Finally, they participated in drafting the Final Report of the Commission.

On behalf of the Commission, I welcome the opportunity to thank the following for their generous assistance in producing these research studies – a project that required the talents of many individuals.

In performing their duties, the research coordinators made a notable contribution to the work of the Commission. Despite the pressures of tight deadlines, they worked with unfailing good humour and the utmost congeniality. I thank all of them for their consistent support and cooperation.

In particular, I wish to express my gratitude to Leslie Seidle, senior research coordinator, who supervised our research analysts and support staff in Ottawa. His diligence, commitment and professionalism not only set high standards, but also proved contagious. I am grateful to Kathy Megyery, who performed a similar function in Montreal with equal aplomb and skill. Her enthusiasm and dedication inspired us all.

On behalf of the research coordinators and myself, I wish to thank our research analysts: Daniel Arsenault, Eric Bertram, Cécile Boucher, Peter Constantinou, Yves Denoncourt, David Docherty, Luc Dumont, Jane Dunlop, Scott Evans, Véronique Garneau, Keith Heintzman, Paul Holmes, Hugh Mellon, Cheryl D. Mitchell, Donald Padget, Alain Pelletier, Dominique Tremblay and Lisa Young. The Research Branch was strengthened by their ability to carry out research in a wide variety of areas, their intellectual curiosity and their team spirit.

The work of the research coordinators and analysts was greatly facilitated by the professional skills and invaluable cooperation of Research Branch staff members: Paulette LeBlanc, who, as administrative assistant, managed the flow of research projects; Hélène Leroux, secretary to the research coordinators, who produced briefing material for the Commissioners and who, with Lori Nazar, assumed responsibility for monitoring the progress of research projects in the latter stages of our work; Kathleen McBride and her assistant Natalie Brose, who created and maintained the database of briefs and hearings transcripts; and Richard Herold and his assistant Susan Dancause, who were responsible for our research library. Jacinthe Séguin and Cathy Tucker also deserve thanks – in addition to their duties as receptionists, they assisted in a variety of ways to help us meet deadlines.

We were extremely fortunate to obtain the research services of first-class specialists from the academic and private sectors. Their contributions are found in this and the other 22 published research volumes. We thank them for the quality of their work and for their willingness to contribute and to meet our tight deadlines.

Our research program also benefited from the counsel of Jean-Marc Hamel, Special Adviser to the Chairman of the Commission and former

Chief Electoral Officer of Canada, whose knowledge and experience proved invaluable.

In addition, numerous specialists assessed our research studies. Their assessments not only improved the quality of our published studies, but also provided us with much-needed advice on many issues. In particular, we wish to single out professors Donald Blake, Janine Brodie, Alan Cairns, Kenneth Carty, John Courtney, Peter Desbarats, Jane Jenson, Richard Johnston, Vincent Lemieux, Terry Morley and Joseph Wearing, as well as Ms. Beth Symes.

Producing such a large number of studies in less than a year requires a mastery of the skills and logistics of publishing. We were fortunate to be able to count on the Commission's Director of Communications, Richard Rochefort, and Assistant Director, Hélène Papineau. They were ably supported by the Communications staff: Patricia Burden, Louise Dagenais, Caroline Field, Claudine Labelle, France Langlois, Lorraine Maheux, Ruth McVeigh, Chantal Morissette, Sylvie Patry, Jacques Poitras and Claudette Rouleau-O'Toole.

To bring the project to fruition, the Commission also called on specialized contractors. We are deeply grateful for the services of Ann McCoomb (references and fact checking); Marthe Lemery, Pierre Chagnon and the staff of Communications Com'ça (French quality control); Norman Bloom, Pamela Riseborough and associates of B&B Editorial Consulting (English adaptation and quality control); and Mado Reid (French production). Al Albania and his staff at Acart Graphics designed the studies and produced some 2 400 tables and figures.

The Commission's research reports constitute Canada's largest publishing project of 1991. Successful completion of the project required close cooperation between the public and private sectors. In the public sector, we especially acknowledge the excellent service of the Privy Council unit of the Translation Bureau, Department of the Secretary of State of Canada, under the direction of Michel Parent, and our contacts Ruth Steele and Terry Denovan of the Canada Communication Group, Department of Supply and Services.

The Commission's co-publisher for the research studies was Dundurn Press of Toronto, whose exceptional service is gratefully acknowledged. Wilson & Lafleur of Montreal, working with the Centre de Documentation Juridique du Québec, did equally admirable work in preparing the French version of the studies.

Teams of editors, copy editors and proofreaders worked diligently under stringent deadlines with the Commission and the publishers to prepare some 20 000 pages of manuscript for design, typesetting and printing. The work of these individuals, whose names are listed elsewhere in this volume, was greatly appreciated.

Our acknowledgements extend to the contributions of the Commission's Executive Director, Guy Goulard, and the administration and executive support teams: Maurice Lacasse, Denis Lafrance and Steve Tremblay (finance); Thérèse Lacasse and Mary Guy-Shea (personnel); Cécile Desforges (assistant to the Executive Director); Marie Dionne (administration); Anna Bevilacqua (records); and support staff members Michelle Bélanger, Roch Langlois, Michel Lauzon, Jean Mathieu, David McKay and Pierrette McMurtie, as well as Denise Miquelon and Christiane Séguin of the Montreal office.

A special debt of gratitude is owed to Marlène Girard, assistant to the Chairman. Her ability to supervise the logistics of the Commission's work amid the tight schedules of the Chairman and Commissioners contributed greatly to the completion of our task.

I also wish to express my deep gratitude to my own secretary, Liette Simard. Her superb administrative skills and great patience brought much-appreciated order to my penchant for the chaotic workstyle of academe. She also assumed responsibility for the administrative coordination of revisions to the final drafts of volumes 1 and 2 of the Commission's Final Report. I owe much to her efforts and assistance.

Finally, on behalf of the research coordinators and myself, I wish to thank the Chairman, Pierre Lortie, the members of the Commission, Pierre Fortier, Robert Gabor, William Knight and Lucie Pépin, and former members Elwood Cowley and Senator Donald Oliver. We are honoured to have worked with such an eminent and thoughtful group of Canadians, and we have benefited immensely from their knowledge and experience. In particular, we wish to acknowledge the creativity, intellectual rigour and energy our Chairman brought to our task. His unparalleled capacity to challenge, to bring out the best in us, was indeed inspiring.

Peter Aucoin
Director of Research

PREFACE

THE RESEARCH PROGRAM of the Commission has as one of its primary foci the internal life and organization of Canadian political parties. Part of the mandate of the Commission is to examine, and to make recommendations on, the nature of internal party processes and the effectiveness with which the parties handle their responsibilities and their obligations to be fair and open toward both their own members and the public at large.

The selection of national party leaders and of candidates in constituencies, and the structure and management of party organizations all represent important and, in recent years, often controversial responsibilities of political parties. These are also responsibilities that have received little study. Given current debates, it is important to gather new data and stimulate fresh insights into them, particularly given calls for reform of political parties both within and outside the parties. For these reasons six separate studies on the internal dynamics of Canadian parties were undertaken on behalf of the Commission.

Two studies, by Keith Archer and George Perlin on the New Democratic Party (NDP) and the Liberal party respectively, probe the workings of leadership campaigns and leadership conventions. Both parties held leadership conventions during the tenure of the Commission and hence these presented ideal opportunities to examine the leadership selection process directly.

Leadership conventions have become controversial in recent years, particularly within the two largest parties, the Progressive Conservatives and the Liberals. The spectre of escalating costs involved in the mounting of an effective campaign for the leadership of a major party, and the tactics sometimes used by leadership contenders or their supporters to recruit delegates at selection meetings of constituency associations, have raised important questions about the need for reform. As Archer notes in his study, many of these problems have been addressed in the NDP by imposing strict expenditure limits on leadership candidates and by direct subsidization of many of the costs they incur. He also examines some proposals for change contemplated for future conventions, such as the direct election of the party leader by the membership at large, a method presently used by the Parti québécois and the Progressive Conservative parties in Ontario and Prince Edward Island and being considered seriously by the federal Liberal party. He discusses the advantages and disadvantages of such innovations as well as the limitations of the NDP's current practices. One of his findings, however, based on a survey of delegates to the 1989 convention, was that NDP delegates were resistant to regulation of leadership contests through government regulations or by an outside body.

George Perlin, in his study of 1990 Liberal leadership convention delegates, using a survey questionnaire specially designed to tap views about the need for reform, points to some of the fundamental dilemmas facing political parties and their memberships. A surprisingly high proportion of delegates agreed that public confidence in the leadership selection process is low. Reforms, in the shape of limits on expenditures by leadership candidates, controls over the selection of delegates and direct election of party leaders by the whole membership, were seen as necessary to restore confidence. The issue of whether the implementation and enforcement of these controls and limits should be achieved through government regulation or left to the parties themselves drew a mixed response from Liberal delegates. While delegates expressed considerable support for reform, they tended to resist specific forms of government intervention, such as having a government agency run leadership conventions directly. At the same time, a clear majority of delegates (63 percent) accepted the principle that the internal affairs of political parties should be "subject to at least partial regulation by public law" given the important public responsibilities of political parties.

In brief, the studies by Archer and Perlin show that members of at least two of the political parties support reform of the leadership selection process, particularly the Liberals, in order to promote greater public confidence in the selection process and in political parties as a whole. At the same time, NDP and Liberal delegates are ambivalent about the role that government should be expected to play in implementing and enforcing new regulations governing the internal affairs of political parties, organizations that have largely regarded themselves as private entities. The issue of public funding of leadership conventions and campaigns also evokes ambivalent responses from delegates. What the Perlin study in particular does show, however, is that within at least the Liberal party there is acceptance of the fact that the public dimensions and responsibilities of parties, and the need to restore public confidence in parties, may well require at least partial or indirect regulation of their internal affairs by government.

The call for the regulation of party activities has also arisen in connection with one of the more critical functions of political parties – the recruitment and selection of candidates at the constituency level. In the present era of media-oriented politics and campaigning, it is common wisdom that the major parties tend to be dominated by the party leader and her or his close advisers and that this "team" tends to be dominant in each party. One of the contributions of the study by Kenneth Carty and Lynda Erickson lies in demonstrating that the candidate selection processes and outcomes are controlled almost completely by constituency associations of the parties, and that these associations have been able, for the most part, effectively to resist interventions by national parties in the selection process. In other words, control by party élites is far from complete, and the bifurcation between the national party apparatus on the one hand and the constituency associations on the other can act as a source of tension and conflict within the parties.

Nomination contests have been a source of controversy in recent years. Instant party memberships, the use of questionable tactics in mobilizing particular communities or special interests and the expenditure of considerable sums of money by candidates are all examples of practices that may need to be regulated. In the case of expenditures, for example, it is possible for candidates to spend far more in winning the nomination than in the actual election itself. It has also been argued that the closed nature of many local associations and inconsistencies in the rules, as well as financial considerations, make it difficult for women and members of visible minorities to obtain nominations. Carty and Erickson provide unique and, in many ways, surprising evidence on many of these issues. They note that the majority of nominations are either uncontested or uncompetitive and that the number of high profile contests involving considerable expenditures of money and mobilization of members are relatively limited and concentrated in a few urban centres. They also note, however, that women tend to face greater competition than men when they place their names in contention and, furthermore, that the lack of standard rules and the informality of the process may contribute to "a veil of ignorance about it that intimidates and excludes outsiders."

Thus, formalization of the process and adoption of specific regulations may be desired not so much in order to control excesses but rather to ensure the appearance of fairness, to promote greater and more meaningful participation by party members and, by making the whole process more visible, to encourage the recruitment of nontraditional candidates. Carty and Erickson conclude that, given the considerable variation in how rules are applied from constituency to constituency, and even in the rules themselves, and the apparent inability of the political parties to enforce national standards or initiate changes, a new balance between local control and national parties may need to be struck.

The organization and structure of political parties, their capacity to mobilize members and, at election time, voters and the broad role played by political parties in any given society is examined in the study on party government by William Chandler and Allan Siaroff and the study on party structures by Réjean Pelletier.

In Canada, in common with most democracies but in contrast to the United States, we have party government. Citizens cast their ballots largely on the basis of political parties; the winning party or parties, singly or in coalition, form the government; in this position they are able to govern and to implement their program so long as they enjoy the confidence of the popularly elected legislature. Party government, as Chandler and Siaroff note, has distinct implications for party organization. It tends to make parties more cohesive and internally centralized. At the same time, the social and political context leads to considerable variation in the form of party organization. They identify three basic contexts: the Westminster parliamentary model operative in Britain, Canada, Australia and New Zealand; the one-party-dominant system found in Sweden and Japan; and coalition systems found in most continental European systems. In the latter two cases, parties tend to be quite potent, having strong roots in and penetrating many important institutions in society, although in coalition systems the power of any individual party tends to be constrained by the presence of other parties in the coalition. In particular, in countries like Germany political parties not only serve electoral purposes but also engage in extensive educational and policy-development activities in between elections through well-established and funded "party foundations."

In contrast, under the Westminster system, parties tend to be considerably weaker: their standing in society is lower; their links with societal groupings and their capacity to structure the vote are limited and they have a much more limited organizational structure, one that revolves mainly around the need to conduct electoral campaigns. Between elections, the role of Canadian parties, for example, is decidedly limited. Applying these insights to the Canadian party system, Chandler and Siaroff stress the implications of that type of relatively weak party organization: the lack of professional staff and in-house expertise means that parties play only a minimal role in policy formulation and implementation. By default, private interest groups are in a much better position to pre-empt political parties in terms of influencing government policy, which in the long run can undermine the basic principles of party government – representation and accountability.

Many of these same themes, as well as the gulf identified by Carty and Erickson between grassroots-level constituency associations on the one hand and central party bureaucracy on the other, resurface in the study on party structure by Réjean Pelletier. He notes how Canadian political parties are essentially oligarchies. Power rests with party leaders and their advisers and, to a lesser extent, with the executive and steering committees of the parties and the parliamentary caucus. In the case of policy development in political parties Pelletier, confirming points made by Chandler and Siaroff, notes that Canadian party structures are designed neither to handle the task of systematic examination of policy nor to allow the involvement of the rank-and-file in this process.

The exception, according to Pelletier, lies with the local associations during nomination time. It is at this level "that rank-and-file autonomy is most apparent and that decentralization most evident." Associations jealously guard their autonomy; party headquarters in turn are loath to interfere, even though in theory (and in law) the party leader can formally withhold his or her approval of the candidate's nomination. What is striking, however, is that this influence on the part of local associations is of short duration. Once the nomination process is complete, control reverts to central party headquarters. Furthermore, when the party is in power, even the party bureaucracy becomes less important. Under those circumstances, according to a senior party official interviewed by Pelletier, "Everything seems to happen on the Hill, originating with the Prime Minister's Office and the regional ministers."

One of the more telling deficiencies of party structure, and of party life, in Canada concerns the state of lethargy into which all parties lapse between elections, and the fact that there are no mechanisms to permit the involvement of the rank-and-file, particularly at the constituency level, in the affairs of the party. As one party official interviewed by Pelletier stated: "If everyone who works on an election arrived on our doorstep tomorrow morning, three years away from an election ... we wouldn't know what to do with them." Here lies one of the more fundamental challenges facing Canadian political parties: integrating Canadians into the internal life and organization of the parties on a systematic and ongoing basis.

The final study, by Keith Archer, examines the unique relationship between the New Democratic Party and organized labour. The NDP is the only one of the major parties to have a formal linkage with another organization, an arrangement that involves financial support for the party, the guarantee of labour representation in forums such as leadership conventions and the party's internal decision-making bodies, and influence over the party's policies. There are at least two issues at stake in this sometimes controversial relationship between labour and the NDP. First, there is the issue of equity among parties. Does the NDP gain an unfair advantage in having the consistent support of a large organization representing the interests of a substantial proportion of the Canadian population? Second, are labour's interests represented adequately in the political system? On the basis of interviews with key officials in different labour unions and in the NDP, and a review of comparative experience, Archer answers "no" to the first question and "yes" to the second. Overall, he argues, the influence of labour on NDP policies is much exaggerated. In addition, as long as certain safeguards remain in place – namely that the party's structures are open and visible, that decisions by unions to become involved in political and community affairs are democratically arrived at and that individual union members retain the right to opt out of paying affiliation fees – both the electorate and trade unionists can judge for themselves whether the relationship is appropriate.

These six studies do not exhaust all aspects relating to the internal life of Canadian political parties. They do, however, bear on what are considered to be among the more important functions and rudiments of political parties: recruitment and selection of party leaders, selection of party candidates, distribution of power and influence within political parties, the internal capacity of parties to handle responsibility for policy development under the system of party government, and representation of outside interests within internal governing structures of parties. The specific studies and findings relate to Canadian political parties and were intended to help inform the deliberations of the Commission in areas such as candidate selection and party finance. The findings and analyses have implications that go well beyond Canadian parties, however. They constitute valuable contributions to our understanding of the internal dynamics of all political parties, and the explicit comparative approach of most of the researchers should facilitate the widespread dissemination of their insights.

Volume 13 forms part of the Commission's publication program, reflecting the importance that the Royal Commission on Electoral Reform and Party Financing attached to original research activities to support its deliberations and recommendations.

As with any multifaceted research undertaking, the completion of this volume, one of 23, is due in no small measure to the help and cooperation of several individuals. To begin, I would like to thank the authors of the research studies, first, for agreeing to contribute their knowledge and expertise, in many instances on short notice, and second, for their cooperation in meeting the deadlines that the exigencies of the Commission imposed. Their task entailed not simply crafting the research studies but also making presentations to the Commission and at research seminars, and responding to requests for information during the time that the Commission's report was being prepared.

Several other individuals in universities, political parties, government and the nongovernment sector assisted by acting as peer reviewers and participants at the research seminars, or by simply being available as resource persons when crucial information was needed on specialized topics. Their willingness to give freely of their time is much appreciated. In particular I would like to thank Grant Amyot, Donald Blake, Kenneth Carty, William Chandler, Jane Jenson, Richard Johnston, Hugh Thorburn and Steven Wolinetz, who willingly shared their time and wisdom on several occasions throughout the life of the Commission.

In addition, I gratefully acknowledge the excellent help and support received from the staff at the Commission in Ottawa and Montreal. They include Paulette LeBlanc, Hélène Leroux, Lori Nazar and Liette Simard, who ensured that the flow of research studies between the coordinator, the researchers and the reviewers moved along appropriate channels and in an expeditious fashion; Richard Herold and Susan Dancause, custodians of the Commission's library; Kathleen McBride, the information system specialist; and Eric Bertram, Peter Constantinou, Keith Heintzman, Hugh Mellon and Donald Padget, the research analysts of the Commission, who spent many late hours preparing background material as well as a number of the research studies. The work of one individual in particular, David Mac Donald, assistant research coordinator with the Commission, proved invaluable in numerous ways, but especially during the preparation of presentations based on the research for consideration by the Commission. To each and every one of them, I would like to extend my appreciation for a job well done.

Finally I would like to express my gratitude to the director of research, Peter Aucoin, the Commissioners, Pierre Fortier, Robert Gabor,

William Knight and Lucie Pépin, and, above all, the Chairman, Pierre Lortie, for the opportunity of working with them and for sharing with me their erudition and experiences concerning that most fascinating of all worlds – the internal workings and dynamics of political parties.

Herman Bakvis
Research Coordinator

CANADIAN POLITICAL PARTIES

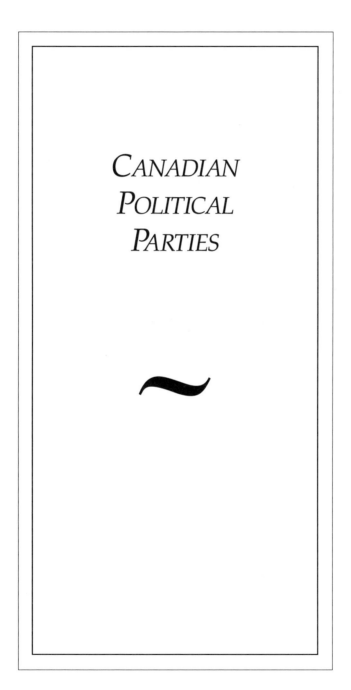

1

LEADERSHIP SELECTION IN THE NEW DEMOCRATIC PARTY

Keith Archer

T HE SELECTION OF party leaders in Canada provides a critical juncture in a party's ongoing development. The relative instability of partisan preferences in Canada, and the increasing reliance on the electronic media to provide political information, have increased the importance of party leaders in shaping the size and contours of a party's base of support (Clarke et al. 1991, 107; Archer 1987). In addition, although all the major parties now have in place a process by which the rank-and-file members are able to review their leader's performance (Wearing 1988a), and ultimately to replace him or her, the fact remains that leaders of the Liberals and New Democrats especially, and to a lesser extent the Conservatives, have tended to hold their positions for long periods of time (Whitehorn 1985, 199).

The rise in importance of the leadership selection process has led to a greater scholarly interest in describing and explaining the way in which party leaders are chosen (see, among others, Smiley 1968; LeDuc 1971; Courtney 1973; Krause and LeDuc 1979; Perlin 1988). However, to date the leadership selection process in the New Democratic Party (NDP) has not been subject to the same level of scholarly inquiry as has recently characterized leadership conventions of the Liberals and Conservatives (but see Morley 1991). Indeed, of the three NDP conventions that selected new leaders prior to 1989, in only one (1971) were the convention delegates surveyed, and in that case the survey instrument was of relatively modest scope (Brodie 1985).

This study attempts to contribute to a fuller understanding of the leadership selection process in the NDP by examining the attitudes and behaviour of delegates to the 1989 leadership convention. The primary data source is a mailed survey questionnaire sent to all delegates in the months immediately following the convention.[1] These data have been supplemented by materials acquired at the convention, by personal interviews with key party officials and by materials obtained through the party office and national archives. Together, they will be used to answer five questions pertaining to the leadership selection process in the NDP:

1. Who are the delegates to NDP leadership conventions, and how are they chosen?
2. What rules does the party use in selecting a leader, and what effect do these rules have on the outcome of the contest? Would different decision rules, such as a Borda count or transferable vote, change the outcome of the convention?
3. What factors determined how delegates would cast their vote over four ballots? Did individuals of different delegate categories (constituency, federal council, central labour, etc.) vote for different candidates, or were other factors more important?
4. How did the party deal with the issue of financing a leadership contest? How much money did the candidates spend, and what role did the party play in setting limits and monitoring campaign expenditures?
5. Was the 1989 leadership convention a success? How did the delegates evaluate this convention, what were its strengths and what were its weaknesses? Should there be fundamental changes to the process of selecting a leader in the NDP?

In answering these questions, an attempt will be made to compare the situation in the NDP with that in the Liberal and Conservative parties. In doing so, the context will be provided to evaluate the degree of conformity or diversity that has developed in the selection of party leaders in Canada, a process that has evolved slowly over time, and one that has developed for the most part outside of the legislative environment.

WHO ARE THE DELEGATES?

Parties vary in the amount of decision-making power held by their parliamentary versus extra-parliamentary wings. Formally, final authority over policy making is held by the national executive for the Conservative party, and by the national convention for the Liberals and New Democrats (Wearing 1988a, 194). Although the Conservatives occasionally hold policy conventions, the primary purpose of conventions is to select party leaders. The Liberals debate policy at conventions more regularly than do the Conservatives, but the leader especially, and caucus to a lesser extent, has considerable latitude to take positions that are at odds with policy developed at convention. As with the Conservatives, the major responsibility of conventions of the Liberal party is to choose a leader.

The NDP takes more seriously its constitutional provision vesting final control over policy in the convention. All NDP conventions are characterized by lengthy debates over matters of policy, and the party publicizes and circulates its official policy manual based on resolutions passed at convention. This is not meant to imply that the party-in-Parliament has no ability to step gingerly around party policy, as it did in 1987 with the help of federal council in modifying its position on NATO. Rather, it suggests that the composition of party conventions is even more important in the NDP than in the other major parties.

Another important difference, at least formally, between the NDP and the other major parties is the way in which leadership contests arise. Both the Liberal and Conservative parties hold a leadership convention on the death or resignation of their sitting leader, or if a leadership convention is called by a party convention following a leadership review (see Wearing 1988a, 195). In the NDP, in contrast, a leadership vote is held at each biennial convention, and is a regular and mandatory part of the convention agenda. As Courtney (1973, 184–85) argues, however, the difference between the NDP and the Liberals and Conservatives on this matter is of more formal than practical significance. In fact, no incumbent leader of the NDP has ever faced a serious challenge over his or her leadership at convention (but see Whitehorn 1985, 199), and on more than one occasion a leader of the CCF or NDP was convinced to stay on as party leader after expressing the intention of resigning (Courtney 1973, 184–85). Nonetheless, there was nothing in the NDP's formal structure that made the 1989 convention different from the 1987 convention. The difference was that in the interim period, Mr. Broadbent, as the sitting leader, resigned. In a formal sense, all NDP conventions are leadership conventions. In practice, it is a short order of business unless challengers emerge, and to date no serious contender has challenged an incumbent.

The representational basis of NDP conventions differs in a number of important ways from that of the Liberals and Conservatives. The latter two parties, for example, feature approximately 18 delegate categories (Courtney and Perlin 1988, 127), and as many as one-quarter of the delegates are ex-officio (Stewart 1988, 156). Ex-officio delegates, who are non-elected, are members of the national and provincial executives, privy councillors, MPs, senators, candidates for office and representatives of provincial parties, among others.

In contrast, the NDP has only six delegate categories, and relies on membership criteria to a greater extent than either of the other parties. Table 1.1 illustrates convention representation at selected NDP conventions between 1969 and 1989. Members of caucus and federal council (who number approximately 130 (see Archer 1990, 29)) are the only ex-officio delegates, and make up approximately 6 to 10 percent of all delegates. Constituency delegates make up approximately two-thirds of delegates, by far the largest group, followed by affiliated unions, usually numbering 20 percent or less. Members of affiliated unions were present at party conventions of the CCF in the 1940s and 1950s, and their position at conventions was continued with the creation of the NDP.

The nature of constituency representation in the NDP is quite different from that of the Liberals and Conservatives and is, at least in part, a consequence of having unions affiliated with the party. The Liberals and Conservatives each award equal convention representation to every constituency in the country. The NDP awards one delegate position to every 50 constituency members for the first 200 members, and one delegate for every 100 members thereafter (Courtney 1986, 109). Constituencies in which the party is strong, and that have a large membership, receive more delegates than those in which membership is small. Although one might question the rationale of effectively penalizing those areas of the country where the party is weak, such as all the provinces east of Ontario, nonetheless it is a system that responds to and counterbalances the representation of affiliated unions based on the size of the union.

Table 1.1
Attendance at federal NDP conventions by delegate status (selected years)
(percentages)

Delegate status	1969	1971	1973	1975	1981	1987	1989
Constituency	61.3	56.1	70.9	66.4	72.0	64.7	68.6
Federal council	8.6	5.3	6.8	6.4	7.2	8.5	4.7
Caucus	1.6	1.2	1.8	1.0	1.9	1.7	1.4
Youth	5.3	5.1	0.7	0.4	1.5	2.7	2.3
Central labour		2.7	4.0	5.0	3.8	5.2	4.6
Affiliated unions	23.2*	29.6	15.7	20.8	13.6	17.3	18.4
N	(1 016)	(1 755)	(1 042)	(1 474)	(1 368)	(1 391)	(2 510)

Source: Archer and Whitehorn (1990b).
*Includes central labour and affiliated unions in 1969.

The affiliates receive one delegate for each 1 000 members of the union, or major fraction thereof who have not "opted out" of affiliation.[2] Although some complain of the "double representation" of unionists – through their union and as individual party members through their constituency association – nonetheless this arrangement was of central importance in bringing labour into a closer relationship with the party at its founding in 1961.

The party also allocates delegate positions to central labour organizations and to members of the New Democratic Youth. The delegates from central labour include representatives of district, regional or national labour bodies (such as provincial federations of labour or the Canadian Labour Congress), as well as the head offices of national labour unions (such as the Canadian Auto Workers (CAW)) or the Canadian head offices of international unions (such as the United Steel Workers of America (USWA)). When central labour delegates are combined with delegates from affiliated unions, total union delegates usually make up one-sixth to one-quarter of all delegates.[3] The New Democratic Youth (NDY) organization is awarded delegates on the same basis as constituencies (Wearing 1988a, 203), and constitutes a relatively modest component (about 2 percent) of total convention delegates.[4]

The way in which delegate positions are awarded in the NDP has given the party's convention a strong regional character. Table 1.2 presents data on the distribution of delegates at the 1989 convention across the delegate categories. These are broken down by province according to three criteria – the number of delegates to which each group was entitled, the number who registered at the convention and the number who responded to the survey questionnaire.

Note the strong skewing of delegates from the West and, to a lesser extent, from Ontario. Well over half (56.3 percent) of the constituency delegates entitled to attend the convention were from the four western provinces, and a further 27.5 percent were from Ontario. In contrast, Quebec was allocated only 9.2 percent of constituency delegates, and the four Atlantic provinces had only 5.4 percent among them. It has been suggested that the city in which the convention is held has a strong effect on the regional distribution of delegates (Whitehorn and Archer 1989). These data lend partial support to that finding. As the 1989 convention was held in Winnipeg, delegates most likely to attend were from Manitoba (168 of 171 eligible delegates actually registered), and there was strong attendance from all of the western provinces. Attendance also was strong from Ontario (93.2 percent), but dropped off dramatically in Quebec (35.7 percent). In addition, with the exception

Table 1.2
Distribution of delegate types at 1989 NDP convention

Delegate category	Number of delegates in percentages		
	Delegate entitlements	Registered delegates	Survey respondents
Federal council	4.4	4.7	4.8
Caucus	1.3	1.4	1.2
Constituency			
British Columbia	11.4	14.2	15.3
Alberta	5.5	6.6	8.5
Saskatchewan	12.7	13.9	13.1
Manitoba	5.4	6.7	7.5
Ontario	17.1	20.2	23.3
Quebec	5.7	2.6	1.5
New Brunswick	1.1	1.1	1.1
Nova Scotia	1.2	1.6	2.2
Prince Edward Island	0.1	0.1	0.1
Newfoundland	0.9	0.5	0.7
Yukon	0.4	0.5	0.7
Northwest Territories	0.5	0.6	0.6
Young New Democrats	1.9	2.3	3.6
Central labour	5.3	4.6	2.7
Affiliated organizations	24.9	18.4	7.0
(Other responses)			5.8
Total	99.8	100	99.7
N	(3 193)	(2 510)	(1 060)

Note: Percentage may not add to 100 due to rounding.

of Newfoundland, attendance remained strong across the Atlantic region, and was very strong from the North.

The regional distribution of convention delegates in the NDP contrasts sharply with that of both the Liberals and Conservatives. The latter two parties provide for an equal number of delegates from each constituency, regardless of the party's strength in the constituency. The nonconstituency delegates, of course, are not subject to the same provision, and thus can provide for some regional distortion. For example, if campus clubs are stronger in one region or province, the result will be more delegates overall from that province or region. Nonetheless, the regional distribution of Liberal and Conservative delegates more accurately reflects the population distribution in Canada. For example, in 1983, 29 percent of Conservative delegates were from Ontario, 24 percent were from Quebec, 28 percent were from the West, 17 percent were from the Atlantic region and 1.5 percent were from the territories. The corresponding figures for the Liberal party in 1984 were 30 percent from Ontario, 25 percent from Quebec, 28 percent from the West, 16 percent from the Atlantic region and 2 percent from the North (Courtney and Perlin 1988, 129–30).

Factors other than region also shape the contours of NDP convention representation. The category to which a delegate belonged was of greater importance in determining delegate attendance than convention location. As one might expect from the exuberance of youth, delegates of the NDY were the most likely to attend, and fully 95.0 percent of all eligible NDY delegates attended the convention. They were followed, in turn, by delegates from constituencies (87.0 percent), federal council (84.9 percent) and caucus (83.7 percent). In contrast, union delegates are much less likely to attend party conventions, even those which are scheduled to choose a new leader. Only two-thirds of the potential delegates from central labour registered at the convention, and even fewer (57.9 percent) did so from affiliated unions.

The same factors can be seen to influence survey response. Whereas approximately 47 percent of all delegates contacted answered the questionnaire, response rates were highest among the youth delegates, and lowest among the delegates from Quebec and from organized labour. As is typical in surveys of NDP conventions, the response rate was very low among union delegates who, although they comprise 18.4 percent of delegates, made up only 7.0 percent of survey respondents. The survey also saw a low response rate among Quebec delegates.[5] Otherwise, the response rate from most provinces was strong, as it was among the remaining categories of delegates.

Several generations of research on political élites in Canada, including legislators and party activists, have revealed some very consistent biases in their sociodemographic profile compared with those they purport to represent (see, for example, Porter 1965; Kornberg et al. 1979). The profile of a typical political activist is a well-educated, middle-aged professional man from one of the two Charter language groups at a middle or upper middle income level. Recent data on Liberal and Conservative conventions have corroborated these general findings, with two major caveats – there has been a significant increase in the proportion of convention delegates who are women, and an increase in the number of delegates under 30 years of age. For example, 45 percent of 1990 Liberal delegates were women, and 40 percent were under 30 (Perlin 1991). For 1983 Conservative delegates,

37 percent were women and 40 percent were under 30 (Wearing 1988a, 202–204).

In general, the sociodemographic profile of delegates to NDP conventions is consistent with the more general finding on party activists, with several caveats. The most important of these is the difference between delegates from the union movement – both central labour and affiliated organizations – and all other delegates. Recalling Porter's findings of a quarter century ago, the labour delegates overall had a substantially lower socio-economic status than other delegates (see table 1.3). For example, whereas almost three in five (57.6 percent) non-union delegates had one or more university degrees, only one in six union delegates had completed university. Similarly, whereas almost half (46.3 percent) of non-union delegates were employed as professionals or managers, less than one-quarter (22.8 percent) of union delegates were similarly employed. On the other hand, almost half (45.5 percent) of the union delegates had blue-collar occupations, compared with only 5.8 percent of non-union delegates. The educational and occupational differences among union and non-union delegates also have a relation to family income levels, although the link is neither strong nor linear. Non-union delegates are more likely to be found among the lower income families (under $40 000) and among the higher income families (over $60 000) than were union delegates, who tended to cluster in the middle income category ($40 000 to $60 000).

The Ontario and western Canadian bias among convention delegates is reinforced by the presence of union delegates. Almost two-thirds of the union delegates are from Ontario (65.7 percent) and another 29.4 percent are from the four western provinces. In contrast, no union delegates in the sample were from Quebec and about 5 percent were from the Atlantic provinces and the territories. The very small representation from Quebec – which has continued to mark the NDP as different from the Liberals and Conservatives – has had a predictable effect on the linguistic distribution. Only 1.7 percent of respondents stated that French was their home language.

On the representation of women and youth, the NDP has moved closer to the Liberals and Conservatives in the proportion of women delegates, but continues to have a small number of young delegates. Once again, differences can be seen among union and non-union delegates. For example, 36.8 percent of the convention delegates in 1989 were women, compared with 33.0 percent in 1987 and 31 percent in 1983 (Archer and Whitehorn 1990b; Whitehorn 1985). Among non-union delegates, 39.5 percent were women, a figure comparable to that obtained at Liberal and Conservative conventions. Among union

Table 1.3
Selected social background characteristics by delegate status

| | | Delegate status in percentages | | |
		Non-union	Union	Total
A. Region	West	59.0	29.4	56.0
	Ontario	30.0	65.7	33.7
	Quebec	2.4	0.0	2.1
	Atlantic and North	8.6	4.9	8.2
B. Gender	Men	60.5	86.3	63.2
	Women	39.5	13.7	36.8
C. Education	High school or less	15.0	42.2	17.8
	College or some university	27.4	41.2	28.8
	One or more university degrees	57.6	16.7	53.4
D. Home language	English	93.2	98.0	93.7
	French	1.9	0.0	1.7
	Both/Other	4.9	2.0	4.6
E. Family income	< $40 000	37.8	25.5	36.6
	$40 001–$60 000	27.8	45.1	29.6
	> $60 000	34.3	29.4	33.8
F. Occupation	Professional/Manager	46.3	22.8	43.9
	White collar/farm	20.2	27.7	21.0
	Blue collar	5.8	45.5	9.8
	Other (homemaker/student/retired)	27.6	4.0	25.2
G. Age	18–30	2.3	0.0	2.1
	31–50	43.6	43.0	43.6
	51–65	30.2	40.0	31.2
	66 +	23.8	17.0	23.1
N		(893)	(102)	(995)

delegates, however, fully 86.3 percent were men and only 13.7 percent were women.

The representation of youth (or lack thereof) continues to differentiate the New Democrat conventions from those of the Liberals and Conservatives. Only 15.0 percent of NDP delegates were 30 years old or younger, less than half the proportion obtained at Liberal and Conservative conventions. Once again, the presence of union delegates produces a further bias toward the representation of middle-aged (31–50 and 51–65) delegates – almost 90 percent of union delegates come from these age groups.

It has been shown that each of the parties has clear biases in the awarding of delegate positions, and that these biases can result in unequal opportunities among individuals to become delegates. Parties create categories of delegate positions, and the nature and size of these categories are determined and adjusted to respond to specific representational goals. In contrast to a general election, which is based on the principle of the equal participation of all citizens, everyone does not have an equal chance to become a party convention delegate. Some individuals can be included under several delegate categories, whereas others may be limited to one. An example may help illustrate the point. Imagine a young woman who holds a membership in an autoworkers local affiliated with the NDP. Assume also that she is working as a provincial coordinator for the Ontario Federation of Labour (OFL). She is an active member of her NDP constituency association, and is also a member of the executive of the NDY. This individual has the opportunity to seek a delegate position at four different entry points – in her constituency, in the NDY organization, in her CAW local and in the OFL. She could also attempt to become a Participation of Women (POW) delegate from her constituency. In contrast, an older man or woman who is not a union member and not involved in the youth group may have only one or two points of entry.

The inequality of opportunity to participate in the process of leadership selection is one of the key features in delegate selection in all the major parties. The principle of "one person, one vote" is applied very crudely in the selection of constituency delegates, and is not applied at all for other categories of delegates. All ex-officio delegates (such as caucus members and federal council for the NDP, and including privy councillors, provincial representatives and many others for the Liberals and Conservatives) are simply awarded delegate status; they are not required to contest it. For each party, the nonconstituency delegate positions are a clear example of representational inequality; they are meant to provide either a reward for party work or a special appeal to a targeted group.

Students and practitioners of electoral politics alike have recognized that the key to winning a public contest lies in either choosing the contestants or defining who is able to vote in the election (Schattschneider 1963). For party conventions, deciding who automatically becomes a delegate, and which positions are open for election is of immense importance. Despite the manifest inequality of opportunity for individuals, the issue of delegate criteria used by Canadian parties should be subject to minimal state regulation. Parties differ on what criteria are important to them and on the relative control each group has over the outcome of the leadership contest. These features – of providing greater or lesser representation to youth, women, provincial representatives or union members, among others – define in important ways what a party represents, and to whom it is appealing for support. Debates on changing representational criteria – and there are many such debates – are most prudently conducted within individual parties. Such debates form a party's character.

THE SELECTION OF DELEGATES

Delegates are selected by different methods according to the category to which they belong. Two categories of ex-officio delegates, federal council and caucus, have delegate status by virtue of their positions. The delegates of central labour and its affiliated organizations are selected by whatever method the organization (i.e., the union or central labour body) chooses to employ. No official record exists as to how these positions are filled and the party sets no requirements for the method of selection. It is suspected that most union delegates are selected by an administrative decision taken by those responsible for maintaining the organization's liaison with the party. It should be noted, however, that for the affiliated organizations, the delegate positions are allocated to relatively small bodies – the union local that chooses to affiliate. Since approximately 700 unions affiliate with the party, most affiliates have only one or two positions to fill (Archer 1985). Thus, it is a highly decentralized decision-making process by which the union delegate positions are awarded.

The two remaining delegate categories – constituency and Youth – are both selected through elections (Wearing 1988a). The delegate selection process has been controversial at recent Liberal and Conservative conventions, especially the "instant Tory" or "instant Liberal" phenomenon of active, last-minute recruiting, the use of delegate slates and the creation of entirely new campus and youth organizations for the allocation of new delegate positions (Courtney 1986, 98; Wearing 1988a). The NDP has not been subject to these pressures to the same degree as the Liberal and Conservative parties. The reason for this is not entirely clear, but is likely owing to a combination of factors. The candidates' spending limit of $150 000, discussed in more detail later, makes it very difficult, and perhaps impossible, for candidates to mount the type of organizational team that can effectively reach into the local constituency organizations to mount recruiting drives. The party's relative lack of electoral success, its condition that members not be supporters of another party and its highly federal (decentralized) structure all contribute to the difficulty of mounting takeovers of constituency associations. In addition, the longevity of membership for many activists, coupled with the culture of an open, democratic institution, could have the effect of making such an organizational effort highly counter-productive. And finally, the party has a relatively early (120 days preceding the convention) cut-off date for new members to take part in the convention.

The result of these factors is that candidates are less able to mount effective and substantial party recruitment drives prior to delegate selection meetings in an attempt to "pack" the meetings before a convention. The costs of doing so are high, given the large number of recruits necessary (50 members for each delegate position for the first 200, 100 members for each delegate thereafter), and the payoffs, factoring in the resentment and alienation of long-time party workers, are relatively modest. Thus, in most areas delegate selection meetings are small events. Table 1.4 illustrates that 64 percent of all constituency delegates were chosen at meetings attended by fewer than 50 people. Most of the remainder (29.9 percent) were chosen at meetings of 50 to 100 people. Only 6.1 percent reported having more than 100 people at the meeting.

In addition, the largest meetings tended to be held in areas where the party was strongest. Over half of the delegates from Saskatchewan were from meetings of 50 to 100, and another 13.9 percent had more than 100 members. At the other extreme, all the delegates from Quebec were chosen at meetings attended by fewer than 50 members, as were all northerners. One supposes that the North's sparse population, rather

Table 1.4
Size of delegate selection meeting by province/region

Province/region	Size of meeting			
	Less than 50 (%)	50–100 (%)	More than 100 (%)	N
British Columbia	53.8	35.0	11.3	160
Alberta	66.7	28.9	4.4	90
Saskatchewan	32.8	53.3	13.9	137
Manitoba	80.5	19.5	0.0	77
Ontario	76.9	21.0	2.1	238
Quebec	100.0	0.0	0.0	16
Atlantic	71.4	26.2	2.4	42
North	100.0	0.00	0.0	13
Total	64.0	29.9	6.1	773

than the NDP's performance (the party forms the government in the Yukon), accounts for the small size of the meetings.

The selection meetings themselves differed from those of the Liberal and Conservative parties in the likelihood of contestation, the incidence of identifying with leadership candidates prior to selection and the use of slates (see table 1.5). For example, whereas one-quarter of Liberal and Conservative constituency delegates are elected without a contest (Carty 1988, 86), fully one-half of the NDP constituency delegates did not face a challenger for the delegate position. In addition, whereas some 41 percent of the Liberal delegates and 48 percent of the Conservative delegates identified themselves as supporters of one of the leadership candidates, only 31 percent of the New Democrats were identified as supporting a candidate. Put another way, more than two-thirds of the NDP constituency delegates were elected without identifying their choice for leader. There was much speculation at the time of the convention that delegates were unenthusiastic about all the candidates. This factor may partly account for the observation that delegate selection meetings in the NDP leadership race took place without reference to preferences for party leader.

Even more pronounced are the differences between the NDP and the Liberals and Conservatives in the use of slates. Whereas almost 40 percent of Liberal and Conservative delegates were elected as part of a slate, only 10 percent of New Democrats followed that route to election. Instead, there appears to be a much greater reliance in the NDP on an individual's personal service and commitment to the party, and less

Table 1.5
Constituency delegate selections in the Liberal, Conservative and New Democratic parties

Cell criteria	Party		
	PC '83	Liberal '84	NDP '89
1. Selection contested	77	75	51
2. Prior identification as supporting a candidate	48	41	31
3. Ran as part of slate	39	38	10
4. Ran identified and on slate	26	24	6
5. Trench warfare (identified slate vs. identified slate)	10	12	2

Source: Data on Liberal and Conservative conventions are from Carty (1988, 86).

Note: Cell entries are percentage of constituency delegates meeting criteria.

on how the individual ranks his or her preferences for party leader. Furthermore, although it is an increasingly common practice among Liberals and Conservatives to run on a slate identified with a candidate – approximately one-quarter in each party did so – that situation remains the exception in the NDP, where only 6 percent claimed to have used that approach. In a scenario aptly described by Carty (1988) as "trench warfare," a slate identified with one candidate is pitted against a slate identified with another. In the selection of constituency delegates to the leadership convention, very few New Democrats (2 percent) engaged in such trench warfare.

Thus, although for New Democrats there is some use of slates and candidate preferences in choosing convention delegates, these tend not to be the norm. Instead, when there is a contest, it has a highly individualistic orientation, highlighting the past service of contestants as party members. For delegates who will spend more time at the convention debating policy than choosing a leader, such an approach to delegate selection seems both predictable and appropriate.

The scope for useful and productive state regulation of the selection of convention delegates ranges from minimal to nonexistent. The parties differ across the full range of delegate selection criteria, often with deliberate intentions. As noted above, each of the parties has large numbers of delegates not chosen by constituency associations. In the NDP, union delegates are a significant minority of delegates, but most union locals have very few (one or two) delegate positions. Applying selection criteria to them would centralize a process that was explicitly and categorically intended to be decentralized (Lewis 1982; Archer 1990). It was a matter of political choice, a choice to be different from the British Labour Party. That choice is best exercised by the party, not by the state. Likewise, the selection of ex-officio delegates is one with little room for useful regulation. Once a party has decided to give delegate status to MPs, or privy councillors or the presidents of provincial wings, there are no selection criteria – one either has those characteristics and becomes a delegate, or one does not.

The area in which regulation may appear more attractive – attractive but unwise – is in the selection of constituency delegates. The selection of convention delegates has generated considerable controversy in recent years, and for good reason. Many of the practices employed, including signing large numbers of new party recruits in the final days before the contest, recruiting heavily on campuses and in ethnic communities, bringing busloads of supporters to the delegate selection meetings and the widespread use of slates, have contributed to the growing cynicism toward the political process. Some have suggested it has even led to a governability crisis in Canada.[6]

However, regulation of delegate selection is problematic for several reasons. Perhaps most importantly, the fact that every biennial convention of the NDP includes the election of the party leader implies that there is no clear distinction in the party, as there is in the Liberal and Conservative parties, between policy conventions and leadership conventions. Thus, it would not be possible to implement a series of regulations pertaining to leadership conventions, and another limited to policy conventions, and expect that they could be applied equally to all parties. The NDP would always fall under the leadership convention regulations. Few would be likely to argue that there is any useful role for the state in regulating how parties formulate their policies, including making regulations on who may participate in the policy-making process. The very idea seems repugnant in a democracy.

In addition, a key to regulating delegate selection is the setting of a cut-off date for new members to participate in the process. An early cut-off date (such as 90 or 120 days preceding the convention) makes a large recruiting drive more difficult, whereas a late date simplifies the task. Parties differ in their reason for conventions, and thus in their preferred cut-off. Those that view leadership conventions mainly as an exercise in public relations or as a forum for the recruitment of new members are more likely to favour a later date. Parties more interested in rewarding past service and in debating policy – both signifying a longer-term commitment to the party – look more favourably on an early cut-off date. In either case, it is not simply an administrative decision that either requires or invites regulation, but rather a difference of perspective and substance.

The delegate selection practices used by the parties may well have contributed to greater public cynicism about the political process. However, there are no solutions to the most problematic features of those practices that can be applied uniformly and neutrally. The conflicting goals of party conventions – which include membership recruitment, policy development, rewards for the party faithful, strengthening of personal networks, representation of specific groups and public relations, combined with selecting a new party leader – ensure that there will be conflicting demands over the nature of delegate selection. However, it is in the very resolution of those conflicting demands that parties define their character and their image. Recent technical changes in candidates' strategic planning, including greater use of opinion research, more delegate tracking and more sophisticated ways of recruiting "instant" party members, have laid bare some of the problems that accompany delegate selection methods used by some of the parties.

It is now up to the parties to respond to those changes and to adjust their delegate selection methods in such a way as to increase public confidence. The growing interest in and movement toward the direct election of party leaders (discussed later) represents one possible solution to the problems of delegate selection.

LEADERSHIP PREFERENCES AND SELECTION RULES

The counter-intuitive argument has been made that the winner of a contest decided by ballot can be someone other than the person with the greatest support among the electors. The most generalizable form of the argument can be found in Arrow's (1961) well-known general impossibility theorem. The implication of the theorem is that there exists no set of rules for aggregating preferences in a democracy that will ensure that the most preferred candidate is elected. The selection of the winner may be more dependent on the rules used in counting preferences than on the actual preferences. Since the rules are to a considerable extent arbitrary, the paradox of voting suggests that the winner is arbitrarily selected. Different rules, under the same preferences, may produce different results (see Brams 1985, 58–60).

The theoretical insights of social choice theory found a practical and controversial application to Canadian politics in Levesque's analysis of the 1983 Conservative leadership convention (Levesque 1983; see the responses by Woolstencroft 1983; Perlin 1983). Levesque argued that Mulroney won the contest because the method of selection eliminated the last place candidate from each ballot. The elimination of John Crosbie after the third ballot led to a showdown between Clark and Mulroney, and Mulroney was preferred to Clark. However, Levesque contends that when the first, second and third place rankings are estimated, Crosbie emerges as the most preferred candidate. The preferences have remained the same; they have simply been counted differently. His conclusion was that the rules prevented the selection of the most preferred candidate. More specifically, in a two-person contest between either Crosbie and Mulroney or Crosbie and Clark, Levesque projected that Crosbie would win.

Levesque's analysis was challenged on two accounts. Woolstencroft (1983) argued that the rules themselves evolved from the process of leadership selection – that is, the method used by the candidates to garner support assumes a simple preference, adversarial system. Candidates premised their strategy on the rules that would be used. While acknowledging the prima facie arbitrariness of the rules, he nonetheless maintains that once they are set, the rules become an integral part of the strategy of delegate recruitment and candidate appeal.

Perlin's critique was more empirical (1983). Examining the preferences of delegates ascertained through a survey questionnaire, he argued that Levesque had overestimated second preference support for Crosbie. Instead, he argued, a substantial proportion of Clark supporters preferred Mulroney to Crosbie. Therefore he claimed that Mulroney would prevail in a two-person contest with Crosbie.

This section will explore the nature of voting during four ballots at the NDP convention. It will examine the effect of preferences on voting and vote shifts across ballots to see whether there is evidence of strategic voting (LeDuc 1971), and to determine the success of the defeated candidates in playing the role of king- (or queen-) maker in delivering their supporters to new candidates. It will then use candidate preference rankings to explore the rank-order placement of the candidates and to assess the effect of the voting rules in selecting Audrey McLaughlin as party leader. The latter part will then follow Levesque's analysis while taking into account Perlin's suggestion that estimates of voter preferences be based on empirical grounds. Woolstencroft's critique is less germane to the NDP since, as was shown in the previous section, the 1989 NDP leadership convention did not feature active and energetic recruitment efforts by the candidates in the period preceding the delegate selection meetings. Therefore, candidates' recruitment does not have a strong effect on the delegates elected to the convention, a factor that should affect relative candidate rankings.

Table 1.6 maps the voting results over the four ballots at the convention. Audrey McLaughlin, the acknowledged front-runner, finished slightly ahead of Dave Barrett on the first ballot, with 26.9 percent and 23.6 percent of the vote respectively. The other major candidates were 10 percentage points or more behind the leaders. The convention rule requiring candidates with the lowest vote total and/or those with fewer than 75 votes to withdraw forced Lagassé off the ballot. Both Waddell and McCurdy withdrew voluntarily after the first ballot. Lagassé freed his delegates, McCurdy moved to support Langdon and Waddell supported Barrett.

The second ballot saw McLaughlin maintaining her lead at 34.3 percent of the vote, although the gap between her and Barrett narrowed somewhat to 2 percent. Langdon's support grew in step with the two front-runners, and de Jong was forced off the ballot. In a moment charged with excitement, and later with controversy, de Jong moved to support McLaughlin. A live wireless microphone had recorded de Jong, minutes earlier, pledging to move to Barrett in exchange for a valued appointment in caucus. However, de Jong chose not to act on that commitment, and instead cast his support behind McLaughlin. The latter was then able to make gains on Barrett on the third ballot. After

Table 1.6
Voting results during four ballots

				Ballot				
	1		2		3		4	
Candidate	N	(%)	N	(%)	N	(%)	N	(%)
McLaughlin	646	26.9	829	34.3	1 072	44.4	1 316	54.7
Barrett	566	23.6	780	32.3	947	39.2	1 072	44.6
Langdon	351	14.6	519	21.5	393	16.3		
de Jong	315	13.1	289	12.0				
McCurdy	256	10.7						
Waddell	213	8.9						
Lagassé	53	2.2						
Spoiled	3	0.1	0	0.0	3	0.1	18	0.7
Total	(2 403)		(2 417)		(2 415)		(2 406)	

Langdon was forced off the ballot, McLaughlin secured victory on the fourth ballot by a comfortable 10-point margin.

Previous research into leadership selection has shown that a considerable proportion of delegates – as many as 25 percent – engage in "strategic voting" at conventions (LeDuc 1971, 100; Krause and LeDuc 1979, 102–105). Strategic voting is defined as voting for someone other than one's first preference. Table 1.7 indicates that a considerable amount of strategic voting was evident at the NDP convention, although the proportion engaging in this activity was less than at previous Liberal and Conservative conventions. Delegates' preferences were determined from a question asking them to rank the seven candidates from their most (1) to least (7) preferred.[7]

Most of the strategic voting that occurred on the first ballot was at the expense of the two front-runners. Of those who ranked Barrett as their most preferred candidate, only 73.6 percent voted for him on the first ballot. For those who ranked McLaughlin first, 80.8 percent gave her first ballot support. For each of the other candidates except Lagassé (for whom the sample size is very small), those ranking the candidate as most preferred were very likely to be first ballot supporters. The level of support ranged from 90.1 percent for Langdon to 97.8 percent for Waddell.

It appears that the only way for candidates to ensure the continued allegiance of their supporters is to continue to perform up to expec-

Table 1.7
Vote on each ballot by first preference on rank order

Vote	Rank-order first preference in percentages						
	Barrett	de Jong	Lagassé	Langdon	McCurdy	McLaughlin	Waddell
Ballot 1							
Barrett	73.6	0	0	1.4	0	1.3	0
de Jong	8.1	96.6	6.7	3.5	1.4	7.8	2.2
Lagassé	2.3	0	80.0	1.4	2.7	1.0	0
Langdon	3.9	0	6.7	90.1	0	3.1	0
McCurdy	3.1	0	6.7	2.1	94.5	2.6	0
McLaughlin	1.6	0	0	0	1.4	80.8	0
Waddell	7.4	2.3	0	0.7	0	3.1	97.8
Spoiled	0	1.1	0	0.7	0	0.3	0
Ballot 2							
Barrett	93.4	6.9	6.7	1.4	11.0	0.8	31.5
de Jong	3.1	80.5	26.7	5.0	20.5	5.0	16.9
Langdon	3.1	5.7	53.3	90.1	45.2	4.4	25.8
McLaughlin	0.4	5.7	13.3	3.5	21.9	89.0	25.8
Spoiled	0	1.1	0	0	1.4	0.8	0
Ballot 3							
Barrett	97.3	26.4	6.7	7.1	27.4	1.6	38.2
Langdon	2.0	16.1	46.7	73.0	26.0	2.1	23.6
McLaughlin	0.8	55.2	46.7	19.1	43.8	95.6	38.2
Spoiled	0	2.3	0	0.7	2.7	0.8	0
Ballot 4							
Barrett	97.7	30.7	0	30.7	33.3	1.3	47.7
McLaughlin	2.3	67.0	100	60.7	64.0	97.9	51.1
Spoiled	0	2.3	0	8.6	2.7	0.8	1.1
N	(258)	(87)	(15)	(141)	(73)	(385)	(89)

tations and to project an image of forward movement (Krause and LeDuc 1979). Once this momentum stops, even supporters begin looking elsewhere to cast their votes. For example, on the second ballot both Barrett and McLaughlin were able to get the support of 90 percent of those who ranked them first. Langdon, buoyed by McCurdy's movement to him, was also able to hold onto 90 percent of those ranking him first. However, de Jong did not receive such an endorsement and there was no visible movement to his camp. Consequently, the movement that did occur was away from him, and his support among those viewing him as their first preference dropped to 80.5 percent.

Similarly, on the third ballot Barrett and McLaughlin both increased their support among those who ranked them first, whereas Langdon's support among those ranking him first dropped to 73.0 percent. By the fourth ballot, Barrett and McLaughlin secured all but a handful of those ranking them first.

Modern conventions for the selection of party leaders – even the NDP's where voting takes place at delegates' tables – provide for a large physical space to accommodate demonstrations by candidates' supporters and the physical movement of supporters during the time between ballots. There is always much hoopla surrounding such movement, and it is widely assumed that candidates are able to deliver their votes when they quit the race and move to support one of their opponents. Furthermore, it is often assumed that such support will remain with the newly endorsed candidate. To what degree are these assumptions valid for the NDP?

Table 1.8 maps delegate movement across the four ballots. Panel A, which shows the relationship between first and second ballot voting, illustrates that both Barrett and McLaughlin retained almost all their first ballot supporters during the second ballot, with Langdon retaining the support of 90 percent of his first ballot supporters. Those who left Langdon split almost evenly between Barrett and McLaughlin. The remaining second ballot candidate, de Jong, managed to hold only two-thirds of his first ballot support, and once again Barrett and McLaughlin were about even in picking up his slippage. Lagassé was dropped from the ballot and freed his supporters, who were more likely to go to Langdon than elsewhere, although the margin was not substantial. Both McCurdy and Waddell voluntarily withdrew, and moved to support Langdon and Barrett, respectively. However, both met with mixed success in delivering their supporters' votes. Less than half of McCurdy's supporters followed him to Langdon; almost one-quarter joined McLaughlin, and about one-sixth voted for Barrett and de Jong. Waddell was even less successful in delivering votes to Barrett, as 36.9 percent of his first ballot voters went to Barrett and 28.7 percent went to McLaughlin.

Both Barrett and McLaughlin were able to maintain their support into the third ballot, including those recently acquired in the second ballot, losing only a handful of supporters in the process. In contrast, Langdon was able to maintain only two-thirds of his supporters, with the remainder moving to McLaughlin over Barrett by a margin of two to one. In his move to McLaughlin, de Jong was able to bring 55.1 percent of his second ballot supporters, with 23.2 percent moving to Barrett. This movement of de Jong supporters to McLaughlin by a

Table 1.8
Vote movement across ballots
(column percentages)

Second ballot vote	First ballot vote						
	Barrett	de Jong	Lagassé	Langdon	McCurdy	McLaughlin	Waddell
Barrett	99.0	14.5	23.1	4.0	15.4	0.6	36.9
de Jong	0.0	66.9	23.1	1.3	16.5	.0	14.8
Langdon	0.0	4.8	30.8	90.0	45.1	1.6	19.7
McLaughlin	1.0	13.8	19.2	4.7	23.1	97.1	28.7
Spoiled	0.0	0.0	3.8	0.0	0.0	0.6	0.0
N	(198)	(145)	(26)	(150)	(90)	(315)	(122)

Cramer's V = .71

Third ballot vote	Second ballot vote			
	Barrett	de Jong	Langdon	McLaughlin
Barrett	99.0	23.2	10.9	0.5
Langdon	0.0	21.0	65.9	0.8
McLaughlin	0.7	55.1	22.3	98.7
Spoiled	0.3	0.7	0.9	0.0
N	(289)	(138)	(220)	(395)

Cramer's V = .75

Fourth ballot vote	Third ballot vote		
	Barrett	Langdon	McLaughlin
Barrett	96.8	32.8	0.4
McLaughlin	3.2	59.3	99.2
Spoiled	0.0	7.9	0.4
N	(343)	(177)	(519)

Cramer's V = .70

margin of more than two to one had an important effect on the outcome. It enabled McLaughlin to extend her lead over Barrett and to maintain the momentum of the convention. Following the third ballot, Langdon was able to deliver his votes to McLaughlin by a two to one margin, and McLaughlin won on the fourth ballot. Thus there appears to be more than rhetoric in the importance ascribed to candidate movement. Although those departing early had less success in delivering their supporters, there was considerable success among those departing after the second and third ballots. And the movement of those in the lead appeared to have an important effect on the outcome of the race.

Overall, more than half the delegates changed their votes at least once during the four ballots (see table 1.9). Looked at from the other perspective, however, more than five in six delegates (84.5 percent) did not change at all, or changed only once. Since Barrett and McLaughlin received just over half (50.5 percent) of the votes on the first ballot, the other half of the delegates had to move at least once, even if the move was to spoil their ballots. Most chose to move once and stay there. For those who moved, some systematic patterns characterized their movement. The most obvious was the first ballot support. Almost all Barrett

Table 1.9
Number of vote changes by delegate type and by first ballot vote

Number of vote changes		Constituency	Federal council	Caucus	Youth	Affiliated unions	Central labour	Total
		A. Delegate type in percentages						
None		45.7	68.6	56.3	28.9	45.9	55.2	47.0
Once		38.5	25.5	37.5	50.0	32.4	34.5	37.5
Twice		13.0	5.9	6.3	18.4	21.6	10.3	13.2
Thrice		2.8	0.0	0.0	2.6	0.0	0.0	2.3
	N	(794)	(51)	(13)	(38)	(74)	(29)	(1002)

Number of vote changes		Barrett	de Jong	Lagassé	Langdon	McCurdy	McLaughlin	Waddell
		B. First ballot vote in percentages						
None		96.0	0.0	0.0	0.0	0.0	95.3	0.0
Once		3.0	83.6	34.6	96.0	37.4	1.9	61.5
Twice		1.0	15.8	53.8	2.7	56.0	2.8	28.7
Thrice		0.0	0.7	11.5	1.3	6.6	0.0	9.8
	N	(199)	(146)	(26)	(150)	(91)	(317)	(122)

and McLaughlin first ballot supporters continued to vote for them across the four ballots (see table 1.9, panel B).

Among the first ballot supporters of other candidates, only Langdon supporters were almost universal in moving only once (96.0 percent), and five in six (83.6 percent) de Jong supporters did likewise. Among Waddell's first ballot supporters, three in five changed their vote only once, and for supporters of Lagassé and McCurdy, the figure dropped to almost one in three. Well over half of Lagassé's and McCurdy's first ballot supporters changed twice, and almost three in ten of Waddell's first ballot supporters did so.

There was also a difference between party insiders and outsiders in the likelihood of vote switching (see table 1.9, panel A). For example, the greatest stability was found in members of federal council, followed by caucus and central labour. Less stable were the constituency delegates and those from affiliated unions. The greatest instability was evident among the youth wing, where only slightly more than one in four did not change their vote across the four ballots.

DID THE BEST (MOST PREFERRED) CANDIDATE WIN?

Did the rules of leadership selection interact with voter preferences to result in a non-optimal choice of winner (Levesque 1983)? The answer to this question requires more information than the voting mechanism itself provides. The voting rules do not allow delegates to supply information on their relative weighting or ranking of candidates. Although delegates are faced with a multicandidate contest, the voting rules allow for only a binary choice – one candidate is preferred, the others are not. Furthermore, the voting rules do not enable delegates to state whether a particular candidate is preferred to *each* of the others.

The survey instrument was used to make a more comprehensive assessment of delegates' candidate preferences to explore further the effects of the voting rules used at the convention. Delegates were asked to rank the seven candidates in order from most to least preferred. In table 1.10, each candidate's ranking relative to every other candidate's ranking can be compared. Focusing on the relative ranking of row (r) and column (c) candidates, the table illustrates the outcome of two-person contests between each of the candidates (r), and among the three strongest candidates (c) – Barrett, Langdon and McLaughlin. Therefore, each cell entry represents the proportion of delegates ranking the row candidate higher compared with the proportion ranking the column candidate higher. To take an example from the table, 42.6 percent of respondents ranked de Jong higher than Barrett, and 57.4 percent ranked

Table 1.10
Outcome of two-person contests based on ordinal preference ranking
(row/column)

	Column contestant		
Row contestant	Barrett	Langdon	McLaughlin
Barrett		43.3/56.7	38.2/61.8
de Jong	42.6/57.4	27.0/73.0	19.4/80.6
Lagassé	19.5/80.5	8.7/91.3	6.4/93.6
Langdon	56.7/43.3		34.2/65.8
McCurdy	40.9/59.1	26.5/73.5	20.1/79.9
McLaughlin	61.8/38.2	65.8/34.2	
Waddell	43.2/56.8	31.5/68.5	23.4/76.6

Barrett higher than de Jong. In a two-person contest between Barrett and de Jong, Barrett would win 57.4 percent to 42.6 percent.

A Condorcet winner is one who can defeat every other candidate in a series of two-person contests. Table 1.10 indicates that McLaughlin is the clear Condorcet winner of the contest. She defeated Barrett 61.8/38.2,[8] she defeated Langdon 65.8/34.2 and she defeated every other candidate by at least a 3 to 1 margin. Note that for Barrett, on the other hand, the margin of victory was large only when facing Lagassé, and was less than 6 to 4 for all others. Furthermore, not only was Barrett preferred less than McLaughlin, but he was also preferred less than Langdon. In addition, Langdon's margin of victory over the remaining candidates (other than McLaughlin) exceeded Barrett's. Recall that McLaughlin defeated Langdon handily. Thus, these data suggest that contrary to the results of the third ballot, which placed McLaughlin first, Barrett second and Langdon third, in fact the delegates' preference ordering placed Langdon ahead of Barrett. However, since McLaughlin defeated Langdon by an even greater margin than her victory over Barrett, the final outcome remains unchanged.

These results can be explained by examining the second preference rankings of all delegates. Table 1.11 compares first preference rankings of all candidates with second preference rankings for Barrett, Langdon, McLaughlin and all others combined. These data illustrate that the major weakness of Barrett's campaign was that he was not a strong second preference of many delegates. In contrast, not only was McLaughlin most popular as a first choice, she was a strong second

Table 1.11
Second preference rankings for top three candidates by first preference

Second preference	First preference rankings in percentages						
	Barrett	de Jong	Lagassé	Langdon	McCurdy	McLaughlin	Waddell
Barrett		21.6	0.0	23.9	13.9	16.8	33.0
Langdon	22.7	19.8	20.0		38.4	52.6	19.8
McLaughlin	38.5	50.0	26.7	50.0	37.8		29.9
All others	33.8	8.6	53.3	26.1	9.9	30.6	17.3

choice. To illustrate, half of de Jong's and Langdon's first preference supporters viewed McLaughlin as their second choice, compared with 21.6 percent and 23.9 percent, respectively, for Barrett. Langdon's strength relative to Barrett was evident mainly among those whose first preference was McLaughlin – they favoured Langdon over Barrett by a margin of 3 to 1. Although these delegates enabled Langdon to be stronger than Barrett, they obviously did not have a similar effect in a contest between Langdon and McLaughlin. Furthermore, even those preferring Barrett as their first choice tended to prefer McLaughlin over Langdon (38.5 percent versus 27.7 percent).

The conclusion that McLaughlin was the most preferred candidate followed by Langdon and then Barrett is confirmed by a Borda count of the preferences of delegates. In a seven-person contest, a Borda count assigns the value of 7 for each time a candidate is mentioned as first preference, a 6 for second preference and so on through to 1 for the least preferred candidate (Brams 1985). These values are then added together for a total preference rating for each candidate. Table 1.12 presents the complete candidate rankings and the Borda count.

Note that McLaughlin received 387 first preference rankings compared with 259 for Barrett and 141 for Langdon. However, Langdon was the most popular second choice, with 328 mentions compared with 149 for Barrett. The factor that helped assure that McLaughlin's campaign would not stall was her strong second preference showing of 267, less than Langdon's but substantially ahead of Barrett's. Applying the Borda count procedure, McLaughlin again emerges as the overall preference of delegates (5 858), followed at some distance by Langdon (5 098). Barrett finishes a very clear third (4 474). Thus, the voting rules used at the convention did alter the standings of the top three candidates. However, the major effect was on the second and third place

Table 1.12
Borda count of rank-order preferences

Preference ranking	Candidate						
	Barrett	de Jong	Lagassé	Langdon	McCurdy	McLaughlin	Waddell
First	259	89	15	141	75	387	89
Second	149	90	13	328	77	267	106
Third	134	134	31	213	151	171	178
Fourth	106	162	63	167	195	114	194
Fifth	84	185	98	95	241	55	222
Sixth	140	228	169	52	201	26	156
Seventh	141	105	589	21	56	19	54
Total Borda count	4 474	3 579	1 811	5 098	3 703	5 858	3 957

Note: Borda formula (Seventh *1) + (Sixth *2) + (Fifth *3) + (Fourth *4) + (Third *5) + (Second *6) + (First *7) = total.

finishers, not on the first. And in a winner-take-all system, the best candidate won.

Research on social choice theory applied to voting has profound implications for our understanding of democracy. The finding that no set of decision rules can guarantee that the most preferred candidate wins should have several policy implications. First, it implies that no single electoral system – whether it is simple preference or a ranking of candidates, whether it uses a plurality or majority decision rule – is superior to all others. Consequently, there is no reason to require parties to use a common system. In fact, it is quite remarkable that the three main parties in Canada have adopted such similar methods for selecting a party leader with almost no regulation from the government. From the perspective of potential regulation, there should be no standing preference either for the status quo or for a single alternative. This is not meant to imply that all electoral systems are equal or that they all have the same effect. They are not all the same. However, it does suggest that no electoral system can be described categorically as "best."

Second, this finding highlights the fact that all electoral systems have an effect on the outcome of the race. Thus, in choosing or designing an electoral system we are not choosing between biased and neutral systems. Instead, the question is what kind of bias do we want? Furthermore, this question is believed to be of greater relevance to political parties than to the state. It is the party's responsibility to define what part of the political spectrum it seeks to cover. The rules of leadership selection play an important role in that process. It is the state's responsibility to ensure that all parts of that spectrum have equal opportunities for institutionalized expression.

DETERMINANTS OF NDP CONVENTION VOTING

The preceding analysis examined both the observed and the hypothetical movement of voters based on their ranking of the candidates. How do these preferences develop? What factors are responsible for influencing delegates to support one candidate over his or her rivals? Are those supporting a particular candidate of like minds in their assessment, or is there evidence of a wide range of reasons, interests, strategies and evaluations that account for the behaviour of individual delegates?

Richard Johnston (1988) recently developed a sophisticated multivariate model to answer similar questions in his analysis of Liberal and Conservative conventions. Focusing on the decision structure underlying individual choice, Johnston posited a model featuring three direct, and two indirect, determinants of voting. He hypothesized that voting can be the result of social background factors, organizational factors and policy and/or ideological differences among delegates. Furthermore, each explanatory factor is a function of a distinctive dynamic underlying the process of convention voting. If the vote is best described by social background characteristics, such as the voter's age, gender, religion, language, region of residence and the like, Johnston suggests (1988, 207) that the proper analogy is the general election among mass electorates. Evidence in support of organizational factors, particularly the distinction between "insiders" and "outsiders," is offered as support for an interpretation of delegate manipulation along the vein suggested by Power (1966; but see Courtney 1986). And evidence supportive of the policy or ideological factors would suggest that the market analogy, under the assumption of maximizing voters, is most appropriate to explain convention delegates' behaviour (Johnston 1988, 206; Downs 1957). In addition to these direct effects, Johnston's model postulates an indirect effect of social background and organizational characteristics on policy and ideology.

Such a model provides a useful approach to evaluate the relative effects of a wide range of potentially important determinants of attitudes and voting behaviour. Its major deficiency is that it fails to examine the full range of potential dynamics of voting. The analogy has been drawn between the dynamics underlying the voting decision at conventions and those motivating the mass electorate during general elections (Krause and LeDuc 1979, 102; Courtney 1986, 101). Johnston's use of this analogy is restricted to identifying it with social background characteristics. However, a substantial body of literature has demonstrated the importance of attitudes toward party leaders in Canadian elections, and the relative weakness of sociodemographic characteristics (see LeDuc et al. 1984; Archer 1987). Many voters base their decisions on their likes and dislikes of the party leaders, independent of their ideological views or policy positions. This is not to deny the potential significance of sociodemographic, organizational or ideological determinants of leadership convention voting. Instead, it suggests that to examine the fit of the mass voting behaviour analogy, measures of attitude toward the candidates should be included.

In this section, the model Johnston developed for Liberal and Conservative conventions is extended to the NDP. In addition, the model has been respecified to include a fourth group, entitled attitudes toward candidates in the set of independent variables. The voting behaviour analogue thus has two separate branches – the group effect, based on sociodemographic characteristics and emphasizing the mobilization of identifiable groups, and the candidate effect model, stressing delegates' attitudes toward the candidates. Anticipating the results of the first stage of analysis, which highlights the importance of attitudes toward the candidates, the second stage then estimates attitudes toward candidates using social background, organizational position, policy positions and ideology as the independent factors.

The Vote

This model was used to generate estimates of the effects of social background, organization, policy/ideology and candidate attitudes on the ranking of preferences and on the four ballots in voting for Barrett, Langdon and McLaughlin (see figure 1.1). In addition, estimates were generated of the effects of background, organization and policy/ideology on attitudes toward the candidates. The analysis begins by examining the determinants of candidate ranking and the vote.

The patterns that emerge in the data tend to be unique to each candidate. In addition to his support among British Columbians, Barrett found disproportionate support among older delegates, and on the final ballot, was underrepresented among the university educated. The gender variable emerges as important in Barrett's relative preference ranking. Men were more likely to rank Barrett positively relative to the other candidates. In addition, Barrett was less likely to be supported by women, other things being equal, than by men on each of the last three

Figure 1.1
A model of the determinants of convention voting

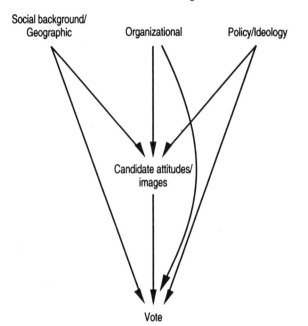

ballots, with the relationship in the final two ballots bordering on statistical significance at the 95 percent confidence interval. If women were less likely to vote for Barrett – and they were – it was not simply because they were mobilized to support others. As shall be seen below, their gender had a powerful impact on their assessment of candidates' characteristics. In other words, women were not blindly led away from Barrett and toward McLaughlin; they were convinced that McLaughlin was the more suitable candidate for the party.

As with Barrett, support for McLaughlin was not strongly influenced, other things being equal, by social background. Her fourth ballot support came disproportionately from the younger delegates, and she was more likely to be supported by women than by men on the last three ballots, although the difference on the final ballot does not achieve statistical significance at the .05 level. Final ballot support also shows greater support in rural areas and New Brunswick, and less support in British Columbia. In addition, while de Jong was still in the race, Saskatchewan residents were less likely to support McLaughlin. When de Jong moved to support her after the second ballot, the negative impact on McLaughlin support from voters living in Saskatchewan disappeared.

Table 1.13
Determinants of support for Barrett

Independent variable	Preference ranking	First ballot	Second ballot	Third ballot	Fourth ballot
A. Social background					
Age	0.008 (0.004)*	0.008 (0.007)	0.002 (0.001)**	0.001 (0.001)	0.002 (0.001)*
Female	-0.42 (0.11)**	0.02 (0.02)	-0.02 (0.02)	-0.04 (0.02)	-0.04 (0.02)
University	0.02 (0.13)	0.05 (0.02)	0.03 (0.02)	-0.03 (0.02)	-0.07 (0.03)*
Rural	0.07 (0.17)	-0.01 (0.03)	-0.02 (0.03)	-0.05 (0.03)	-0.07 (0.04)
Metropolitan	-0.21 (0.12)	-0.01 (0.02)	-0.01 (0.02)	-0.03 (0.02)	-0.01 (0.03)
Francophone	-0.40 (0.45)	-0.09 (0.08)	-0.05 (0.08)	-0.08 (0.09)	-0.08 (0.09)
Working class	-0.16 (0.12)	0.01 (0.02)	-0.005 (0.02)	-0.01 (0.02)	0.01 (0.02)
Upper class	-0.07 (0.13)	-0.04 (0.02)	-0.01 (0.02)	-0.01 (0.03)	-0.02 (0.03)
Public sector	-0.03 (0.11)	-0.03 (0.02)	-0.01 (0.02)	-0.01 (0.02)	-0.01 (0.02)
Catholic	0.23 (0.16)	-0.05 (0.03)	-0.003 (0.03)	0.004 (0.03)	0.01 (0.03)
British Columbia	0.26 (0.16)	0.10 (0.03)**	0.16 (0.03)**	0.09 (0.03)**	0.00 (0.03)
Alberta	0.07 (0.18)	0.03 (0.03)	0.11 (0.03)**	0.07 (0.04)	-0.01 (0.04)
Saskatchewan	-0.40 (0.17)*	-0.02 (0.03)	0.02 (0.03)	0.05 (0.03)	-0.04 (0.04)
Manitoba	0.07 (0.18)	0.02 (0.03)	0.05 (0.03)	0.02 (0.04)	0.01 (0.04)
Quebec	-0.39 (0.40)	0.03 (0.07)	-0.06 (0.07)	-0.10 (0.08)	0.05 (0.09)
New Brunswick	-0.93 (0.42)*	0.01 (0.07)	0.04 (0.08)	-0.02 (0.08)	-0.02 (0.09)
Nova Scotia	-0.24 (0.30)	0.02 (0.05)	-0.03 (0.05)	-0.04 (0.06)	0.03 (0.06)
Prince Edward Island	-0.71 (0.78)	-0.12 (0.14)	-0.18 (0.15)	0.21 (0.16)	0.02 (0.17)
Newfoundland	0.47 (0.58)	0.03 (0.10)	0.002 (0.10)	-0.03 (0.12)	-0.08 (0.12)
Territories	-0.63(0.47)	0.01 (0.08)	-0.03 (0.08)	-0.09 (0.09)	-0.13 (0.09)
Immigrant	-0.14 (0.15)	0.009 (0.02)	-0.01 (0.03)	-0.01 (0.03)	-0.03 (0.03)
B. Delegate status					
Affiliated union	0.44 (0.23)*	0.11 (0.04)**	0.11 (0.04)**	0.12 (0.04)**	0.11 (0.04)*
Federal council	0.05 (0.27)	0.08 (0.05)	0.17 (0.05)**	0.12 (0.05)*	0.04 (0.06)
Central labour	0.03 (0.32)	0.16 (0.06)**	0.19 (0.06)**	0.13 (0.06)*	0.03 (0.07)
ND Youth	-0.01 (0.29)	-0.04 (0.05)	0.03 (0.05)	0.01 (0.06)	-0.02 (0.06)
Small meeting	0.12 (0.12)	-0.01 (0.02)	0.03 (0.02)	0.04 (0.02)	0.04 (0.03)
C. Policy position					
NATO	-0.11 (0.05)*	-0.01 (0.01)	-0.01 (0.01)	-0.003 (0.01)	-0.1 (0.01)
Free trade	-0.14 (0.06)*	0.01 (0.01)	0.01 (0.01)	0.003 (0.01)	0.01 (0.01)
Meech Lake	-0.01 (0.05)	0.01 (0.01)	0.003 (0.009)	-0.001 (0.1)	-0.02 (0.01)
Distinct Quebec	-0.004 (0.04)	-0.02 (0.01)**	-0.01 (0.01)	-0.02 (0.01)*	-0.02 (0.01)
Leader cut off	0.01 (0.05)	0.02 (0.01)**	-0.001 (0.008)	-0.01 (0.01)	-0.02 (0.01)
Left-right	0.02 (0.04)	-0.003 (0.008)	0.006 (0.008)	0.02 (0.01)*	0.001 (0.01)
D. Attitudes toward candidates					
Likeable	0.68 (0.14)**	0.11 (0.03)**	0.07 (0.03)**	0.06 (0.03)*	0.06 (0.03)*
TV image	0.23 (0.12)**	-0.01 (0.02)	-0.02 (0.02)	0.02 (0.02)	0.06 (0.03)*
Policy positions	0.54 (0.17)**	0.19 (0.03)**	0.21 (0.03)**	0.17 (0.03)**	0.09 (0.04)*
Competence	0.81 (0.17)**	0.11 (0.03)**	0.17 (0.03)**	0.19 (0.03)**	0.18 (0.03)**
Unite party	-0.12 (0.21)	0.14 (0.04)**	0.04 (0.04)	-0.02 (0.04)	0.002 (0.04)
Tough decisions	0.52 (0.14)**	0.10 (0.02)**	0.11 (0.03)**	0.11 (0.03)**	0.11 (0.03)**
Respect from leaders	0.35 (0.16)*	0.07 (0.03)**	0.09 (0.03)**	0.12 (0.03)**	0.12 (0.03)**

Table 1.13 (cont'd)
Determinants of support for Barrett

Independent variable	Preference ranking	First ballot	Second ballot	Third ballot	Fourth ballot
Regions	0.23 (0.19)	0.06 (0.03)	0.11 (0.04)**	0.06 (0.04)	0.04 (0.04)
Win elections	0.88 (0.16)**	0.08 (0.03)**	0.20 (0.03)**	0.25 (0.03)**	0.32 (0.03)**
Labour ties	0.06 (0.12)	-0.02 (0.02)	-0.01 (0.02)	-0.02 (0.02)	-0.002 (0.02)
Intercept	3.52 (0.45)	-0.09 (0.08)	-0.12 (0.08)	0.04 (0.09)	0.20 (0.09)
R^2	.55	.57	.63	.62	.59
N	(901)	(901)	(901)	(901)	(901)

Notes: Standard error in parentheses.
*$p < .05$; **$p < .01$.

The social background determinants of Langdon's support had a number of interesting features. Women were more likely than men to rank him more highly, but that attitude did not translate into more votes. On the contrary, women were less likely than men to vote for Langdon on the second and third ballots, a relationship that achieved statistical significance for the second ballot, and which bordered on significance for the third. One suspects that in the absence of McLaughlin's candidacy, Langdon would have received disproportionate votes from women. However, in this particular contest, the support of women was moved away from Langdon to McLaughlin. The strongest social background determinants of Langdon's support are found in the province of residence measures. Residence in the three westernmost provinces had a strong negative impact on his support, with the impact being strongest in British Columbia and Saskatchewan. Nova Scotians, in contrast, were strong Langdon supporters over the second and third ballots.

The most important organizational factor in the 1989 NDP convention was union membership. Union delegates were more likely to support Barrett than were constituency delegates. Interestingly, the results are stronger on the first three ballots than on the fourth. Union delegate status had a negative effect on McLaughlin's support, although the effects for both Barrett and McLaughlin were tempered when the two candidates went head to head on the fourth ballot. The strong effect of union membership variables illustrates that, as a group, their mobilizational capacity is substantial. The fact that these coefficients were not even larger is important, and is based on the divisions in the labour movement over candidate endorsements. For example, Shirley Carr, the Canadian Labour Congress president, supported Barrett, whereas Leo Gerard (Steelworkers) and Bob White (Autoworkers) endorsed McLaughlin.

In addition to his support from labour, Barrett was also able to secure the disproportionate support of federal council, a group that overall was somewhat unsupportive of McLaughlin. It is worth noting that, once again, while the coefficients remain in the same direction on the final ballot (i.e., negative for McLaughlin, positive for Barrett),

Table 1.14
Determinants of support for Langdon

Independent variable	Preference ranking	First ballot	Second ballot	Third ballot
A. Social background				
Age	0.0001 (0.003)	-0.0001 (0.001)	-0.0001 (0.001)	-0.001 (0.003)
Female	0.23 (0.08)**	0.001 (0.02)	-0.06 (0.02)**	-0.04 (0.02)
University	0.04 (0.10)	-0.03 (0.02)	-0.05 (0.03)*	-0.03 (0.03)
Rural	0.18 (0.14)	0.002 (0.03)	0.004 (0.03)	0.03 (0.03)
Metropolitan	0.04 (0.10)	0.02 (0.02)	0.01 (0.03)	-0.01 (0.02)
Francophone	-0.35 (0.36)	0.14 (0.08)	0.20 (0.10)*	0.16 (0.09)
Working class	-0.01 (0.09)	0.0001 (0.02)	-0.02 (0.03)	0.02 (0.02)
Upper class	-0.16 (0.11)	-0.03 (0.02)	-0.06 (0.03)*	-0.05 (0.03)*
Public sector	0.07 (0.09)	0.01 (0.02)	-0.02 (0.02)	0.03 (0.02)
Catholic	0.12 (0.12)	-0.01 (0.03)	0.03 (0.03)	0.02 (0.03)
British Columbia	-0.36 (0.13)**	-0.12 (0.03)**	-0.19 (0.03)**	-0.11 (0.03)**
Alberta	-0.29 (0.14)*	-0.07 (0.03)*	-0.08 (0.03)*	-0.02 (0.04)
Saskatchewan	-0.83 (0.13)**	-0.11 (0.03)**	-0.21 (0.03)**	-0.09 (0.03)**
Manitoba	-0.29 (0.15)	-0.05 (0.03)	-0.12 (0.04)	0.02 (0.04)
Quebec	0.53 (0.33)	-0.001 (0.07)	-0.07 (0.40)	0.09 (0.08)
New Brunswick	0.20 (0.34)	-0.03 (0.08)	-0.08 (0.09)	-0.12 (0.09)
Nova Scotia	0.10 (0.24)	-0.01 (0.05)	0.20 (0.06)**	0.16 (0.06)**
Prince Edward Island	0.48 (0.64)	0.15 (0.14)	0.04 (0.17)	0.08 (0.16)
Newfoundland	-0.85 (0.44)	-0.18 (0.10)	-0.30 (0.18)*	-0.15 (0.18)
Territories	0.15 (0.36)	-0.10 (0.08)	-0.22 (0.09)*	-0.16 (0.09)
Immigrant	0.01 (0.12)	-0.02 (0.03)	0.03 (0.03)	0.08 (0.03)
B. Delegate status				
Affiliated union	0.13 (0.18)	0.02 (0.04)	0.03 (0.05)	-0.01 (0.05)
Federal council	0.21 (0.21)	-0.002 (0.05)	-0.02 (0.06)	0.002 (0.05)
Central labour	-0.27 (0.27)	-0.02 (0.06)	-0.03 (0.07)	0.01 (0.07)
ND Youth	0.14 (0.23)	0.04 (0.05)	-0.02 (0.06)	0.05 (0.06)
Small meeting	-0.09 (0.10)	0.01 (0.02)	-0.002 (0.02)	0.05 (0.02)
C. Policy position				
NATO	0.04 (0.04)	-0.003 (0.009)	-0.01 (0.01)	-0.003 (0.01)
Free trade	0.03 (0.05)	-0.01 (0.01)	-0.01 (0.01)	0.004 (0.01)
Meech Lake	0.01 (0.04)	0.001 (0.01)	0.004 (0.01)	-0.01 (0.01)
Distinct Quebec	0.03 (0.03)	0.001 (0.01)	0.004 (0.01)	0.0001 (0.01)
Leader cut off	0.002 (0.04)	0.002 (0.01)	-0.01 (0.01)	-0.01 (0.01)
Left-right	0.11 (0.04)**	-0.01 (0.01)	-0.001 (0.01)	-0.005 (0.01)

Table 1.14 (cont'd)
Determinants of support for Langdon

Independent variable	Preference ranking	First ballot	Second ballot	Third ballot
D. Attitudes toward candidates				
Likeable	0.51 (0.16)**	0.29 (0.04)**	0.15 (0.04)**	0.11 (0.04)**
TV image	0.25 (0.22)	-0.10 (0.05)*	-0.06 (0.06)	0.02 (0.06)
Policy positions	0.69 (0.11)**	0.11 (0.02)**	0.12 (0.03)**	0.10 (0.03)**
Competence	0.37 (0.14)**	0.15 (0.03)**	0.20 (0.04)**	0.14 (0.04)**
Unite party	0.32 (0.18)	0.04 (0.04)	0.04 (0.05)	0.05 (0.05)
Tough decisions	0.37 (0.16)*	0.14 (0.03)**	0.14 (0.04)**	0.10 (0.04)*
Respect from leaders	0.05 (0.15)	0.04 (0.03)	0.03 (0.04)	0.17 (0.04)**
Regions	-0.003 (0.19)	0.02 (0.04)	0.003 (0.05)	-0.07 (0. 05)
Win elections	0.23 (0.23)	0.14 (0.05)**	0.23 (0.06)**	0.21 (0.06)**
Labour ties	0.12 (0.11)	0.04 (0.02)	0.02 (0.03)	-0.004 (0.02)
Intercept	4.63 (0.37)	0.15 (0.08)	0.38 (0.09)	0.23 (0.09)
R^2	.35	.47	.43	.38
N	(910)	(910)	(910)	(910)

Notes: Standard error in parentheses.
*$p < .5$; **$p < .01$.

they lose their statistical significance. In fact, the organizational factors tended to have their strongest ceteris paribus effect early in the contest. By the final ballot, most had decreased in statistical significance beyond the critical value.

The data indicate that ideology had a very weak direct effect on voting, and the effect of policy positions was mixed. Ideology had no significant effect on any of the ballots for McLaughlin and had a positive effect for Barrett on only one of the four ballots. Those on the left of the party were more likely to place Langdon higher on the preference ranking, but those attitudes had no significant effect on the likelihood of voting for Langdon. In addition, none of the policy questions had a significant impact on Langdon's support. Barrett's support was measurably reduced among those who believed that Quebec constitutes a distinct society, a result of Barrett's position during the campaign that the party and country should turn their attention away from Quebec and toward other matters. McLaughlin's support was increased among those agreeing that the Meech Lake Accord is unacceptable. Again, however, it is worth noting that on the important fourth ballot, no issue divided the supporters of McLaughlin and Barrett, and voters' attitudes toward left or right ideological self-placement had no independent effect.

Table 1.15
Determinants of support for McLaughlin

Independent variable	Preference ranking	First ballot	Second ballot	Third ballot	Fourth ballot
A. Social background					
Age	0.004 (0.003)	-0.001 (0.001)	-0.001 (0.001)	-0.001 (0.001)	-0.003 (0.001)**
Female	0.10 (0.08)	-0.08 (0.02)**	0.07 (0.02)**	0.06 (0.03)*	0.03 (0.03)
University	-0.02 (0.09)	0.01 (0.03)	0.02 (0.03)	0.04 (0.03)	0.04 (0.03)
Rural	0.02 (0.12)	-0.03 (0.04)	-0.03 (0.04)	0.07 (0.04)	0.12 (0.04)*
Metropolitan	0.09 (0.09)	0.01 (0.03)	0.04 (0.03)	0.05 (0.03)	0.03 (0.03)
Francophone	-0.25 (0.32)	-0.08 (0.09)	-0.16 (0.010	-0.03 (0.010	0.13 (0.10)
Working class	-0.04 (0.09)	0.01 (0.03)	0.01 (0.03)	-0.01 (0.03)	-0.01 (0.03)
Upper class	-0.02 (0.09)	0.01 (0.03)	0.03 (0.03)	0.06 (0.03)*	0.02 (0.03)
Public sector	0.05 (0.08)	0.01 (0.02)	-0.01 (0.02)	-0.01 (0.02)	0.01 (0.03)
Catholic	-0.04 (0.11)	-0.02 (0.03)	-0.02 (0.04)	-0.06 (0.04)	-0.05 (0.04)
British Columbia	0.08 (0.11)	0.07 (0.03)*	0.02 (0.03)	-0.04 (0.03)	-0.15 (0.04)**
Alberta	0.08 (0.12)	-0.01 (0.04)	0.005 (0.04)	-0.01 (0.04)	0.001 (0.04)
Saskatchewan	-0.20 (0.12)	-0.11 (0.03)**	-0.13 (0.04)**	0.03 (0.04)	-0.05 (0.04)
Manitoba	-0.04 (0.13)	-0.03 (0.04)	-0.01 (0.04)	-0.02 (0.04)	-0.03 (0.04)
Quebec	0.01 (0.28)	0.20 (0.08)*	0.11 (0.09)	-0.01 (0.09)	-0.02 (0.09)
New Brunswick		0.06 (0.09)	0.16 (0.09)	0.20 (0.10)*	0.21 (0.10)*
Nova Scotia	-0.55 (0.21)**	-0.05 (0.06)	-0.09 (0.07)	-0.09 (0.06)	-0.06 (0.07)
Prince Edward Island	-1.42 (0.55)*	0.04 (0.17)	0.04 (0.18)	-0.004 (0.18)	-0.20 (0.18)
Newfoundland	0.001 (0.38)	-0.005 (0.09)	0.15 (0.12)	-0.01 (0.13)	-0.03 (0.13)
Territories	0.19 (0.29)	0.17 (0.09)*	0.14 (0.09)	0.07 (0.09)	-0.08 (0.10)
Immigrant	0.10 (0.10)	0.0002 (0.03)	0.04 (0.03)	-0.03 (0.03)	0.05 (0.04)
B. Delegate status					
Affiliated union	-0.32 (0.16)*	-0.06 (0.05)	-0.13 (0.05)*	-0.10 (0.05)*	-0.09 (0.05)
Federal council	0.09 (0.18)	0.04 (0.05)	-0.04 (0.06)	-0.14 (0.06)*	-0.04 (0.06)
Central labour	-0.15 (0.23)	-0.14 (0.07)*	-0.22 (0.07)**	-0.17 (0.07)*	-0.12 (0.08)
ND Youth	-0.10 (0.20)	-0.05 (0.06)	-0.07 (0.06)	-0.08 (0.06)	-0.02 (0.07)
Small meeting	-0.16 (0.08)	-0.03 (0.03)	-0.05 (0.03)	-0.09 (0.03)**	-0.05 (0.03)
C. Policy position					
NATO	-0.08 (0.04)*	-0.004 (0.01)	0.01 (0.01)	0.01 (0.01)	0.01 (0.01)
Free trade	-0.01 (0.04)	-0.01 (0.01)	0.02 (0.01)	0.01 (0.01)	0.02 (0.01)
Meech Lake	0.05 (0.04)	-0.006 (0.01)	0.01 (0.01)	0.03 (0.01)**	0.02 (0.01)
Distinct Quebec	0.07 (0.03)*	0.01 (0.01)	0.001 (0.009)	0.01 (0.01)	0.01 (0.01)
Leader cut off	0.07 (0.03)*	0.003 (0.01)	-0.002 (0.01)	0.01 (0.01)	0.01 (0.01)
Left-right	-0.02 (0.03)	-0.01 (0.01)	-0.01 (0.01)	0.001 (0.01)	-0.002 (0.01))
D. Attitudes toward candidates					
Likeable	0.31 (0.10)**	0.12 (0.03)**	0.06 (0.03)*	0.06 (0.03)*	0.06 (0.03)
TV image	0.18 (0.09)*	0.02 (0.03)	0.02 (0.03)	0.01 (0.03)	0.03 (0.03)
Policy positions	0.37 (0.11)**	0.17 (0.03)**	0.14 (0.03)**	0.09 (0.03)**	0.04 (0.04)
Competence	0.35 (0.12)**	0.22 (0.03)**	0.23 (0.04)**	0.21 (0.04)**	0.11 (0.04)**
Unite party	0.23 (0.10)*	-0.02 (0.03)	0.03 (0.03)	0.07 (0.03)*	0.09 (0.03)**
Tough decisions	0.17 (0.11)	0.12 (0.03)**	0.14 (0.03)**	0.15 (0.04)**	0.12 (0.04)**
Respect from leaders	0.35 (0.11)**	0.05 (0.03)	0.06 (0.03)	0.09 (0.03)**	0.05 (0.03)

Table 1.15 (cont'd)
Determinants of support for McLaughlin

Independent variable	Preference ranking	First ballot	Second ballot	Third ballot	Fourth ballot
Regions	0.20 (0.10)*	0.04 (0.03)	0.03 (0.03)	-0.04 (0.03)	0.05 (0.03)
Win elections	0.55 (0.10)**	0.10 (0.03)**	0.17 (0.03)**	0.25 (0.03)**	0.30 (0.03)**
Labour ties	-0.18 (0.10)	-0.005 (0.03)	-0.02 (0.03)	-0.03 (0.3)	-0.04 (0.03)
Intercept	4.24 (0.31)	0.04 (0.09)	0.08 (0.10)	-0.001 (0.10)	0.23 (0.10)
R^2	.50	.56	.55	.56	.51
N	(926)	(926)	(926)	(926)	(926)

Notes: Standard error in parentheses.
*$p < .05$; **$p < .01$.

In view of the fact that the NDP is often described as a programmatic (as opposed to a brokerage) party, it may appear counter-intuitive that policy and ideology would play only a minimal role in the selection of party leader. Previous leadership contests, such as the showdown between Lewis and Laxer in 1971, suggest that when there are significant and salient differences between the candidates on major issues of policy, the delegates will respond by casting their ballots according to their positions on those issues, a finding that has been corroborated with research on mass publics (Archer and Johnson 1988). When leadership candidates do not differ measurably on policy, then delegates will choose according to other criteria. In the 1989 convention, the most compelling criteria were more generalized attitudes toward the candidates.

Tables 1.13 to 1.15 illustrate the marked effect on voting choice of attitudes toward the candidates. Furthermore, the coefficient emerging particularly strongly for each of the candidates, and especially for Barrett and McLaughlin, was their perceived ability to win the next federal election. If delegates believed that a candidate could help win elections, there was a strong pull for support, other things being equal. The delegates were not looking for someone necessarily on the left or right of the party, or someone who would champion one issue position over another. They wanted a winner. From that perspective, the selection of a leader in the NDP in 1989 was similar to that found in the Conservative and Liberal parties (Martin et al. 1983; Goldfarb and Axworthy 1988).

Other attitudes toward the candidates also had a significant effect on voting. The perception that he or she was competent and could make tough decisions was important for all the candidates. But there were also factors in which the candidates, particularly McLaughlin and Barrett, differed. For example, the perception that the candidate had a positive TV image did not differentiate McLaughlin supporters, and barely achieved significance for Barrett on the last ballot, a curious finding given the importance attached to winnability. Candidate likeability was more important in the earlier than the later ballots, as were the candidates' policy positions. Note that across the four ballots, likeability and policy positions decreased in importance for Barrett and McLaughlin, and by the fourth ballot were no longer significant predictors of McLaughlin support.

There was an important difference between McLaughlin and Barrett in the voters' perception of their ability to unite the party. Although it characterized Barrett's first ballot supporters, the perception that he could unite the party did not strengthen his position. Apparently, many delegates thought that a Barrett victory, particularly in the later ballots, would be divisive for the NDP. Just the opposite was true for McLaughlin. Her perceived ability to unite the party became more important across the four ballots, and by the fourth when she went head to head with Barrett, it had a strong positive effect on her support. Barrett, on the other hand, projected the image of being able to get respect from international leaders, apparently in reference to his long career as premier or opposition leader in British Columbia. The perceived ability to appeal to all regions of the country, and the likelihood of strengthening party ties with organized labour, had no measurable effect on the support for the major candidates. Thus, to reiterate, it was the perception of her as a winner for the party in federal elections, combined with perceived competence, ability to make tough decisions and to unite the party, that propelled McLaughlin to victory in 1989.

Determinants of Attitudes toward Candidates

Why did some delegates perceive McLaughlin as more likely than Barrett to help win a federal election, and perceive her as being competent? Were there any characteristics of delegates that systematically led them to develop positive images of some candidates and negative (or at least less positive) images of others? To answer these questions, estimates were generated of the effect of social background, organizational position, and policy and ideology on delegates' perceptions of the attributes of Barrett, Langdon and McLaughlin (not presented in tabular form).

Gender and favourite son or daughter loyalties exerted the strongest effects from the delegates' backgrounds. Women were much more likely than men to give McLaughlin a positive evaluation on all attributes. Barrett was favoured, although less strongly, by men. McLaughlin was strongly rewarded by residents of the territories, and Barrett received strong evaluations from British Columbia.

Among the organizational factors, the union variables once again emerge as important predictors. Overall, labour delegates perceived McLaughlin more negatively than did nonlabour delegates, whereas for Barrett, where the union effect was present, it was positive. Union delegates were not substantially more negative toward McLaughlin on all the attributes, but those areas in which their evaluations were less positive are instructive. For example, labour delegates were less likely than others to perceive McLaughlin as able to help win the next election, able to unite the party and competent to lead the party. In contrast, labour, and especially central labour, saw Barrett as taking attractive policy stands and as being competent, able to make tough decisions and able to elicit respect from international leaders.

The policy issue with the greatest positive effect for McLaughlin was the view that Quebec constitutes a distinct society. This important clause in the ill-fated Meech Lake Accord did not have the additional baggage of Senate reform, federal transfer funds reform and other aspects of the Accord that were less popular with New Democrats. Those agreeing on the distinctiveness of Quebec were less likely to support Barrett; the issue had no effect on Langdon's support. Perhaps surprisingly, delegates' positions on Canada's participation in NATO and on the free trade issue also had very little impact. Their positions on these issues simply did not affect their perceptions of the candidates' attributes.

Ideology had a role to play in the leadership selection, although not a profoundly important one, and not one, as we saw previously, that persisted to the final ballot. Barrett tended to be associated with the party's ideological right wing, although it must be noted that the party's right wing does not extend to the right of centre. Langdon, on the other hand, received disproportionate support, and positive evaluations, from those who place themselves on the party's left. Based on her support, it would appear that McLaughlin placed herself at the position of the Downsian median voter, or at some location that neither inspired nor repelled ideologues of the left or right. Consequently, ideology had almost no measurable impact directly on her support, or indirectly on attitudes toward her attributes.

FINANCING THE LEADERSHIP CONTEST

Money has been called the mother's milk of politics (Jesse Unruh, quoted in Stanbury 1986). The analogy suggests that a well-financed political party or candidate, like a well-nourished suckling baby, possesses the necessary conditions for good health and strong growth. But the analogy ends there. There exists an almost perfect relationship of supply and demand between a mother and her nursing child, in which the mother rarely produces too much or too little milk. There is, after all, a fixed amount of milk which any baby can consume, and the mother's supply will usually soon adjust to provide the amount demanded.

The financing of political parties and candidates provides a highly distorted reflection of this relationship. For one thing, there appears to be no definite point at which a party's or candidate's appetite for funds is satiated. By illustration, in the 10 years between 1977 and 1986, expenditures in the Liberal party increased from $4.2 million to $11.1 million, for Conservatives from $4.2 million to $14.1 million and in the NDP from $3.1 million to $15.2 million (Stanbury 1989, 352),[9] a rate of growth that would alarm even the most committed nursing mother. Likewise, as we shall see, there has been tremendous growth in the funds spent by candidates seeking the leadership of the parties. The parties have responded to these increased demands in different ways, with some being more and others less likely to set limits on expenditures. Consequently, the rules outlining the financing of leadership contests are quite different in each party, with the greatest difference being between the NDP and the others.

The Liberal party established a spending limit of $1.65 million per candidate in 1984 (Wearing 1988b, 73), a limit that was adjusted to $1.7 million in 1990. During the 1984 contest, the party required candidates to file financial statements, but these were not released publicly. It has been estimated that John Turner spent $1.6 million in 1984 compared with $1.5 million for Jean Chrétien, $0.9 million for Don Johnston and $0.6 million for John Roberts (ibid.). For the 1990 leadership contest, the limit of $1.7 million related only to the official campaign period itself, and most of the candidates spent funds both within and outside that period. Total spending reported by Jean Chrétien and Paul Martin was $2.1 million, and for Sheila Copps $0.75 million (Perlin 1991). The Conservatives in 1976 asked candidates to submit accounts of expenditures and receipts and all complied except Brian Mulroney. In that year Mulroney's expenditure was estimated at $343 000, compared with reported expenditure for Joe Clark of $168 000. During the 1983 contest, the party had no internal regulations regarding either limits or reporting of expenditures (Wearing 1988b, 78). However, it has been estimated that Clark's expenditures ranged from $800 000 to $1.5 million; John Crosbie's were estimated at $1.5 million and Mulroney's as high as $2 million. Thus, the leadership candidates for the Tories increased their spending between five- and tenfold in seven years. Both parties allege to have observed a limit on individual contributions of $10 000, although the lack of public reporting of individual contributions makes this impossible to verify.

For the NDP, money has historically been less plentiful (if not less important) in leadership contests, and the party has been much more inclined to regulate, or at least impose guidelines on, campaign expenditures. For example, in 1975 the party issued a document to leadership candidates outlining the rules and suggesting how they should be observed (New Democratic Party 1975). Leadership candidates could spend a maximum of $15 000, of which $1 000 would be reimbursed from the party for the party-organized candidates' tour and for mailing costs. Thus, New Democrats could spend only between one-tenth and one-twentieth of the amount estimated for Conservatives the following year. In addition, candidates were required to appoint official agents responsible for filing both an interim report (at the time of the convention) and a final report. Through that statement candidates were required to disclose all revenue and expenditures, including the identification of all contributors of $10 or more.

For the 1989 convention, the NDP issued a more detailed statement of rules governing the leadership contest (New Democratic Party 1989). The new rules called for the appointment of a chief electoral officer (Donald C. MacDonald), and candidates were required to appoint an official agent. Once again, the agents filed interim financial statements at the time of the convention, and a final statement by 1 July 1990. The party established a spending limit of $150 000 per candidate, which also was a small fraction (less than one-tenth) of the limit used by the Liberal party six months later. That limit was inclusive of candidates' spending on the party-organized candidates' tour. The party reimbursed candidates' spending on the tour to a maximum of $5 000. Thus, in effect, candidates net fund-raising (after deducting the federal revenue-sharing fee, discussed below) was limited to $145 000.[10] Contributions from individuals, unions or other organizations were limited to $1 000, and disclosure was required for all contributions, including contributions in kind exceeding $100.

All the candidates stayed well below the spending limit in 1989 (see table 1.16). The largest expenditures were by McLaughlin ($129 000) and Barrett ($114 000), which were 85.7 percent and 76.0 percent of the allowable limit, respectively. None of the remaining five candidates spent as much as one-half the allowable limit. As well, none of the candidates' fund-raising, together with the candidates' tour rebate, was sufficient to cover total expenditures, as of 1 July 1990 when the candidates were required to file their final statements. Langdon came closest to covering all his expenses, falling short by only $35.47. However, Waddell, McLaughlin, Barrett and de Jong had substantial shortfalls necessitating either a prolonged period of post-convention fund-raising by the candidates, or a decision by the candidates to personally absorb substantial costs.

In a feature first used in the 1989 contest, the party, following a ruling by Elections Canada, considered contributions to the leadership campaign as tax-creditable political contributions (New Democratic Party 1990).[11] The contributions were payable to the federal party on behalf of a candidate, and the funds were then transferred back to the candidate, minus a 15 percent "revenue-sharing" fee to the federal party. Thus, to a considerable extent, the NDP moved toward public financing, or at least public supplementing of the financing of the 1989 leadership contest.

The party enforces its regulations governing the financing of leadership contests mainly through the reporting process itself. The chief electoral officer is charged with monitoring expenditures and does so through the submission of the two (interim and final) statements. Based on the interim statements, the chief electoral officer makes a report to the convention, so that at the time of voting, delegates are apprised of the candidates' reported expenditures. At that time, the convention delegates in effect decide on the propriety of the expenditures of each candidate.[12] Other than the vote at the convention itself, the party has

Table 1.16
Leadership campaign revenue and expenditures

Candidate	Campaign expenditures ($)	Campaign revenues ($)	Surplus (deficit) ($)	Expenditure as percent of limit
Barrett	113 986.98	94 505.15	(19 481.83)	76.0
de Jong	42 516.85	42 515.85*	(26 935.73)	28.3
Lagassé	11 891.62	10 300.39	(1 591.23)	7.9
Langdon	52 461.91	52 426.44	(35.47)	35.0
McCurdy	72 891.54	68 364.08	(4 527.46)	48.6
McLaughlin	128 575.50	111 051.46	(17 524.04)	85.7
Waddell	39 256.00	30 048.00	(9 208.00)	26.2

Source: New Democratic Party, "Final Financial Statement of Candidates for Leadership" (to 30 June 1990).

*Includes loan of $26 935.73 to candidate.

two sanctions it can use to ensure that candidates abide by its spending limits and disclosure requirements. The first is financial. The party is committed to paying the costs of the all-candidates cross-country tour, to a maximum of $5 000. These funds can be withheld if candidates fail to comply with the spending and disclosure rules. More significantly, the party relies on moral suasion and the personal integrity of candidates to ensure that its rules are followed. To date, these have been sufficient to guarantee that no candidates spend funds beyond a level acknowledged by the party to be appropriate for the financing of a bid for the party's leadership.

The financing of leadership contests is one area that could profit from greater state regulation. Full public disclosure of all revenues (including an acknowledgement of all individual contributions of $100 or more) and expenditures is long overdue, for obvious reasons. The system of disclosure used annually by political parties in their fiscal period returns, or the system used by the NDP in 1989, could serve as a model for public disclosure of the financing of all leadership campaigns. The receipting of contributions to leadership contestants now appears well established, having been used by both the Liberals and the New Democrats. However, at present these funds compete with the general contributions to political parties, and fall under the same ceilings for tax-creditable reimbursements. In recognition that a party's responsibilities continue, and likely increase, during a leadership contest, contributions to such contests should be tax-creditable over and above the current limits for contributions to parties.

With respect to establishing limits on individual contributions to leadership campaigns or on campaign expenditures, there is little merit in across-the-board regulations for all parties. Many candidates borrow heavily in the early period of a campaign to establish a budget that allows for systematic planning of the campaign, hoping and expecting to raise funds to offset those costs. The experience of the NDP in 1989 suggests that many candidates' fund-raising drives fall short of these goals, with the result that many have a high personal expenditure. Limiting the size of individual contributions may have the effect, and apparently did have the effect for the NDP, of placing many candidates in breach of the rules. One way around this is to exempt the candidates' personal contributions from the spending limits. However, exempting candidates from the spending limits will result in the rules favouring more affluent candidates. Provided that reasonable spending limits are set, the inequality that can arise from differences in candidates' contributions to their own campaigns can be limited, although an effect will remain. The problem is most severe where candidates borrow heavily in anticipation of a successful fund-raising campaign and are left responsible for substantial personal contributions when this does not occur.

The issue of limiting campaign expenditures is a complex one. Many would agree that basic precepts of fairness require that limits be placed on the amount of money that any candidate can spend. However, experience suggests that the parties differ dramatically in their perception of what constitutes a reasonable amount. For New Democrats, $150 000 was deemed to be fair and sufficient in 1989. For the Liberal party six months later, the amount was more than 10 times greater. Although some people, including some potential Liberal candidates, complained that their limit was too high, no Liberals appear to have suggested that $150 000 was adequate. The figure they discussed most often was $500 000. And yet, in view of the fact that none of the New Democrat candidates' spending even approached $150 000, and for most was less than $75 000, it is apparent that a limit such as $500 000 would be inappropriate for the NDP. In deference to fairness and in light of differences between parties, the most prudent course is to encourage parties to set and enforce their own spending limits, again using the NDP's experience in 1989 as a model.

SATISFACTION WITH THE OUTCOME

There are several ways of gauging whether delegates to the NDP convention considered the experience to be successful. One way is to examine evaluations of the winning candidate relative to the other declared candidates. A post-convention survey, such as the one used for the present analysis, should help reveal whether the campaign was embittering and divisive for those whose favourite candidate lost. Another way is to go beyond the declared field of candidates to examine delegates' satisfaction with the winning candidate relative to the potential candidates for leadership. And a third is to examine delegates' satisfaction with the process of the convention itself, including the system of determining delegate entitlement and the larger question of the appropriateness of using party conventions to choose a leader. This section explores delegate satisfaction with the outcome of the contest by examining each of these questions in turn.

The Winner Relative to Other Declared Candidates

How do the delegates feel about Audrey McLaughlin relative to the declared field? The data on candidate preferences already presented showed that McLaughlin was the Condorcet winner – she could defeat every other candidate in a one-on-one contest. She had the highest first preference ranking and the second highest second preference ranking.

In addition, she was less likely than any other candidate to be ranked either last or second last in delegates' preferences. She did not evoke a lot of antipathy. When asked to use a 100-point feeling thermometer to gauge their feelings in favour of the candidates, delegates rated her 74.1, almost 10 points above the next highest candidate (Langdon at 65.3), and more than 13 points above her fourth ballot opponent, Barrett (60.8).

Furthermore, McLaughlin was not a dark-horse candidate slipping virtually unknown to victory, as Clark had done at the Conservative convention in 1976 (Brown et al. 1976). When asked, "Going into the convention, which candidate did you think was most likely to win?" 60.5 percent of respondents answered McLaughlin, 20.2 percent said Barrett and 10.0 percent thought either Barrett or McLaughlin would win. Thus, over 70 percent expected a McLaughlin victory, and most expected the final ballot to include McLaughlin and Barrett. When asked to describe how they felt about the outcome of the contest, a large majority (72.7 percent) said they felt either very satisfied or somewhat satisfied, compared with only 13.5 percent who felt somewhat or very dissatisfied. The remainder (12.8 percent) were undecided.

Although there appeared to be some sense of dissatisfaction, and perhaps embitterment, among delegates, as there is almost bound to be in a zero-sum contest of winners and losers, such feelings were held by a relatively small number of delegates. The much greater tendency of non-Barrett supporters to rank him negatively – more than a quarter (26.5 percent) viewed him as their least or second least preferred candidate – suggests that a Barrett victory would have been much more controversial and divisive. McLaughlin's wider appeal is also indicated by the finding that two-thirds of delegates (66.0 percent) thought her victory would strengthen the party, whereas only one in six (18 percent) believed it would weaken the party. The remainder (16 percent) believed it would have no effect. In light of the available alternatives, delegates were pleased with McLaughlin. There remains a residue of doubt about her selection, and about her ability to strengthen the party. Nonetheless, she is seen to possess enough positive attributes, or at least to not possess an overabundance of negative attributes, to enable the majority of delegates to rally around her leadership. Whether she is able to maintain that support will be very much a function of the way she handles her responsibilities as party leader.

The Winner Relative to Other Potential Candidates
Although McLaughlin was the most popular candidate contesting the leadership, it is much less certain whether she was the most popular New Democrat at the time of the convention and at the time of the

survey. One of the recurrent themes of commentaries on the contest during the campaign was its lacklustre character because many prominent New Democrats had chosen not to run. Given that theme, delegates were asked if they preferred anyone over all the declared candidates. A majority (51.8 percent) said yes, 40.7 percent said no and 7.5 percent were undecided or did not know. As might be expected, several non-candidates stood out as highly attractive to the delegates, with one being exceptionally popular. Stephen Lewis, former leader of the Ontario NDP, and son of former federal party leader David Lewis, was identified by almost half (47.5 percent) of those preferring someone to all the declared candidates. He was followed at some distance by (now) Ontario premier Bob Rae (18.4 percent), MP Lorne Nystrom (14.2 percent) and CAW president and NDP vice-president Bob White (8.7 percent). The remarkable finding that over half the delegates preferred someone other than the declared candidates suggests that McLaughlin's support, although widely distributed, was not very deep.

Satisfaction with the Process

The process by which the NDP chooses a leader, as noted previously, is distinct from the Liberal and Conservative processes in a number of ways, among the most prominent of which is the allocation of constituency delegates. The awarding of delegates on the size of constituency parties has resulted in an overrepresentation of the West, primarily, and Ontario to a lesser extent, and the underrepresentation of Quebec, primarily, and the Atlantic region. Delegates were asked whether they were in favour of "changing the system of constituency representation to grant equal numbers of delegate entitlement to all constituencies." Approximately seven out of every eight delegates with an opinion were opposed. While recognizing that it may present difficulties for the party in convention to act as an instrument of intra-state federalism, the delegates were inclined to see the merits of a system that rewards areas of strength rather than those of weakness. Furthermore, since unions are awarded convention delegates based on union size, there is a strong justification for continuing to use membership size as a criterion in awarding delegates to constituencies as well.

The issue of constituency representation at conventions is increasingly debated as parties move away from conventions and toward party-wide voting on leadership contests. First introduced in Canada by the Parti québécois, the one person, one vote method of selecting leaders was recently used by the Ontario and Prince Edward Island Conservative parties. The federal Conservatives at their 1989 annual meeting directed the executive to investigate the issue of direct election of leaders (Woolstencroft 1991), and the federal Liberal party, at its 1990 leadership convention, agreed to put such a system in place before the selection of its next leader. The matter was raised at the 1989 NDP convention and referred to a committee for further study. As a result, delegates to the NDP convention were asked the following question:

> The NDP constitution committee is to consider the possibility of replacing leadership conventions with a "one member, one vote" system, and to report to the next party convention. Are you in favour of a change to a "one member, one vote" system to choose party leader?

More than half of all respondents (52.4 percent) favoured the change to a "one member, one vote" system, slightly more than one-third (35.8 percent) were opposed and 11.9 percent were undecided or did not answer. Thus, there appears to be very substantial support for replacing the selection of leader by convention to the selection of leader by party membership. Putting in place such a system involves deciding on a number of technical but nevertheless very important matters. For example, does the vote take place every two years, as it does at present, or will this vote on the party leader be eliminated? How do the interests of organized labour and other groups such as the NDY find representation, if at all, in such a system? In considering such questions it is useful to reflect on the experience of parties that have used the direct election method.

The Parti québécois adopted the method in 1984 with little debate and little consideration for alternatives (Latouche 1991, 226–27). Quite remarkably, the party had existed for 16 years under one leader without having any formal rules for leadership selection. The new system was adopted because of its perceived strong democratic and open character and because it was thought that a "return to the people" might reverse the party's flagging position in the polls (ibid., 227). The model adopted was a pure one person, one vote system – all party members may vote, and the votes are summed. If no candidate receives a clear majority, a run-off between the top two contestants is held.

This system eliminates rewards for long-term party work, and all members have an equal say in leadership selection, regardless of the length of time an individual has held a membership, or the depth of commitment. There is little doubt that, in the short term, the method used by the PQ in 1985 gave the party an infusion of new energy and enthusiasm. In the period leading up to the vote, party membership increased by over 50 000, an increase of 57 percent (Latouche 1991, 230–32). But this contest, connected as it was with the departure of René Lévesque, the party's founder and a charismatic presence within the party and the province, may well be highly atypical. The membership gains experienced in 1985 were very short-lived, and within two years they had all been lost (Latouche 1991). And yet, the votes of short-term party members counted every bit as much as those who had been with the party from the outset, and who continued to be active party members. Furthermore, for all the rhetorical appeal of more "democracy" through direct election, it is difficult to escape the irony that this method in the PQ attracted only one candidate in 1988 when used for only the second time.

The experience of the Ontario and Prince Edward Island Conservative parties with the direct election of leaders suggests that it is highly questionable that this method leads to greater public participation. For example, in the Ontario Conservative contest of 1990, although almost 16 000 people voted, this was similar to the number who participated in delegate selection meetings during the two 1985 conventions (Woolstencroft 1991, 271). In the PEI Conservative leadership contest in 1990, the number of party members voting in the direct election (fewer than 900) had actually declined from the number of delegates who participated in leadership selection under the previous delegate system (approximately 1 400).[13]

The failure of direct election to produce substantially higher rates of participation is likely a result of the requirement that voters purchase a party membership to exercise a vote. In contrast to the system of primary elections in the United States, in which all those registered as supporters of a party may vote (i.e., all avowed *party identifiers*), direct election of the leader in Canada has always been limited to *party members*. The party membership fee, typically $10 a year, appears to be such a disincentive that most party supporters choose not to participate. There was a further disincentive for PEI Conservatives in 1990. The party superimposed direct election by all party members onto the convention setting. To vote, delegates had to purchase a party membership ($10), register at the convention ($15) and attend the convention in Charlottetown. Some of the candidates saw the financial costs of attending the convention as an important barrier to recruitment.[14]

Thus, it is highly debatable whether direct election of leaders results in a more open, democratic and participatory process. On the other hand, encouraging greater participation by adopting state-sponsored voter registration and state-run leadership contests appears problematic. A primary election system is premised on the assumption that both (or all) parties are choosing their leaders at the same time. In the United States, at any given moment a voter is registered as a supporter of the Democratic or Republican party, and limited to voting in the primary for only one party. However, with a variable time frame for leadership selection, the primary system is open to significant abuse. For example, a voter could claim to be a Liberal during a Liberal primary, a Conservative during a Conservative primary and a New Democrat during a New Democratic primary and vote in each of them.

Staggered leadership contests are an important feature of Canadian politics because of the role played by the leader of the defeated party. In the United States, the defeated presidential candidate has no role to play in institutionalized partisan politics, and therefore there is no need to review his or her performance. In Canada, the leader of a defeated party becomes the leader of an opposition party in Parliament, where his or her performance is open to review almost immediately following an election. However, it is neither necessary nor desirable to review the leader of the victorious party at that time.

It was noted previously that the direct election method would emphasize political equality among all electors. Furthermore, it was argued that parties may sometimes wish to reward some individuals or provide special representation to particular sections of the party. For example, at present the NDP gives more delegate seats to constituencies with a large membership than to those where it is small. As well, affiliated unions, central labour bodies and several other groups are given delegate positions. The model adopted by the Ontario Conservatives helps to reconcile the conflict between political equality and special rewards. The party used the constituency as the basic electoral unit and awarded 100 electoral votes to each. The constituencies varied in size from 23 members in the smallest to 961 in the largest (Woolstencroft 1991, 270). Candidates were awarded electoral votes in direct proportion to the number of votes received in each constituency. This system could be applied in a more generalized format to include the representation of all important groups within a party. For example, in the NDP a proportion of electoral votes could be allocated to constituencies, with others being awarded to affiliated unions, central labour, the NDY, federal council and caucus.

The portrayal of the direct election method as more open, equal and democratic than the delegate system used widely at present has provided it with substantial prima facie appeal. Some of the claims made by its proponents appear to be highly questionable in light of the experience of parties that have adopted it. As a social democratic party, the New Democrats may nevertheless find the appeal of greater democratization too difficult to resist. If direct election is adopted, it will likely be a variant of the Ontario Conservative party model, with a continued place for important groups within the party.

CONCLUSION

This study examined the leadership selection process in the NDP by focusing on the 1989 leadership convention. It also provided a comparative context by examining the NDP convention in relation to Liberal and Conservative conventions.

Similarities and differences were found between NDP conventions and those of the other two parties. All have a large majority of constituency delegates, but these are chosen quite differently, with the NDP's constituency delegates clustering in areas of party strength. A surprising number of NDP constituency delegates did not face an opponent in the delegate selection process, and the use of slates is not popular in the party. The NDP has a slightly smaller proportion of women than the Liberals and Conservatives in convention, and a much smaller percentage of youth delegates. These findings are particularly characteristic of union delegates.

The voting rules of the convention had some impact on the standings of the candidates, but did not influence the selection of the winning candidate. Barrett was not the second most preferred candidate, as voting at the convention suggested, because of the large number of delegates with negative feelings toward him. In a two-person contest, Langdon would have defeated Barrett. However, since McLaughlin was a Condorcet winner, there was no voting cycle operative.

The major determinants of voting are found in the attitudes of convention delegates toward the candidates. Of particular importance was the perception that the candidate could lead the party to electoral victory. The formation of positive and negative candidate evaluations was strongly affected by gender, by the favourite son or daughter effect, by status as a union delegate and by attitudes toward the distinctiveness of Quebec.

The NDP has played a relatively active role in regulating the financing of leadership campaigns. It has placed a relatively low limit on spending, requires public disclosure of contributions over $100 and prohibits contributions of more than $1 000. The party also uses the practice of official agency. The chief electoral officer makes a report to convention to inform delegates of the candidates' spending. In 1989, for the first time, the party issued tax receipts for political contributions for the financing of the leadership contest.

Overall the delegates viewed the experience as a success, although probably as a limited success. They were pleased, but not ecstatic, about the selection of McLaughlin as leader. There was a certain scepticism among some delegates about her ability to strengthen the party and lead it to electoral victory, although those who believed she could strengthen the party were highly supportive of her candidacy. There was also a sense of disappointment that some high-profile party activists, especially Stephen Lewis, decided not to enter the race. The process of constituency delegate entitlements was satisfactory for most delegates, as long as the party chooses its leader at convention. However, the Task Force on Party Structure is examining the proposal of "one member, one vote" for leadership selection, but has not yet brought a recommendation to convention on this matter. The data indicate that although the delegates are far from unanimous in their views, at present the "one member, one vote" method receives the support of a majority of delegates. Although there is majority support in principle, it is not clear whether a particular detailed proposal will receive a similar level of support. But one thing is clear: it will be decided by the party in convention.

NOTES

This study was completed in April 1991.

Collection of data was funded by the Research Grants Committee of the University of Calgary, the President's Fund of the Social Sciences and Humanities Research Council of Canada (SSHRCC) and a general research grant from SSHRCC. In addition, financial or material support, or both, were provided by Professors John Courtney, Ken Carty and Alan Whitehorn, and the Department of Political Science at the University of Calgary. Research assistance was provided by Lori Hausegger and Martin Bennett. The federal office of the NDP was particularly helpful in the administration of the survey, and in providing other information and assistance. I wish to thank Dick Proctor, Terry O'Grady and Brian McKee from the federal office of the NDP for facilitating this research, as well as Professors Alan Whitehorn and Herman Bakvis and the anonymous reviewers for their helpful comments. None of the individuals or institutions listed share responsibility for the analyses or interpretations in this study.

1. In total, 2 510 delegates registered at the 1989 convention. The federal office provided address labels for 2 291 delegates (it had no current address for the remainder), and 39 were returned as undeliverable; thus, 2 252 questionnaires were delivered and 1 060 were completed and returned for a response rate of 47 percent.

2. All members of unions affiliated with the NDP have the right to "opt out" of affiliation with the party. Those who opt out do not contribute any of their union dues to the party.

3. At the 1971 convention, union delegates were almost one-third (32.3 percent) of all delegates, indicating that when labour's position within the party is challenged, as many perceived to be the case with Jim Laxer's leadership bid (Brodie 1985), organized labour can and does respond with a large number of delegates, albeit with far less than 50 percent of voting delegates.

4. This situation contrasts markedly with the Liberals and Conservatives: approximately 40 percent of their delegates are under the age of 30.

5. The low response rate for union delegates, combined with their greater likelihood of supporting Barrett, accounts for much of the underestimation in Barrett support in the survey.

6. This argument was made by one of the anonymous reviewers of this paper.

7. The data on delegate preferences in tables 1.7 to 1.12 are taken from the survey of delegates, whereas the ballot results in table 1.6 are the official results of the convention. In general, the survey data conform well to observed convention data, although there are several cases in which there are important disparities. For example, at the convention 18 delegates spoiled their ballot on the fourth ballot (table 1.6), whereas the survey data indicate that 20 people reported spoiling their fourth ballot (table 1.7). This small difference is the result of people misreporting their true behaviour, or those choosing not to vote interpreting their action as spoiling their ballot (note that 2 417 ballots were cast on the second ballot, but only 2 406 on the fourth). In either case, the error is well within the expected margin. For a discussion of the error in underreporting Barrett support, see note 8.

8. Note that these data overestimate McLaughlin's support and underestimate Barrett's support among respondents. In general, Barrett's support in the survey is about six percentage points less than at the convention. McLaughlin's support is similarly overestimated by about 6 percent, and the other candidates' support is accurately mapped. This is the result of the relatively low response rate of union delegates, who were disproportionately supportive of Barrett, as well as the more generalized finding from post-convention or post-election studies that such studies overestimate the support of the winning candidate. However, the size of the error in estimation, and the fact that it applies only to McLaughlin and Barrett support, adds to the confidence in the reliability of the data on relative voter preferences. In particular, the relative preference standings for Barrett and Langdon are unaffected by the error.

9. For the NDP, this also includes federal party transfers to the provincial parties.

10. Any surplus funds were required to be donated to the party's national office.

11. Interview with Dick Proctor, 15 August 1990.

12. Interview with Donald C. MacDonald, 21 September 1990.

13. Data on voting at PEI Conservative conventions were provided by the party's provincial office.

14. Interview with Barry Clark, candidate for leadership, 19 December 1990.

REFERENCES

Archer, Keith. 1985. "The Failure of the New Democratic Party: Unions, Unionists and Politics in Canada." *Canadian Journal of Political Science* 18:353–66.

———. 1987. "A Simultaneous Equation Model of Canadian Voting Behaviour." *Canadian Journal of Political Science* 20:553–72.

———. 1990. *Political Choices and Electoral Consequences: A Study of Organized Labour and the New Democratic Party.* Montreal: McGill-Queen's University Press.

Archer, Keith, and Marquis Johnson. 1988. "Inflation, Unemployment and Canadian Federal Voting Behaviour." *Canadian Journal of Political Science* 21:569–84.

Archer, Keith, and Alan Whitehorn. 1990a. "Opinion Structure Among New Democratic Party Activists: A Comparison with Liberals and Conservatives." *Canadian Journal of Political Science* 23:101–13.

———. 1990b. "Organized Labour in the New Democratic Party." Paper presented at the Annual Meeting of the Canadian Political Science Association, Victoria.

Arrow, Kenneth J. 1961. *Social Choice and Individual Values.* New Haven: Yale University Press.

Brams, Steven J. 1985. *Rational Politics: Decisions, Games and Strategy.* Washington, DC: CQ Press.

Brodie, M. Janine. 1985. "From Waffles to Grits: A Decade in the Life of the New Democratic Party." In *Party Politics in Canada.* 5th ed., ed. Hugh G. Thorburn. Scarborough: Prentice-Hall.

Brown, Patrick, Robert Chodos and Rae Murphy. 1976. *Winners, Losers: The 1976 Tory Leadership Convention.* Toronto: James Lorimer.

Carty, R.K. 1988. "Campaigning in the Trenches: The Transformation of Constituency Politics." In *Party Democracy in Canada: The Politics of National Party Conventions,* ed. George Perlin. Scarborough: Prentice-Hall.

Clarke, Harold D., Jane Jenson, Lawrence LeDuc and Jon H. Pammett. 1991. *Absent Mandate: Interpreting Change in Canadian Elections.* 2d ed. Toronto: Gage.

Courtney, John C. 1973. *The Selection of National Party Leaders in Canada.* Toronto: Macmillan.

———. 1986. "Leadership Conventions and the Development of the National Political Community in Canada." In *National Politics and Community in Canada,* ed. R. Kenneth Carty and W. Peter Ward. Vancouver: University of British Columbia Press.

Courtney, John C., and George Perlin. 1988. "The Role of Conventions in the Representation and Accommodation of Regional Cleavages." In *Party Democracy in Canada: The Politics of National Party Conventions,* ed. George Perlin. Scarborough: Prentice-Hall.

Downs, Anthony. 1957. *An Economic Theory of Democracy.* New York: Harper and Row.

Goldfarb, Martin, and Thomas Axworthy. 1988. *Marching to a Different Drummer: An Essay on the Liberals and Conservatives in Convention.* Toronto: Stoddart.

Johnston, Richard. 1988. "The Final Choice: Its Social, Organizational, and Ideological Bases." In *Party Democracy in Canada: The Politics of National Party Conventions,* ed. George Perlin. Scarborough: Prentice-Hall.

Kornberg, Allan, Joel Smith and Harold Clarke. 1979. *Citizen Politicians: Canada.* Durham: Carolina Academic Press.

Krause, Robert, and Lawrence LeDuc. 1979. "Voting Behaviour and Electoral Strategies in the Progressive Conservative Leadership Convention of 1976." *Canadian Journal of Political Science* 12:97–135.

Latouche, Daniel. 1991. "Universal Democracy and Effective Leadership: Lessons from the Experience of the Parti Québécois." In *Leaders and Parties in Canadian Politics: The Experience of the Provinces,* ed. R.K. Carty, Lynda Erickson and Donald E. Blake. Toronto: Harcourt Brace Jovanovich.

LeDuc, Lawrence. 1971. "Party Decision-making: Some Empirical Observations on the Leadership Selection Process." *Canadian Journal of Political Science* 4:97–118.

LeDuc, Lawrence, Harold D. Clarke, Jane Jenson and Jon H. Pammett. 1984. "Partisan Instability in Canada: Evidence from a New Panel Study." *American Political Science Review* 78:470–84.

Levesque, Terrence J. 1983. "On the Outcome of the 1983 Conservative Leadership Convention: How They Shot Themselves in the Other Foot." *Canadian Journal of Political Science* 16:779–84.

Lewis, David. 1982. *The Good Fight: Political Memoirs.* Softcover ed. Toronto: Macmillan.

Martin, Patrick, Allan Gregg and George Perlin. 1983. *Contenders: The Tory Quest for Power.* Scarborough: Prentice-Hall.

Morley, Terry. 1991. "Leadership Change in the CCF-NDP." In *Leaders and Parties in Canadian Politics: The Experience of the Provinces,* ed. R.K. Carty, Lynda Erickson and Donald E. Blake. Toronto: Harcourt Brace Jovanovich.

New Democratic Party. 1975. "Rules and Suggestions for the Conduct of the Leadership Contest of the New Democratic Party of Canada – 1975." Ottawa.

———. 1989. "Leadership Rules." Ottawa.

————. 1990. "Memorandum to Official Agents for Federal NDP Leadership Campaigns, Re Tax Receipting." Ottawa.

Paltiel, Khayyam Z. 1989. "Political Marketing, Party Finance and the Decline of Canadian Parties." In *Canadian Parties in Transition: Discourse, Organization, and Representation,* ed. Alain G. Gagnon and A. Brian Tanguay. Scarborough: Nelson Canada.

Perlin, George. 1983. "Did the Best Candidate Win? A Comment on Levesque's Analysis." *Canadian Journal of Political Science* 16:791–94.

————, ed. 1988. *Party Democracy in Canada: The Politics of National Party Conventions.* Scarborough: Prentice-Hall.

————. 1991. "Attitudes of Liberal Convention Delegates toward Proposals for Reform of the Process of Leadership Selection." In *Canadian Political Parties: Leaders, Candidates and Organization,* ed. Herman Bakvis. Vol. 13 of the research studies of the Royal Commission on Electoral Reform and Party Financing. Ottawa and Toronto: RCERPF/Dundurn.

Porter, John. 1965. *The Vertical Mosaic.* Toronto: University of Toronto Press.

Power, C.G. 1966. *A Party Politician: The Memoirs of Chubby Power,* ed. Norman Ward. Toronto: Macmillan.

Schattschneider, Elmer E. 1963. *The Semi-sovereign People.* New York: Harper and Row.

Smiley, D.V. 1968. "The National Party Leadership Convention in Canada." *Canadian Journal of Political Science* 1:373–97.

Stanbury, W.T. 1986. "The Mother's Milk of Politics: Political Contributions to Federal Parties in Canada, 1974–84." *Canadian Journal of Political Science* 19:795–821.

————. 1989. "Financing Federal Political Parties in Canada, 1974–1986." In *Canadian Parties in Transition: Discourse, Organization, and Representation,* ed. Alain G. Gagnon and A. Brian Tanguay. Scarborough: Nelson Canada.

Stewart, Ian. 1988. "The Brass Versus the Grass: Party Insiders and Outsiders at Canadian Leadership Conventions." In *Party Democracy in Canada: The Politics of National Party Conventions,* ed. George Perlin. Scarborough: Prentice-Hall.

Wearing, Joseph. 1988a. *Strained Relations: Canadian Parties and Voters.* Toronto: McClelland and Stewart.

————. 1988b. "The High Cost of High Tech: Financing the Modern Leadership Campaign." In *Party Democracy in Canada: The Politics of National Party Conventions,* ed. George Perlin. Scarborough: Prentice-Hall.

Whitehorn, Alan. 1985. "The CCF-NDP Fifty Years After." In *Party Politics in Canada.* 5th ed., ed. Hugh G. Thorburn. Scarborough: Prentice-Hall.

———. 1988. "The New Democratic Party in Convention." In *Party Democracy in Canada: The Politics of National Party Conventions,* ed. George Perlin. Scarborough: Prentice-Hall.

Whitehorn, Alan, and Keith Archer. 1989. "The NDP and Territoriality." Paper presented at the Annual Meeting of the Canadian Political Science Association, Quebec.

Woolstencroft, Peter. 1983. "Social Choice Theory and the Reconstruction of Elections: A Comment on Levesque's Analysis." *Canadian Journal of Political Science* 16:785–89.

———. 1991. " 'Tories Kick Machine to Bits': Leadership Conventions and the Ontario Conservative Party." In *Leaders and Parties in Canadian Politics: The Experience of the Provinces,* ed. R.K. Carty, Lynda Erickson and Donald E. Blake. Toronto: Harcourt Brace Jovanovich.

2

ATTITUDES OF LIBERAL CONVENTION DELEGATES TOWARD PROPOSALS FOR REFORM OF THE PROCESS OF LEADERSHIP SELECTION

George Perlin

T HE LEADERSHIP SELECTION process in parties may be evaluated from a variety of perspectives. This study is concerned with the extent to which that process conforms to norms of democratic legitimacy. The premise of the analysis here is that the public's confidence in the wider system of party politics will be influenced by its impression of the way the parties conduct their internal affairs. The study will first consider criticisms that suggest the existing process of leadership selection in the Liberal and Progressive Conservative parties does not meet standards of democratic legitimacy. Then, on the basis of a survey of delegates to the Liberal leadership convention of 1990, the study will examine the attitudes of participants in the process to proposals for reforming it. Finally, the study will comment on the implications of these attitudes for the future development of the leadership selection process, concentrating on the question before the Commission of whether the process should be regulated by the state.

THE EVOLUTION OF THE LEADERSHIP CONVENTION
In 1919 the Liberal party became the first federal party to choose its national leader in a convention of delegates representing all of the

party's constituent elements. In 1927 the Conservative party adopted the same procedure. Since then, with one exception, the convention has been the method of leadership selection used by both parties.[1]

The need to bring the parties' practices into line with popular conceptions of democracy was an important factor in the development of this method of selecting a leader. In provincial politics the convention had begun to replace selection by party notables early in the century. It was a time when the legitimacy of the whole system of party politics was being challenged by ideas of direct democracy which had developed in the United States.[2] There is no evidence to link the Liberal party's decision to choose its leader by convention in 1919 directly to these ideas, but the decision was made as the pressure for democratic reform was reaching its peak. The very existence of the Liberal and Conservative parties was being challenged by the Progressive movement, which advocated various devices of direct democracy as a means to end a party politics that was claimed to be corrupt, élitist and unresponsive to citizens. The election of 65 Progressives in 1921 sent a clear message to the established parties. Although there were other reasons for the Liberals and Conservatives to make leadership selection by convention a permanent feature of their internal government,[3] by doing so they were demonstrating that they understood the new spirit of democracy in the country. To be sure the convention was an institution, not of direct democracy, but of representative democracy, but it was markedly different from the practices of the past in that it provided a significant opportunity for citizen participation.

There was no serious challenge to the legitimacy of the convention for the better part of 60 years. But in the 1960s significant changes in the technology of political communications and the nature of convention politics were to have a very important effect on the way in which the convention was viewed.

The critical change in the technology of political communications, of course, was the central role assumed by television. As television became the principal medium of political communication, it affected views of leadership selection in two ways.

First, the central position of the leader in Canadian party politics was dramatically accentuated. The nature of television is to emphasize personalities. The national party leaders, formerly known at best only as disembodied voices on the radio, were now seen regularly in the living rooms of Canadians. Political conflict was expressed through their images on national television. The competition among parties was transformed into a competition among their leaders.[4]

Second, the leadership convention became a much more visible part of the political process. Up to this time conventions had been conducted more or less in private, attracting media attention only after they met and then receiving only limited coverage, often not even on a daily basis.

In 1967, for the first time, the convention became a major television event, covered virtually continuously from beginning to end. By 1983 television coverage had been widened to incorporate regular reports on television news programs, dealing with every phase and element of the process from the time of the calling of the convention. A similar pattern of coverage developed in the print media, with newspapers assigning staff to full-time convention coverage, providing regular reports throughout the pre-convention period and producing special convention-week sections and editions.

As a result of these changes, leadership selection has acquired a much more central place in the portrayal of politics to voters, and leadership politics has come under much closer public scrutiny.

As this was occurring there were changes in the character of convention politics. Early conventions were relatively small gatherings, usually attended by fewer than 1 300 delegates and never by more than 1 600. Delegates were selected informally, often by a handful of local party members who did not even bother to call a selection meeting; there was little pre-convention campaigning; and delegate support was mobilized through personal contacts by the candidates or intermediaries. Since the 1960s convention politics has assumed a very different form. The critical factor in this change has been the growth in the size of conventions and the broadening of the base of participation in delegate selection. At the 1967 and 1968 conventions, for the first time, there were more than 2 000 delegates. At the conventions of 1983 and 1984 there were more than 3 000, and at the Liberal convention of 1990 there were 4 670. There has been a similar growth in the number of people attending delegate-selection meetings. Some meetings to select delegates for the 1990 convention were attended by more than 2 000 party members. It seems likely that, country-wide, from 75 000 to 100 000 people may have taken part in the selection of delegates for the 1990 convention. The need to appeal to an ever larger number of delegates and to the tens of thousands of party members engaged in selecting delegates has compelled candidates to devise ever more elaborate and sophisticated campaigns, availing themselves of all the techniques of political mobilization that have been developed to win the votes of mass electorates. Candidates now make extensive national tours before the convention, attempt to influence the selection of delegates by establishing local organizations in the constituencies, seek wide coverage in the mass media, conduct polls, use direct mail and telemarketing to appeal for the support of party activists and delegates, maintain computerized data banks to track delegate preferences and attitudes, and stage elaborate convention-week events to maintain the morale of their supporters and give their campaigns the aura of success.

As the convention came under closer public scrutiny, there were elements in this new style of convention politics, as well as older features of the convention, that raised questions about how well this method of leadership selection stood up to the norms of democratic practice.

CRITICISMS OF THE PROCESS

Very little is known directly about what opinions the public has formed of conventions because there has been almost no research into these opinions. The only study that reports having asked an evaluative question about leadership selection in the federal parties is a survey done for the Commission.[5] Only 40 percent of the respondents in this survey said they were satisfied with the way in which leaders are chosen. (Thirty-one percent said they were dissatisfied and 29 percent did not express an opinion.) Unfortunately, since this survey was not designed to explore opinions about specific elements of the process, it offers no evidence about what might have provoked this low level of satisfaction. However, some inferences about public attitudes may be drawn from analyses by journalists, scholarly commentaries and testimony before the Commission.

One set of criticisms of the convention has focused on issues of representation.

First, while recurring amendments to apportionment rules have progressively extended the representation accorded the parties' mass memberships, these rules have continued to provide a substantial role in conventions for unelected delegates. The balance of voting power lies with the elected representatives of the constituency associations and local units of affiliated student and women's organizations, but delegates from the constituency associations, which are the basic units of mass participation in the two parties, made up only 56 percent of the PC convention in 1983, 57 percent of the Liberal convention in 1984 and 69 percent of the Liberal convention in 1990.

There is good reason in a system of parliamentary democracy to ensure a place for the parties' legislative élites in the selection of the party leader. Since the leader's authority can be exercised only through the structure of the parliamentary party, the leader must be able to command the confidence of his or her colleagues in the parliamentary party.

But the categories of ex officio delegates go well beyond the parties' members of Parliament to include organizational élites at both the federal and provincial levels. Whether or not this can be justified, the result is that élites continue to be portrayed as exercising inordinate influence in conventions. Indeed, it is common for commentators to attribute convention results to the activities of élites (Stewart 1988a).

Second, there has been recurring criticism of conventions because of the class bias in the backgrounds of delegates. Every study of Liberal and Conservative conventions has found that two-thirds or more of the delegates come from the wealthiest, best-educated and highest-status occupational groups in the Canadian population. Convention politics in the Liberal and Progressive Conservative parties are dominated by high-status groups.

All studies of political participation have found higher levels of activism among the better-off and better-educated. The reasons include the fact that these people are more interested in politics and have more time to devote to public affairs. But there are also structural barriers to political activism by people of lower socio-economic status. In the case of conventions the obvious structural barrier is the cost of participation. With travel, food, accommodation and registration fees, the expenses for the average delegate can now be expected to exceed $2 000. The parties have provided some financial support to equalize disparities in travel costs but otherwise have failed to deal with this problem.

Third, although the parties have adopted rules to ensure representation from the constituencies for women, and although they have special categories of delegates to represent women's organizations, they have not achieved gender equity in the structure of their conventions. Under the constitutions in effect in 1983 and 1984, one-third of the delegates from each constituency had to be women. Both parties also provided for representation from women's organizations. As a result of these affirmative action provisions the proportion of women delegates to Conservative conventions increased from 19% in 1967 to 37% in 1983, and the proportion of women delegates to Liberal conventions increased from 18% in 1968 to 40% in 1984.[6] In 1986 the Liberal party adopted regulations that require gender equality among all delegates selected by constituency associations and youth clubs. Coupled with the representation provided to women's organizations, this change increased the number of women eligible to attend the Liberal convention of 1990 to 45%, almost but still not quite gender parity.

One reason the parties have not been more successful in giving women equitable representation is that the party élites, represented through ex officio delegateships, remain predominantly male. Only about 10% of the ex officio delegates to the 1983 Conservative convention and 11% of the ex officio delegates to the 1984 and 1990 Liberal conventions were women. This is another aspect of the problem created by the continued allotment of delegateships to the parties' élites.

Fourth, although affirmative-action rules have helped the parties reduce the gender imbalance at conventions, they have created a new form of imbalance by substantially overrepresenting young people. The number of delegates under the age of 30 attending Conservative conventions grew as a result of affirmative action rules from 20% in 1967 to 27% in 1976 to 40% in 1983. In the Liberal party it grew from 20% in 1968 to 30% in 1984 and 36% in 1990. The number of delegates aged 24 or younger made up close to one-third of the Conservative convention in 1983 and 26% of the Liberal convention in 1990.

The protection of a role for young people in conventions can be defended from the parties' perspective on the grounds that it keeps the parties in touch with the opinions of first-time voters, helps them recruit new members into their élites and provides a continuing supply of energetic workers for election campaigns. But the affirmative-action rules for young people have been so open-ended that conventions are in danger of coming under the dominance of the parties' youth wings. That has happened because the parties' constitutions provide for the representation of clubs at all recognized post-secondary educational institutions. Thus there is the possibility for the creation of hundreds, indeed perhaps thousands, of additional delegates. The parties also require that one-third of the delegates elected by constituency associations be youth delegates (30 or younger).

These rules for protecting young people have a distorting effect on representation in at least two ways. For one thing, of course, there is an obvious imbalance in the representation of age-based interests. This is a matter of increasing importance as society engages in debates about such issues as the allocation of social spending, retirement policy and employment policy. In addition there is an indirect effect on the representation of other kinds of interests. This is dramatically illustrated by the fact that 19% of the delegates to the Liberal convention in 1990 were students, a situation that clearly distorts the representation of socio-economic interests – both because it reduces representation from other occupational groups and because students tend to be from higher-status backgrounds.

A second set of criticisms has focused on the delegate-selection process. One problem arises from the fact that the parties have adopted procedures to facilitate broad participation in delegate-selection meetings. These meetings have been effectively open to participation by any person who chooses to declare him- or herself a party member. Membership fees are nominal, and membership lists are kept open for extended periods, often right up to the day of the delegate-selection meeting. Both parties have left the constituency associations to decide when and where delegate-selection meetings will be held. However commendable the objectives, these rules have permitted the "packing" of delegate-selection meetings by candidates and by single-interest and extremist groups. Rival groups have been willing to mobilize "any warm body" to get a vote at a meeting.

This practice has grown rapidly. In 1990 more than 80% of the constituency delegates to the Liberal convention said they had run on slates, whereas in 1984 the number was less than 40%.[7]

Probably no aspect of convention politics has done more to bring the process into disrepute than the packing of delegate-selection meetings. This form of political activity simply as a form of activity has been portrayed as illegitimate. Making it worse has been the fact that some meetings have been packed with people who have little interest in, understanding of or commitment to the choices they are being asked to make. This image of packed meetings became a stereotype for the delegate-selection process during the Conservative convention campaign in 1983 through a videotaped scene, shown often on television, of men from a street mission, described as "derelicts," disembarking from a bus to vote at a delegate-selection meeting. There have also been frequent references to participation in these meetings by groups of new immigrants, some not yet even citizens, who understood so little of the process that they had to be guided through every stage. The fact that the recruits for packing have often been drawn as a bloc from ethnic minority communities has added another, particularly unpleasant, aspect to the attention packing has received. This is because the reporting of these meetings has sometimes evoked images that could well contribute to racism.[8]

Another problem in the process of delegate selection is that the rules of apportionment have undermined one of the most fundamental norms of democratic process: the principle of equality in voting rights. Some party members have been able to get more than one vote because they are eligible to vote in elections for different categories of delegates. As John Courtney has pointed out, for example, a female university student under age 30 in the Progressive Conservative party in 1983 could vote four times – for constituency youth delegates, constituency senior delegates, campus club delegates and women's association delegates (Courtney 1983, 8).

There is no way of knowing how many party members actually vote for more than one category of delegate because there have been no systematic studies of voting in delegate-selection meetings. But anecdotal evidence from interviews with party élites and youth organization members, and published complaints from party members who feel they have been treated unjustly by the rules that permit multiple voting, suggests the practice is fairly common in both parties. Despite the manifest inconsistency of multiple voting with democratic principles, the parties have made no effort to eliminate it.

The rules for delegate elections have also been criticized for allowing people to vote who are not eligible to vote in elections for public office. The minimum age for voting in delegate elections is 14, and there is no requirement that participants be Canadian citizens. Again, because there has been no research about the people who vote at delegate-selection meetings, there is no way of telling how many of them are actually ineligible to vote in public elections. Judging by the proportion of Liberal delegates in 1990 who were under the voting age (3%), the number is probably small. But the fact the rules permit even a small number of people who are not eligible voters to have a voice in the choice of party leaders has been a source of complaints.

Another criticism in this area focuses on the integrity of the processes by which delegates have been chosen from campus clubs. Open-ended rules for representation from campus clubs have encouraged candidates' organizations to establish new clubs on a wide scale and, in many cases, to seek accreditation for delegates chosen under uncertain circumstances from clubs of doubtful legitimacy. The parties have curbed the worst abuses of these rules, the creation of "instant" campus clubs, by establishing cut-off dates for the registration of clubs, but there continue to be questions about the selection procedures followed by the campus clubs.

A third set of issues that has attracted much criticism arises from the power of money in convention campaigns. Campaign costs have grown rapidly with the development of the new style of convention politics. Some candidates in the 1983 and 1984 conventions spent more than $1.5 million. In 1990 both the Chrétien and Martin campaigns spent more than $2 million, which, even allowing for inflation, is four to five times what any candidate spent in the conventions of 1967 and 1968.

Being able to raise such sums is important, and not just to ensure that the candidate can get his or her message through to the delegates. One of the criteria by which journalists and delegates are likely to judge a candidate is his or her ability to conduct an effective national campaign. Indeed, as Fletcher (1988, 100) has pointed out, simply having "the capacity to raise funds" is one of the indicators journalists use in judging the seriousness of a candidacy.

The large amount of money required makes it difficult for candidates to compete on an equal footing. Few candidates have been able to raise the large amount of money required. That this is a deterrent is demonstrated by the decision of Lloyd Axworthy, clearly a candidate of national stature, not to contest the Liberal convention in 1990 because he could not raise enough money to mount an effective campaign.

The large sum required also forces candidates to rely on contributions from wealthy individuals, groups or corporations. Manifestly, this discriminates against candidates who do not have access to the main source of such contributions: corporations. It has been argued that this is a particular problem for women candidates because they are not well-connected to the parties' networks of corporate donors (Wearing 1988, 81).[9] It also discriminates against candidates whose opinions are at variance with those of corporate contributors.

A more general issue raised by the high cost of a leadership campaign, which goes to the very heart of the matter of legitimacy, is the power of money to determine or appear to determine the outcome of the process. This point was made in several submissions to the Commission, reflecting a number of different interests and ideological perspectives.[10] Since the conventions of 1967 and 1968, the charge has been made repeatedly from within the parties that the integrity of the process has been compromised by the appearance that money influences convention outcomes. There have been complaints both about spending and about the size and sources of contributions.

The parties themselves have recognized the problem and made efforts to introduce some form of control over the financing of leadership campaigns, attempting to limit spending and require disclosure of contributions. But these rules have been more or less ineffective – if not counterproductive – because of the controversy they have generated or, more seriously, because they have been broken.[11] The underlying problem is that in the absence of legal regulation the parties have no way of enforcing these rules.

PROPOSALS FOR REFORM

The criticism of the existing system of leadership selection has engendered proposals for three kinds of major reforms.

First, there have been proposals for changing the method of leadership selection to give rank-and-file party members more direct and complete control in systems similar to American primary elections. Some call for a convention made up entirely of elected delegates, others for replacing the convention with a system in which members vote directly for the leader. Two provincial parties have already used direct election – the Parti québécois in 1985 and 1988 and the Ontario Conservative party in 1990 – and the federal Liberal party appears to be moving in the same direction. Direct election was first discussed by the Liberals in 1984 in the context of a general discussion of proposals to introduce more democracy to the party's internal government. A meeting on the party constitution held during the 1990 convention voted to authorize a task force to work out a method of direct election to be put to a convention on reform of the party constitution in the fall of 1991 (subsequently rescheduled for February 1992). This vote has been construed as an endorsement of the principle of direct election. However, since the meeting at which it took place was attended by fewer than one-fifth of the delegates and there was no way of knowing how representative they may have been of the full convention, it was not clear how accurately this vote reflected delegate attitudes and, therefore, it was not clear whether a full convention would endorse direct election.

The argument for direct election is that it is more democratic, giving rank-and-file party members full control over the choice of the leader; that it avoids the unfairness of apportionment rules that permit multiple voting; that it can be regulated more effectively to prevent the kinds of abuses that have occurred in delegate selection for conventions; and that for all these reasons it is more likely to promote public confidence in leadership selection. Conventions are defended on the grounds that they ensure that every region, no matter how weak a party's electoral base within it, has a voice in the party's deliberations; that they provide a forum in which representatives of the diverse interests the party seeks to incorporate can work out accommodations; that as a deliberative body in which the opinions of party élites can be heard and in which participants have close contact with representatives of every element of the party, it is better equipped than a mass-based election to make informed and wise judgements about the competence of leadership candidates; that it has been an effective mechanism for the recruitment of new activists for the party; and that because of the attention it attracts from the media it is a means of getting valuable publicity for the party.

Second, there have been proposals to reform the financing of leadership campaigns by applying to them the same principles that have been used in regulating the financing of parties in their external activities. These proposals have included campaign spending limits, spending disclosure requirements, contribution limits, the disclosure of the sources of contributions, restrictions on the sources of contributions and public subsidization for campaign expenses.

Third, it has been argued that leadership selection should be brought under public regulation. Most of the proponents of this view maintain that there is a need for effective sanctions to enforce regulations governing campaign finance, but some people go so far as to propose public regulation and administration of the process by which leaders are chosen. One such proposal is that Canada should adopt a system of voter registration like that in the United States, which allows voters who declare a party affiliation to vote in party primaries. Another is that the parties give Elections Canada responsibility for delegate elections or voting by party members in a system of direct election.

Proponents of public regulation argue that only the authority of the state, buttressed by sanctions enforceable by law, can ensure the integrity of leadership elections. Those who oppose public regulation argue that, as private organizations, parties should be left to establish principles of internal government consistent with their own values and that if they do not conduct themselves in a manner consistent with public expectations the public can express its disapproval by not voting for them.

THE SURVEY OF LIBERAL DELEGATES

How do party members who have participated in the existing system view these proposed reforms? To answer this question a mail survey of delegates to the 1990 Liberal leadership convention was conducted for the Commission in the fall of 1990.

The questionnaire was mailed to 4 670 delegates. One hundred and thirty questionnaires were returned unanswered because of invalid addresses; 1 507 questionnaires were completed by delegates and returned, a return rate of 32.3%, which is close to that which would be expected for a mail survey. The representativeness of the sample was tested by comparing data for known characteristics of the whole delegate body with those of the sample. Comparisons were made for delegate type, province, gender, language and voting choice. Generally there was a close similarity between the characteristics of the sample and those of the delegate body as whole. The only notable exception was in the distribution of the sample by province. Delegates from Quebec made up 18% of the sample, compared to 23% in party records of those eligible to attend the convention. Controls using the other variables suggested this was due, not to an under-sampling of any particular group, but rather to a generally lower response rate from Quebec. There is no evidence in the analysis of the data that this had any significant effect on the overall distribution of attitudes in the sample.

The questionnaire dealt with attitudes related to the specific interests of the Commission. Although it would have been useful to ask about other attitudes, the large number of questions needed to deal with the issues before the Commission made this impracticable. Delegates were also asked about their voting behaviour at the convention, their participation in the convention campaign, their social characteristics, the processes (for those who were elected) by which they were chosen, and their experience and positions in the party. Since there were surprisingly few statistically significant differences in attitudes along any of these dimensions, the data are presented primarily in the form of distributions representing the aggregate opinions of delegates. Where there were significant differences between subgroups, they are reported in the text.

Delegate Attitudes toward the Convention

There is an obvious parallel between current public attitudes toward the political process and public attitudes 70 years ago, when the parties turned to the convention as the method of leadership selection. Opinion polls show that large numbers of citizens do not trust politicians and doubt their honesty, that large numbers feel they have no voice in political decisions, that politicians are unresponsive to their concerns and that there is need for reforms to the political process.[12]

These attitudes are an important consideration in delegate opinions of the current system of leadership selection. Fifty-eight percent of them said they were very concerned about the effect of low levels of confidence in politicians on the level of confidence in the political process as a whole, and 33% said that they were concerned (see tables 2.1 and 2.2). Fifty-one percent said they believed the decline in confidence in politicians is a result of "the way the whole process of party politics is conducted" rather than of the conduct of some individuals. And 74% said they believed that "the way in which the selection of party leaders has been done and/or some of the things that have happened in leadership convention campaigns" have had some part in creating low levels of confidence in the integrity of politicians.

Most of the delegates wanted extensive changes to the system. The most dramatic change they wanted is in the method of leadership selection. When asked how they think the leader should be chosen, only 18% said the convention system "much as it is now." Fifty-five percent said they wanted the leader chosen by direct election. Another 24% favoured one of two forms of convention made up entirely of elected delegates (see table 2.3).

Some variation among subgroups might be expected in delegate views of the two systems, reflecting the way different groups have fared

Table 2.1
Delegate opinions about low levels of voter confidence

	%
Many public opinion surveys have reported that levels of voter confidence in the integrity of politicians, regardless of what party they represent, are quite low. Do you believe this is a reaction to the behaviour of just some individual politicians or that it is a reaction to the way the whole process of party politics is conducted?	
Reaction to the conduct of some individuals	44
Reaction to the way the whole process is conducted	51
How concerned are you about the possible effect of this attitude on the overall level of confidence in the political process in Canada? Very concerned, concerned, a little concerned, not concerned?	
Very concerned	58
Concerned	33
A little concerned	8
Not concerned	1
Do you think the way in which the selection of party leaders has been done and/or some of the things that have happened in leadership convention campaigns have had any part in creating low levels of public confidence in the integrity of politicians?	
Yes	74
No	25

Note: "No opinion" responses have not been reported in any of these tables. They normally range from 2 to 5%. Unless otherwise stated the number of cases in all tables is 1 507.

Table 2.2
Concern among delegates about effect of low voter confidence on overall confidence in the political process, by selected other responses

	% of each level of concern who hold opinions shown in the left column			
	Very concerned (*N = 866*)	Concerned (*N = 482*)	A little concerned (*N = 124*)	Not concerned (*N = 21*)
Believe the way leadership campaigns have been conducted has helped create low levels of confidence in politicians	80	70	56	57
Believe low levels of confidence are a reaction to the way the whole process of party politics is conducted	58	45	34	33
Believe internal affairs of parties should be subject to at least partial public regulation	66	61	48	48

Table 2.3
Delegate views of how party leader should be chosen

	%
By a convention of delegates allocated and chosen pretty much as delegates to the 1990 convention were allocated and chosen	18
By a convention made up entirely of delegates elected by the riding association members	8
By a convention made up entirely of elected delegates mostly from the riding associations but also including delegates elected by youth, aboriginal people, and women's organizations	16
Not by a convention, but by a direct vote of all party members	55

in the convention system. The people who have benefited most from the convention are young people, in particular students, because affirmative-action rules have given them a disproportionately large voice in convention decisions. In fact, the convention, and not direct election, was supported by a majority of student delegates and, generally, by all delegates 24 years of age or younger. But, even among student delegates, 45% supported direct election.

Support for the two systems might also be expected to vary by province, since people from the smaller provinces have proportionately more influence in conventions (because of the allocation of delegates by constituency and to certain categories of officials by province) than they might have if apportionment were based on population. This expectation was only partially fulfilled. The convention was supported by majorities in Prince Edward Island and Newfoundland, but direct election was supported by majorities in Nova Scotia and New Brunswick. The convention also did better than might have been expected in Ontario – where the two systems were supported by roughly the same number of delegates (48%). Support for direct election was greatest in the four western provinces, exceeding 60% in all four.

There were no other significant variations in patterns of group support for the two systems.

The delegates were asked to compare direct election and the convention in several areas related to the arguments that have been made for the two systems. The question asked which system they thought would do the better job in each area. The distribution of their responses is shown in table 2.4.

What is most striking in table 2.4 is the fact that 68% of the delegates said direct election would do a better job than the convention of promot-

Table 2.4
Delegate evaluation of convention and direct vote
(percentages)

	Convention	Direct vote	Both the same
Which system of leadership selection, a convention system or a system in which the leader is chosen by a direct vote of all the party members, would do the better job in respect to each of the following?			
Representing regional interests	29	50	17
Selecting the most competent leader	31	50	17
Recruiting ethnic minorities into the party	35	37	23
Promoting confidence in the integrity of the process	15	68	13
Representing women's interests	32	39	25
Limiting the influence of extremist groups	26	56	13
Getting favourable publicity for the party	55	30	11
Representing Aboriginal people	42	34	20
Recruiting young people into the party	52	30	15
Reconciling and accommodating conflicting interests	33	42	19
Keeping down the costs of leadership campaigns	18	63	15

ing confidence in the integrity of the process. Even among those delegates who said they favoured retention of the convention, in either its present form or some modified form, a plurality (44%) said direct election would be better than the convention at achieving this purpose. (Only 30% said the convention would do a better job.) These data clearly point to a connection between delegate concern about the legitimacy of the process and support for direct election. This connection is substantiated by two other pieces of evidence. First, there is an association between delegate concern about low levels of confidence in politicians and support for direct election. Support for direct election is strongest among delegates who said they are "very concerned." Second, delegates who believe the conduct of leadership politics has contributed to low levels of confidence in politicians are more likely than other delegates to support direct election (see table 2.5).

Table 2.5
Opinions of delegates who support direct election of party leader on questions
related to confidence in the political process

	% who support direct election	N
Believe decline in confidence is result of conduct of some individuals	44	667
Believe decline in confidence is result of way whole process is conducted	64	767
Level of concern with decline in confidence		
Very concerned	60	866
Concerned	51	482
A little concerned	40	124
Not concerned	30	21
Has the way leaders have been chosen helped cause the decline in confidence in politicians?		
Yes	62	1 121
No	32	370

Most delegates also rejected some of the principal arguments made on behalf of the convention (see table 2.4). Only 29% said the convention would be better at representing regional interests,[13] only 31% said it would be better at selecting the most competent leader and only 33% said it would be better at reconciling and accommodating conflicting interests.

There are only two areas in which a majority of the delegates said the convention would be better. Fifty-five percent said it would be better at getting publicity for the party and 52% said it would be better at recruiting young people into the party.

The delegates' evaluations of the two systems were least clear in their assessments of which system would be better at representing the interests of particular groups. Thirty-two percent thought the convention, and 39% thought direct election, would be better at representing women; 35% thought the convention, and 37% thought direct election, would be better at recruiting ethnic minorities; and 42% thought the convention, and 34% thought direct election, would be better at representing Aboriginal people. It should be noted that women and men had different views on which system would be better at representing women's interests. A plurality of women said direct election, and a plurality of men said the convention. This difference is probably explained by the fact that many men see affirmative-action rules for representation in conventions as benefiting women, even though, despite the existence of these rules, women have not achieved representation proportional to their share of the population.

The need to limit the length of the questionnaire made it impossible to explore in detail what form of direct election the delegates would prefer. However, they were asked about one matter of particular interest. Critics have argued that direct election, if based on the principle that every party member's vote is of equal weight, would be likely to weaken the influence in the choice of the leader of parts of the country where the party is weak because in those places it is likely to have fewer active members. For this reason it has been suggested that in a direct election an equal number of votes should be given to each constituency or a fixed number of votes to each province, proportional to the size of its population. Delegates were asked for their views of these two systems as opposed to a system in which the vote of every party member everywhere in the country had exactly the same weight. Only 28% said they would want balloting based on the allocation of an equal number of votes to each riding, and only 14% said they would want votes allocated by province, whereas 53% said they preferred the straight one-person–one-vote system. Surprisingly enough, there was no significant regional variation in response to this question.

The Rules of Participation

In view of the criticism that the parties' delegate-selection meetings are not open enough, delegates were also asked about participation in leadership elections. Most of them favoured open participation. Thus 63% said, "Participation in the delegate selection process is a legitimate way for various interest groups to make sure their views are heard in the party," whereas only 35% said, "Particular ethnic, issue and other forms of interest groups should not be organized as groups to vote for slates of delegates to conventions." And 57% said, "The recruitment of people who know very little about politics and the party to vote for delegates is a good thing because it gets new people involved in the party and helps to educate them about politics," whereas only 39% said, "People who know very little about politics and the party should not be recruited to vote for delegates to conventions." The delegates were also asked about eligibility for voting in leadership elections. Though most of them favoured open participation, they did not extend that to people who are not Canadian citizens. Eighty-seven percent said they opposed voting by non-citizens, a practice that, as we have observed, is claimed to be common in delegate-selection meetings. And most of them were also opposed to the current rules that permit people as young as 14 to vote for delegates. Fifty-nine percent said the minimum age should be 18 or older. In short the delegates wanted leadership elections to be open, but they wanted participation to be governed by the same criteria of eligibility as elections to Parliament.

The Issue of Public Regulation

It has been argued, as was noted earlier, that the best way for the parties to ensure the integrity of leadership elections would be to place their administration under public regulation. The model commonly cited is that of the United States, where eligibility to vote in primary elections is determined by the laws of state legislatures and where state electoral officials run the primaries.

Most of the delegates did not want government involvement in the management of leadership elections (see table 2.6). Sixty-two percent said they were opposed to a system of voter registration in which voters could declare a party affiliation in order to establish their eligibility to vote in party constituency nomination or leadership elections; 60% said registration to vote in party leadership elections should be done by party officers rather than by Elections Canada; and 60% said party officials, rather than Elections Canada, should run party leadership elections.

But the rejection by delegates of these specific forms of intervention in election management does not mean that they rejected all forms of government intervention.

Opinion among them was almost equally divided between those who believed that the electoral laws should "establish some common standards and principles to govern the selection of leaders in all parties which are officially registered under the law" and those who believed that "the parties should be left entirely on their own to decide by what standards and principles they will select their leaders."

Moreover, most of them (63%) accepted the principle that, because of the importance of the public responsibilities of parties, their internal affairs should be "subject to at least partial regulation by public law."

And 59% said, "There should be a code of ethics to which parties *must* subscribe before they can become eligible for financial benefits under election and party expenses legislation" (see table 2.7).

Those who approved of a mandatory code of ethics were asked what they would want the code to cover. More than half the delegates who answered this question mentioned items related to campaign finance (see table 2.8).

Table 2.6
Delegate attitudes toward public regulation

	%

A *Which of these statements better represents your opinion?*

Political parties should be free to regulate their internal affairs by their own rules, as they think best. **36**

or

Political parties have important public responsibilities and their internal affairs should be subject to at least partial regulation by public law. **63**

B To help establish eligibility for voting in party leadership elections or to elect delegates to leadership conventions, would you favour the adoption of a system in Canada in which voters registering to vote had the option to declare a party affiliation?

Yes **34**
No **62**

C Even if you do not agree with adopting a system like this, do you think registration to vote in these elections should be done by Elections Canada (the staff of the Chief Electoral Officer) or that it should continue to be done by officers of the party riding associations?

Elections Canada **34**
Officers of the riding associations **60**

D If the election of the Liberal party's leader is based on a system in which all of the members vote, should that system be run by Elections Canada or by officials of the party?

Elections Canada **37**
Officials of the party **60**

E *Which of these statements better represents your opinion?*

Electoral law should establish some common standards and principles to govern the selection of leaders in all parties which are officially registered under the law. **48**

or

The parties should be left entirely on their own to decide by what standards and principles they will select their leaders? **49**

F If contributions to leadership candidates are to be regulated, should the regulation be done by each party under its own rules or should it be done by public law under legislation such as the *Election Expenses Act*?

By each party under its own rules **34**
By public law **64**

G If spending by leadership candidates is to be regulated, should the regulation be done by each party under its own rules or should it be done by public law such as the legislation governing election expenses?

By each party under its own rules **40**
By public law **57**

Table 2.7
Delegate attitudes toward a code of ethics for parties

	%
It has been suggested that there should be a code of ethics to govern the conduct of political parties. What is your opinion of this idea?	
There should be a code of ethics to which parties *must* subscribe before they can become eligible for financial benefits under election and party expenses legislation.	59
There should be a code of ethics to which parties should be asked to subscribe *voluntarily*.	27
There should not be a code of ethics.	11

Table 2.8
Areas that delegates want a code of ethics to cover

	% who mentioned item first	% who mentioned item either first or second
Delegate selection	6	12
Campaign funding	17	23
Vote buying	1	2
Financial disclosure	3	6
Party membership	5	8
Conflict of interest	1	3
Patronage	—	1
Expenditures	4	7
Staff conduct	1	1
Candidate conduct	4	7
Advertising	1	2
Election of officers	1	1
Nomination process	1	2
Election process	2	4
Accountability	—	1
Miscellaneous/vague	4	9
All/everything	3	3
Did not answer	47	—

Attitudes toward Regulation of Campaign Finance

There was widespread agreement among the delegates on the need to reform the financing of leadership campaigns (see tables 2.9 and 2.10):

- 90% wanted spending limits on campaigns.
- 87% wanted candidates to be required to make detailed disclosure of how they spend their campaign funds.
- 88% wanted some form of disclosure of the sources of campaign contributions.
- 56% wanted limits on the size of contributions.

And to ensure enforcement most delegates wanted the financing of leadership campaigns regulated by law. Sixty-four percent said contributions should be regulated by law, and 57% said candidate spending should be regulated by law.

The survey did not ask delegates for proposals on specific spending limits, since without data about costs there did not seem to be any realistic standard of assessment. Instead delegates were asked if they would approve of a formula like that used for establishing constituency spending limits for parliamentary elections; this formula is based on the number of registered voters in the constituency. Two-thirds of them said yes.

Most delegates supported fairly stringent disclosure requirements for campaign contributions, as shown in table 2.9. Twenty-six percent wanted disclosure of the sources of *all* campaign contributions, 31%

Table 2.9
Delegate attitudes toward disclosure of names of contributors

	%
Existing federal law requires candidates and parties to disclose the names of contributors of donations in excess of $100. What is your opinion of requiring disclosure of contributions to leadership candidates?	
There should be *no* requirement for disclosure of contributions to leadership candidates	11
There should be disclosure of *all* contributions	26
There should be disclosure of contributions over	
$100	31
$250	6
$500	11
$750	1
$1 000	9
$5 000	4

Table 2.10
Delegate attitudes toward limits on size of contributions

	%
There should be *no* limits on the size of contributions	41
There should be a limit of	
$100	3
$500	6
$1 000	13
$2 000	3
$3 000	2
$4 000	1
$5 000	17
The limit should be higher than $5 000	11

wanted disclosure of all contributions over $100 and 6% wanted disclosure of all contributions over $250.

The data in table 2.10 show that there was less concern about the size of contributions. Forty-one percent of delegates said there should be no limits at all, 17% would set the limit at $5 000 and 11% would set it at a figure higher than $5 000.

Opinion was divided about whether there should be proscriptions on the kinds of sources from which candidates can accept contributions. Forty-six percent said they would only permit candidates to accept contributions from individuals; 52% opposed this form of restriction. Of the latter group more than half said they would not impose any restrictions on the kind of group or organization from which candidates could receive contributions. Three percent would prohibit contributions from charities, 3% from "special interests" and 1% from large corporations.

Seventy-nine percent of the delegates said candidates should not be allowed to accept contributions from non-Canadian sources.

Delegate opinion on the penalties for candidates who break laws regulating spending and contributions varied widely (see table 2.11). Twenty-four percent would permit fines up to $100 000 for spending violations, and 24% would permit fines up to $100 000 for violations of contribution regulations. In both cases some delegates – 4% for violations of contribution regulations and 4% for violations of spending regulations – would permit even higher fines; in each case just over 2% favoured jail terms. On the other hand, the number who would limit fines to $5 000 – $10 000 was 24% for contribution violations and 20% for spending violations.

Table 2.11
Delegate support for certain penalties for violations of contribution and spending regulations by leadership candidates

Penalty	Contribution violations	Spending violations
Fines up to $5 000	15	12
Fines up to $10 000	9	8
Fines up to $25 000	10	11
Fines up to $50 000	10	10
Fines up to $100 000	24	24
Other (please specify)		
More than $100 000	4	4
Jail	2	2
Other fine	9	10
Other	10	10

Some delegates (approximately 11%) who wanted spending and contributions regulated by party rules rather than by law also said they would impose fines (without specifying levels or saying how such penalties could be enforced). Sixteen percent said they would disqualify a candidate who broke spending regulations; 14% said they would disqualify a candidate who broke contribution regulations.

As can be seen in section A of table 2.12, a majority of the delegates wanted leadership candidates to be eligible for some form of state subsidy for their campaigns. Fifty-five percent believed there should be some direct state reimbursement of a candidate's expenses "subject to the establishment of certain eligibility requirements and spending limits." Forty-two percent supported reimbursement of half a candidate's expenses, as is now provided for candidates for the Commons; 7% supported reimbursement of a smaller proportion, and 6% a larger proportion.

Eighty-eight percent of the delegates also believed there should be tax credits for contributions to candidates' campaigns. Sixty-two percent said tax credits should be permitted if the donations are made through the parties, and 26% said they should be permitted for contributions made directly to candidates.

Seventy percent of the delegates also believed national television networks should be required to provide some free time to the parties for leadership campaigns – 34% favoured free time for candidate debates,

Table 2.12
Delegate attitudes toward public subsidization of leadership campaign expenses

	%
A Which of these statements best represents your opinion of state reimbursement of leadership candidates for campaign expenses?	
Leadership candidates should not be able to get any of their expenses reimbursed by the state.	42
or	
Subject to the establishment of certain eligibility requirements and spending limits, leadership candidates in officially registered parties should be able to get half their expenses reimbursed by the state, as is now provided for candidates for election to the Commons.	42
or	
Subject to these requirements and limits, leadership candidates in officially registered parties should be able to get reimbursement at a level of less than half of their expenses. (Please specify.)	7
or	
Subject to these requirements and limits, leadership candidates in officially registered parties should be able to get reimbursement at a level of more than half of their expenses. (Please specify.)	6
B Which of these statements best represents your opinion?	
Contributors to leadership campaigns in officially registered parties should be able to claim tax credits for their donations, as is now provided for contributors to election campaigns and parties, if the donations are made through the parties.	62
or	
Contributors to leadership campaigns should be able to claim tax credits for donations made directly to candidates.	26
or	
Contributors to leadership campaigns should not be able to claim tax credits for their contributions.	9

Table 2.12 (cont'd)

	%
C *Which of these statements best represents your opinion?*	
When officially registered parties are choosing a leader, the national TV networks should be required to provide free time to the parties for candidate debates.	34
or	
Subject to certain candidate eligibility requirements, the national TV networks should be required to provide some free time for individual candidates.	12
or	
Subject to the eligibility requirements, the national TV networks should be required to provide free time for *both* candidate debates *and* for individual candidate messages.	24
or	
The national TV networks should *not* be required to provide any free time for party leadership campaigns.	29

12% for individual candidates and 24% for both debates and individual candidates.

An important question that arises if candidates are to have support from the state is whether all candidates should receive it, or whether there should be limits on eligibility of candidates to prevent abuses of the system. Delegate opinions on criteria of eligibility are shown in tables 2.13 and 2.14. Most delegates seemed to favour fairly easy access for leadership candidates to state support. Thirty-six percent said a candidate should not have to be nominated by some minimum number of party members to benefit from the tax credits system, and 21% said a candidate should be made eligible for this benefit if he or she could get nominated by 10 party members in 25 ridings. Nor did they believe candidates should be required to make substantial (refundable) deposits in order to benefit from tax credits. Twenty-eight percent said there should be no deposit, 13% would require a deposit of less than $5 000, 11% would require a deposit of $5 000 and 13% would require a deposit of $10 000.

However, a majority of the delegates believed public support should be conditional on public regulation of spending. Eighty-four percent said candidates should be required to meet spending limits and disclose how they spent their funds if contributors to their campaigns are to be given tax credits, and 87% said candidates should have to meet these conditions if they receive reimbursement for their expenses.

Table 2.13
Delegate opinions of eligibility for tax credits

	%
A If candidates in leadership campaigns are to benefit from tax credits to contributors to their campaign funds, it has been suggested they should have to be nominated by some minimum number of registered party members in some minimum number of ridings. What is your opinion?	
There should be *no* requirement to qualify for this benefit	36
Nomination by 10 registered party members in 25 ridings	21
Nomination by 10 registered party members in 50 ridings	25
Nomination by 10 registered members in a larger number of ridings	5
Nomination by 10 registered members in less than 25 ridings	4
B If candidates in leadership campaigns are to benefit from tax credits to contributors to their campaign funds, it has also been suggested they should have to make a substantial financial deposit, refundable if they attain a minimum level of support in the voting. What is your opinion?	
They should *not* have to make a substantial deposit	28
They should have to make a deposit of	
under $5 000	13
$5 000	11
$10 000	13
$20 000	12
$30 000	5
$40 000	1
$50 000	8
more than $50 000	2

There is one striking variation in delegates' attitudes toward proposals for state subsidies. Whereas only 9% said they opposed tax credits, 42% opposed any form of public reimbursement of expenses. On the face of it, reimbursement is not much different from a tax credit, which is a tax expenditure. How, then, is the greater opposition to reimbursement to be explained? External evidence suggests the answer lies in different attitudes toward the role of money in the process. Some people believe that a candidate's ability to raise money from private contributors is a measure of his or her credibility as a candidate. They believe that those who are genuinely of national stature will be able to attract financial support. (Cf. Wearing 1988, 81–82.) From this perspective candidates do not need direct subsidies. If they are worthy they will be able to raise the funds they need from private contributions. In contrast, advocates of reimbursement may be inclined to accept the argument that factors other than the inherent merit of a candidacy – such as a candidate's opinions on issues or a candidate's connections

Table 2.14
Delegate opinions of eligibility for reimbursement for campaign expenses

	%
If there is to be some reimbursement from public funds for candidates in leadership campaigns, what minimum level of support, if any, would you require the candidate to attain before qualifying for reimbursement?	
None	19
5 % of the votes cast on the *first* ballot	12
5 % of the votes cast on *any* ballot	8
10 % of the votes cast on the *first* ballot	14
10 % of the votes cast on *any* ballot	8
15 % of the votes cast on the *first* ballot at a convention or in a direct vote of the membership	20
15 % of the votes cast on *any* ballot	9
Over 15 % of the votes cast on *any* ballot	2

to corporate donors – determine how much he or she can raise from private contributions. From this perspective the reimbursement of expenses would be a fairer means of providing state support to candidates because it would equalize competition and prevent the power of money from determining the choice of a leader.

We would expect a more benign attitude toward the role of money to be held by people from the more privileged elements in society and by people who have been successful in raising money under the existing system of private finance. Therefore, if this interpretation is correct we would expect opposition to state reimbursement to be highest among delegates from higher-status backgrounds, holders of élite positions in the party and, probably, among men (since it has been argued that women have had difficulty in getting access to the established sources of party funding). In fact, this is the case. Opposition to reimbursement was significantly greater among people in the highest-status occupations – professionals, corporate executives and owners of big and small businesses (averaging just over 51%); among people with total family incomes of $80 000 to $100 000 or of more than $100 000 (49% in both groups); among occupants of élite positions in the party, both at the national level and in the constituencies (averaging 52%); and men (47% compared to 35% of women). It is interesting to note that this pattern of cleavage occurs only in the responses to the question about reimbursement.

On every other question about financial reform there are no significant variations among subgroups – with one exception. The exception is that on other questions dealing with state regulation, women were more likely to support state regulation than men.

Sixty-nine percent of women, compared to 59% of men, wanted contributions regulated by law, and 64% of women, compared to 52% of men, wanted spending regulated by law. The explanation for this difference poses an interesting analytical question that the survey is not designed to answer. One possibility is that many women believe, because of the experiences they have had in trying to achieve equal opportunity both within the party and outside it, that reform is only effective when it is supported by the law.

CONCLUSIONS

Some Observations on Direct Election

This research shows that Liberals want, or are prepared to make, important changes to the process of leadership selection.

It is not surprising that most of the delegates supported greater regulation of leadership campaign finance, for this reform would extend to the internal affairs of their party principles that have been accepted in public elections for nearly two decades. However, the delegates who supported direct election are proposing a reform that is a fundamental break with existing practice. How is this to be explained?

The support by a majority of Liberal delegates for direct election of leaders, in particular in the one-person–one-vote form that most of them want, is a clear manifestation of a society-wide movement toward direct democracy. Large numbers of Canadians believe that government is élitist and unresponsive. They see the cause for this in the way party politics is conducted. They seek to change it by breaking down the rigidities of party discipline, establishing new means of calling elected officials to account and creating opportunities for citizens to participate directly in political decisions.

Although there is nothing in the survey to prove that delegate support for direct election of leaders is a response to this social movement, there are two bits of evidence that support this thesis. First, the data show that while both types of reform that the delegates support are connected to their concern about low levels of public confidence in the process, the link between this concern and support for direct election is somewhat stronger (see table 2.15). Second, as we have already seen, most delegates, regardless of the system they preferred, believed direct election would do better at promoting confidence in the system.

There has as yet been little analysis of what lies behind the social pressure for direct democracy. It seems to come from two very

Table 2.15
Delegate opinions of effect of leadership politics on low confidence in politicians,
by selected other responses

	% of those who say conduct of leadership politics has contributed to low levels of confidence in politicians	% of those who say conduct of leadership politics has *not* contributed to low levels of confidence in politicians	
		%	V
Believe low levels of confidence are a reaction to the way the whole process of party politics is conducted.	57	31	.17[a]
The internal affairs of parties should be subject to public regulation.	67	50	.13[a]
There should be common standards for leadership selection in all parties.	53	33	.15[a]
Contributions to leadership campaigns should be regulated by public law.	69	49	.15[a]
Spending by leadership candidates should be regulated by public law.	62	42	.13[a]
There should be reimbursement for leadership campaign expenses.	56	49	.07[b]
The selection system that will best promote public confidence in the process is direct election.	73	52	.17[a]
Support direct election of leader.	62	32	.20[a]
N	(1 121)	(370)	

[a]Differences significant at .0001.
[b]Differences not significant.

different kinds of groups. One can be identified with values of the kind that Inglehart has called "post-materialism" – embracing values such as environmentalism and feminism.[14] Challenging entrenched interests, the advocates of these new ideas have been concerned with the whole structure of power in society. As a result they have sought changes in the processes of governance as well as changes in the goals of public policy. The other groups that have taken up proposals for direct democracy are people with a wide variety of grievances over the direction of government and society over the past two or three decades. They include people who oppose what they see as the burdens imposed by the interventionist state, moral conservatives who have failed to win government support for their causes, and people who dislike the policies of multiculturalism and official bilingualism that have been promoted by the federal government for the past 20 years. In the case of these people, direct democracy is part of the wider agenda of conservative populism.[15]

Thus the advocates of direct democracy are to be found across the ideological spectrum, within existing parties, outside parties and in new parties. The rapid growth of the Reform Party has been the most visible and most dramatic manifestation of the appeal of direct democracy, but the Liberals, Progressive Conservatives and New Democrats have all in different ways sought to incorporate its ideas. It is in this context that the attraction of direct election as a method of leadership selection can best be understood.

There is good reason to expect that direct election of leaders will be widely adopted. Once one party uses this method, its more democratic aura will put pressure on other parties to use it as well. In fact, there is evidence that it already has substantial support in other parties. The NDP at its 1989 convention authorized a study of direct election, and a survey by Keith Archer (1991) of delegates to the 1989 convention found that 53% supported it. In a survey of constituency presidents for the Commission, R.K. Carty (1991) found direct election to be supported by majorities in all three of the established parties as well as the Reform Party. Among NDP presidents it was supported by 57%, among Liberals by 68%, among Conservatives by 52% and among Reform Party presidents by 69%.[16]

The adoption of this radical change in the method of leadership selection would have important implications both for the process of leadership selection and for party politics more generally. Four of these implications are particularly noteworthy.

First, direct election would add to the complexity of the relationships between leaders and their parties. There is already instability in these relationships because, whereas leaders are chosen, and may be removed, by party conventions, they must exercise their authority through, and are accountable to, their colleagues in the party in Parliament. The difficulties inherent in this situation have been compounded by the fact that the parliamentary party and the party convention represent different institutional and social interests because of the way the convention has been designed. This dual line of accountability of leaders has created strains in both the Liberal and Progressive Conservative parties. Leaders acceptable to one body have found themselves in difficulty because they have not been acceptable to the other. The conflict this has produced has impaired their control of party resources and undermined their effectiveness in appealing for public support.[17] This form of internal conflict is all the more likely if the parties decide to choose their leaders by direct election and retain the convention as their general governing body – which seems to be the intention of the Liberal party.[18] This will create a situation in which leaders will be chosen by one group of party members, can be removed by a second and must govern through a third – all composed in different ways and, therefore, representing different interests.

Second, one of the distinctive characteristics of the convention has been the fact that it incorporates principles of territorial representation, thus ensuring that places where a party was weak electorally would be represented in the choice of its leader. If parties using direct election adopt a strict one-person–one-vote apportionment system of the kind favoured by most Liberal delegates, the leaders they choose are more likely to represent the interests of regions where the party is strong, thus making it more difficult for them to build support in other regions.

Third, with direct election the balance of group interests represented in the selection of leaders will be very different. The people choosing leaders will no longer be predominantly from higher-status groups, women are likely to have a more equitable role and the representation of young people is likely to be reduced.

Fourth, the adoption of direct election may also be expected to have an effect on the style of leadership politics. Because candidates will have to appeal directly to tens and perhaps hundreds of thousands of voters, the mass-politics character of campaigns will be accentuated. Candidates will have to rely much more on the mobilization techniques of electoral politics, in particular making more extensive use of the mass media. As a result money is likely to become even more important in leadership politics.

The Role of the State in Leadership Selection

From the Commission's perspective the most important finding of this study is the desire of a majority of Liberal delegates to bring leadership campaign finance under state regulation. Of course, it does not necessarily follow that state regulation is in the public interest.

State regulation can be argued to be justified because, given the central role of parties in the political process, the state has an interest in ensuring that everything they do is consistent with the norms of democratic legitimacy. It is all the more warranted when the party leadership is involved, because no decision the party makes is more important to the political process than the choice of its leader. Leaders enjoy transcendent authority in their parties, they are the principal representatives of their parties in the competition for public office and they are the nominees of their parties to fill the most important office in government. Indeed, the leaders of *all* parties officially recognized in Parliament, as soon as they are chosen, occupy positions of formal responsibility in the state, endowed with special privileges and supported by special resources. It was argued before the Commission that this in itself is sufficient grounds to justify state intervention in the selection of leaders.[19] Rod Murphy, speaking on behalf of the New Democratic Party, put it this way in his oral submission to the Commission:

> I do not believe that leadership candidate campaigns within a federal political party are just private business or an in-house business. A person who is running for the leadership of a political party is also running to be the Prime Minister of Canada, and we believe that it is important that we have some knowledge of who has donated to that campaign. We also have a right in our society to insist that there is some limitation on how that campaign is run and to make sure it is an open and fair campaign, and I think that also means that we are talking about control or limitations over the funding, whether or not the tax system is used. We do not believe that the position of Prime Minister of Canada should be up for the highest bidder. (Murphy 1990, 86–87)

If the principle of state intervention is accepted, there is still the question of how widely it should be applied. There are two issues here. First, should all, or only some, parties be eligible to receive benefits that may be conferred in the form of state support for leadership campaign financing? American law virtually precludes government support for presidential nomination campaigns in third parties by making it very difficult for third parties to get official recognition.[20] Canadian party and election finance law has generally been much more permissive, and a majority of Liberal delegates believe it should remain unchanged.[21] It is in this context that principles for extending the benefits of public financing to leadership candidates have to be seen. Put briefly, there is no obvious justification for denying these benefits to candidates in any party that qualifies for public subsidies under other provisions of the law.

The second question is whether parties should have to submit to state regulation of the financing of their leadership campaigns if they do not want to. Some parties object in principle to state regulation of their internal affairs. Thus, Gerry St. Germain (1990, 27), president of the Progressive Conservative Party of Canada, told the Commission, "The view of the Progressive Conservative party on this subject ... is that parties should continue to operate under the current system free of government regulation in relation to the selection of party leaders." St. Germain argued that responsible parties, because they know the public's interest in the issue, "will themselves set guidelines or regulations relating to the process of leadership selection" (ibid.). The divergence of opinion on this issue among parties can be seen in Carty's study for the Commission of the attitudes of constituency presidents. Carty asked officials about the principle of public regulation of internal party affairs, using the same question as this study. Of those who answered, 57% of Liberals and 78% of New Democrats said, "Political parties have important public responsibilities and their internal affairs should be subject to at least partial regulation by public law," whereas 58% of Conservatives and 57% of Reform Party members said, "Political parties should be free to regulate their internal affairs by their own rules as they think best."

As we have seen, a majority of Liberal delegates would require regulation of all parties whose leadership candidates receive any form of state subsidy for their campaigns – such as tax credits for contributions. But the endorsement by a majority of Liberal delegates and majorities of Liberal and NDP officials of the principle that, because of their public responsibilities, the internal affairs of parties should be subject to at least partial state regulation implies the need for a more comprehensive standard. Those who hold this view might well argue that leadership campaign contributions and spending should be regulated in any party that receives any financial benefit from the state (including, for example, tax credits for contributions to election campaign expenses).

The movement to adopt direct election as the method for choosing leaders poses another problem. Some parties may not want to adopt it, and those that do may do it in different ways; some, for example, may incorporate some principle of territorial representation, as both the Ontario Conservatives and Ontario Liberals have done.[22] Therefore any system of public regulation of leadership campaign finance is likely to have to deal with a number of very different selection procedures. American experience suggests this need not pose insurmountable difficulties, for American laws on campaign finance have had to accommodate substantial differences in delegate selection procedures, ranging from various forms of primary elections to delegate selection by state party caucuses and state party conventions. However, the need to deal with differing procedures suggests that regulation will be complex and may best be done, not by defining specific rules, but by establishing general principles that may be applied in different ways. This suggests the best approach might be to define standards and principles within a mandatory code of ethics for parties seeking benefits under party and campaign finance law, a proposal that, as we have seen, was supported by 63% of the Liberal delegates.

One last question about the role of the state concerns the scope of state intervention. Although a majority of Liberal delegates did not want state management of leadership elections, the application of public law to the financing of leadership campaigns may require some state intervention in the management function. For example, if there is to be public subsidization of campaigns and it is based on some formula tied to the size of party membership, regulatory officials would have an interest both in the definition of membership and in the procedures by which it is verified. Beyond this, once the principle of state intervention in one aspect of the process is accepted, the ground used to justify it may be used to justify intervention in any aspect of the process. If the parties are unable to prevent the kinds of practices that have been criticized in delegate elections, there may be a case for broader state regulation. In this regard there is a practical problem to be dealt with if parties adopt direct election for choosing their leaders. The task of ensuring that elections of this kind (held simultaneously at hundreds or thousands of locations across the country) are conducted fairly will present a daunting challenge to the parties' administrative structures. It may be that this is a task that can only be done through some form of state intervention.

Ultimately, public opinion will determine whether there is a need for state involvement in party leadership elections. This does not mean that there is now or is likely to be widespread public demand for state intervention.[23] Rather, what is important is the general mood of the public and how the parties themselves believe they can best respond to that mood. The mistrust of parties expressed in the wave of populism that swept large sections of the country after the First World War was a major cause of the first great reform in leadership selection: the transfer of authority over leadership selection from party caucuses to conventions. A similar sentiment is part of public attitudes toward politicians and the political system in Canada today. There is no direct evidence linking low levels of confidence in politicians to opinions of the politics of leadership selection, but, as we have seen, most of the delegates who participated in the Liberal convention in 1990 believe this link exists. Equally important from the perspective of judging the need for state regulation is the fact that most of these delegates evidently believe that public confidence in the process can be ensured only by such regulation.

NOTES

I would like to thank Professor Keith Archer, Professors André Blais and Elisabeth Gidengil, and Professor R.K. Carty for providing me with the data from their surveys.

1. The only occasion when it was not used was in the succession to R.J. Manion in the Conservative party during the Second World War. In 1941 a conference of Conservative members of Parliament and representatives of provincial and constituency associations that had been called to organize a leadership convention decided instead to ask Arthur Meighen to assume the leadership for a second term. When Meighen resigned after his defeat in a by-election in February 1942, the party called a convention to choose his successor.

2. For a full discussion of the circumstances under which the parties adopted the convention method of leadership selection, see Courtney (1973, chap. 4).

3. Courtney (1973) refers, among other things, to the desire of the parties' élites to encourage wider participation in their extra-parliamentary activities, to ensure that the selection of the leader included regional interests that were not represented in the parliamentary party and to promote internal party cohesion.

4. Professor Ken Carty's seminal article on the development of parties in Canada points out the important connection between changes in the technology of communications and the evolution of the role of leaders in Canadian parties and politics. See Carty (1988b).

5. The survey was conducted by telephone in the autumn of 1990 with a national sample of 2 947 (Blais and Gidengil 1991).

6. The number of women attending a Conservative convention under rules changed since 1983 might well be smaller. The party has reduced the quota for women among constituency delegates to two out of seven, and it has not imposed a gender quota on representation from campus clubs or a newly established category of youth constituency clubs, each of which is entitled to elect three delegates.

7. For a discussion of this aspect of convention politics in the 1983 and 1984 conventions see Carty (1988a).

8. This point was made in testimony before the Commission by Peter Dotsikas (1990, 10636) of the Canadian Hellenic Foundation: "The more visible your group is, the more of a stigma there is." Referring to the attention given to the influence of members of the Sikh community in delegate selection in the 1990 Liberal leadership campaign, he described the way they were identified and "the things that people say about the Sikh community" as "revolting."

9. Elizabeth Burnham (1990, 6464), speaking on behalf of the Committee for '94, a non-partisan group of women political activists, made this point in referring to the campaign for the Liberal leadership by Sheila Copps in 1990: "One of [Ms. Copps's] fund raisers, Joe Cruden, a professional fund raiser from Toronto, says political donations are the most sensitive any corporation makes, and the decision inevitably is made by the Chief Operating Officer. Most are male. Ms. Copps' chances are diminished by her sex."

10. Nancy Riche (1990, 25) of the Canadian Labour Congress, describing elements of the system of representation at conventions as "undemocratic," argued that the power of money contributed significantly to the effectiveness of these elements. She added, "Regrettably no one knows the strings attached to the support given to the candidates by unknown supporters during a leadership race." Ron Nicholls (1990, 8810) of the Calgary Chamber of Commerce, in arguing for the need for controls in leadership campaigns, said, "It gets down, I guess, then in a moral point of view, … to be the person who can raise the most dollars gets to win, and I think that if you keep throwing money at it, you can probably win a nomination or win a leadership."

11. The Liberal party's administration of financial regulations in 1990 was more effective than what either the Liberals or Conservatives had achieved at earlier conventions, but it still generated controversy. Among the problems were the following: (1) Some candidates complained that spending limits were so high that they had no practical effect. Only two candidates were able to raise amounts close to the spending limits: Jean Chrétien and Paul Martin, who each reported spending just under $1.7 million during the period covered by the regulations and a total of approximately $2.1 million for the whole campaign. Sheila Copps spent just under $500 000 for the period covered by the regulations and a total of approximately $750 000. (2) The regulations did not cover substantial expenditures made before the actual calling of the convention. (3) The party's leadership expenses committee complained of serious differences with the party executive over whether the committee had the authority to make the regulations or had to have its regulations approved by the executive. These differences focused on "the decision concerning the information which would be made public after the convention, and especially, … who would set the spending limit" (Liberal Party of Canada 1990). (4) The committee also expressed concern about the effectiveness of its sanctions in ensuring compliance and urged that there should be "more strict and enforceable sanctions" (ibid.). For an elaboration of some of the difficulties with the administration of financial regulations at earlier conventions see Wearing (1988, 78).

12. See, for example, the CBC-Globe poll for October 1990 and Gregg and Posner (1990, 54).

13. The only province from which a plurality of delegates said the convention would be better was Prince Edward Island.

14. For a discussion of the application of Inglehart's ideas to Canadian politics see Nevitte et al. (1989).

15. I have attempted to describe some of the factors that have led to the development of this new conservative populist movement elsewhere. See Perlin (1991).

16. Professor Carty's survey was done by mail in the spring of 1991 (Carty 1991). His sample comprised 145 PCs, 131 Liberals, 126 New Democrats and 49 Reform Party members.

17. The best-known examples of this problem are to be found in the Conservative party, but John Turner's difficulties in the Liberal leadership from 1984 to 1988 demonstrate that this is not just a Tory problem.

18. Section 16, article 4, of the Liberal constitution adopted in 1991 continues to provide for a leadership review vote at the party convention "next following a federal general election."

19. See, for example, the brief submitted to the Commission by Professor William Christian (1990). Several witnesses made the same argument.

20. Only one third-party candidate has qualified for federal subsidies in American presidential nomination campaigns since funding was first made available in 1974. For a brief discussion of the American system of funding for presidential nomination campaigns see Sorauf (1988, 189–205).

21. The questionnaire gave delegates the condition of eligibility under existing law and asked if they would make it easier or harder for a party to become registered or if they would continue the present requirement unchanged. Sixty-three percent said they would leave the requirement as it is. Eleven percent said they would make it easier and 22% said they would make it harder.

22. When the Ontario Conservatives used direct election in 1989, they counted votes by constituency, allocating 100 votes to each constituency and distributing these votes proportionally among the candidates on the basis of their share of the votes cast by the members. In 1992, the Ontario Liberals elected delegates for each constituency who were required to vote on the first ballot on the basis of the candidate preferences expressed by members of the constituency association. After the first ballot delegates were free to vote as they thought best.

23. The survey for the Commission suggests most citizens think regulation of leadership politics should be left to the parties. However, since the respondents were not asked for their views of specific elements of convention politics, it is difficult to judge how they interpreted the question or how well they understood its implications (Blais and Gidengil 1991).

BIBLIOGRAPHY

Archer, Keith. 1991. "Leadership Selection in the New Democratic Party." In *Canadian Political Parties: Leaders, Candidates and Organization,* ed. Herman Bakvis. Vol. 13 of the research studies of the Royal Commission on Electoral Reform and Party Financing. Ottawa and Toronto: RCERPF/Dundurn.

Blais, André, and Elisabeth Gidengil. 1991. *Representative Democracy: The Views of Canadians.* Vol. 17 of the research studies of the Royal Commission on Electoral Reform and Party Financing. Ottawa and Toronto: RCERPF/Dundurn.

Brodie, Janine. 1988. "The Gender Factor and National Leadership Conventions." In *Party Democracy in Canada: The Politics of National Party Conventions,* ed. George Perlin. Scarborough: Prentice-Hall.

Burnham, Elizabeth. 1990. Testimony before the Royal Commission on Electoral Reform and Party Financing, Toronto, 8 May.

Carty, R.K. 1988a. "Campaigning in the Trenches: The Transformation of Constituency Politics." In *Party Democracy in Canada: The Politics of National Party Conventions,* ed. George Perlin. Scarborough: Prentice-Hall.

———. 1988b. "Three Canadian Party Systems: An Interpretation of the Development of National Politics." In *Party Democracy in Canada: The Politics of National Party Conventions,* ed. George Perlin. Scarborough: Prentice-Hall.

———. 1991. *Canadian Political Parties in the Constituencies: A Local Perspective.* Vol. 23 of the research studies of the Royal Commission on Electoral Reform and Party Financing. Ottawa and Toronto: RCERPF/Dundurn.

Christian, William. 1990. Submission to the Royal Commission on Electoral Reform and Party Financing. Ottawa.

Courtney, John C. 1973. *The Selection of National Party Leaders in Canada.* Toronto: Macmillan.

———. 1983. "The Morning After: Delegate Accountability." *Parliamentary Government* 4 (2): 8–9, 15.

———. 1986. "Leadership Conventions and the Development of the National Political Community in Canada." In *National Politics and Community in Canada,* ed. R. Kenneth Carty and W. Peter Ward. Vancouver: University of British Columbia Press.

Dotsikas, Peter. 1990. Testimony before the Royal Commission on Electoral Reform and Party Financing, Toronto, 31 May.

Fletcher, Frederick J. 1977. "The Prime Minister as Public Persuader." In
Apex of Power: The Prime Minister and Political Leadership in Canada, ed.
Thomas A. Hockin. Scarborough: Prentice-Hall.

Fletcher, Frederick J., with the assistance of Robert J. Drummond. 1988.
"The Mass Media and the Selection of National Party Leaders: Some
Explorations." In *Party Democracy in Canada: The Politics of National Party
Conventions,* ed. George Perlin. Scarborough: Prentice-Hall.

Gregg, Allen, and Michael Posner. 1990. *The Big Picture: What Canadians
Think About Almost Everything.* Toronto: MacFarlane Walter and Ross.

Kirkpatrick, Jeane. 1976. *The New Presidential Elite.* New York: Russell Sage
Foundation and the Twentieth Century Fund.

Krause, Robert, and Lawrence LeDuc. 1979. "Voting Behaviour and Electoral
Strategies in the Progressive Conservative Leadership Convention of
1976." *Canadian Journal of Political Science* 12:97–135.

Lele, J.K., G.C. Perlin and H.G.T. Thorburn. 1985. "The National Party
Convention." In *Party Politics in Canada.* 5th ed., ed. Hugh G. Thorburn.
Scarborough: Prentice-Hall.

Liberal Party of Canada. 1990. *Report of the Leadership Expenses Committee.*
Ottawa.

Murphy, Rod. 1990. Testimony before the Royal Commission on Electoral
Reform and Party Financing, Ottawa, 12 March.

Nevitte, Neil, Herman Bakvis and Roger Gibbins. 1989. "The Ideological
Contours of 'New Politics' in Canada: Policy, Mobilization and Partisan
Support." *Canadian Journal of Political Science* 22:475–503.

Nicholls, Ron. 1990. Testimony before the Royal Commission on Electoral
Reform and Party Financing, Calgary, 22 May.

Perlin, George. 1991. "The Progressive Conservative Party: An Assessment
of the Significance of Its Victories in the Elections of 1984 and 1988." In
Party Politics in Canada. 6th ed., ed. Hugh G. Thorburn. Scarborough:
Prentice-Hall.

Perlin, George, Allen Sutherland and Marc Desjardins. 1988. "The Impact of
Age Cleavage on Convention Politics." In *Party Democracy in Canada: The
Politics of National Party Conventions,* ed. George Perlin. Scarborough:
Prentice-Hall.

Riche, Nancy. 1990. Testimony before the Royal Commission on Electoral
Reform and Party Financing, Ottawa, 13 March.

St. Germain, Gerry. 1990. Testimony before the Royal Commission on
Electoral Reform and Party Financing, Ottawa, 21 September.

Sorauf, Frank J. 1988. *Money in American Elections*. Boston: Scott, Foresman.

Stewart, Ian. 1988a. "The Brass Versus the Grass: Party Insiders and Outsiders." In *Party Democracy in Canada: The Politics of National Party Conventions*, ed. George Perlin. Scarborough: Prentice-Hall.

———. 1988b. "Class Politics in Canadian Leadership Conventions." In *Party Democracy in Canada: The Politics of National Party Conventions*, ed. George Perlin. Scarborough: Prentice-Hall.

Wearing, Joseph. 1988. "The High Cost of High Tech: Financing the Modern Leadership Campaign." In *Party Democracy in Canada: The Politics of National Party Conventions*, ed. George Perlin. Scarborough: Prentice-Hall.

3

CANDIDATE NOMINATION IN CANADA'S NATIONAL POLITICAL PARTIES

R.K. Carty
Lynda Erickson

1. PARTIES, CONSTITUENCIES AND THE NOMINATION PROCESS

POLITICAL PARTIES ARE organizations that nominate candidates for elected office. Many of them do other things as well; no two of them seem to share identical motives or operational practices; very often they have to compete with other kinds of organizations (even in the electoral market-place) for resources and support. But it is the activity of nominating candidates that distinguishes parties. Groups that do this are regarded as parties, those that do not are called something else.

Canada's system of electoral law and regulation clearly recognizes that nomination is the critical activity that defines parties. The *Canada Elections Act* makes this the sole substantive requirement of any group seeking to register as a political party. No matter what else it may or may not do, by nominating 50 candidates to contest a general election under a (distinctive) common label, any organization is entitled to be registered as a party. It is through this process of labelling candidates that parties come to make their principal contribution to the conduct of electoral democracy and responsible government as it is practised in Canada.

One might expect that a process so central to parties and elections would be carefully regulated by the *Canada Elections Act*. After all, its provisions typically provide for exhaustive control of most aspects of electoral activity. But such is not the case. Despite the fact that nominating is the test of a party, the process is treated as if it were the ad hoc business of small groups of autonomous electors. The Act does limit the advertising of nomination meetings, but in the context of restricting total election expenses; it provides for a candidate veto by party leaders, but in the context of providing for ballot labels. Otherwise the regime can best be characterized as essentially permissive with respect to how parties nominate their candidates.

In recent years, this permissiveness has come to be seen by some Canadians as a problem that demands reform. In part, this change in attitude reflects a changed view of political parties. No longer are they seen simply as private organizations of electors: rather, they are recognized as integral parts of the constitutional system of government. That perspective led to their recognition and registration in the 1970s, and to the increasing regulation of many of their financial and broadcasting activities at election time (Paltiel 1970). Those reforms could be seen as institutionalizing the parties' role in the electoral process (Courtney 1978). Calls to regulate nominations propose to take this process a step further by using the power of the state to govern the internal affairs of the parties. This suggestion appears to have been driven by three factors that characterize contemporary patterns of party life.

First, despite some claims that Canadian politics is too competitive, recent decades have seen large parts of the country dominated by one party or another. Thus, until recently, Quebec operated as a Liberal fortress in national politics, while Alberta returned no one but Conservatives. Even the New Democrats, if unable to hold sway over an entire province like their larger opponents, had well-established strongholds. This pattern has meant that in substantial numbers of constituencies, capturing a particular party's nomination was tantamount to winning election to the House of Commons. Given that Canadians have decided that the electoral process must be regulated to ensure fairness and equity, many would argue that similar procedures ought to be extended to the candidate nomination process – if that is where the really significant decision is being taken. This argument seems all the more compelling, given the other two changes that appear to be taking place.

The second factor reflects recent mobilization activities of interests attempting to capture party agendas and organizations for their own purposes. Groups concerned with a single issue (e.g., abortion), or which represent some identifiable social group (e.g., an ethnic community), have begun to move in and take over local party associations. They nominate one of their own and in doing so, often drive out the party regulars. Ultimately this is a politics of exclusion that is destructive of the traditional inclusive practices of brokerage and accommodation that have long characterized Canadian party politics (Stasiulis and Abu-Laban 1990). It is the desire to constrain this sort of fragmentation of the parties that has led to calls for extending the *Canada Elections Act* to cover party nominations.

The third development that has spurred proposals for reform has been a perceived escalation in the costs of Canadian elections. The nomination process has apparently not been spared this inflation and press reports of nomination battles in the 1980s indicated that, in some extreme cases, would-be candidates were spending tens of thousands of dollars – more than they would be legally allowed over an entire general election campaign. Whatever the extent of these practices, they have led to a perception that the equity intentions of the election expense regime are being compromised and undermined. This has led to a call to extend the finance provisions of the *Canada Elections Act* to the nomination process, and so to regulate it as elections now are.

When all three forces are brought together, they form an image of the modern nomination process as one in which groups are routinely able to penetrate local party associations and buy a nomination, and therefore often a seat in the House of Commons. This is, of course, an exaggerated scenario. There is little evidence that many constituencies have reached this stage, but it is a determination to avoid this that has fuelled the case for reform.

Any attempt to change the candidate nomination process, be it by the parties themselves, interested electors, or the state through its electoral system, must start with a clear understanding of how the process currently operates. Despite the arguments of those critical of it, there is no clear systematic portrait of how it works or what factors seem to make a significant difference to who gets nominated. In a summary essay written a decade ago, Robert Williams (1981, 89) commented: "It is difficult to generalize about the process ... because no two cases are precisely the same and there may be considerable variation between the written rules and the actual practices ... In its essence, candidate selection in Canada ... is idiosyncratic, highly decentralized, and partisan."

This study is designed to provide a systematic empirical investigation of contemporary Canadian party nomination procedure and activity. As a benchmark analysis, it is largely descriptive; it seeks to identify the essence of the process and to map out the variables on which important differences exist.

Inherited Traditions
The origin of much political practice in Canada lies in the experience of the post-Confederation mid-19th century, and nomination activity is

no different. The political system at the time was one where the institutions of democracy (a secret ballot, universal franchise, impartial electoral administration) were only slowly developing. It was essentially a rural society of self-dependent producers tied to local markets where voters were oriented to the concerns of their local communities. Members went to Parliament to represent their constituencies, for that is where their elections were won.

Political parties in this formative period were little more than coteries of notables, a parliamentary caucus gathered together behind a leader. There was no formal national party organization, and there were no permanent structures and no regular national conventions of members (Carty 1988). Indeed, in this period our contemporary notion of party membership, implying as it does some organization for the citizen to be a member of, had little relevance. At best electors might be known as party supporters, tied to their party through the leading political figures of their locale. Such a system was inevitably highly decentralized, with partisan practices evolving to suit local conditions. Parties necessarily left much to their local activists to decide, so much so that ridings might go uncontested: in the period up to the First World War, there was not a single general election that did not see some seats won by acclamation.

During those early decades, national parties were held together by an elaborate and extensive patronage network that ran from the top of the public service right down to the lowest-level employee in the country's smallest villages. In that system the incumbent MP, or alternatively a party's defeated candidate, was the crucial link, and so came to be a well-known figure of local importance (Stewart 1980). Not surprisingly, incumbents or previous candidates were not readily or easily challenged. A presumption naturally grew that such men would have first claim on a renomination. And it always was a man, for the disenfranchisement of women up to the First World War meant they could not be nominated and so could play only a peripheral role in party politics.

For the most part, local party activists established and maintained the habit of coming together in a recognized meeting to settle on and nominate their candidate at election time. This they did in their own way, for there were no national party constitutions to set standards or to govern them. Practice varied considerably, but the predominant pattern appears to have been some form of representative local assembly at which delegates or spokesmen were present from as many as possible of the areas (polls, rural districts, or towns) in the constituency. Sometimes those attending would have been elected, in other cases they would simply be accepted as representative of known party supporters. Whatever the case, this practice of a recognizable constituency party meeting publicly to choose its candidate became accepted as the standard, legitimate nomination process (Siegfried 1966, 119).

While obvious nominations could make the local meeting something of a formality, real contests could also occur. Often several notable local figures might be nominated only to withdraw in favour of an agreed-upon candidate, but in the absence of such a consensus, several ballots would be cast until the party's nominee emerged. In that climate, the constituency would normally opt for a local man, someone well known as a friend and neighbour, someone whom the locals believed could represent them personally. This was not a system, like that in the United Kingdom, where outsiders could easily be parachuted in, or where members did not have to establish close ties to those they sought to represent.

Thus, with the institutionalization of political parties in Canada, grew powerful norms governing candidate selection. The local partisans had the right to decide who their candidate would be, and they determined how he would be chosen. Whatever the form, the process was expected to provide for widespread participation to ensure that the candidate was genuinely representative of local party interests. Though incumbents might find an easy road back, it was not uncommon for them to subject themselves to renomination by their supporters. These norms left the nomination process decentralized and the particulars in any single constituency dependent on the vagaries of local conditions. No doubt this reinforced the parochialism of early Canadian political life; it also gave the local associations a vital and autonomous decision-making part to play in parties that were otherwise focused on activity in the national capital. This was a prerogative that constituency activists jealously guarded: it distinguished their local associations from those in similar parliamentary systems, such as Britain or Australia, where the national party organization took a much more active part in the selection of candidates.

But other, quite different practices were adopted to supplement these established nomination procedures during the years of the second party system – from the First World War to the Diefenbaker revolution. They involved the central party apparatus taking a much greater part in the candidate identification and nomination process. Several different influences were at work behind this development. Parties now believed that they ought to run a candidate in every constituency, no matter what the electoral prospects. In part this was driven by broadcasting regulations which rewarded parties that had more candidates by providing them with increased air time (Courtney 1978, 43). But it meant that outsiders might have to help find candidates for hopeless ridings.

As the governing Liberal party evolved an organization tied together by powerful regional (cabinet minister) bosses, candidate nominations often came under the influence and control of these figures (Whitaker 1977, 183). Not surprisingly this was most pronounced in areas where an active local association was not so crucial to electoral success (Meisel 1962, 120–25). Thus, for example, in large parts of Liberal Quebec or Newfoundland, local parties took on a vestigial quality and candidates were increasingly nominated by fiat. On occasion, Newfoundland candidates for federal elections were announced in a press release from the premier's office. In the CCF, on the other hand, party officials took an active supervisory role, but for sharply different reasons. In order to prevent infiltration from Communists, the party's provincial councils would insist on approving local candidates and would veto unacceptable candidates.

Nevertheless, these practices which gave the party leadership greater control over their candidates did not sweep away established local prerogatives (Scarrow 1964). They did add to the complexity of nomination processes, often by operating through the old forms. During these same years, protest parties such as the Progressives were working to counteract these centralizing tendencies by arguing that the nomination process had to be even more responsive to local control (Morton 1967, 223–24). The net impact of all this activity seems to have been to legitimate the interest of the wider party organization in a constituency's candidate selection processes. The immediate consequence was to increase the diversity of candidate selection processes among parties and regions across the country. However, these developments provided little or no challenge to the position of incumbents who were generally assured of near automatic renomination if they wished.

The current period, starting from the mid-1960s, marks the maturing of modern Canada. Many social groups, long excluded from the nation's corridors of political power, were beginning to make demands to be included. The electorate had grown more quickly in the decades after the war than it had in any other western democracy, and the subsequent multicultural challenges to traditional conceptions of the country led to many of these ethnic groups seeking to nominate members of their own communities. The publication in 1970 of the *Report* of the Royal Commission on the Status of Women in Canada clearly articulated the claims of Canadian women to fuller opportunities to participate in public life.

The contemporary period has also seen a sharp increase in the institutionalization of party organization in Canada, and this has affected candidate nomination no less than other areas of party activity. Some of this change has been driven by the decisions of the early 1970s to recognize and register parties, to put party labels on the ballot, and to set in place an elaborate electoral expense and party finance regime that quickly transformed the parties from among the poorest in the western democratic world to ones of relative affluence. The other major influence was the expansion of participation and the growth of extra-parliamentary party organizations. Conventions in the two traditional governing parties are no longer held just when the leadership is vacant, but are regular events. As these conventions can depose leaders as well as choose them, they are an important locus of authority in the party. That has meant that the parties have been driven to standardize the relationships between their local associations and the provincial and national organizations (e.g., on matters such as convention delegate selection), and so have increasingly sought to have constituency associations adopt a common riding association constitution.

In terms of changing local candidate nomination practice, two particular developments must be noted. The first is the apparent growth of open and often divisive local contests involving the mobilization of individuals with no previous history of party activity, whose loyalty is directed solely to the candidate who attracts them to the meeting. Much the same thing was going on with respect to choosing delegates to national leadership conventions and the two undoubtedly reinforced one another. By the end of the 1970s, this phenomenon of aggressively contested nominations was spreading and the National Film Board even made a film (*The Right Candidate for Rosedale*) about one well-publicized case that might have served as a primer on how to conduct such a campaign. Inevitably, the renomination of incumbents began to come under challenge, and even prominent MPs discovered they could suddenly be unseated by their own constituency associations. One dramatic instance of this occurred in Edmonton during the 1984 general election when Marcel Lambert, a 27-year parliamentary veteran, former cabinet minister and Speaker of the House, was out-manoeuvred in a long four-ballot nomination by a 30-year-old rival at a meeting attended by a thousand local activists.

The second specific change in party nomination practice came with the decision to put party labels on the ballot. As the provision in the *Canada Elections Act* was written, the national party leader was required to certify local candidacies for this purpose. But this also had the consequence of giving the leader a veto over individual local candidates whom he or she might choose not to certify. Conservative leader Robert Stanfield used this power in 1974 to veto a candidate selected in New Brunswick, and in 1988 Prime Minister Mulroney vetoed the candidacy of a former minister (Sinclair Stevens in Ontario), while Reform leader Manning vetoed a candidate chosen in British Columbia. There may have been other cases where the possibility of such action constrained local associations from choosing someone unacceptable to the party leadership.

Public veto of a locally chosen candidate is the bluntest possible way for a party to assert that national considerations must prevail over local interests. Yet the very existence of the veto leads to calls and pressures for its use by groups outside the constituency wishing to pursue their own agendas. Perhaps the best example of this is the veto of Sinclair Stevens in 1988 by Mr. Mulroney. By all accounts, much of the demand for this came from Conservatives in other provinces who believed the standards they were being required to meet also had to be enforced in Ontario (Fraser 1989, 178).

Though these changes echo well-developed themes in the candidate nomination process, they pull it in competing directions. More open competitive nomination meetings reinforce the traditions of local autonomy and sovereignty; the leader's veto strengthens the hand of the central party apparatus. This is a formula for internal tension, made all the more difficult by the fact that significant numbers of local party activists are concerned about central-local relations, but party members are divided over which position they favour.

It is difficult to be precise about the prevalence of internal party discontent over local constituency battles. Contemporary press accounts in the past few years emphasize its disruptive impact on constituency organizations, but they may exaggerate the extent of this by focusing only on ridings where such internal conflict has developed. However, the plea for the reform and regulation of the nomination process made by Albina Guarnieri (1990), MP for Mississauga East, in her brief to the Royal Commission on Electoral Reform and Party Financing, suggests that even some of the winners in these contests believe the process is now more destructive than creative. It is this same widespread discontent that is driving the growing movement to change the party leadership selection process. Delegate selection meetings, like candidate nomination meetings, are now seen by too many partisans as vulnerable to non-party interests. Liberal Guarnieri told the Commission that she knew nearly 10 percent of those in her association were also Conservative party members, while almost a quarter of the Conservative association members were also Liberals. Partisans realize this makes a mockery of the process and deprives committed party members of effective control over who their candidate will be.

At the same time, party activists are clearly reluctant to allow much interference from outside the constituency. The tradition of local autonomy in the choice of the candidate is strong and deeply ingrained. Even the current leader's veto is widely opposed by Liberals and Conservatives. At recent national leadership conventions delegates were asked if they thought the party leader had the right to reject a local candidate or if the locally chosen candidate had to be accepted. As table 3.1 indicates, the majority of activists in the two large parties believe in the local autonomy position. This is most strongly held by ordinary constituency delegates, but a majority of the others (mainly ex-officio delegates) also accept this proposition. One might reasonably assume that this would be even more strongly supported by partisans who do not get to national conventions.

Despite these recent changes and emerging internal party tensions, a century of practice continues to weigh heavily on candidate nomination practices. But before turning to look at how these inherited traditions are currently playing themselves out, it is necessary to examine one further aspect of the parties: their constitutions. In the past two decades, the parties have worked toward standardizing many of their activities so that their constitutions have become much more

Table 3.1
Liberal and Conservative party activists' attitudes to local nomination autonomy
(percentages)

On local nominee, party leader	Conservative		Liberal	
	Constituency delegates	Other delegates	Constituency delegates	Other delegates
Right to reject	32	46	36	49
Has to accept	69	54	64	52
	(502)	*(410)*	*(743)*	*(538)*

Note: The data are taken from the 1983 Conservative and the 1984 Liberal national leadership convention delegate surveys provided by G. Perlin (Queen's University). The delegates are divided between those chosen by constituency associations and all others.

The respondents were asked to choose which of the following better represented their opinion:
a) "The party leader should have the right to reject a candidate nominated by a constituency association if that candidate does not accept the policies established by the leader."
  OR
b) "The party leader should always have to accept the candidates nominated by constituency associations."

significant documents. It is to these, and their relevance for the nomination process, that we now briefly turn.

The Party Constitutions

The long tradition of constituency primacy with respect to candidate nomination is reflected in the constitutions of the national parties. All are permissive, all make it clear that the local constituency association has the prerogative of nominating candidates for federal elections. This right is constrained only in the most general way by modest membership qualifications and what could best be described as an override provision that allows the party to intervene in exceptional cases. Surprisingly, no reference is made to the role of the leader that is created by the provisions of the *Canada Elections Act*.

Both the Liberal and New Democratic parties have federal organizational forms. Their constitutions leave the local nomination process to be specified in their provincial or territorial affiliate's constitutions, though they do specify that membership in them is open only to those who are not members of any other political party. But, as Albina Guarnieri's comments (1990) suggest, this rule is often more honoured in the breach than the observance. Inevitably, this decentralization leads to a diversity of practice within the same party; e.g., the BC NDP has a series of provisions governing appeals of nomination contests, the Manitoba party none; the Ontario Liberals' constitution has rules governing nomination finances, but there are none in the New Brunswick party. As long as these national parties retain a decentralized federal structure, this variation will persist.

Though the Progressive Conservative and Reform Party constitutions tie their constituency associations directly to the national party, neither is significantly more directive as far as nomination practice is concerned. The rules are left to be specified in local associations' constitutions subject only to age provisions for party membership, a local resident qualification for constituency association membership, and a minimum notice requirement for a nomination meeting. The Reform Party's national constitution goes furthest when it urges party members to "conduct a thorough search to find the best possible candidate," as if to confirm that the national party knows it has an interest in this area but realizes that the traditional right to choose remains with the constituency associations.

Any complete picture of how parties nominate candidates requires examination of how the process actually works. Very often the informal, unwritten rules of local practice override written constitutional forms, especially when the latter have been adopted only on the urging of someone in a remote provincial or national office. The evidence from our 1988 Candidate Nomination Survey project will help us in gaining more complete insight into the nomination process.

The 1988 Candidate Nomination Survey

Williams (1981) was right when he noted that the idiosyncratic, decentralized character of the nomination process made it difficult to generalize about it. But more important was a complete absence of any systematic data that might be used in a comprehensive analysis. It was to fill just this gap that we decided to conduct, at the time of the 1988 general election, a nation-wide survey of constituency nomination practices. The intention was to provide data for a first analysis of the process which could then serve as a benchmark for subsequent, more sophisticated studies.

Timing was a major constraint, since many nominations are held only after an election is called, and so it was impossible to conduct a survey before then. But at the same time, there would be obvious difficulties in getting returns during a campaign when potential informants were preoccupied with the election itself. The solution was a mail survey conducted immediately after election day, with the expectation that memories of the nomination would still be fresh enough to provide basic information about riding association activity.

At election time, constituency parties must provide two names for the public record, that of the candidate and his or her official agent. This made both of them obvious target respondents in a constituency-focused survey. While local campaign managers or association presidents would have made equally good (sometimes better) sources, there are great difficulties in obtaining a comprehensive and reliable list of them during a campaign. For a number of compelling reasons, it was decided to send the questionnaire to the official agents rather than to the candidates.

First, we believed that the prospects of agents returning the questionnaire would be less influenced by the outcome of the contest or the status of the winner. In other words, losers might not be as keen, in the aftermath of rejection at the polls, to complete the survey as winners would. Ministers and frontbenchers would not have as much time to do so as backbenchers. These considerations seemed less likely to influence the agents, who by the very nature of their activities in the electoral process must play a somewhat more detached and administrative role.

Second, candidates were more likely to have a one-sided view of the nomination process: that of winners. They had, after all, been successful in getting their party's nomination. Since we wished to pose a number of questions about that process, we sought as objective an account of it as possible. Agents were thought to be more likely to provide it than the successful nominees. The difficulty was that some agents might have had little involvement with the local party at the nomination stage, but, in our view, they were likely to be the rare cases. It was possible that such individuals might choose not to return the questionnaire, but there was no reason to think they would be clustered in any particular settings.

Finally, agents were thought likely to respond in larger numbers because one of their major tasks in the electoral process was to keep records and fill out the required forms for the chief electoral officer in the aftermath of the election. Perhaps the questionnaire would elicit some "duty calls" responses and help increase the return rate.

While the use of official agents had its advantages, there were disadvantages to using a single informant from each constituency association. One person might have only limited information on his/her association and its nomination process. In some instances, a few respondents indicated they did not know the answer to every question; in other cases, some of the agents' knowledge on specific issues was limited. This was most likely true of details concerning past party membership figures, nomination meeting attendance, and for some of the questions concerning pre-nomination activity, including spending. Thus, as with much survey material, the broad outlines drawn in these data tend to be more telling than the specifics recounted in them.

Given that the intention was to map out the basic patterns of the party candidate nomination process, we decided to survey only the three large national parties. Only they nominated a full slate of serious candidates – in 1988 they nominated among them 56 percent of all those who ran – and only their candidates were successful. None of the nine other registered parties nominated even enough candidates to be able to win the election. One, the Reform Party of Canada, had then a constitution prohibiting it from nominating candidates east of the Manitoba–Ontario border. This meant that it could nominate in, at most, 30 percent of the nation's constituencies. Smaller parties did not, then, incorporate much of the regional and cultural variation in Canadian political life, yet it was the impact of many of those basic variables that the survey sought to map.

Questionnaires were mailed immediately after the election, with both French and English versions sent to agents in Quebec and appropriate areas of Ontario and New Brunswick. Those agents were

invited to return whichever version they preferred. Cost precluded a
follow-up mailing. The overall return rate was 41.5 percent. As table 3.2
indicates, the returns are representative of region (including the nation's
principal metropolitan centres), party, and language group. One-third
came from winning constituency associations (which is what one would
expect in a three-party system) and, as will be seen later in the study,
the proportion of ridings with incumbents appears to be representative of the country.

In a final check for representativeness, the distribution of the
survey sample was compared with that of all (885) major party associations on an objective measure of competitiveness (see the third
section of this study). As with the rest of the indicators, these figures
suggest that the sample reflects the diversity of local constituency
nomination practice and experience – at least in 1988. The 1988 election was somewhat unusual in this respect, for it followed the second
largest landslide in Canadian history. That left Conservative incumbents in ridings they had not held before in this century and may have
altered local parties' nomination practice in many of them.

The questionnaire itself sought to collect information on a number
of distinct aspects of party nominating activity. The first set of

Table 3.2
1988 Candidate Nomination Survey: breakdown of returns
(percentages)

		Returns	All constituencies
Party			
Liberal	34		
Conservative	31		
NDP	35		
Language			
English	78		
French	22		
Region		Returns	All constituencies
Atlantic		9	11
Quebec		24	25
Ontario		36	34
West		29	29
The North		1	1
Competitiveness of local association*		Returns	All associations
Safe		23	22
Good chance		22	24
Unlikely		19	12
Hopeless		35	42

*This is the objective measure of competitiveness defined in section 3.

questions asked about the form and process used by the local association. This was followed by a number of items concerned with the competitive nature of the nomination and the extent and character of any campaign waged by prospective nominees. There was then a series of questions on the searching and screening activity carried out by the local association where, among other things, the objective was to discover what institutional attempts were being made to recruit women candidates. Finally, the last two sections of the questionnaire collected information on the candidate and the agent. The data set was then supplemented with 1988 constituency-level information provided by the chief electoral officer and Statistics Canada's summary of key census variables grouped by electoral districts. The questionnaire we used appears as an appendix to this study.

The remainder of this section deals with the basic institutional arrangements used by the three national parties to nominate their candidates. This serves as a necessary prelude for exploring the dynamics of nomination activity and competition from a number of different perspectives.

Party Nomination Meetings

The survey data leave no doubt that a local nomination meeting, open to all party members, is the universally accepted method for choosing a party candidate. For the 1988 election, 98 percent of all respondents reported their association had such a meeting. The handful that did not were divided between the Liberal and Conservative parties with the single largest group of them in Liberal constituency associations in Quebec. But what is most striking is how exceptional these instances were. This suggests that naming candidates in ways other than by an open party meeting is likely to be seen as abnormal and therefore suspect. This helps to account for the strong local opposition that emerged in the few constituencies in 1988 where party leaders attempted to reserve the riding for star candidates who were to be parachuted in (Fraser 1989, 164–65). It also explains the resistance of constituency activists to leadership vetoes of their locally selected candidates, as noted above.

Nomination meetings are under the control of the local associations and in two-thirds of the cases this meant the established local executive set the timing as they saw fit (and perhaps to the advantage of a candidate they favoured), while in a further 20 percent, it was determined by the full association. Most of the rest were set by party officials in ridings where their local support was weak or badly organized: in 1988 the large majority of such cases (71 percent) were Liberal or New Democrat associations in Quebec. Older practices of having a series of meetings across the constituency, or a single meeting with delegates coming from all corners, now seem largely anachronisms made unnecessary by modern transportation in all but a few electoral districts. A single meeting was held in 94 percent of the ridings, and it was open to any and all members of the local association in 95 percent of the cases.

Rules about membership in local associations inevitably vary from area to area. For local groups this is often a problem in urban areas where constituency boundaries do not always follow natural social ones, or where redistributions may suddenly leave partisans cut off from people they have worked with for a long time. As a result, many local association constitutions allow a certain proportion of non-resident members. The Conservative party is least accommodating on this: its national constitution restricts non-resident voting to members of the local executive. Over half (52 percent) of the responding associations reported having non-resident members, though three-quarters of them said such members constituted less than 10 percent of their local membership. As can be seen in table 3.3, the Conservative party differs from the other two in having much lower rates of local non-residency. This is what one would expect, given its constitutional prohibition. Indeed, from that perspective, the fact that more than a third of Conservative associations report non-resident members is surprising. It suggests that local practice can be somewhat oblivious to formal national constitutional norms on matters that impinge on local prerogatives.

The other important aspect of local membership is the length of time individuals must be members before they are entitled to participate in the nomination. A long waiting period would indicate a more disciplined, institutionalized approach to party membership, a short one evidence of an open and thus potentially very penetrable process. While there are some differences among the parties (the Conservatives

Table 3.3
Non-resident membership in local associations
(percentage of constituency associations)

Non-residents permitted	Liberal	PC	NDP	All
Yes	58	36	59	52
No	42	64	41	48
	(113)	(100)	(126)	(339)

generally have shorter time requirements, the New Democrats more often longer ones), the basic message of the data is that Canadian parties require very little commitment from individuals in exchange for the right to vote at nomination meetings (table 3.4). The majority of riding associations in all three parties demand somewhere between one week and one month. Given that this may be the associations' single most important task, it seems a remarkably modest standard. It makes the parties open and vulnerable to outside interests. At the same time, it might well prove difficult to regulate associations whose membership is so fluid and unevenly institutionalized.

As we noted above, nomination meeting dates are set by the local association, though this is often done within time periods set by the national party office. In 1988 the timing of nomination meetings was complicated by uncertainty as to what constituency boundaries might apply during the general election. Had an election been held in the first half of the year, the scheduled redistribution would not have taken effect. Nevertheless, as table 3.5 reports, almost half of the constituency associations held nomination meetings before 1 July, and a handful of them then had to hold another because of the redistribution. Equally striking is the fact that fully 80 percent of the party nominations had been completed by the time the election was called, at the beginning of October, for 21 November. Given that the *Canada Elections Act* does not now cover the period between elections, it might not easily be extended to provide for the regulation of most nomination activity.

It is perhaps worth noting that the Conservative party was the best prepared when the prime minister called the election: over 91 percent of their candidates had been nominated. Both opposition parties still had over 20 percent to nominate. That may reflect some organizational superiority on the Conservatives' part as well as the presence of a large

Table 3.4
Membership requirements of nomination meeting participants
(percentage of constituency associations)

	Liberal	PC	NDP
One week or less	25	46	15
8–15 days	17	28	13
16–30 days	38	23	45
30 days or more	21	3	28
	(97)	*(89)*	*(116)*

number of incumbents. It is also likely one of the natural advantages provided the government party by its right to name the election date.

There is little doubt that these meetings are definitive. The leaders rarely use their veto, though it was publicly applied twice in 1988, and few nomination outcomes are appealed to higher party bodies. In the survey, only 6 percent appealed and in the vast majority of cases, the original nomination was upheld.

The data on membership commitments suggest that constituency associations are under-institutionalized. There is further support for this interpretation in table 3.6, which provides some indicators of the extent to which local associations have formalized their nomination process, or are attached to the recruitment activities of the national party apparatus. Relatively few have any guidelines concerning nomination expenses. Somewhat more NDP associations have such rules, but their general absence among the three parties is surprising in light of the attention given to this issue in the press and all the parties' attempts to use such guidelines in their national leadership selection processes. While such rules might be difficult to enforce, the presence of guidelines would signal an attempt by the local parties to establish a code of ethics for their internal use.

It is equally apparent that most riding associations are not "helped in finding a candidate by party officials from outside the riding." Such involvement is most common in the NDP, but that is only to be expected, given that party's substantial areas of organizational weakness east of the Ottawa River. However, as this is a way in which local and national candidate recruitment interests and activities can be integrated, the fact that fewer than one in five associations get such help suggests that parties' nominations are most often carried on in splendid isolation from one another.

Table 3.5
Timing of constituency association nomination meetings: 1988 general election
(percentage of constituency associations)

Before 1988	1
1 January–30 June	42
1 July–1 October	36
After election call	20
	(368)

Table 3.6
Constituency association nomination processes
(percentage of constituency associations)

Constituency associations that have:	All		Liberal	PC	NDP
	%	N			
Nomination expense guidelines	14	339	10	13	19
Outside help to find candidate	18	357	17	12	24
Formal search committee	49	351	50	26	67

Our last indicator of a structured process is the presence or absence of a formal candidate search committee in the riding. As one might expect, given the numbers of incumbents, search committees in 1988 were far less common in Conservative ridings than in those held by the other two parties. But between the two opposition parties there were marked differences, with search committees being considerably more common in NDP than in Liberal associations. This is noteworthy because, as the analysis of recruitment processes below will demonstrate, such mechanisms can play an important role in increasing the numbers of women who participate in the process.

Finally, table 3.7 provides some evidence about the size of local association memberships and the proportions of party members who actually come to the nomination meetings to vote. Without comparative data, it is difficult to know what to make of these absolute numbers. Our general assessment is that they reveal fairly low levels of participation. The average constituency has nearly 60 000 electors, while the typical (median) constituency association has but 532 members: 44 percent of the constituency parties in the country have fewer than 500 members; just under a third of them have a thousand or more. The figures on the proportions turning out to the nomination meeting, arguably the most important decision taken by the association, support this portrait of limited party involvement. On average, only about a third of a riding's membership attends. As will be seen later, participation rates are influenced by a number of obvious contextual variables, but the general pattern is clear. Nomination meetings, the first stage in the public electoral process, attract and involve relatively few Canadians. This makes the candidate selection process one in which those citizens who do participate see that they

Table 3.7
Participation in nomination meetings
(percentage of constituency associations)

Association membership size	
0–100	11
101–499	33
500–1 000	24
1 001+	31
Mean	975
Median	532
	(308)

Nomination meeting turnout	
< 20	28
20–36	23
37–54	25
> 55	24
Mean	39
Median	36
	(248)

are having an influence. This also makes it one that can be manipulated with relatively few resources.

Conclusion

Several features of the Canadian nomination process stand out and bear being summarized here. Most important is that, unlike nominations in some other parliamentary systems, it is deeply rooted in the local communities that lie at the heart of Canadian society. In this it reinforces – and itself is strengthened by – the powerful geographical impulses that are at the centre of Canada's territorially organized electoral system.

This tradition is manifested in a nomination system organized and controlled by local constituency associations whose members often resent any outside interference. By and large, they do not want to be told when or how to nominate their candidate nor do they appreciate being instructed on who they should select to be their standard-bearer. However, the other face of these associations is that of a rather loosely structured, informally disciplined organization. There are apparently few standard rules, the most limited membership requirements, and uneven connections to the wider party establishment.

But parties exist to nominate candidates under a common label, to impose common obligations on many local candidates in exchange for the promise of nation-wide political success. The Canadian system recognizes that this implies that parties as national institutions have distinctive interests, one of the most important being the mix of candidates their local associations nominate in their name. This is why the electoral system gives the national party organizations, through the leaders, control over the label.

Successful regulation of the nomination process will require finding a framework that can accommodate these traditions and interests. As the first reflects a local, populist, and essentially participatory impulse while the latter shows the increasingly formal, institutional requirements of a national organization, the accommodation is not likely to be an easy one. Recent events in British Columbia, which have seen the Supreme Court intervene to overturn a (provincial) party nomination, ordering that the meeting be reconvened and the nomination recontested, suggest that partisans are increasingly prepared to force the issue and courts to take it up (see *Gray* 1990).

With this picture of the basic framework within which nominations are conducted in mind, the focus of the remainder of this study will be the politics that direct them.

2. THE CONTESTS FOR PARTY NOMINATIONS

Nominating candidates for Parliament is largely the business of the nation's political parties. Independent candidates no longer have much realistic chance of electoral success in normal circumstances. Yet for all that, the party nomination process remains part of the informal, unwritten aspect of the constitutional processes that order Canadian political competition and choice. As previously noted, nomination activity is everywhere characterized by a powerful and pervasive localism as well as a remarkable lack of formal structure.

The localism that provides much of the dynamic of constituency-level political activity means not only that local forces are important to the process and outcome of nomination contests, but that there is considerable variation in many aspects of party nomination from riding to riding. The lack of formal structure – evidenced by the absence of uniform national party rules, very limited membership requirements, almost no financial constraints, and uneven candidate search mechanisms – means there is ample scope for the operation of informal norms and raw political might. But neither of these basic features of the process means that it is without characteristic shape.

Subsequent sections will explore the impact on party nomination activity of the competitive context the local association inhabits and those special cases marked by the presence of an incumbent MP, the manner in which the parties are responding to the demand for more women candidates, and the extent to which there are regular differences between parties and/or regions. To set the stage for these analyses, this section maps out the patterns that can be seen in local nominations. We pose several basic questions: How contested are party nominations? What forces, be they groups or issues, drive them? Does it appear that nominations are being bought? What can be deduced from the data about the state of local party association democracy? This last question is really the heart of the matter, given that the power to nominate candidates constitutes the central gatekeeping role in Canadian electoral politics.

Media Images of Party Nominations

Much of the growing public interest in the processes by which political parties choose their candidates comes from accounts in the media. In particular, the rise of investigative journalism has given the electorate vivid newspaper portraits of nomination contests that go far beyond the traditional reports of public meetings that simply recount speeches made and votes taken. As often as not, these stories emphasize conflict and dwell on the dissatisfactions of losers.

While a detailed content analysis of the Canadian media's treatment of party nominations remains to be done, table 3.8 summarizes a simple first assessment. It indicates what observant readers of the *Globe and Mail* in the four months (1 June–30 October) before the 1988 general election would have seen. That paper was used because of its superior coverage of national politics and its claim to being Canada's national newspaper. (In fact, though stories referred to nominations in nine provinces, 81 percent of stories concerned Ontario ridings. Obviously, a full study of the media would require broader coverage.) Over the four months, 93 separate nomination stories appeared, a rate of almost one a day.

Two-thirds of the nomination stories featured a reference to a contested nomination while almost 30 percent described local conflicts created by the mobilization of new party members. In one-fifth of the stories, there was a reference to some individual or group being so dissatisfied with the fairness or outcome of the party's process that it wanted or planned to appeal it to some other party body. If *Globe and*

Table 3.8
Media images of party nominations

Globe and Mail stories reporting	%
Contested nominations	66
Conflicts over mobilization	28
Appeals	19
Local-national conflict	10
Ethnic mobilization	5
Nomination expenses	4
Local issue	0
	(93)

Notes: All stories in the *Globe and Mail*, 1 June–30 October 1988, that reported nominations.
Data collection and summary by B. O'Neill, University of British Columbia.

Mail readers thought they were getting a representative portrait of the nomination of candidates in Canadian general elections, then they must have believed it to be an essentially disruptive and cacophonous process. More subdued sub-themes in this information flow were the recruitment of instant partisans, sometimes from the urban ethnic communities, tensions between the local and national party, and the high cost of some exceptional nomination campaigns. After documenting the experiences of the major parties in nominating their candidates, we will return to these media images to consider how well they match the portrait that respondents drew.

The Nomination Meeting

Although local meetings are almost universally held to name party candidates, it is clear that local associations no longer wait for the writs to be issued before nominating their candidate. As seen in table 3.5, only about one-fifth of the major party nomination meetings now take place after the election is called. This obviously makes it difficult to use the *Canada Elections Act* to regulate the process. Indeed, any attempt to do so might see more nominations pushed back into the pre-election period. Would this matter? The point is that the timing of the process is not neutral and may itself be a factor in shaping the sort of candidate who is nominated. The data allow some specific inferences to be made about the critical influences at work in this process.

National party strategists now regularly make use of nomination freezes (periods when a national party does not permit its local associations to hold a valid nomination meeting) as part of their ongoing electoral strategy. This sort of effort to manage the process is partially aimed at ensuring that particularly desirable candidates come forward. Thus, for instance, the NDP delayed holding nomination meetings in the period before the 1988 election, believing that many potential women candidates – or those new to the party – could not commit themselves too early for family or career reasons. The party's managers believed that if local associations held early meetings, other candidates might capture the nominations. They also knew that skilful local politicians could manipulate the nomination meeting date to their advantage.

Incumbents are particularly sensitive to this advantage, knowing that a nomination held well in advance of the election period can effectively forestall a local challenge. It was Sinclair Stevens' use of just such a ploy that left the prime minister with no alternative but a public veto of his candidacy. But Stevens was not the only MP who saw an advantage in early nomination. Fully two-thirds of the incumbents who got themselves renominated did so by 30 June (three months before the election was called) as compared to only 40 percent of non-incumbents. By the time the writs were issued, only 5 percent of incumbents remained to be nominated while 25 percent of non-incumbent candidates were in the same situation. Clearly, established politicians do not see any marked advantage in having a well-publicized nomination meeting during the campaign. They appear to prefer the relative safety of early anonymity.

This argument implies that anything that encourages earlier nominations may work to the advantage of those already well placed in the system. However, the story is not quite so straightforward. Since newcomers who wish to penetrate and capture a local political party need time to do so, they are less likely to manage it once an election campaign is under way. Thus, post-writ nomination contests are less likely to have involved the recruitment of supporters, or the mobilization of ethnic groups, than are those held somewhat earlier.

The nomination meetings now held after the election is called might be described as among the most politically marginal. As noted previously, they are more likely to occur in the opposition parties. These riding associations make up almost half the instances in which external party officials had to arrange for holding the nomination meeting, and they are twice as likely to have outside party help in finding a candidate. As will be demonstrated in the next section (table 3.16) these are ridings the party does not expect to win. As an example, consider Quebec in 1988: by the time the election was called, all but 3 percent of the Conservative candidates had been nominated, yet 45 percent of the

New Democrats' standard-bearers in the province remained to be found.

This argument indicates that much of the important nomination politics in parties may have escaped from the traditional electoral period back into the internal dynamics of local constituency associations. However, before one can rest on such an analysis it is necessary to examine the nomination contests themselves. It turns out that contests are the exception rather than the rule, and that local democratic choice is as much a matter of form and opportunity as of practice and reality.

Running(?) To Run

Commonplace portraits of local constituency association nomination meetings have party members gathering together, hearing a few worthy colleagues proposed as their candidate, and then choosing among them. More elaborate versions refer to the mobilization of new members by aspiring nominees, or to the salience of local issues. As previously noted, media accounts focus on how conflictual much of this is. The fact is that the typical party nomination is not like that at all.

Perhaps the most important aspect of the process needing emphasis is that most party nominations are not contested. As table 3.9 indicates, two-thirds of all party nominations are won by acclamation, a further 20 percent have just two potential nominees, while only one in seven meetings sees more than two individuals competing for the right to run in the election as the party's official candidate. Even these multi-candidate contests are only modestly competitive: 54 percent of them were won on the first ballot.

As one might expect, this general pattern of rather uncompetitive nomination contests varies depending on who is in the running. It has been shown that incumbents manage to have earlier nomination meetings and it comes as no surprise that almost 90 percent of them are not opposed. Some are, and a few are dramatically unseated, but

Table 3.9
Competitiveness of local nominations
(percentage of riding associations)

Number of candidates	All	First ballot winner	Incumbent running	No incumbent	Former MP running	Woman contesting
1	65	—	88	57	41	39
2	20	100	10	24	30	30
3+	15	54	2	19	30	30
	(359)	(355)	(93)	(266)	(27)	(104)

the old tradition of acclaiming a local member evidently remains a powerful norm.

Yet even in those instances where no incumbent is present, the majority (57 percent) of party nominations are not contested. Only one-fifth of the constituency associations in this situation have contests with several candidates. One reason for these low levels of competitiveness is the undesirability of many such nominations (see the discussion around table 3.18). It is also likely that in some ridings the local party establishment works behind the scenes to find a candidate and stage-manage his or her nomination. No comprehensive measure of the extent of that activity is available, but in one constituency association in five, the respondents reported that someone was either talked into or out of becoming a candidate. In some ridings (4 percent) both activities were acknowledged.

Former MPs do not get the deference that incumbents do, at least they did not in 1988, when 60 percent (well above average) faced a contest for their party's nomination. It is possible that 1988 was not a typical year, for 70 percent of those seeking to return to Parliament in that election were Liberals who had served under Pierre Trudeau's leadership. Many Liberal activists were anxious to put that period of their history behind them. Women were the other group that was more likely to have to fight for a nomination. Where women were running, only 40 percent had the comparatively tranquil path of an uncontested nomination meeting. A later section will explore in greater detail the parties' efforts to recruit more women into electoral politics as candidates.

These figures speak only to the (limited) amount of competition for party nominations. Table 3.10 shows something of what the contests were about. For the most part, they were not driven by issues. In only one-quarter of the contested constituency associations was "any specific issue, concern or local matter ... at the heart of the nomination contest" and the two most frequently mentioned issues were free trade (which pervaded the wider national election) and the particular candidate. This generally issueless cast to nomination contests is reflected in the fact that local issues were infrequently mentioned in reports about the bases on which individuals attempted to mobilize support for the associations' nominating meetings.

Recruiting new people – party outsiders – to come to a local nomination meeting is now common, though it was reported to have occurred twice as frequently where there was a contested nomination. Though recruitment of instant members for this purpose has the potential to generate considerable animosity and adverse publicity, it is striking how relatively infrequently it becomes "a source of internal

Table 3.10
The basis of nomination competition
(percentage of all constituency associations)

Number of candidates	Contests with a specific issue	Supporters recruited	Recruit-ment controversial	Recruitment from			
				Volunteer assoc.	Ethnic groups	Women's interest groups	Local single issue
1	19	42	2	47	6	4	5
2	26	82	19	67	15	15	7
3+	25	83	24	72	30	23	15

Note: Horizontal percentages. Thus in row 1, 19 percent of all one-candidate nominations reported that there was a specific issue in the local nomination contest.

controversy in the local association." Naturally, that is more likely to happen in the most contested cases or the most divided party (in 1988 this conflict primarily affected the Liberals), but this practice now seems to be accepted as an essential aspect of contemporary nomination politics.

The data also testify to the variety of social bases underlying the recruitment of supporters into local constituencies, the most common being the large variety of local voluntary associations found in most Canadian communities. Using ethnic groups or women's interests to canvass for support appears to be far less common, and accounts of using either unions/professional associations or church groups were reported in only a handful (7 and 3 percent respectively) of constituency associations.

While individual constituencies are not immune from pitched battles, this is largely a portrait of a process typically neither disciplined nor driven by issues or distinctive social groups. Candidates for nomination apparently find their support in an ad hoc, particularistic fashion. Incumbents, of course, are rarely contested, so are under less pressure at this stage in the electoral process. But the figures for those local party associations with no incumbent are virtually identical to those for all ridings, suggesting that the pattern described here is the norm.

Most individuals involved in nomination contests accept their outcome. Only 6 percent of the associations in our survey reported having the decision "appealed to a higher party body." Though the very small numbers make it difficult to identify much that is distinctive about those contests, they do not appear to have been ones in which there were unusual membership recruitment campaigns. If anything, nominations that were appealed were twice as likely to have been fought over some issue than were all nominations. This tentative finding hints that the informal cast to the local parties' processes might not be strong enough to withstand nomination battles that were characterized by strong policy conflicts.

Nomination Contests and Constituency Mobilization

The previous section demonstrated that participation rates in local party constituency associations and their nomination meetings were generally low (table 3.7). There is, needless to say, enormous variation in the size and strength of constituency memberships from party to party and across the country. As one would expect, parties that hold a constituency typically have bigger memberships than those that do not. That is probably one of the reasons why they won the seat, and an MP's presence and resources are a continuing stimulus to organization and activity. In this section we turn our attention to how local membership and the mobilization of new members condition the nomination process, and then what a contested nomination implies for a constituency party association.

Given the considerable variation in constituency sizes and the levels of local political activism, comparisons of the actual numbers of individuals joining and participating in local party associations do not reveal very much. Instead, the rates of mobilization and nomination meeting turnout must be examined for a measure of the openness of the process and the impact of a contested nomination on a local party organization.

Nominating the local candidate is undoubtedly the one task that gives local party members the most opportunity to play a significant and relatively autonomous part in the electoral process. For that reason, one might expect that local association membership would increase up to the nomination meeting date. Certainly the common practice of recruiting supporters specifically for nomination contests (table 3.10) stimulates such membership growth. But recruiting new members is only half the story; they must also come to the meeting and participate to have an impact on the outcome.

Since the presence of an incumbent makes a significant difference to a local association, it is important to take that into account. On the one hand, an incumbent's local associations will have a larger regular membership to begin with and so be less likely to have large growth rates in the period before an election. And the absence of a contest may depress participation in the formal nomination meeting. On the other hand, an incumbent's natural resources are such that any nomination challenge is likely to be fought extremely vigorously. Local parties with no incumbent will normally have smaller memberships and so be vulnerable to much greater mobilization campaigns by aspiring nominees. The patterns of all these pressures in 1988 can be seen in table 3.11.

For an indicator of the mobilization of new members, the rate of growth of a local association's membership between 1986 (midway between the two general elections) and the time of the constituency nomination meeting has been used. Given that the range of membership change is from –73 percent to +2 500 percent, these averages must be treated with considerable caution (the median change is just +25 percent) but the pattern seems clear and as predicted. The prospect of an open (no incumbent) nomination generally leads to a marked growth in membership and if there is a contest, the average rate of growth is about 275 percent. Where an incumbent is ensconced, the distinction between an acclamation and a contest for the nomination is much sharper. Where an MP is being routinely renominated, the average membership increase is just 34 percent, but it is 10 times that when an MP faces a contest. Challenging an MP clearly requires a much more aggressive mobilization of support which is met by a defensive response in kind.

But these rates of mobilization do not lead to large local party memberships. Even in the fiercest battle, where an incumbent was challenged, the average constituency association averaged only some 2 700 people at the time of the nomination. This was over twice the average size of non-incumbent associations whose nominations were contested, and more than five times the size of uncontested non-incumbent cases. That means that the average membership in uncontested associations

Table 3.11
Mobilization and participation for nominations
(constituency associations averages)

	Constituency association growth: 1986–88				Nomination meeting turnout			
	Incumbents		No incumbent		Incumbents		No incumbent	
Number of contestants	%	N	%	N	%	N	%	N
1	34	59	163	114	38	35	28	86
2	321	6	275	41	62	8	44	47
3+	–		287	37	–		50	45

with no incumbent was just 500. Even accepting that many of those nominations are not particularly desirable in that they represent normally unwinnable seats, simple arithmetic suggests that winning many of these nominations would require rather little. That being so, the fact that so few are contested indicates what low levels of competition characterize Canadian party life.

The data in table 3.11 reinforce this point by demonstrating that membership turnout at nomination meetings is relatively low. It increases with the degree of competition, but even in contested open seats still averages less than 50 percent. When an incumbent is being contested, the average turnout climbs to over 60 percent, more evidence that these (very few) cases induce the most aggressive contests. The simple truth is that, in most cases, the majority of party members do not bother to turn out to vote at nomination meetings, even when they are contested.

The Costs of Winning a Nomination

Recruiting members, fighting nomination contests, and turning supporters out to vote at an evening meeting some weeks or months before a general election campaign is under way costs money. There is currently no state regulation of the process and only a small minority of local constituency associations have any party rules governing nomination financing (table 3.6). In an attempt to provide a first approximation of the amounts of money that are currently being spent, respondents were asked, "How much, would you estimate, did the winning candidate spend on his/her nomination campaign?"

These figures refer to the ultimate nominee and not to any opponents, so they provide only a partial portrait of nomination campaign expenditures. At the same time, we have no obvious absolute or comparative standard by which to judge them. Because they are rather crude estimates, no impression of precision will be given by reporting numbers in a table. Instead, the patterns of spending they reveal are described below.

On balance the data suggest that the characteristic nomination battle in a local Canadian party association does not cost the winner very much. Over a third of the nominees were reported to have spent nothing at all, 70 percent had spent $500 or less, and only 21 percent were thought to have spent more than $1 000 on their successful nomination. There were, however, accounts of up to $30 000 having been spent, meaning that some exceptional cases helped pull the average cost to about $1 400. But the more important point is that the median cost was just $100.

A number of interesting and predictable variations occur in the patterns of nomination spending. Many of them are interrelated, and will be discussed later, but bear noting here. On average, Liberals spent more on their nominations than did those in the other two national parties in 1988. As one might expect, incumbents spent less – about a third of what non-incumbents had to – but then they had all the advantages of an MP's local office and parliamentary franking system. Contested nominations cost about three and a half times more than uncontested ones, but the more important factor appears to have been the character of the nomination campaign. Where supporters were recruited to come to the nomination meeting, costs were, on average, nine times those of contests where no such mobilization campaign was necessary.

Perhaps equally interesting are several dimensions that do not themselves appear to be directly related to nomination spending. The existence of local spending guidelines is associated with lower average spending, but the differences are not large. The presence of a more formal party nomination process, signalled by the existence of a local candidate search committee, makes no difference to the average amounts of money that winning nominees spend. Finally, men and women winners spend virtually the same amounts of money on their nomination contests.

One last feature of this process deserves attention here, in this overview of nomination spending patterns. The data show that nominees selected after the election was called spent only about a quarter of what their colleagues did who had been nominated in the three months before the issuing of the election writs. No doubt that reflects differences in the kinds of constituencies nominating in these two time periods, but it may also indicate that candidates are more prone to husband resources once the real election is on and they are under full media scrutiny.

Managing(?) Nominations

To this point the focus has been on the formal public aspect of the nomination process in the constituency associations. As in all politics, some significant activity always takes place behind the scenes to set the stage for the public rituals and, in many cases, outside pressures are brought to bear on local activists to make the right decision, or perhaps simply to help them find a candidate. Neither of these dimensions of the process is particularly easy to tap with a mail questionnaire, for the subtleties and possible variations seem infinite. The responses to several questions do, however, give a first – albeit crude – approximation of the extent of some of this activity.

As table 3.12 indicates, formal search committees exist in almost half the local associations. While they are far more common in instances where there is no incumbent MP, they are still to be found in 16 percent of incumbents' ridings, suggesting they may be a regular part of some organizations' formal structure. There are two sides to candidate recruitment: convincing good potential nominees to offer their services and discouraging those whom key local party activists believe unsuitable or unacceptable. The former apparently happens twice as frequently as the latter, but both go on and in a few constituencies do so simultaneously. That actively encouraging candidates seems more common than discouraging them is consistent with a generally uncompetitive process. However, in as many as 10 percent of the local parties with no incumbent, local party figures thought it necessary to dissuade certain would-be parliamentarians. The small numbers make it impossible to draw much of a portrait of those cases in 1988. It does seem that candidates are twice as likely to be recruited (encouraged to run) where there are search committees, but aspirants are also twice as likely to be dissuaded by such committees.

Ridings with incumbents rarely need outside help to find a candidate, but those without one – and limited prospects of electing an MP – often have difficulty identifying and selecting a candidate. One-quarter of the associations with no incumbent reported having help from party officials from outside the riding. In over half the cases, such help was provided by provincial-level figures, with national officials being used in only one case in five. That suggests that national party strategists possess only a limited or indirect capacity to shape their teams of candidates, even where vacancies occur. For the most part, this outside help

Table 3.12
Organizing the nomination
(percentage constituency associations)

	All	Incumbent	No incumbent
Search committee	48	16	60
Candidate persuaded to run	17	5	22
Potential candidate discouraged	8	2	10
Outside help to find candidate	18	—	24
Outside help produced controversy	4	—	4
Outside pressure for woman	21	5	26

does not "become a matter of local party controversy" and in 8 percent of the instances where it does, the riding has ended up with more than one individual contesting the nomination.

Finally, just over one constituency association in five reports "any outside encouragement for the local party to choose a woman candidate," with most of those cases being in non-incumbent situations. This implies that the parties are at least directing their efforts to increasing the recruitment of women in ridings where there is a reasonable prospect of having them nominated. On the other hand, the large majority of local associations do not appear to be getting a clear message that the national parties are serious about attracting more women candidates. That may be because no convincing message to that effect is being transmitted along party channels, or because local associations are not inclined to listen to advice on who their candidate should be, or both. These issues of recruiting women are discussed in more detail later in this study.

Conclusion

The evidence of this section indicates that local party nominations can best be characterized as relatively uncompetitive, modest events. Incumbents have the considerable advantage of being able to influence the timing of the meeting, but are rarely challenged. Nominations are now, more often than not, the occasion for recruiting new members into the local association and while such mobilization can engender conflict, such campaigns seem to be accepted as legitimate and normal. And while costs vary widely, the average nominee spent only about $1 400 in a campaign to gain the nomination. As will be seen later in this study, this general portrait can be sharply altered in particular circumstances but any variations can only be understood against this backdrop.

This account of the nomination process might well come as a surprise to regular readers of the press. The media's portrayal of intensely fought local battles mirroring participatory local associations is not the norm. This is evident from the images presented in the *Globe and Mail*, as compared with the patterns revealed by the national survey data (table 3.13).

It appears that nominations are only half as likely to be contested as newspapers' stories would suggest, and only a third as likely to produce conflict over the recruitment of new members into the local associations. That being so, it is also not surprising to learn that local dissatisfaction, as indicated by attempts to appeal the meeting's decision, is far less common than media reports imply. Similarly, the extent

Table 3.13
Image v. reality
(percentages)

Nomination meetings	Press image*	Constituency reports**
Contested	66	35
Conflicts over recruitment	28	9
Appeals	19	6
Local-national conflict	10	4
Specific issue	0	21

*Globe and Mail reports – see table 3.8.
**Constituency association survey.

of conflict between local activists and national party officials appears to be exaggerated. Although in about 20 percent of cases constituency associations reported there was a local issue of some importance to the participants, this feature of nomination contests seems to be ignored by the media. There was little reflection of this in the coverage of party nominations in 1988.

But if the media do not provide a realistic portrait of the typical, average nomination, that is because such cases are routine – they aren't news. However, it is also fair to say that the idea of the average nomination is something of a delusion. As subsequent sections will show, the process varies depending on the context. We begin by considering the political realities facing a local association as it names its candidate.

3. THE POLITICAL CONTEXT OF NOMINATIONS

Nominations can take place in a number of distinct political contexts insofar as any individual local party association is concerned. The position a constituency association finds itself in as it moves to select its candidate is a fundamental determinant of its behaviour and the course of its nomination politics. Our analysis of the process implicitly adopts a topology of nominations based on its two most salient dimensions: the presence of an incumbent, and the competitiveness of the local association. These dimensions are features of all ridings, whatever their demographic profile, though later sections examine the extent to which regional or partisan effects modify their working.

These two dimensions dictate the basic topology of nomination contests because they set the terms that govern what parties need to do, i.e., find a candidate, and what the nominees can then expect. Clearly, the dynamics of any nomination contest change with the presence of an incumbent who has signalled his or her intention to seek renomination. Such individuals have a wide variety of resources at their disposal and, as has already been seen, they can make a real fight of it (table 3.11). But the eventual nominees' electoral prospects may very well be as relevant. Some associations occupy ridings that are considered safe for their party, others will be more competitive, while still others are recognized as almost hopeless. Given the localism that prevails in Canadian political life, aspiring MPs (unlike many in Britain) are not expected to prove their mettle by first running in hopeless situations. This suggests that there ought to be few resources expended over undesirable nominations, and that the candidate selection problems of such associations will be of a different order. Their task will be to find a respectable candidate.

This section sets up the analysis by exploring the effects of these two dimensions on the nature of selection, on the competitiveness of the nomination process itself, on the pre-selection campaign, and on the spending levels in these various political circumstances. Given that the fundamental factor at work is invariably the existence of an incumbent, it begins by looking at incumbency and candidate selection.

Incumbents and Selection

In all democracies where the processes of candidate selection have been examined, incumbent legislators are the most successful individuals among those who seek their party's nomination (Gallagher and Marsh 1988). In Canada, the tradition of incumbent renomination began early and has continued even when other party practices surrounding candidate selection have been modified. Renomination occurs partly because incumbents have a number of resources with which to mobilize support in the face of a challenge to their candidacy. As members of Parliament they have, in local ridings, offices that serve as contact points between them and their local party members, and their position as the community's representative in Ottawa attracts attention from the local media. As a result, they typically have a higher local profile than other members of their local party.

More importantly, party norms at both the local and national level work to prevent challenges to incumbents from arising. Such norms seem to be rooted in the view that to challenge a member is to criticize the team that represents the party in Parliament, which in turn reflects badly on one's party. Thus, while competition for candidacies could be portrayed as furthering local party democracy, competitors who seek to unseat an incumbent are not normally viewed from that perspective, especially inside the party. In actual practice, however, local party organizations do not have to work actively to limit incumbent challenges. In only a couple of the associations with sitting members seeking re-selection did the local organization, in 1988, attempt to discourage other potential or would-be candidates.

Party norms concerning incumbency are of only limited protection to MPs. After all, other norms about accessibility and local party democracy require (at least) the forms and mechanisms, if not the fact, of competition. In practice, incumbents have to face at least a pro forma selection meeting: of the associations surveyed, all but 4 percent with incumbents seeking re-selection had a formal meeting to ratify their candidate. With the virtual universality of such meetings, it is not surprising that there are occasions when challenges to incumbents do arise and that in a few instances, incumbents are not re-selected.

Because they are so few in number in the sample, this analysis of the phenomenon of challenged incumbents must be tentative. But a few observations are possible. First, incumbent challenges were not limited to the parties' safest seats. If anything, incumbents were challenged in local associations whose electoral prospects at the time of the nomination were judged more equivocally (see table 3.14), and whose success in the election was marginally poorer than that of local associations with unchallenged incumbents.

Second, there is a hint of party differences in the figures: a third of Liberal incumbents in the sample faced a contest at their nomination meeting, compared to 9 and 12 percent, respectively, of Conservative and NDP incumbents. The fewer challenges to government members

Table 3.14
Incumbent challenges and local competitiveness
(percentages)

Perceived competitiveness of local party	Incumbent challenged	
	No	Yes
Safe seat	63	40
Good chance	37	50
Unlikely	—	10
	(78)	(10)

Note: The questionnaire asked: "[W]hen the party was nominating the candidate, how did the local association assess the chances of victory in the constituency? Was the riding considered by your party to be: safe, good chance, unlikely, hopeless?"

may reflect the greater premium governments place on matters of internal party solidarity, which is reflected in the reluctance of active party members to challenge their local MP. The difference between the Liberals and New Democrats may, on the other hand, be testimony to the stronger internal norms of solidarity in the NDP, stemming from their historical experience as a minority movement.

A third observation about incumbent challenges is the prevalence of mobilization efforts and their effects on local membership levels. As already observed, active recruitment of people from outside the parties appeared to be common in these contests, and although the local associations grew substantially, this activity was not without its critics. In the sample, eight of the eleven constituencies with a challenged incumbent indicated that "the candidates actively recruit[ed] supporters to join the party and come to the nomination meeting to support them." When asked about recruitment activities, just over half of these associations indicated that it was a source of internal controversy in their local party. This is a much higher level of internal tension than existed in other cases where active recruitment campaigns existed (compare to table 3.10).

A final observation about these contested nominations concerns their costs. The winning candidates clearly spent more on their preselection campaigns than did uncontested incumbents. Slightly more than half of the latter group spent no money on a nomination campaign and their average spending was a mere $61, while virtually all of the former group spent some money and their average spending was about $2 700. However, the spending of these contested incumbents was essentially similar to that of other candidates who faced contests. The difference measured was a mere $46. Though incumbent challenges in the U.S. system of candidate selection have bred the phenomenon of huge candidate war chests, in Canada the response in such cases so far appears to have been relatively modest.

Competitiveness and Selection

To explore the impact of electoral context requires finding ways to define and measure local competitiveness. Because of the volatility of Canadians' voting habits, a party's past performance in a riding is often only a rough guide to its future success in that constituency. Predicting the competitiveness of a local association before the 1988 election, when most local parties were nominating their candidates, was complicated by a remarkable fluidity in the public's partisan preferences, the unusually high Conservative party vote in the previous election, and the introduction of new constituency boundaries with the redistribution of 1987.

Not surprisingly, given the uncertain indicators – and the enthusiasm of partisanship – almost half of the respondents in the sample chose a moderately optimistic option to describe their local association's assessment of its chances of local victory: 49 percent said their party considered it had a "good chance." A further 19 percent said their local party considered the riding to be a "safe seat" for their party. This suggests that from the perspective of the local party organizations, there were many competitive and, hence, attractive candidacies. Yet for prospective candidates, the personal and other demands of running for a candidacy and for legislative office are substantial. So, for them, the enthusiasm of partisanship may be more tempered when they assess the attractiveness of their party's chances. Past party performance may play an equally significant role in their decisions about whether or not to contest a candidacy.

In order to show the effect of competitiveness on party activity and on prospective candidates, both *perceptions* of local competitiveness at nomination time and the local parties' *performance* in the last election deserve attention. This requires two measures of competitiveness: one based on a survey question concerning the local party's assessment of its chances of victory; the other based on local party performance in the 1984 general election. For the performance-based measure, a party's percentage lead, or percentage distance from the lead (based on the new 1987 constituency boundaries), was calculated and four categories of competitiveness were determined. Because it was well understood by prospective candidates and other party people that the Conservative vote in 1984 was atypically high, that was taken into account in characterizing the competitiveness of local party associations: Conservative party associations were assigned higher threshold levels for the various categories.

The four categories of competitiveness were assigned as follows:

Safe Seat:

Conservative	party won seat by margin of at least 15%
Liberal and NDP	party won seat by margin of at least 5%

Good Chance:

Conservative	party won seat by less than 15% or was within 5% of winner

Liberal and NDP	party won seat by less than 5% or was within 15% of winner

Unlikely:

Conservative	party lost seat and vote share was 5–15% behind the winner
Liberal and NDP	party vote share was 15–30% behind the winner

Hopeless:

Conservative	party vote share was more than 15% behind the winner
Liberal and NDP	party vote share was more than 30% behind the winner

Although this set of categories still left the Conservative party with approximately three-quarters of the safe seats and virtually none of the hopeless seats, this measure does allow an alternative test for the effects of competitiveness. While the two measures of competitiveness are

Table 3.15
Competitive measures as predictors of electoral success
(percentages)

Electoral success in 1988	Perceived competitiveness of local association			
	Safe	Good chance	Unlikely	Hopeless
Won	77	31	8	—
Lost	24	69	92	100
	(68)	(170)	(88)	(24)

	Competitiveness assessed on 1984 result			
	Safe	Good chance	Unlikely	Hopeless
Won	83	43	13	2
Lost	17	57	87	98
	(86)	(82)	(71)	(130)

correlated ($r = .63$), the one based on the 1984 vote was a slightly better predictor of success in the 1988 election (table 3.15).

How does competitiveness affect the nature of selection and the nomination procedures within local associations? In some respects, not very much. Selection procedures vary little in terms of format, and what variability exists is unrelated to competitiveness. Nor do competitive riding associations have more – or less – stringent eligibility rules for participation in selection. The length of time that members must have belonged to the party in order to participate in candidate selection is unrelated to either perceptions of local competitiveness or the party's past performance. The same is true of party rules with respect to the participation of non-constituency residents.

Only the timing of the nomination meetings differs with local competitiveness (table 3.16). Even taking account of the incumbency factor, we found those associations that considered their chances of victory to be low held their meetings later, presumably because of their difficulty in attracting prospective standard-bearers. Those few uncompetitive associations that did hold their nomination meetings comparatively early had more contested nominations. Fifty-four percent of those that held their nomination meetings before 30 June of the election year had contested nominations. Only 10 percent of associations that held their meetings after the election call had contests.

While the formal elements of selection do not typically vary in relation to the competitive circumstances of the local associations, some of the pre-selection activities do, at least when there is no incumbent

Table 3.16
Perceived party competitiveness and timing of selection
(percentages, no incumbent contesting)

Timing of nomination	Perceived competitiveness		
	Safe or good chance	Unlikely	Hopeless
No meeting	—	2	—
Before 1988	1	1	—
1 January–30 June	43	27	13
1 July–1 October	37	40	29
After election call	18	29	58
	(150)	(85)	(24)

Table 3.17
Candidate search activity by local competitiveness
(percentages, no incumbent contesting)

| Local party had: | Perceived competitiveness of local association* | | | |
	Safe	Good chance	Unlikely	Hopeless
Search committee	13	57	73	58
Outside help	7	21	28	46
	(15)	(131)	(86)	(24)

*Read, for example, as 13% of seats perceived as safe had a search committee.

(table 3.17). Local search committees, outside party assistance, and organizations that talked their candidates into running were more frequent when the electoral prospects of local associations were not very good. While it is obvious that less competitive associations would have a greater need for search committees in order to find a candidate, the fact that such committees are seldom found in local associations with the best electoral prospects is an indication that they are not primarily used as a means to shape the character of party caucuses.

At the other end of the spectrum, among associations whose electoral prospects are considered bleak, the propensity to mount search committees is compromised, probably by small local memberships. There, outside party assistance in finding candidates is more likely. It is interesting that such outside assistance is virtually absent in safe ridings, again suggesting the limited input of party organizations in shaping or developing the character of the party teams they put in office.

The most significant effect from the competitive context, by whatever way measured, is on the number of people who contest a nomination. Once the associations in which incumbents sought re-selection are excluded, the relationship is straightforward. The more competitive the local association, the greater the likelihood of a nomination being contested. But past party performance, rather than local party judgements of their competitiveness, is a moderately better predictor of the numbers contesting a nomination. Using party perceptions of competitiveness, we found that even in those associations that considered the seat a safe one for their party, over 40 percent of their candidates won the nomination by acclamation. This was true of none of the candidates from associations characterized as safe by the performance criteria. On the other hand, using either criterion, 47 percent of candidates from associations considered to have a good chance of winning won their nominations by acclamation (table 3.18).

Once nominations are contested, does the competitiveness of the local association affect the nature of the campaign that precedes the formal selection? The evidence on this is ambiguous. For example, recruitment of outside supporters was not related to the local party's past electoral performance, although there was some variation with party perceptions of competitiveness. But still, no matter how parties viewed their election prospects, competition for the local candidacy was, more often than not, the real signal that recruitment activities were occurring. Even in those constituencies where prospects for victory were judged by the local party to be unlikely or hopeless, when there was competition for the nomination, prospective candidates actively recruited supporters in 70 percent of the associations.

The data suggest that once a constituency candidacy is contested, the mobilization effects of pre-selection campaigns are not systematically related to the competitiveness of the local associations. The contest

Table 3.18
Nomination competition by local association competitiveness
(percentages, no incumbent contesting)

Number contesting local nomination	Perceived competitiveness			
	Safe	Good chance	Unlikely	Hopeless
1	43	47	71	79
2	14	26	22	17
3 +	43	28	7	4
	(14)	(131)	(85)	(24)

Number contesting local nomination	1984 electoral competitiveness			
	Safe	Good chance	Unlikely	Hopeless
1	–	47	58	68
2	47	21	26	21
3 +	53	32	16	11
	(17)	(53)	(70)	(124)

Table 3.19
Pre-selection spending of winning contestants by electoral competitiveness of local associations
(contested associations)

Perceived competitiveness of local association	Mean spending	
	$	N
Safe seat	8 686	11
Good chance	2 566	60
Unlikely or hopeless	824	28

itself, and not the competitiveness of the local party, appears to be the primary fuel for recruitment and membership growth.

The same is not as true of spending. There does appear to be a relationship between a local party's competitive situation and the amounts winning candidates are thought to have spent on their nomination battles. This is especially apparent when the perceptual measure of competitiveness is used (table 3.19). The average spending level of successful aspirants who fought nomination battles in safe ridings was more than 10 times that of the winners in ridings perceived unlikely or hopeless, and over three times that of the winners in associations considered to have a good chance of electing a member.

Conclusion

"Is an incumbent seeking re-selection?" is the most important question to be asked when characterizing a local association's nomination process. Despite the fact that local parties go through the process of calling an open meeting to nominate their candidate, seldom are incumbents challenged. This means that incumbents have to spend very little money on assuring their renomination.

A small number of incumbents are challenged in every election, a practice that sustains democratic norms of responsibility and accountability in local party associations. These are the contests that generate the greatest internal conflicts, for inevitably many local party members, loyal to their MP, will resent and resist any challenge. As shown in table 3.11, incumbent challenges produce the largest membership recruitment campaigns – and those meetings have the largest turnouts. It is also true that those contests are the most disruptive, for such activity is far more likely to provoke controversy than it would in a nomination contest where there is no incumbent. Yet for all that, contested incumbents do not appear to spend any more money on their nominations than do contested non-incumbent nominees. The advantages enjoyed by incumbents are not primarily monetary, though they are no less important for that.

In the real world, some nominations are far more attractive than others simply because they hold out greater promise of election to Parliament. The data suggest that this makes little difference to the ways in which local associations conduct their nominations, with the exception of a greater use of formal search committees and outside party assistance where the riding offers less hope and so, presumably, is less attractive to aspiring MPs.

Not surprisingly, the local party's competitive position does make a difference to how many individuals contest the nomination. There are more contests in better seats. But the data indicate that once there is a contest for the nomination, the general form and character of campaigns do not seem to vary much regardless of the competitive context of the constituency – with one obvious exception: individuals spend more to win a contested nomination in ridings with good electoral prospects than they do in others. It is in these relatively few cases that the costs of winning a nomination are beginning to grow beyond the reach of ordinary Canadians.

4. THE NOMINATION OF WOMEN CANDIDATES

Of the various groups that have demanded more access to nominations and the attendant entry this provides to the House of Commons, none have been more organized and vocal in the last two decades than women. The publication in 1970 of the *Report* of the Royal Commission on the Status of Women, with its chronicle of the dismal record of female candidacies, marked a turning point. Since then, women from within and without the party organizations have increasingly demanded that the parties sharply raise the number of women they nominate, particularly in constituencies that hold the promise of victory. In response, the national organizations of all three major parties have signalled their interest in greater gender balance in their caucuses. Yet the proportion of women elected to the House of Commons in the 1988 election was still only 13 percent.

To what extent does the selection process contribute to the under-representation of women in the House? What has been the record of selection and the various parties' efforts for women? How and where are women being nominated? And to what extent do particular features of party selection work in favour of women being nominated, and of being nominated in ridings where they have a chance of winning? These questions are at the heart of this section, beginning with a discussion of the parties and women candidates prior to the 1988 election.

The Parties and Women Candidates

Until 1984, women candidates who were well placed competitively were an unusual phenomenon in Canadian general elections. This was partly because the total number of women candidates was not very high, but it was also because women were primarily nominated by so-called fringe parties and/or in seats where their party's chances of winning were not good. In the 1980 election, while 14 percent of all candidates were women, more than two-thirds of them ran for one of the minor parties or as Independents (Brodie 1985). Only 8 percent of major party nominees, and 5 percent of the winning candidates, were women.

Between the 1980 and 1984 elections a number of factors, including increased visibility and organizational strength of the Canadian women's movement, raised the saliency of women's concerns about representation in the political domain. In addition, with growing evidence of gender differences in voting preferences in the United States and the subsequent appearance of that phenomenon in Canadian public opinion polls (Brodie 1985), the issue of women's votes had become increasingly relevant to politicians. Within the parties, there were indications of an interest in expanding the numbers of women running as part of the parties' teams, although activities directed toward women's representation varied (Erickson 1991).

While the 1984 election did not see any increases with respect to the percentage of women candidates, their distribution among parties and in winnable ridings did change. A majority of women who ran for Parliament did so as candidates for one of the three major parties, and the proportion of winning candidates who were women doubled. Among the major parties, women comprised 8 percent of Conservative candidates, 15 percent of Liberal candidates and 23 percent in the NDP. But whether these changes were in response to party efforts to recruit women, or whether more women sought out major party candidacies, is not known.

Yet while they were no longer as uncommon in competitively placed candidacies, the number of women nominated as candidates in 1984 was still not substantial and women were again disproportionately selected by local associations that had little prospect of electing a member. The success rates for men who ran for one of the three national parties was 36 percent, for women it was 21 percent. That this latter figure was as high as it was, was only because of a number of unexpected Conservative party victories in Quebec, the province where that party ran almost half of its women candidates.

For the 1988 election, women's organizations were especially active in designating increased female candidacies as an immediate objective, and emphasizing their importance for the realization of greater gender equity in national institutions (Canadian Advisory Council on the Status of Women 1987). The national leadership of the three major parties indicated that they, too, would like to see expanded numbers of women in their caucuses. The leaders articulated a commitment both to increasing the proportions of women candidates running for the parties and to improving the overall competitive prospects of many of them. Yet the reality of the highly localized system of candidate selection limited the capacity of the national party organizations to deliver on such commitments. The mechanisms for direct intervention were either unavailable or the parties were unwilling to use them. The use of the leader's veto as a means of ensuring the nomination of women in certain constituencies, or effecting the nomination of a minimal proportion of women candidates, does not appear to have been contemplated by any of the parties.

Indirect activities, including workshops for women and identifying particular individuals for encouragement to run, were undertaken, although there were party differences in the extent of such activities and the degree to which they were centrally directed. The NDP was the most aggressive in its programs and the most centralized and systematic in its encouragement of prospective women candidates. In both the Liberal and Conservative parties, programs were more decentralized and efforts to encourage women more informal (Erickson 1991).

Women Candidates in the 1988 General Election

With the 1988 election, the proportion of female candidates increased only modestly over 1984: from 15 to 19 percent. There was some regional cast to the distribution, with proportionately more women nominated in Quebec (22 percent) and Ontario (21 percent) than in the other three regions. The proportion of women candidates was smallest in Atlantic Canada, at 14 percent, marginally lower than the Prairies' 15 percent. British Columbia was just on the national average. An argument that these regional differences are manifestations of different regional cultures does not stand up when the data are compared with the proportion of women in provincial elections. The pattern in the gender distribution of candidacies both within and between regions in the 1988 national general election differed from the pattern of recent provincial elections (table 3.20). For example, whereas Saskatchewan had one of the smallest

Table 3.20
Women candidates in national and provincial elections
(percentages)

	Candidates who were women	
	Provincial	National
Atlantic Canada		14
Newfoundland (1989)	8	13
Nova Scotia (1988)	21	15
New Brunswick (1987)	16	7
Prince Edward Island (1989)	25	36
Quebec (1989)	18	22
Ontario (1990)	23	21
Prairies		15
Manitoba (1990)	21	9
Saskatchewan (1986)	25	12
Alberta (1986)	18	19
British Columbia (1986)	21	19

Source: provincial data supplied by the Royal Commission on Electoral Reform and Party Financing.

Note: National – 1988; provincial – as noted.

proportions of female candidates in the federal election, it had the largest percentage of any in the most recent provincial elections. On the other hand, Quebec, where the federal percentage was highest, had the third lowest provincial figure.

The partisan distribution of female candidacies in 1988 was similar to that of 1984. Again, the majority (58 percent) of women candidates ran for one of the three major parties and the rank order of the parties remained the same. Twenty-eight percent of NDP, 18 percent of Liberal, and 13 percent of Conservative candidates were women.

But to what extent were those women who were nominated by the three major parties selected to run in less competitive ridings? Election statistics suggest that women continue to be disproportionately found in losing ridings. Only 23 percent of them won seats in the 1988 election, compared to 36 percent of their male counterparts.

This inference concerning women and winnable seats is confirmed by plotting the electoral results by the measure of local competitiveness based on the 1984 election results. Looking at all of the candidacies of the three major parties, women are disproportionately represented in those which fell into the categories of unlikely or hopeless seats,

Table 3.21
Candidate sex and local competitiveness
(all candidates in the three major parties)

Competitiveness of local party (based on 1984 performance)	Female (%)	Male (%)
Safe seat	12	25
Good chance	18	26
Unlikely	14	12
Hopeless	56	38
	(171)	(706)

while only 12 percent of the women compared to 25 percent of the men ran in seats characterized as safe for their parties (table 3.21).

The regional pattern on the willingness to nominate women in good seats is similar to the earlier one on their nomination generally. The figures are best in Quebec and worst in Atlantic Canada (table 3.22). None of the female candidates in the four easternmost provinces were nominated by local associations with safe seats, whereas 24 percent of male candidates were. By contrast, in Quebec, almost as high a proportion of women as men were nominated in ridings considered safe. Despite its comparatively higher proportion of women candidates, Ontario does not do as well on this measure, falling considerably behind Quebec and surpassed by British Columbia.

As table 3.23 suggests, the pattern also differs by party, although this partly reflects the differential distribution of competitive seats. More than half of all Conservative party candidates were classified as having safe seats, but only a third of that party's women were in safe candidacies. For the Liberals, the women who ran for the party were as likely as their male counterparts to be running in the few safe seats the party had, but they were somewhat less likely to be placed in ridings where the party had a good chance and more likely to be placed in a hopeless candidacy. This latter pattern was similar among New Democrats, although their women candidates were even more likely to be placed in constituencies considered unlikely or hopeless.

We observed in the previous section that the performance of a local association in the 1984 election was but one indicator of the competitiveness of the local party, and that local perceptions of their competitive circumstances at the time of the local nomination should also be part of the analyses of the nomination process. The survey

Table 3.22
Safe seat candidacies by sex and by region

	Safe candidacies*		
	Women (%)	Men (%)	Ratio**
Atlantic	—	24	—
Quebec	19	23	.89
Ontario	11	25	.44
Prairies	8	28	.29
British Columbia	14	21	.67

*The figures represent the percentage of candidates in each category who were running in seats classified as safe for their party.
**Percentage of women candidates who ran in safe seats/percentage of men candidates who ran in safe seats.

Table 3.23
Parties' candidacies by sex and competitiveness of local association
(percentages, all ridings, 1988 general election)

Competitiveness of local party	Female	Male	All
Progressive Conservative party			
Safe seat	33	53	51
Good chance	47	30	32
Unlikely	17	11	12
Hopeless	3	5	5
Liberal party			
Safe seat	8	9	9
Good chance	20	29	27
Unlikely	16	17	16
Hopeless	57	46	48
New Democratic Party			
Safe seat	5	8	7
Good chance	5	18	14
Unlikely	12	6	7
Hopeless	79	69	71

data for this subjective measure reveal that women's placement in less competitive seats is not as pronounced as the electoral measure suggests. Still, only 10 percent were nominated to candidacies characterized as safe, compared to 22 percent of male candidates (table 3.24). Of all the safe seat candidates, 90 percent were men.

Table 3.24
Perceived competitiveness of the riding and the sex of candidates
(percentages)

Perceived competitiveness of local party	Female	Male
Safe seat	10	22
Good chance	52	47
Unlikely	32	24
Hopeless	6	7
	(69)	(275)

The Selection of Women and the Local Nomination Process
Given what has been shown about incumbency, safe seats, and incumbent re-selection, it should be expected that some of the over-representation of men in safe-seat candidacies is a result of incumbency. With so few women incumbents and so many safe seats occupied by incumbents, there are few avenues in any one election for women to gain safe seats. In the survey, four-fifths of the local associations with safe seats had incumbents seeking renomination. But only 9 percent of these incumbents were women. Of course incumbents can be – and sometimes are – challenged at their nomination meetings. Yet with the limited success rate of such challenges, and the finding that challenges tend to be launched in less competitive ridings, women's entry into safe seats via challenges is unlikely to be successful without some marked modification in party practices.

With many electorally competitive nominations taken up by uncontested incumbents, the ones remaining attract not just women, but more contestants generally: local parties with no incumbents seeking re-selection were four times more likely to have a contest for their nomination.

In section 2 we described the phenomenon of uncompetitive selection. The norm for party selection is that local candidates are chosen by acclamation and local party members typically have no choice among aspiring candidates. While this may have some negative implications for party democracy, for candidates, the circumstances of selection by acclamation are more salutary. They do not have to face the financial implications of a selection contest or the possibility of a divided constituency association as a result of a battle for the nomination. Yet these benefits do not fall equally to women and men candidates: in their bids for nomination, women faced competition more frequently than did their male counterparts. Sixty-one percent of associations

Table 3.25
Women aspirants and the competitiveness of nominations
(percentages)

	Woman sought nomination	No woman sought nomination
Acclamation	39	71
Competition	61	29
	(106)	(211)

where a woman sought the party nomination had a contest for the position. This is compared to 29 percent of those associations where only men sought the nomination (table 3.25). A similar story holds for those who won their party nominations. Forty-seven percent of the women candidates, compared to only 31 percent of the men, faced another contestant at their nomination meeting. Even when those who were incumbents are excluded, more male candidates (61 percent) had been selected by acclamation than female candidates (47 percent).

Although women faced a competitive selection more frequently than did their male counterparts, there is no evidence that the party members who decide such contests prefer male candidates. When both women and men sought the local nomination, women won over half the time (54 percent). Indeed the record of local associations may be more than even-handed when it comes to choosing between women and men. In almost half of these cases, more men than women were on the selection ballot, while there were more women than men in only 10 percent of these contests.

Still, the data do indicate that when women ran against one or more men, they were most successful in smaller, somewhat less electorally competitive associations. And while these contests were no less likely to involve recruitment campaigns, the number of new members at nomination time tended to be smaller in those associations that women won. Perhaps not surprisingly, then, men who won mixed contests seem to have spent more on their pre-selection campaigns than did women victors, although the mean difference was only in the order of $600. Nonetheless, the figures, although based on only a few associations, do suggest that even in contests for the most desirable candidacies – those classified as safe or having a good chance of success – when the number of male and female contestants was equal, women were as likely or even more likely to win than were men (table 3.26).

While local selection may be a factor in limiting the nomination of

Table 3.26
Candidate sex by local competitiveness
(local associations with equal number of males and females in a nomination contest)

Gender of candidate selected	Perceived competitiveness	
	Safe or good (%)	Unlikely or hopeless (%)
Female	64	60
Male	36	40
	(14)	(10)

	Competitiveness on 1984 result	
	Safe or good (%)	Unlikely or hopeless (%)
Female	56	71
Male	44	29
	(9)	(17)

women, the data do not support the view that this is because the grass-roots membership discriminates against women. The problem, it seems, is that women do not contest candidacies to the same extent as men: in the survey, women sought nominations in only 37 percent of the local associations in which incumbents were not running, whereas men did so in 84 percent of those associations.

This leads us to ask about the role of the party organizations in all of this. What, if anything, did they do to affect the number of women nominated? To answer this question requires examination of the pre-nomination period and party activities prior to the stage at which local members made their selection.

Party Pre-Selection Activities and the Nomination of Women

If parties are committed to the nomination of more women, recruitment practices should reflect this commitment by the identification and encouragement of prospective women candidates. While our measures of such activities are indirect, we can infer from the data that party efforts can have an impact.

Search committees are one aspect of local association activities that can make a difference to both the participation of women in local contests and the nomination of women to candidacies, at least in associations where incumbents do not seek re-selection. Where incumbents signal their wish to return to Parliament, any search committees are assumed to be largely formal exercises, given party norms concerning incumbency. But in other associations, when the local party had a candidate search committee, women contested 43 percent of the nominations and won 30 percent of them. By comparison, where the local party had no such committee, women contested only 27 percent of the nominations and won 16 percent of them.

In addition to merely searching out possible candidates, local associations are sometimes more explicit in encouraging reluctant individuals to run. When asked if the local association had to talk its candidates into running, 18 percent said yes. Although the small number involved requires conclusions about them be tentative, the evidence again suggests that recruitment practices can be especially encouraging to women. Twenty-nine percent of the candidates who were talked into running were women, compared to 19 percent of the rest. Moreover, the majority of women talked into running did so for local parties whose electoral success was judged by the party to be at least good. On this, women may have done better than the male candidates. A majority of men talked into running did so for local parties whose electoral chances were considered by their own party to be unlikely or hopeless.

In looking at the influence of search committees, a party effect was also sought. Did such structures contribute to the nomination of women in all parties, or was it more limited? The findings (in ridings with no

Table 3.27
Search committees by party
(non-incumbent associations only)

Party	Local search committee		
	Yes (%)	No (%)	N
NDP			
Women aspirant(s)*	52	28	107
Woman candidate	42	18	112
Liberal			
Women aspirant(s)	37	24	99
Woman candidate	20	14	105
PC			
Women aspirant(s)	26	30	39
Woman candidate	10	19	42

*Cell entries are percentages of local associations in which at least one woman ran for the nomination.

incumbents) suggest that the role of search committees can be variable. The NDP was more likely to have such committees, and the presence of such committees in local NDP associations was more likely to result in female aspirants contesting the local nomination and female candidates being nominated (table 3.27). For the Liberals, the figures are not as striking, but they do suggest a similar pattern: search committees produce more women aspirants and more women candidates. It is among Conservative associations that the pattern breaks down. Although these observations are based on a small number of constituencies, it appears that local search committees do not function here for women as they do in the other two parties.

While riding associations sometimes receive help from outside party officials in seeking candidates to run in their constituency, the distribution of this assistance indicates it is rarely used by the party organizations as a means to install their preferred candidates – whether female or male – in winning ridings. Only 7 percent of non-incumbent local associations that thought they had a safe seat said they had help from outside party officials in finding a candidate.

If the assistance of such outsiders did not contribute to the nomination of women in safe candidacies, what about instances where the prospects were at least good? Here, it seems, such help may have added to the numbers of women: they were nominated more than twice as often when outside assistance was reported than when it was absent (table 3.28). Some of this apparent effect is attributable to party differences: Conservative party associations, which were least likely to have had such outside help, were also least likely to nominate women. But 40 percent of the Liberal and NDP associations that had such party help nominated women, compared to 22 percent of those that reported no such assistance.

Table 3.28
Outsiders and the selection of women candidates:
non-incumbent associations
(safe or good chance candidacies only)

Local party had assistance in candidate search	Percentage of women candidates nominated
Yes	44
No	18
	(142)

Given the degree of local autonomy in the nomination process, and the limited use of outside officials in the search for local candidates, national parties wishing to achieve more gender parity in their candidate lists must also rely, to an important degree, on more indirect methods. These include simply encouraging their local associations to nominate women. Given that the national leadership of all three parties had declared an interest in expanding the numbers of women nominated, it was anticipated that many local associations would report having been encouraged by their party to choose a female candidate. Yet this was not our finding: fewer than a fifth of the associations reported this was true in their case. Even excluding ridings where incumbents sought re-selection, only 21 percent reported national or regional level encouragement and most (83 percent) of this occurred in one party, the NDP. Among non-incumbent associations, only 2 and 8 percent, respectively, of the Conservatives and Liberals reported such encouragement, compared to 43 percent of the NDP.

But was this encouragement really effective? The data suggest it may have been. Among non-incumbent associations that reported receiving it, women were more likely to contest the local nomination and to be chosen as the local candidate.

As it is primarily the NDP that reports such encouragement and as it is also the party tending to nominate more women, the question arises as to whether this is simply a party effect. To answer this question, the pattern within NDP associations was examined. Among those organizations reporting extra-local encouragement to choose a woman candidate, 56 percent had at least one woman contesting their nomination and 53 percent chose a woman as their candidate (table 3.29). By comparison, this was true of only 37 and 22 percent, respectively, of NDP associations not reporting such encouragement.

Table 3.29
NDP efforts to increase female candidacies
(non-incumbent associations)

Local association encouraged by party to choose woman candidate	Women			
	Contested		Nominated	
	%	N	%	N
Yes	56	43	53	45
No	37	57	22	60

Unfortunately, because only a small number of Liberal and Progressive Conservative associations reported this phenomenon, it is not possible to confirm whether the apparent success of such efforts is party-specific.

Conclusion

While the parties have improved their record on nominating women candidates in the 1980s, the increase in female candidacies in the 1988 election was modest and their overall electoral success was not changed much from the previous election. Nor has the rank order of the parties altered in terms of the proportions of women selected. The NDP nominated the largest number of women and the Progressive Conservatives the smallest.

Across the regions, the pattern of female candidacies varied from Atlantic Canada, with the lowest proportion of women candidates and none nominated in what were considered safe seats, to Quebec, with the highest proportion and the best record on women nominated in safe constituencies. These regional differences in federal politics were not consistent with the regional patterns of female candidacies at the provincial level, suggesting that efforts to explain regional differences in terms of regional cultures are inappropriate.

Incumbency was a major factor limiting the nomination of women to safe candidacies and meant that those women seeking nominations tended to face more competition when they did place their names in contention. But the evidence also suggests that grassroots party members do not disproportionately favour men, and may even favour women when they run against men.

Some practices do appear to work in favour of more women running, although their effects may vary by party. Local search committees, regional and national party assistance in finding local candidates, and explicit encouragement for some local ridings to nominate women candidates can contribute to women both seeking nominations and winning them. But party-specific effects suggest that none of these factors per se are sufficient to produce more women nominees at the local level.

5. THE REGIONAL DIMENSIONS OF PARTY SELECTION

It has become a truism to observe that much of Canadian politics is written in regional terms. The parties' histories, patterns of electoral support, and organizational structures all have important regional dimensions. The rules and practices of local constituency selection might then be expected to reflect regional organizational and political mores and vary accordingly. Systematic differences may be especially apparent in Quebec, given its long history of Liberal dominance federally, its clear separation of federal and provincial political organization, and its recent development of an electoral reform agenda and innovative system of party finance. This section will examine the various rules and practices of selection from a regional perspective, looking for patterns that suggest regional distinctiveness.

In seeking regional dimensions, five regions will be used as units of analysis: Atlantic Canada, Quebec, Ontario, the Prairies and British Columbia. Alternatively, when the data suggest such analysis is appropriate, Quebec will be compared with the rest of Canada. Although this sort of regional analysis does not exhaust the possibilities of territorial differences, e.g., differences between the provinces within Atlantic Canada and those of the Prairies, the small sample size in these regions limits reliable exploration of such possibilities. For northern Canada, where the parties face particular problems because of the vast territory and small numbers of people, this kind of study is insufficient to analyse its differences.

This analysis of region and selection begins with a look at the general format of meetings, and the formal rules and guidelines that govern the process within local associations.

Selection Format, Rules and Structures: The Local Dimension

As we observed in the first section of this study, some aspects of the nomination process are virtually uniform across the country. With few exceptions, candidates are chosen at local nomination meetings open to the general membership of the local constituency association. Although the largest number of associations that did not have meetings is found in Quebec, even there they constitute less than 5 percent of the total. In another few associations (3 percent) meetings were held, but they were open only to delegates from smaller parts of the constituency and not to the general membership. These were also more regionally concentrated: they were more prevalent in the constituencies in Atlantic Canada, where they characterized 12 percent of the associations. But neither of these variations is substantial and the overall picture remains one of very considerable uniformity in the basic format for choosing party candidates.

Although the general method for selection is standardized, this is not true of the rules governing membership in the local association. Residency requirements virtually divided the sample in half and, as described in section 1 of this study, there are some clear party differences between the Conservatives on one hand and the Liberals and New

Democrats on the other (table 3.3). To this must be added a regional dimension. In Atlantic Canada, only 17 percent of the associations allowed non-resident members, while on the Prairies, this was true of 23 percent. But Quebec and Ontario associations, perhaps reflecting the exigencies of urban ridings, were much less restrictive. Sixty-nine and 63 percent, respectively, allowed for non-resident members. And as table 3.30 illustrates, these regional variations are not explained by party differences. While Conservative party associations are, in every region, the ones least likely to allow non-resident members, with the exception of British Columbia, their restrictiveness varies across regions in a pattern similar to that of the other two parties. Conservative riding associations are least likely to have non-resident members in Atlantic Canada and the Prairies and more likely to have them in Quebec and Ontario.

Like membership requirements, the length of time individuals must be members before they can participate in nominations varies across the sample, although the requirements are not typically very demanding. Only 18 percent of the sample associations required participants to have been party members for more than 30 days, while 27 percent required a time period of only a week or less.

Conditions for participation varied primarily between parties, with Conservative associations the least and NDP the most demanding. Although the numbers within the groups in the sample are small and consequently not very reliable, they do suggest that there is no clear regional pattern across all three parties except, perhaps, a contrast between the more open approach practised on the Prairies and the stricter requirements in British Columbia. On the Prairies, 51 percent of associations required that members belong for only a week or less

Table 3.30
Regional patterns of non-resident local association membership

| | | Party | | | |
Region	All (%)	Liberals (%)	Conservatives (%)	NDP (%)	N
Atlantic provinces	17	25	—	29	29
Quebec	69	74	48	79	83
Ontario	63	74	45	68	129
Prairies	24	14	24	33	59
British Columbia	51	87	22	52	37

in order to participate, and as few as 6 percent demanded more than 30 days' membership. Among the Conservatives, no associations required longer than 30 days and 87 percent asked only a week or less (table 3.31). In British Columbia, almost 70 percent of the associations in the sample required more than 30 days' membership, including 90 percent of NDP associations and 80 percent of the Liberal ones. Even the requirements of Conservative associations in BC were more

Table 3.31
Membership requirements for nomination meeting participants by region and party

Region	Length of membership	Liberals (%)	Conservatives (%)	NDP (%)	N^c
Atlantic provinces	7 days or less[a]	22	70	33	25
	over 30 days[b]	22	—	—	
Quebec	7 days or less	8	20	30	73
	over 30 days	31	10	15	
Ontario	7 days or less	30	40	4	116
	over 30 days	14	—	21	
Prairies	7 days or less	26	87	26	53
	over 30 days	5	—	11	
British Columbia	7 days or less	—	25	—	32
	over 30 days	80	12	90	

[a]Percentage of local associations with a membership requirement of 7 days or less.
[b]Percentage of local associations with a membership requirement of over 30 days.
[c]Number answering items on membership requirements.

Table 3.32
Spending guidelines by region

Region	Spending guidelines	
	%	N
Atlantic provinces	16	32
Quebec	20	79
Ontario	8	124
Prairies	14	63
British Columbia	21	38
All	14	336

demanding than the party's norm, with half of them requiring more than 15 days. But the larger story in this is the highly uneven character of local requirements within regions and the limited institutionalization of party membership across the country.

Another set of possible rules about the selection process concerns nomination expenditures. But as noted in the first section, comparatively few local associations regulate this aspect of candidate selection, and the evidence of table 3.32 suggests few regional differences on this dimension of local party practice. More associations in British Columbia and Quebec report guidelines than in other provinces, but the differences between them and most of the others are not substantial. Looking within regions by party does not sharpen this picture, except with respect to the differences between Ontario and Quebec which become most clear among Liberal and Conservative associations. In Quebec, 22 percent of Liberal and Conservative associations had expenditure guidelines compared to only 6 percent of their counterparts in Ontario. But more generally, in whatever region and within whichever party, such guidelines are surprisingly uncommon.

While constituency associations in Quebec (and in BC) are somewhat more structured when it comes to spending guidelines for their nomination campaigns, this is not true of the search committee phenomenon. As already observed, local search committees are rarely established when incumbents wish to run again, and this is no less true in Quebec than elsewhere. But a look at constituencies with no incumbents seeking re-selection reveals that Quebec is rather distinctive for its lack of formal structure in the search process (table 3.33). In every other region, more than half of these non-incumbent associations have search committees, and in Ontario almost three-quarters of them do. Yet

Table 3.33
Local search committees by region
(non-incumbent associations only)

	Local search committee	
Region	%	N
Atlantic provinces	52	25
Quebec	36	61
Ontario	74	97
Prairies	61	49
British Columbia	68	32

in Quebec, only 36 percent of respondents indicated that such committees existed in their local association.

Regional-National Input

Although our picture of selection is one which is highly localized, we
have evidence of at least three means by which the regional and/or
national party apparatus may play a role in the process. The first, public
use of the leader's veto, is rarely used. The other two include the umpire
role that may be demanded of outside officials in instances where nominations are appealed, and assistance in the recruitment of prospective
candidates. Both of these activities turn up some interesting differences
between Quebec and the other regions.

First, with respect to appeals, the Quebec respondents were more
likely to indicate the decisions of their local nomination meetings
were taken to a higher body. Over 85 percent of all appeals recorded
in the sample occurred in that province (table 3.34). They constituted 23 percent of the nominations in Quebec, and were distributed
across all three parties.

Second, although the distribution is a more complex one, there is a
suggestion that among the non-incumbent constituency associations,
outside party help in finding candidates was more likely to be reported
by the Quebec respondents (table 3.35). Thirty-seven percent of Quebec
associations said they had such assistance, compared to 20 percent of
associations in the rest of the country. Of course, parties are more likely
to seek (and accept) outside help in finding candidates when their competitive circumstances are weak. And to be sure, in hopeless circumstances,
regional differences fade. But among constituency associations where
the chances of electoral success were judged to be good or safe, outside
party help was more often observed in Quebec. Thirty-four percent

Table 3.34
Regional appeals of nomination outcomes

Region	Nomination appealed	
	%	N
Atlantic provinces	—	32
Quebec	23	83
Ontario	2	133
Prairies	—	66
British Columbia	2	41

Table 3.35
Outside party assistance in candidate search by region
(non-incumbent associations only)

| | Outside party help | | | |
| | All contexts | | Safe/good chance | |
Region	%	N	%	N
Atlantic provinces	24	25	23	13
Quebec	37	59	34	38
Ontario	19	97	12	56
Prairies	25	48	20	20
British Columbia	16	31	6	17

reported such assistance, compared to only 14 percent in the rest of the country (table 3.35). Even among those that judged their electoral success unlikely, similar Quebec/non-Quebec differences were recorded.

Although these figures must be treated with caution, since they may not tell the whole story on regional-national relations among local associations, the two sets of findings do suggest a pattern: that is, a less localized, more integrated process exists in Quebec. That Quebec respondents were also more likely to say that the party, not the local association, determined the date for nomination meetings adds to a picture of greater involvement of outside party officials. In Quebec, 19 percent of selection dates were determined by the party, whereas this was true of only 2 percent of the non-Quebec meetings. All of this is consistent with most accounts of the history of federal parties in that province, where regional leaders from the federal Liberal party caucus wielded power vis-à-vis local organizations by virtue of their position as the usual governing party. In the other two parties, the weakness of local party organizations fostered dependency on outside party resources. But again, it is important not to overemphasize this difference between Quebec and the other provinces, for despite these indicators of the role of the outside party it still appears that such input from outside party officials is not the norm.

Regional Contests and Campaigns

In looking at regional contests and campaigns, three questions are of concern to us. The first is whether candidacies are more contested in some regions than others. The second concerns the kind of mobilization that occurs in the context of selection campaigns and whether it differs by region. The final one is whether the apparent costs of candidacies vary by region.

As seen in the second and third sections of this study, the presence of incumbents is one of the most significant factors in reducing competition for local nominations. Beyond that general pattern are some modest regional differences between Quebec and the Prairies, on one hand, and the rest of the country on the other (table 3.36). In the former, contests for nominations in associations in which no incumbent was seeking re-selection were substantially fewer: 29 percent compared to 53 percent in the other regions.

It might be expected that some of this difference in competition for candidacies was attributable to more meagre election prospects, especially on the Prairies, where only 12 percent of the non-incumbent riding associations were classified as having safe seats or a good chance of winning, and the election prospects of fully 63 percent were rated as hopeless. In Quebec, the constituency competitiveness of the non-incumbent candidacies was somewhat better: 21 percent were in safe seats or had good election prospects, while 50 percent were hopeless. In the rest of the country, a third of the non-incumbent candidacies were in safe seats or ones with good election prospects, and 40 percent were hopeless. But even controlling for local electoral competitiveness, the numbers, although small, suggest that the lesser incidence of competition for Prairie and Quebec candidacies is not just a function of fewer attractive candidacies (table 3.37). Ironically, proportionately more incumbents (24 percent) were challenged in Prairie constituencies than elsewhere (9 percent). Moreover, as will be shown, mobilization patterns in both regions suggest the number of contestants

Table 3.36
Contests for local selection by region
(non-incumbent associations only)

Region	Candidacies contested	
	%	N
Atlantic provinces	48	25
Quebec	29	62
Ontario	54	98
Prairies	29	48
British Columbia	52	31

on the final selection ballot may not tell the whole story about competition for nominations.

To an important degree, the recruitment of supporters from outside the parties varied with how competitive the nominations were, and in local associations where more than one person was placed on the nomination ballot, regional differences were small (table 3.38). However, larger differences were apparent in associations whose candidate was chosen by acclamation. In Quebec and the Prairie region, candidates who were ultimately unchallenged were more likely to have recruited supporters to join the party to support them at the nomination meeting. In Quebec, in over half of the constituencies where the candidate was

Table 3.37
Contests for local selection by region and local competitiveness
(non-incumbent associations only)

	Candidacies contested					
	Good prospect*		Unlikely		Hopeless	
Region	%	N	%	N	%	N
Quebec	31	13	33	18	26	31
Prairies	50	6	36	11	20	30
Rest	75	51	46	40	40	63

Note: Local association competitiveness based on 1984 election.

*Safe or good chance candidacies.

Table 3.38
Regional patterns of nomination mobilization
(percentage constituency associations)

	Supporters actively recruited			
	Uncontested nominations		Contested nominations	
Region	%	N	%	N
Atlantic provinces	32	19	77	13
Quebec	55	62	82	17
Ontario	36	73	86	58
Prairies	44	45	78	18
British Columbia	22	23	75	16

nominated by acclamation, that candidate had actively recruited people to the party to support her/his nomination. While it is unclear whether these candidates were unchallenged because of their recruiting success, the lower competition in Quebec might be partly attributable to this recruitment phenomenon.

The results of all of this, in terms of the numbers who were involved in selection meetings across the country, do not, as we argued earlier, produce a picture of a very participatory process (table 3.39). Even in those local associations that saw competition, the mean turnout was only 714 members. While there were some regional differences on this, the variability between regions was not significantly greater than the variability within them. The only substantial difference in the turnout numbers was for competitive selection meetings in Quebec, where the average was less than 400, compared to the rest of the country, where the average turnout was 760.

Table 3.39
Number of members at nomination meetings by region
(average number at nomination meetings)

Region	All	Uncontested nomination		Contested nomination	
Atlantic provinces	611	160	(13)	1145	(11)
Quebec	221	127	(25)	390	(14)
Ontario	426	132	(48)	692	(53)
Prairies	302	89	(33)	651	(14)
British Columbia	412	124	(15)	1059	(16)

Note: Figures in parentheses are numbers of nomination meetings.

Table 3.40
Average nomination spending by candidates by region

Region	All		Uncontested		Contested	
	$	N	$	N	$	N
Atlantic provinces	993	26	205	16	2 255	10
Quebec	1 464	62	1 036	46	2 697	16
Ontario	1 752	106	624	60	3 222	46
Prairies	1 126	51	416	37	3 000	14
British Columbia	672	33	400	18	998	15

Note: N = number of candidates on whom average spending figures are based.

Spending levels among successful candidates did not track those of turnout. Rather, those regions with the highest turnout numbers, the Atlantic region and British Columbia, were just those where campaign spending may have been lowest, whether all nominations are considered or just those where there were contests (table 3.40). The Quebec sample stands out for the significantly higher level of spending among uncontested candidates: mean spending among unchallenged Quebec candidates was $1 036 compared to an average of just $411 in the other regions. But in the overall spending equation, the competitiveness of local parties – and party differences themselves – overshadow what are really modest regional differences.

Conclusion

Regional differences in the structure and practices of candidate selection are muted. Uniformity in the general format for selection is considerable, and where local rules and structures do vary they do so unevenly, revealing no consistent regional pattern to the institutionalization of the process. A regional dimension was found in residency requirements for local members, but for rules on length of party membership required of selection participants, guidelines on nomination expenditures for aspiring candidates, and the presence of local candidate search committees, the only substantial regional difference among local associations was the lack of local search committees in the Quebec parties.

The role and influence of outside party structures and officials are limited across all regions: neither appeals to higher party structures, nor assistance from outside party officials is the norm in any region. However, while the picture of a very locally based process holds true even for Quebec, it is there that a more integrated process exists, with more apparent input from outside officials. This, we suggest, is consistent with most accounts of the history of the federal parties in Quebec.

There were some apparent regional differences in the prevalence of contested nominations, with fewer in Quebec and the Prairies. Some of the difference is explained by the higher proportion of electorally hopeless candidacies, although this is more true of the Prairies than it is of Quebec. The greater incidence of pre-nomination mobilization on the Prairies and in Quebec, and the higher pre-nomination spending by acclaimed Quebec nominees also suggest that some contests were averted by aggressive pre-nomination recruitment.

Among contested candidacies, regional differences in the incidence and effects of mobilization were not substantial, with the exception of Quebec where the numbers of people attending nomination meetings were clearly smaller. Otherwise, variations within regions were as great as variations between them. This was equally true of spending levels among successful candidates. Party differences and inequalities in the electoral prospects of local constituencies over-shadowed regional differences.

6. THE PARTIES AND CANDIDATE NOMINATION

Through the various descriptions and analyses of candidate selection we have seen some evidence of party differences in aspects of this process. In this section, these and other observations concerning the parties and candidate nominations are brought together in order to document both party differences and similarities, and to create more coherent and nuanced portraits of the parties.

Expectations of party differences come partly from the particular historical roots of the NDP, as compared with those of the Liberals and Conservatives. As a party whose forerunner, the CCF, was predicated upon the principles of grassroots participation combined with an ideo-logical commitment to socialism, the NDP has inherited a mixed tradi-tion (Young 1969). Local control is an important aspect of grassroots participation. But so, too, is centralized activity an important means by which to meet socialist organizational principles and to retain some ideological coherency. In the nomination process, these two traditions seem to pull the party's members in opposite directions. On one hand, the requirements of membership and voting in local ballots may be more rigorous, reflecting a tradition of party decision-making controlled by a committed membership which takes local democracy seriously. On the other hand, the central organization of the party may be more active and influential as it seeks to steer and direct constituency associations in order to achieve the organizational and ideological objectives of the party.

But these traditions may be both confounded and reinforced by another aspect of the NDP – its electoral weakness in significant parts of the country. That political reality may lead local constituency associations to relax some of the requirements for membership and participation, while reinforcing the need for central party activity to assist weak local associations. Accordingly, this analysis differentiates, where possible, those aspects of NDP practices which may reflect the party's distinct traditions from those attributable to its competitive position in ridings.

While documenting the similarities and differences between the NDP and the other two parties, we also looked for patterned differences between the Liberals and Conservatives. Where they occur, they may reflect the differences between government and opposition parties, and especially the impact of the very much larger number of incumbent members seeking re-selection in the Conservative party. But that is not to ignore the possibility that as separate organizations, with their own distinct histories, the Liberals and Conservatives may have developed unique organizational cultures and practices that have made their way into the selection process.

Selection Rules and Structures: The Local Dimension

It has already been observed that the general format of selection through local nomination meetings, open to the local membership, has few exceptions. That no exceptions are found among NDP associations, and that they rarely occur in the other two parties, is testament to the important symbolism of local control. But in other respects, such as membership requirements, the elements of local organizational democracy are weaker and more uncertain. Moreover, the patterns of party differences on those do not always match the simple characterization of the NDP as distinctively restrictive. Rules and practices are clearly more variable than that model would suggest: the Liberals and Conservatives are neither consistently different from nor consistently similar to either the NDP or to one another.

Consider, first, local residency requirements. The Conservative party's national constitution works to make non-resident membership in Conservative associations far less common than is the case for either the Liberals or the NDP. On the other hand, the percentages of the Liberal and NDP associations that allow non-resident members are virtually identical (table 3.3). Nor, as seen in the discussion of regionalism, does restrictiveness in residency requirements among Liberal and NDP associations vary by region. There is, in other words, no indication in the data that NDP rules are less restrictive only in regions where the party is particularly weak.

In practice, however, this apparent similarity between the Liberals and NDP breaks down. While 58 and 59 percent, respectively, of those parties' associations allow non-resident members, the mean proportions of non-resident members in associations that allow them differ sharply (table 3.41). NDP associations resemble their Conservative counterparts in this regard with a mean proportion of 4 percent non-resident members compared to the 10 percent among Liberal associations. Thus, while more NDP than Conservative associations do permit non-residents to join, the extent to which they depart from the practice of local residents selecting local candidates aligns them more with Conservative than with Liberal experience.

When we turn to the time requirements that local parties set for membership participation in nomination balloting, a different pattern

Table 3.41
Proportions of non-resident members by party
(only associations which permit non-residents)

Party	Average proportions (%)	N
Liberal associations	10	52
Conservative associations	4	30
NDP associations	4	64

is apparent. Here, the NDP is more restrictive than the other two parties: compared to both the Liberals and Conservatives, more of their local associations require in excess of 30 days' membership and fewer of them require only a week or less (table 3.4). However, while the sample sizes within provinces are small, they do suggest that NDP requirements are less rigorous in regions where the party has been least successful electorally (table 3.31). But what was unexpected is how little the New Democrats differ from the Liberals. Compared to Conservative associations, among which fewer than 4 percent required members to have belonged for more than 30 days in order to take part in nomination ballots, 21 and 28 percent, respectively, of Liberal and NDP associations had such requirements.

The final two indicators of structure in the local selection process are more consistent with a model of the NDP as the party that takes local participation and local democracy more seriously. The first indicator, the establishment of local search committees, implies a greater formal commitment to having the local organizations active in producing prospective candidates. The second, the development of guidelines for local nomination expenses, suggests a concern that the conditions of local democracy include those of a level playing field among the participants.

On the first indicator, the data suggest that NDP local associations are more likely to have search committees, and that the difference between them and the other two parties is not simply a function of the weaker electoral position of the NDP. Looking at local associations where incumbents were not seeking re-selection, the survey shows 70 percent of the NDP sample had a local search committee, as compared to just over half of the Liberal and Conservative samples (table 3.42). This difference is not diminished when the focus shifts to those associations whose electoral chances are rated as good or better. Similarities across the parties exist only when their chances of electoral success are judged to be unlikely or hopeless. As already noted in the discussion of women candidates, the implications of local search committees in the NDP extend beyond their role in expanding activities at the local level. They also include the implementation of organizational commitments, such as the selection of greater numbers of women candidates.

On the second indicator, guidelines for nomination expenses, few local associations in any of the parties gave evidence of having established such provisions. But 48 percent of those that did were NDP associations, although the differences between the parties were not significant (table 3.43). That difference is much more marked, however, in those associations where the nomination was contested. In those cases, more than four times as many NDP as Liberal or Conservative associations had established guidelines. While guidelines were more prevalent among NDP associations when their nominations were contested, they actually appear to have been less prevalent in contested Liberal and Conservative associations, where they were presumably more needed.

Table 3.42
Local party search committees by party
(non-incumbent associations only)

| | Local selection committee | | | |
| | All instances | | Safe/good seats | |
Party	%	N	%	N
Liberal associations	54	110	46	61
Conservative associations	51	43	43	28
NDP associations	70	113	65	57

Table 3.43
Local guidelines for nomination expenses by party

| | All constituencies | | Contested nominations | |
Party	%	N	%	N
Liberal associations	10	110	7	45
Conservative associations	13	105	6	33
NDP associations	18	124	29	41

Extra-local input

As documented earlier, intervention and influence from party bodies and officials outside the local constituency were not frequent occurrences in 1988. But it was suggested that, in the NDP, this phenomenon might be anticipated more frequently, as the party attempts to meet certain organizational principles, and indeed, there were two ways in which the national party did exercise influence in the selection process.

The first was by placing a restriction upon the timing of nominations. The second was by encouraging local associations to choose a woman candidate. In the latter case, such encouragement resulted in more women candidates being selected in the NDP than in the Liberal or Conservative parties.

For the Liberals and Conservatives, such influence was more unusual, although Prime Minister Mulroney's veto of the candidacy of former cabinet colleague Sinclair Stevens provided a dramatic public exception to normal practice. The Liberals did place a nomination freeze upon their local constituencies, but this was lifted much earlier than that of the NDP – and neither Liberal nor Conservative riding associations reported much encouragement from outside party figures to choose women candidates.

The remaining party differences in the role of extra-local party structures were limited. Nominations, for example, were rarely appealed to higher party bodies and although more of this was recorded by the Liberal associations, the differences between the parties were very small.

There were some party differences in the extent to which outside party assistance was given in the search for local candidates, with about a quarter of the NDP associations indicating that they had received such help, as compared to 17 percent of the Liberal, and just 12 percent of the Conservative ones. But as table 3.44 indicates, these differences virtually disappeared in those associations where incumbents were not a factor. Then, Conservative and NDP associations looked identical in the

Table 3.44
Outside party assistance in candidate search by party
(non-incumbent associations only)

Party	%	N
Liberal associations	18	108
Conservative associations	28	43
NDP associations	28	111

proportions that had outside help, while the differences with the Liberals were not significant.

Party Contests and Campaigns

Next to incumbency, the most important factor influencing the competitiveness of a nomination is the electoral circumstance of a local association. Not surprisingly, the competitiveness of a nomination also reflects differences in the parties' national standings. Competition was most likely in non-incumbent Conservative associations, least likely in non-incumbent NDP ones. A control for local competitiveness reinforces this interpretation: among associations with safe seats, or a good chance of victory, Conservative associations still had proportionately more contests for their nominations in 1988 (table 3.45). This, and the incidence of contests among the various Liberal and NDP associations, suggests that the attractiveness of the governing party and local competitiveness count for more in nomination politics than do party traditions.

Some party differences in the character of nomination contests were anticipated, but in many respects, the parties were more similar than they were different. In all parties, a majority of associations saw prospective candidates actively recruit supporters to join the party, although this was less frequent among NDP associations than Liberal or Conservative ones (table 3.46). In none of the parties was the recruitment of new members particularly controversial, although Liberal associations were more likely to report such a controversy than either Conservative or NDP associations. In terms of the groups from which prospective candidates recruited new members, the party patterns were basically similar – with a few exceptions. NDP recruiters were more

Table 3.45

Competitiveness of local nominations by party and past electoral performance
(non-incumbent associations only)

Competitive position based on 1984 performance	Percentage of nominations contested					
	Liberal		Conservative		NDP	
	%	N	%	N	%	N
Good chance	57	28	77	26	56	16
Unlikely	36	33	40	10	48	27
Hopeless	39	51	*		24	70

*Too few to calculate.

likely to turn to unions or professional groups (27 percent of NDP associations reported prospective candidates mobilizing supporters in such groups) as compared to their Liberal and Conservative counterparts (fewer than 5 percent of these associations reported such recruitment). Conservatives were less likely than Liberals or New Democrats to recruit from ethnic groups, while Liberal nominees were less likely to recruit from women's groups than their NDP and Conservative counterparts. In all three parties, recruitment was most frequent from local voluntary associations and most nomination contests did not revolve around a specific issue.

Finally, party differences were clearly apparent in the pre-nomination expenditures of non-incumbent nominees (table 3.47). On average, the Liberals spent most. For uncontested nominations, there was only a small difference between Conservatives and New Democrats, but it was a different matter in contested situations: there, the NDP average was less than half that of the Conservatives. But while these

Table 3.46
Nomination competition in the parties
(contested nominations: percentage of all associations)

| | | | Recruitment from | | | |
Party	Supporters recruited	Recruitment controversial	Volunteer assoc.	Ethnic groups	Women's interest groups	Local single issue	Contests with a specific issue
Liberal	92	26	72	24	10	14	28
PC	88	15	64	15	21	9	21
NDP	65	18	68	24	27	7	25

Table 3.47
Candidate pre-selection spending by party for contested and uncontested nominations
(averages for non-incumbent associations only)

	Uncontested		Contested	
Party	$	N	$	N
Liberal	1 752	51	4 036	42
Conservative	633	9	2 335	20
NDP	208	59	1 070	31

Note: N = number of candidates on whom average spending figures are based.

inter-party differences are striking, it is important to note that they mask very considerable differences within each of the parties.

Conclusion

Party differences in nomination structures and format do not support the notion that NDP politics is significantly different from that of the other two national parties. NDP associations do typically require longer membership for the participants in local selection, and they are more likely to have local party structures such as search committees and to have guidelines for nomination expenses. But Conservative party associations more often limit non-resident membership than do those of the NDP, and Liberal associations are frequently as restrictive in length of membership required for participation. There is also evidence that, in the NDP, extra-local influence is occasionally used to effect organizational goals, but as in all of the parties, intervention from outside bodies is infrequent.

The competitiveness of constituency nominations was primarily a function of incumbency and local parties' electoral chances, and not any distinctive party cultures. Moreover, the contests themselves were remarkably similar among the parties. Recruitment of outside supporters by prospective candidates was widely practised, although less so in the NDP; recruitment was not often controversial and the groups from which aspiring nominees recruited their support did not differ much from party to party. What, in fact, may have distinguished the three parties' contests the most were the levels of spending among *some* of their candidates.

7. NOMINATIONS AND CANDIDATES

Canadians appear to take the process by which they nominate local candidates for election pretty well for granted. Despite the complaints about abuses that occur in most elections, there has been little real change in over a century in the processes commonly used by the political parties. This is perhaps the more noteworthy considering virtually all other areas of party organization and life have been transformed over that period (Carty 1988). But for all that, the nomination process is not just a matter of simple, familiar and informal constituency politics. There are several puzzles worth noting that must be dealt with by anyone seeking to reform the process.

On the one hand, the process retains its parochial focus: local associations are jealous of their right to set their own rules, maintain their own practices, and determine their own candidate. It is in this way that party members ensure that they can inject the impulses of their distinctive communities into national political life. Yet, on the other hand, our analysis of the practices of local associations in nominating their candidates indicates that there is remarkably little systematic variation in the structure and processes they adopt. Unlike much else in Canadian politics, there is no significant regional or partisan variation, only modest elaborations on a remarkably common theme. There appears to be a surprisingly homogeneous national process at work, with only competition (in the form of contested nominations or a competitive riding context) making a difference to the dynamics of individual candidate selections.

This combination of a national process managed by autonomous local associations generates a unique set of frustrations and tensions within the parties and among those interested in shaping the mix of candidates presented for election. The widespread acceptance of common processes would seem to suggest common rules and procedures. Yet differences among constituency associations' particular practices indicate that the national parties have had only modest success in setting national standards. And even where attempts have been made (as with the residence rule in the Conservative party), they have so far proved difficult to enforce. However, some observers and critics of the parties have pointed to these constituency differences not as a strength of the system, but as evidence of local corruption or a lack of will on the part of the parties.

On no issue, in recent years, has this been so true as that of increasing the number of women selected as candidates (Brodie and Vickers 1981, 326). Given that the parties have made some progress in enforcing rules about the number of women who must be in constituency associations' delegations to leadership selection conventions, advocates of increasing the number of women candidates believe the parties' nomination rules should be written in the same spirit. Certainly, the major parties' public statements suggest that they want to increase the number of women who run under their label. And as seen in the fourth section of this study (see especially tables 3.27 and 3.28), where the national party is able to involve itself in the local process, or where the local association reports the party actively encouraged it to search for a woman candidate, the probability of selecting a woman candidate increased. The real story, however, is how few associations in good competitive situations were in either of those categories. It is difficult not to conclude that most activists, believing that nomination is a local prerogative, simply ignored the signals being sent by the national parties, or at least thought they imposed no requirement on their constituency. Local associations continue to choose candidates more or less as they please. It is difficult to see how the national party organizations could themselves increase the number of women candidates without altering this basic relationship with their local associations.

Beyond this puzzle as to whether candidate selection is a national process in local clothing, or a parochial event parading under a national label, is the apparent curiosity of the contests themselves. With loose structures, informal organizations, few rules and small memberships, the large majority of local constituency parties are open and easily permeable. In the large majority of cases, money is not a significant factor in nomination politics. But despite all this, two-thirds of the major parties' candidacies are not contested. As it would be difficult to design a party regime that was more hospitable to participation, the question of why there is so little competition remains.

This section takes up these two aspects of candidate nomination in Canada (its uncompetitiveness and the local-national balance) in an attempt to throw more light on them. In both instances the data at hand do not allow us to tell the complete story, but they do permit us to begin sketching out some aspects of the workings of these dimensions of constituency party organization and activity in Canadian parties.

An Uncompetitive Nomination Politics

The second section of this study showed that despite media-generated impressions to the contrary, most party nominations in Canada are not contested at the local candidate selection meeting. Some uncontested nominations are to be expected. Where a local party has an incumbent member who is doing a good job and who wishes to be renominated, one might normally expect that he or she would not be challenged. A few in any election will be, because either the party or some local activists (sometimes both) want to be rid of the member, and local challenges have been the way of doing this in Canada for over a century. Naturally, such situations can produce the most vigorous nomination contests of all, but they are dramatic events precisely because they are infrequent. While the presence of incumbents does limit competition, in a three-party system they can never occupy more than a third of the spaces and with normal retirements this means that something in the order of three-quarters of the nominations are open. (In the 1988 Candidate Nomination Survey, one-quarter of the responding associations had an incumbent seeking the nomination.)

If some local party associations do not have a contest for their nomination because of their strength in the riding (hence an incumbent), others do not have one because they are so weak. Where there is no chance of local victory, there are unlikely to be many seeking a candidacy (an exception is in a governing party where losing an election may entail few costs while offering the chance of influencing local patronage). In 1988, 7 per cent of the constituency associations claimed they estimated their local election chances as hopeless at the time they were nominating their candidate. This figure seems low. In part it reflects the general volatility and uncertainty that characterized Canadian politics over the elections of 1979, 1980 and 1984. But a larger part is due to an unrealistic sense of optimism in NDP associations before the 1988 election. Only 9 percent of them estimated their prospects as hopeless, though five times that proportion (42 percent) went on to lose their deposit. In any event, 80 percent of the nominations in all of the ridings perceived as hopeless went uncontested.

Taking the strong (incumbents) and weak (hopeless) associations into account still leaves something over two-thirds of the nominations available. But as seen in the first two sections of this study, the majority of these are still not contested. Now, there may be no puzzle in this at all. It may simply be that extraordinarily few Canadians want to become members of Parliament. Certainly the rate at which MPs leave the House suggests that many choose not to stay long. Assuming, however, that this is not simply a supply problem, what do the data reveal about the way the nomination process is working in those ridings that are open and should be the natural targets of groups trying to penetrate the Canadian political system?

Of the constituency parties with no incumbent member in 1988, 58 percent were optimistic about their prospects when nominating, and rated their riding as either safe or a good chance. These were the local constituency associations (44 percent of all in the three national parties) that offered the best prospect for those seeking a nomination that might be converted into a seat at the general election. Table 3.48 reveals something of these most desirable ridings, distinguishing between those that were contested and those that were not.

Perhaps the most remarkable finding reported in the table is its basic one: almost half (46 percent) of these local associations had an uncontested nomination meeting. While there can be little doubt that local élites were managing their party's nomination in the ridings, the rather small average size (600 members) of their associations constituted little barrier to anyone who might have contemplated seeking the nomination, given that formal rules are minimal and nomination meeting turnouts are generally low (see table 3.11).

There is also a marked party difference in the degree to which these good nominations are contested. In 1988, comparatively few of the governing Conservative party's good nominations went begging. This

Table 3.48
Contested nominations in desirable seats
(percentages)

| | All | Party | | | Timing | | Membership | |
		Lib	PC	NDP	Pre-writ	Post-writ	2–30	>30 days
No contest	46	46	22	58	44	54	38	57
Contested	54	54	78	42	56	46	62	43
N	(145)	(61)	(27)	(57)	(117)	(26)	(87)	(21)

Note: Desirable seats = riding where the local association had no incumbent and perceived the seat to be either "safe" or a "good chance."

presumably reflects the greater attractiveness there is to being on the government side in the Canadian House of Commons. By definition, however, a government party (this was especially so in 1988, given the size of the 1984 victory) is likely to have fewer of these good nominations available. The other side of this coin is that the opposition parties' good seats are relatively less attractive. In the case of the NDP, which has never formed a national government (or been the official opposition), almost 60 percent of its best prospects went uncontested. Even in the absence of comparative data, this figure seems extraordinarily high. This suggests that there are significant numbers of potentially easy access points (uncontested good nominations) available for individuals wanting into the system. However, most of them are on the opposition side of the party system.

In section 5 of this study, we noted some modest regional differences in the propensity to contest nominations – something that appears equally true for the available desirable seats we are considering here. In both Quebec and the Prairies, unlike in the other three regions, the majority of such nominations were uncontested. Given that these were areas of Conservative strength in 1984–88, this presumably reflects something of the partisan dynamic discussed above. It also indicates that there are significant parts of the country where individuals do not come forward and fight – even over good nominations.

Table 3.48 points to two other structural aspects of the nomination process that may be related to its competitiveness. The first has to do with the timing of the meeting. Those held before the writ is issued are more likely to be contested, the majority of those held after are not. In some ways this finding is counter-intuitive, especially when we recall that the bulk of these ridings are in the opposition parties. Nominations held before an election is called require an individual to make a more indefinite public commitment. For many, family and career responsibilities make this difficult. Certainly this has been an argument advanced by minority or excluded groups (for instance, women) who have argued that the present system works against them. On the other hand, once the writ has been dropped, politically interested individuals are expected to proclaim their allegiances, and the time commitment required in becoming a candidate is more sharply defined. For a good nomination, one might think this would increase the number of potential candidates and thus, contested nominations. The lack of competition revealed in the data might be explained by a reluctance to engender intra-party conflict in the election period, but more of it may simply be due to the fact that there are relatively few (18 percent) desirable seats left at that point, and most of them are in the opposition parties.

Membership requirements appear to be related to the likelihood of competition for a good nomination. Those local associations with modest membership requirements are more likely to be contested than those that have, by Canadian standards, more stringent tests (30 days or more). This certainly makes sense, given the central role that mobilizing new supporters now seems to play in candidate nomination battles. There is also a party dimension to this, for it was the opposition Liberal and NDP associations that were most likely to have had the longest membership requirements in 1988.

While we have only limited data on the active management of candidate recruitment, table 3.49 provides a first glance at the behind-the-scenes activity in the constituencies. It records the influence of

Table 3.49
Managing nominations in desirable seats
(percentages)

	All	Search committee present	Talked candidate into running	Discouraged would-be candidate	Outside help finding candidate
Frequency		53	16	11	19
No contest	46	47	41	56	78
Contested	54	53	59	44	22
	(145)	*(76)*	*(22)*	*(16)*	*(27)*

Note: Desirable seats = riding where the local association had no incumbent and perceived the seat to be either "safe" or a "good chance."

search committees, the active encouragement or discouragement of particular individuals, and the impact of party officials from outside the riding on the extent to which these most desirable constituencies saw a contest for their nomination. Two aspects of this sort of activity should be remembered. First, with the exception of candidate search committees, all of these activities are reported infrequently. Second, when they occur, they are more likely to exist where the party's prospects are seen as hopeless. In desirable ridings, these kinds of structured candidate recruitment processes (all but search committees) are clearly the exception rather than the rule.

In only about half of the cases where local party associations had a desirable nomination available did they create a candidate search committee. This suggests either an informal approach to recruitment, or a belief in a laissez-faire, supply-side nomination process. In neither instance does the party, as an institution, take the opportunity to try and give shape to its caucus. As the table also indicates, the presence of such search committees does not affect the degree to which the nomination is contested. The use of such committees does not markedly increase the choice offered to ordinary party members over who their candidate will be, though it did make a modest difference for both Liberal and NDP associations in 1988.

In the small, rather intimate world of local party associations, one would expect much discussion and debate over who should be the candidate, especially in desirable seats. This, it might seem, would lead to efforts to persuade particular individuals to run for the nomination, or to discourage persons who were advancing their own cause but were generally thought to be unsuitable.

Our survey asked about such activity, though it may underestimate the extent of it, since not all can be known by a single respondent. Even so, there seems to have been rather little of this activity in these ridings. Where it is reported to have gone on, it produced predictable results: nomination contests are more frequent where people have been talked into running; they are less likely when individuals have been actively discouraged by key party activists.

Finally, when outside party officials are reported to have been involved in helping to find a candidate for a good nomination, there is seldom a contest for that nomination. It is not clear why this happens and the small number of occurrences suggests that each case may be different. No doubt it reflects a hesitancy by party outsiders to push a candidate onto an association, except in situations where no one has emerged locally. But if this is so, it means that the party is regularly denying itself the ability to recruit particular individuals, or particular groups, into its caucus. After all, it is these ridings that offer the greatest prospects for bringing new people into Parliament.

This portrait of what ought to be the most sought-after nominations is instructive. It suggests that under the guise of tradition and the rationale of local autonomy, the national political parties, as independent organizations, have largely abdicated any significant role in the nomination of their candidates. It is, then, misleading to argue that Canadian political parties as national institutions are responsible for recruiting men and women into political life. They hardly even act as gatekeepers to the system. More typically, they exist as rather general electoral syndicates that lend their name to the activities of local groups. The parties' parliamentary candidates are either self-selecting (and so reflect an apparently limited supply of would-be MPs), or they are the product of informal parochial cliques pushing forward an agreed-upon representative.

Yet at the same time, this is a very open and undefined system. Despite widespread agreement on how local parties ought to name their candidates, the very lack of standard rules and the permeability of the process may create a veil of ignorance about it that intimidates and excludes outsiders. It might well be that a more formally structured process would also be one that would facilitate participation. More individuals might find it possible to seek a candidacy if the procedures were clearly and publicly delineated, and more party members might then have a real part in choosing their candidate. If that were the case, then it might even be possible for the national parties to influence who stood in their name.

This brings the study back to the candidates themselves. The final subsection looks at the party candidates who are, after all, the products of this nomination process.

And the Nominees Are ...

The Canadian House of Commons is full of middle-aged, middle-class, well-educated males because they are the ones the three national parties largely nominate in the constituencies where they have much prospect of electing a member. Perhaps the most noticeable variation in this ongoing story has been the recent decline in the political attractiveness of lawyers as candidates. Courtney's (1988, 204) analysis of the 1984 general election noted that the lawyers' "numbers in the House of Commons slipped below 20 percent for the first time." The basis for this is clear: lawyers are now being nominated in far fewer constituencies; the data indicate that they made up little more than 10 percent of the three parties' candidates in 1988 (table 3.50). This does suggest that striking changes in the candidate mix can occur quickly.

The table also indicates that few federal constituency associations nominate men or women who have had experience in local or provincial elected office. The absence of former provincial politicians is now of long standing and it reflects the separation of federal and provincial party life common to much of the country in the last half-century. Virtually all of the small number who enter national politics do so in their home communities and in safe or good-chance ridings. Significantly, a third of them are from Atlantic Canada, where traditional patterns of party organization, including strong ties between provincial and federal parties of the same name, persist. Local politics is a more common recruiting ground for federal candidates, but here, too, those with such experience to offer are far more likely to take a nomination in a good seat rather than in a hopeless cause. Nominees with service in local elected office are twice as common among Liberals and Conservatives as they are among New Democrats, though what this particular partisan difference means is not clear. The more important point is surely that the parties are largely recruiting political amateurs to the country's national Parliament.

A second dimension of this phenomenon of nominating amateurs is the short history of party involvement that many candidates have. The evidence suggests that a quarter of all nominees (30 percent of non-incumbents) joined the political party that nominated them during the

Table 3.50
Candidate characteristics in the 1988 election
(percentages)

Principal occupations	
Business/management	22.1
Law	11.2
Education	12.6
Professional (unspecified)	12.6
Political experience	
Provincial legislature	4.9
Local government	24.3
Local resident	77.6
Party membership (year joined)	
1988	10.5
1984–87	14.7
1980–84	16.2
1970s	32.0
Pre-1970	26.7

life of the last Parliament, while 10 percent actually joined during the election year itself. These are hardly men and women well schooled in the party and its traditions. They are conscripts who cannot realistically be expected to play an active and independent role in party affairs. But, given that the wider party has so small a role in their recruitment, it can hardly expect more. At the same time, local associations that send individuals with such weak party roots to Ottawa can hardly expect these parliamentarians to stand up to the caucus leadership in any systematic fashion.

As the data also indicate, most nominees are residents of the local constituency they seek to represent. While just over 20 percent are not, that is probably not a large proportion, given the increasing number of ridings now within the major metropolitan centres and the frequency with which the boundaries of the electoral map change. It is this predilection for choosing a local man or woman as their candidate that no doubt reinforces party members' opposition to the leadership veto and makes it difficult for the party establishment to come into a riding and designate who the candidate will be.

Tables 3.51 and 3.52 follow up on these last two points and consider how the nomination process appears to contribute to the extent of amateurism (as indicated by recent party membership) and localism (as indicated by the selection of a constituency resident) among election candidates. To focus on the recruitment aspect of local associations' activity, those cases where a sitting MP is ensconced have been excluded, and only non-incumbent nominations examined.

On the issue of the length of a nominee's party membership, there is not much difference among the parties in the proportion of recent members, i.e., those who joined between 1984 and 1987, though the Conservatives have a somewhat larger percentage (but smaller number) of instant (joined in 1988) partisans among their new candidates (table 3.51). That may simply be a function of a governing party's advantage in attracting previously uninvolved individuals into public life. There are some sharp regional variations, with Quebec having twice as many candidates with recent memberships (59 percent) and British Columbia only half as many (16 percent) as the nation as a whole. The finding for Quebec likely stems from the political upheavals of the 1984 election in that province.

Though the differences are not particularly large, the proportion of instant party members is higher in ridings that did not name a candidate until after the election was called and/or had to talk their nominee into running. These are the situations in which a local association cannot easily find a traditional candidate, so that there is a

Table 3.51
Party membership of non-incumbent candidates
(percentages)

Membership	All	Liberal	PC	NDP
Instant*	14	13	17	13
New**	17	18	15	18
	(251)	(106)	(42)	(103)

		Nomination		
Membership	Post-writ	Search committee	Talked into running	Woman candidate
Instant	19	15	23	17
New	24	12	12	14
	(62)	(147)	(52)	(59)

	Constituency perceived as		
Membership	Safe/good chance	Unlikely	Hopeless
Instant	10	17	22
New	18	16	22
	(136)	(83)	(23)

*Instant = candidate joined party in 1988.
**New = candidate joined party in 1984–87 period.

greater likelihood of nominating an instant party member as the local standard-bearer.

Constituencies where electoral prospects are good do not have the same difficulty in finding a candidate. As a result, they are only half as likely as hopeless causes to end up nominating an instant party member. This keeps down the proportion of the latter actually elected to the House of Commons. That is surely a good thing from the perspective of party members concerned for the integrity of party policy and the participation of committed activists. However, the opposite side of this coin is that if outsiders can generally be nominated only in the least attractive (in the electoral prospects sense) constituencies, then it does become more difficult for the parties to bring new people into Parliament.

That said, these data on party memberships confirm the picture this study has drawn of an open and permeable nomination process. The problem does not seem to be that Canadians have a closed system.

Indeed, if the parties move to tighten the requirements on who can participate in the selection process, they might also want to give some thought to considering whether there ought to be party membership requirements for candidates. Some such conditions might work to strengthen the importance and autonomy of the parties as meaningful institutions.

Table 3.52 focuses on the extent to which constituency associations appear to prefer local residents as their nominees. This is not surprising in a country long preoccupied by geography, and whose electoral system is territorial in organization. Three-quarters of the constituency parties nominated a local man or woman in 1988, and there was no significant difference between those with incumbents and those without. In the non-incumbent cases, the Tories were somewhat more likely to have had a local candidate than either of their opponents, but they also had far fewer open seats to begin with. There is little regional variation on this, though British Columbian constituencies were somewhat less likely to nominate a local person in 1988.

If there are positive local predispositions toward nominating constituency residents, then one might expect that where outside help was required to find a candidate, or where there was no choice (an acclamation), the proportion of non-residents would be higher. Table 3.52 suggests that this is, indeed, the case. It also indicates that women candidates are slightly less likely to be locals. To the extent

Table 3.52
Localism of non-incumbent candidates
(percentage local residents)

	%	N
All non-incumbents	74	273
Party		
Liberal	74	115
Conservative	81	44
NDP	72	114
Nomination		
Acclamation	69	152
Outside involvement	60	63
Woman candidate	70	66
Constituency		
Safe/good chance	77	151
Unlikely	67	87
Hopeless	75	24

that women are trying to break into the system, or that parties are trying to attract greater numbers of women candidates, they may need to be more sensitive to the strength of this factor in constituency candidate selection decisions.

This localistic bias makes its impact on the House of Commons because seats that are seen as safe, or offering a good chance, more frequently choose a local resident as their candidate than do those where electoral prospects are rated as unlikely. And the former win more. This is not so true in hopeless situations. Those constituency associations choose a local as frequently as do the best seats, although few of those candidates are likely to get to the Commons except in unusual circumstances – such as 1984.

This brief look at the candidates indicates that the structures and processes adopted by Canadian parties make a difference to the characteristics of the candidates nominated and so, ultimately, to the composition of Parliament. Different processes will bias the outcomes of nomination politics, not only by altering the relative importance of particular strategic resources (such as money), but also by altering the value placed upon potential candidates' personal qualities. Of the latter, the current bias of constituency-based party associations for a local candidate seems especially salient. It reflects the parochial cast of much grassroots party organization in Canada and obstructs the national parties' efforts to alter the cast of their parliamentary caucuses. Any attempt to reform the nomination process must start there. Changes to it can best be assessed in terms of how, if at all, they shift the internal party balance of power between national and local interests.

APPENDIX

Constituency _____

1988 Constituency Survey

Lynda Erickson, Simon Fraser University
Kenneth Carty, University of British Columbia

Thank you very much for taking a few minutes to fill out this question-naire. We would appreciate it if you could put it in the mail today. Naturally we shall be glad to share the results of this survey with you. If you would like a copy of our findings please include a card with your name and address or drop us a line:

> *1988 Constituency Survey*
> *Department of Political Science*
> *University of British Columbia*
> *Vancouver, B.C.*
> *CANADA V6T 1W5*

Nomination Format

This first set of questions concerns the formal process used by the constituency to choose its candidate. [Please check the appropriate box.]

1. When did your constituency association hold its nomination meeting?
   - ❏ did not hold one
   - ❏ 1984–86
   - ❏ 1987
   - ❏ Jan. 1–June 30, 1988
   - ❏ July 1–Oct. 1, 1988
   - ❏ after election called (Oct. 1, 1988)

2. Who determined when the local association would select its candidate for the election?

   _____

3. If the original nomination meeting was held before redistribution was finalized did you hold another meeting to nominate for the new boundaries?
   ❏ Yes   ❏ No
   If yes, was the outcome the same?
   ❏ Yes   ❏ No

4. If there was no constituency association meeting how was the party nominee decided?

   _____

   Who took the decision as to who would be the candidate?

   _____

5. If there was a constituency association meeting what form did it take?
   - ❏ a single meeting
   - ❏ a series of meetings in different riding centres
   - ❏ other (*please specify*) _____

   Was the nomination meeting:
   - ❏ open to all party members
   - ❏ composed of delegates from small parts of the constituency
   - ❏ other (*please specify*) _____

6. What was the size of the constituency association's membership in mid-1986?

   _____

7. What was the size of the constituency association at the time of the nomination?

   _____

8. How many constituency association members voted in the selection of the candidate?

   _____

9. How long before the nomination meeting did an individual have to be a party member in order to be entitled to vote?

   _____

10. Are non-constituency residents entitled to be local association members?
    - ❏ Yes   ❏ No

    If yes, what proportion of your constituency association members are non-resident?

Nomination Contests

This section includes a number of questions concerning the competitive aspect of the nomination process in your constituency.

1. Was an incumbent MP running for renomination?
   - ❏ Yes   ❏ No

   If yes, was the MP renominated?
   - ❏ Yes   ❏ No

2. Was a former MP (not an incumbent) seeking the nomination?
   - ❏ Yes   ❏ No

   If yes, was that individual chosen the candidate?
   - ❏ Yes   ❏ No

   Which election had he/she previously won? _____

   Had one of the candidates run unsuccessfully in previous elections?
   - ❏ Yes   ❏ No

   If yes, was that individual chosen the candidate?
   - ❏ Yes   ❏ No

3. How many individuals sought the nomination at the meeting?

  ❑ one, it was an acclamation
  ❑ two
  ❑ three
  ❑ four
  ❑ more, please indicate how many_____
  ❑ none – no meeting was held

4. How many of the candidates seeking the nomination were women?

  _____

5. Taking all aspects of the nomination process in your constituency into account, how would you compare it with your party's 1984 nomination? Was 1988:
  ❑ more competitive
  ❑ less competitive
  ❑ about the same

6. Was the decision of the local nomination meeting appealed to a higher party body?
  ❑ Yes   ❑ No
  If yes, to whom?_____

  _____

  What was the outcome?

  _____

7. How many ballots did it take to choose the party candidate?
  ❑ acclamation
  ❑ one
  ❑ two
  ❑ three
  ❑ four
  ❑ more (*please specify*) _____

8. Did the candidates actively recruit supporters to join the party and come to the nomination meeting to support them?
  ❑ Yes   ❑ No

9. Was the process of recruiting support a source of internal controversy in the local association?
  ❑ Yes   ❑ No

10. If support was canvassed before the meeting was it on the basis of: (please tick as many as relevant in your constituency)
  ❑ voluntary association membership
  ❑ unions or professional associations
  ❑ ethnic group affiliations
  ❑ women's interests

❏ single issues of local importance
   (*please specify*) _____
   ❏ church-based groups
   ❏ other (*please indicate*) _____

11. How much, would you estimate, did the winning candidate spend on his/her nomination campaign?

   _____

12. Does your local party association have guidelines for nomination expenses?
    ❏ Yes   ❏ No

13. Was there any specific issue, concern or local matter(s) that was at the heart of the nomination contest in your local association for this election?
    ❏ Yes   ❏ No
    If yes, what was it?

    _____

Candidate Search Process

Some questions on the process by which potential candidates were identified by the party.

1. Did the local constituency association have a candidate search committee?
   ❏ Yes   ❏ No

2. Was the local constituency party helped in finding a candidate by party officials from outside the riding?
   ❏ Yes   ❏ No
   If yes, which party level did they represent?
   ❏ national
   ❏ regional (provincial)
   ❏ both the above
   ❏ other (*please specify*) _____

3. If party officials from outside the constituency were involved in the candidate selection process did that become a matter of local party controversy?
   ❏ Yes   ❏ No

4. Did the local association discourage some potential or would-be candidates from seeking the nomination this time?
   ❏ Yes   ❏ No

5. Did the local association have to "talk its candidate into running"?
   ❏ Yes   ❏ No

6. Was there any outside encouragement for the local party to choose a woman candidate?
   ❏ Yes   ❏ No

If yes, did it come from:
- ❏ national party
- ❏ provincial party figures
- ❏ local women's groups
- ❏ other (*please specify*) _____

7. When the party was nominating the candidate how did the local association assess the chances of victory in the constituency? Was the riding considered by your party to be:
- ❏ safe
- ❏ good chance
- ❏ unlikely
- ❏ hopeless

The Candidate

A few questions about the candidate chosen to represent your party in the constituency.

1. What is the candidate's age? _____

2. How would you describe the candidate's occupation?

_____

3. Is the candidate ❏ male ❏ female

4. Has the candidate held elected public office before? (please check as many as relevant)
- ❏ House of Commons
- ❏ Provincial Legislature
- ❏ local government (council or board)
- ❏ other (*please specify*) _____
- ❏ none

5. What is the candidate's mother tongue?
- ❏ English
- ❏ French
- ❏ other (*please specify*) _____

6. What is the candidate's religion?

- ❏ Roman Catholic
- ❏ Protestant (*denomination*) _____
- ❏ Jewish
- ❏ Non-Christian (*please specify*) _____
- ❏ none

7. Has the candidate been a resident of the constituency over the past four years?
- ❏ Yes ❏ No

8. When did the candidate first become a member of the party?
   - ☐ in 1988
   - ☐ 1984–87
   - ☐ 1980–84
   - ☐ 1970s
   - ☐ 1960s
   - ☐ _____ (*please specify*)

The Official Agent

Finally, some questions on the position and role of the candidate's official agent.

1. Was your appointment as the official agent a decision made by:
   - ☐ the constituency party executive
   - ☐ the candidate
   - ☐ a party official from outside the constituency
   - ☐ other (*please specify*) _____

2. Have you been an official candidate's agent in a previous federal general election?
   - ☐ Yes   ☐ No
   If yes, which one(s)? _____

3. Is the party reimbursing you for your services?

   ☐ Yes   ☐ No

4. Have you been to any training programme for agents?
   - ☐ Yes   ☐ No
   If yes, who organized it?
   - ☐ my party
   - ☐ the Chief Electoral Officer
   - ☐ other (*please specify*) _____

5. What is your regular occupation?

   _____

6. As agent were you a full, active member of the constituency campaign planning committee?

   ☐ Yes   ☐ No

ABBREVIATIONS

c.   chapter

B.C.S.C. British Columbia Supreme Court

R.S.C.   Revised Statutes of Canada

REFERENCES

Brodie, J. 1985. *Women and Politics in Canada*. Toronto: McGraw-Hill Ryerson.

Brodie, J., and J. Vickers. 1981. "The More Things Change ... Women in the 1979 Federal Campaign." In *Canada at the Polls, 1979 and 1980,* ed. H. Penniman. Washington, DC: American Enterprise Institute for Public Policy Research.

Canada. *Canada Elections Act*, R.S.C. 1985, c. E-2.

Canada. Royal Commission on the Status of Women. 1970. *Report*. Ottawa: Information Canada.

Canadian Advisory Council on the Status of Women. 1987. *Women and Politics: Becoming Full Partners in the Political Process*. Ottawa: CACSW.

Carty, R.K. 1988. "Three Canadian Party Systems: An Interpretation of the Development of National Politics." In *Party Democracy in Canada,* ed. G. Perlin. Scarborough: Prentice-Hall.

Courtney, J.C. 1978. "Recognition of Canadian Political Parties in Parliament and in Law." *Canadian Journal of Political Science* 11:33–60.

———. 1988. "Reinventing the Brokerage Wheel: The Tory Success in 1984." In *Canada at the Polls, 1984,* ed. H. Penniman. Durham: Duke University Press.

Erickson, L. 1991. "Women and Candidacies for the House of Commons." In *Women in Canadian Politics: Toward Equity in Representation,* ed. K. Megyery. Vol. 6 of the research studies of the Royal Commission on Electoral Reform and Party Financing. Ottawa and Toronto: RCERPF/Dundurn.

Fraser, G. 1989. *Playing for Keeps*. Toronto: McClelland and Stewart.

Gallagher, M., and M. Marsh. 1988. *Candidate Selection in Comparative Perspective*. London: Sage Publications.

Gray v. Parton, B.C.S.C., Vancouver Registry No. A902 881, 25 October 1990.

Guarnieri, Albina. 1990. Submission to the Royal Commission on Electoral Reform and Party Financing.

Meisel, J. 1962. *The Canadian General Election of 1957*. Toronto: University of Toronto Press.

Morton, W.L. 1967. *The Progressive Movement in Canada*. Toronto: University of Toronto Press.

Paltiel, K.Z. 1970. *Political Party Financing in Canada*. Toronto: McGraw-Hill.

Scarrow, H. 1964. "Nomination and Local Party Organization in Canada: A Case Study." *Western Political Quarterly* 17 (1): 55–62.

Siegfried, A. 1966 [1906]. *The Race Question in Canada*. Toronto: McClelland and Stewart.

Stasiulis, D., and Y. Abu-Laban. 1990. "Ethnic Activism and the Politics of Limited Inclusion in Canada." In *Canadian Politics: An Introduction to the Discipline*, ed. A.G. Gagnon and J. Bickerton. Peterborough: Broadview Press.

Stewart, G.T. 1980. "Political Patronage Under Macdonald and Laurier, 1878–1911." *American Review of Canadian Studies* 10 (1): 3–26.

Whitaker, R. 1977. *The Government Party*. Toronto: University of Toronto Press.

Williams, R. 1981. "Candidate Selection." In *Canada at the Polls, 1979 and 1980*, ed. H. Penniman. Washington, DC: American Enterprise Institute for Public Policy Research.

Young, W.D. 1969. *The Anatomy of a Party: The National CCF, 1932–1961*. Toronto: University of Toronto Press.

4

PARTIES AND PARTY GOVERNMENT IN ADVANCED DEMOCRACIES

William M. Chandler
Alan Siaroff

THE SCOPE OF this project confronted us with the challenge of pursuing its very broad comparative implications while at the same time delving into the substance and specifics of party organizations. To ensure some balance between two such potentially divergent objectives, we opted first to establish a broad comparative foundation. The introductory section of this study is therefore dedicated to the task of constructing a comprehensive framework to be filled in by more specific and targeted considerations.

From the outset, it was essential to address explicitly the problem of institutional settings, because all social organizations including political parties are both products of and influences on the environments in which they exist. Having established this background in the first section on the role of political parties, our analysis then turns to the more specific considerations of the character of individual parties, with a view to identifying patterns of internal organization. In the third section we address comparatively questions of party finance, the implications of which are now generally accepted to be of vital importance for understanding the workings of modern party organizations.

Finally, we give particular attention to German parties. Postwar German experience has been widely judged to be not only an economic success story but also a well-operating democratic system. The German case represents a version of party government that falls between the highly competitive (e.g., Commonwealth) and the hegemonic party (e.g., Japanese) extremes. Given the objective of assessing the capacity of parties to perform basic functions within democratic regimes, German parties appear especially interesting because they constitute highly developed, complex organizations having considerable resources, expertise and permanence. They therefore serve as valuable examples of modern party organizations.

Taken together, our survey of the role of parties in parliamentary regimes allows us to integrate our discussion in the study's final section around the question of the implications for Canada. We have chosen to reserve this discussion for the end because we remain convinced that the comparative assessment and analysis of party life is best presented when it is not confounded with various, sometimes controversial, policy implications.

THE ROLE AND NATURE OF POLITICAL PARTIES

Political parties normally lack formal constitutional status, yet they are central to the workings of democracy. Parties play such an essential role that we commonly use the term "party government" as a shorthand description of the governmental process. They are the primary, and in some systems the only, mechanism for the recruitment of elected officials and government leadership.

In democratic systems, parties operate as the crucial intermediaries linking rulers and the ruled. The most basic party function is that of representation, involving the translation of public opinion to political leaders. This occurs through the articulation of programmatic alternatives and the aggregation of diverse interests. In the electoral arena, parties have as their primary goal the maximization of votes in order to take or hold power. Once this goal is achieved, the winning party or coalition then acts on policy and value choices previously presented to the public through the parliamentary process.

When one looks beyond this vision of pure party government, however, to examine the reality of party practice, it becomes less clear how well parties actually perform these functions essential to the democratic state. In Canada, as in many other working democracies, political parties are often viewed by the public with a degree of cynicism and distrust which implies doubts about their ability to perform democratic tasks effectively. If the capacity of parties to fulfil their representational roles is in doubt, this may be due in part to their own internal characteristics; that is, to those organizational dynamics that constitute the basic elements of internal party management.

Of course, parties of whatever nature never operate in a void but rather within existing laws and customs – ideally of a democratic character. Indeed, the nature, functions and goals of a political party are determined to a considerable extent by the institutional context in which it operates. These contextual factors will be detailed in this section.

As a starting point, we may ask what it is that political parties do. Parties are generally seen to play roles involving the organization of society and/or the "transmission" of public concerns. As Sartori stresses, "Parties are *the* central intermediate and intermediary structures between society and government" (1976, ix, emphasis in original; cf. Katz 1986, 31). By extension, parties are assumed in some way to "govern," or at least are thought to be central to the governmental/democratic process. Such assertions should probably be taken as working hypotheses rather than as verified propositions, because there is doubt about how effectively some parties are able to play this intermediary role.

Sartori's general definition of the role of parties implies a range of potential functions that parties may perform. These have been usefully summarized by Anthony King (1969) as follows:

- structuring the vote;
- the integration and mobilization of mass publics;
- the recruitment of political leaders;
- the organizing of government;
- the formation of public policy; and
- the aggregation of interests.

King goes on to argue that "to the extent that these functions are performed in liberal democracies, parties themselves have only a limited part in this." Parties thus "do" less than imagined. One should note, however, that King's analysis is largely based on the United States, the United Kingdom and France; that is, nations with relatively weak party systems, two of which operate within presidential systems. He does not dwell on nations such as Germany, Austria and Italy, where stronger parties prevail. It is more likely that such parties can and largely do perform the aforementioned functions (Ware 1987, 112).

The six functions proposed by King require examination in greater detail. By definition, all democratic parties compete in free elections, and thus vote structuring occurs everywhere. King does not, however, distinguish parties primarily concerned with maintaining their electoral base from those seeking to maximize it. This is an important distinction involving goals and governing styles.

The integration of mass publics refers to a socialization function in which both individuals and social groups come to support the entire democratic system through loyalty to their own party. Kirchheimer (1966) refers to the "antebellum (before the First World War) mass parties of integration," which were typically rooted in a particular social milieu (e.g., class, confessional or linguistic subculture). Yet one should also note that parties after the Second World War in Germany, Austria and Italy played a significant integrative role.

King's third and fourth functions – leadership recruitment and the organization of government – are interrelated, for they refer respectively to the "reach" and "grasp" of parties, that is, to the breadth and depth of their control over the polity (King 1969, 131–32). These points are essential to explaining whether political parties possess the capacity to govern, in the sense of "authoritatively allocating values" and setting policy on specific issues. In turn, this relates to King's fifth function, the ability to formulate policy (autonomously).

His sixth and final function is the often-stated "interest aggregation," a term with two meanings. The loose definition is that parties merely "take account" of a wide range of interests (King 1969, 138). This implies a general, perhaps strictly electoral, concern for various interests which remain, however, autonomous from the parties – that is, in clearly separate interest organizations or social movements. The second sense of interest aggregation implies a tight accommodation of selected, related interests through and within party structures. In this sense, parties and certain key groups are bound together as stable partners with considerable organizational and membership overlap. These various functions can be summarized around three general goals of political parties, as noted in figure 4.2: first, the goal of subculture defence, that is, the desire to integrate and speak for certain related interests; second, the goal of controlling state power, that is, to (be able to) implement coherent and effective policies consistent with a party's basic values or ideology; and third, the goal of vote maximization, that is, the desire to be as electorally successful as possible – even if this means compromising certain values. Of course, the sacrifice of basic value positions may imply that electoral success becomes an end in itself. All three goals can at times overlap and thus reinforce party activity, but they (especially all three together) are more likely to produce conflict within parties. Furthermore, the argument will be made here that certain types of parties correspond to specific and identifiable goal-patterns.

In anticipation of the relevance of this analysis to Canada, the hypothesis may now be advanced that if parties are truly aggregative, they will also perform a national unity function.

Party Influence and the "Party-State"

It follows that the power of political parties may be greater in one nation than in another. Indeed, it is reasonable to hypothesize that party influence is enhanced by:

1. Parliamentary rather than presidential systems. In the former, the government is dependent on continuous parliamentary support (best achieved through a disciplined party). In the latter, an elected president has a separate power base and can normally appoint cabinet ministers with limited concern for legislative majorities or the minister's party affiliation (if any). In the mixed case of the French Fifth Republic, in which governments are responsible to both president and parliament, incompatible majorities may constrain presidential authority and test the viability of party government.

2. Unitary/centralized systems rather than federal/decentralized ones. Under federalism, there is a tendency for division between national parties and provincial/state parties. Of course, there are variations across federal regimes. Within Canadian and especially Australian party organizations, the provincial/state level has historically had great influence. In Austria the effect of regionalism depends on the specific party. This is also true in unitary Britain, where the Liberal Democrats have separate Celtic wings. In Germany – leaving aside the exceptional organizational autonomy of the Bavarian Christlich-Soziale Union (CSU) from the Christlich-Demokratische Union (CDU) – the parties seem strikingly nationalized and integrative despite the federal order.

3. Systems in which voters may choose only a single representative from those presented by competing parties, with each individual candidate being selected by the party itself. Where voters have a choice of multiple candidates from one party (as in Japan's multi-member districts) or where voters determine party candidates (as in American primaries), candidates are forced to develop their own bases of support independent of party (such as the *koenkai* for Japanese Liberal Democratic Party (LDP) deputies). Such systems ultimately weaken party government. In general, the direct public funding of political parties rather than individual candidates enhances party government, without of course being a sufficient condition.

4. Systems in which political parties are the primary channel for public participation, demand articulation, and decision-making. Where other forces in society fill these roles, party government will be displaced or in extreme cases rendered nonexistent (Katz 1986, 55–59).

Such factors allow us to distinguish between systems which tend to either minimize or maximize the opportunities for party influence and control. Where institutional constraints systematically favour maximal governing roles for parties, we can expect to see the flourishing of strong party organizations. These parties in turn reinforce a pattern of authority which we may designate as strong party government or even the party-state. Indeed, in some nations parties are so powerful that they shape much of society outside of the traditional political domain (what Sjöblum calls a high "partyness of society"; that is, a high degree of party penetration of society). Correspondingly, where parties and party government are highly legitimate in society, one finds a high "public opinion of parties" (Sjöblum 1987, 157). A high "partyness of society" overlaps with the notion of a "party-state," in which two traits are especially striking: first, parties have a broad symbolic role as defenders of the democratic system, and are thus perceived as a "good" in themselves; and second, parties have extensive penetration of the polity, possibly into society as a whole, but most clearly into the bureaucracy and para-state organizations (Dyson 1982).

This "party-state" pattern has typically developed in nations where democracy was established or restored following an era of authoritarian rule. In these cases, other sociopolitical forces were tainted by association with the discredited authoritarian regime. Examples of this include Italy, Austria and Germany. In the Federal Republic of Germany, the constitutional role of parties is made explicit in the Basic Law. Article 21 provides that "the political parties shall participate in the shaping of the political will of the people. They must be freely established. Their internal organization must conform to democratic principles" (*The Law on Political Parties* 1987).

The pattern of democratic development has been rather different in Japan because there the bureaucracy played the key role in the early postwar years, with strong parties developing only much later. Generally, a party-state is more likely to emerge in nations with an historic tradition of a strong state, long periods of single-party dominance and the relatively early replacement of local élites by national party organizations in the organizing of elections (Ware 1987, 195–97).

Lastly, the assumption is that the government "does something" or indeed many things within a given society. However, where the scope of government remains very narrow in terms of the "authoritative allocation of values" – as in Switzerland or the United States – then even a strong party can induce only limited party government. Conversely, where the tasks of the public sector are defined broadly, the state has a stronger interventionist role and party government increases, other things being equal (Katz 1986, 45–46).

Power is a finite quantity. Therefore to the extent that parties and party politicians control decision-making, other actors will be correspondingly less powerful. Conversely, where nonparty actors are more influential, then party power will be constrained. One can think of four main alternatives to political parties in the policy-making process:

1. *Bureaucracy* plays a key role in the formulation and implementation of policy. It reinforces traditional modes of policy-making and stable policy patterns. Political parties, however, may espouse sharp shifts in policy direction – a situation fraught with potential conflict. In all nations there is the general issue of the relative control that cabinet ministers can exert over their own administrative apparatus. Conversely, this may be seen as a question of the dependence of politicians on the expertise built into the career civil service. This may even generate the phenomenon of a ministry/department "capturing" its minister and converting him/her into a de facto spokesperson. Yet in systems where the bureaucracy is often the source of new policy, and/or where it has interest groups for clients, then political parties may be effectively by-passed. Seen historically, it is very important whether political parties developed prior to, simultaneously with, or after the formation of, a professional bureaucracy (Daalder 1966, 60).

2. Where *interest groups* have a privileged role in policy formation through various neo-corporatist arrangements, in countries such as Sweden and Austria, the ability of both governments and parties to act on their own desires is constrained. Corporatist modes of policy-making create legitimate and semi-autonomous "chambers" or "boards" of conflict resolution. This phenomenon has the effect of segmenting important components of public policy (e.g., incomes policy, or *Tarifautonomie* in Germany). Such a system limits governmental control. It has the corresponding advantage of removing many contentious issues from partisan parliamentary debate but in the process also reduces the scope of party government. Moreover, in Austria, Switzerland and Germany it is common for interest representatives to sit in parliament. In Austria, for example, the head of the trade union confederation has also been the speaker. As Pelinka stresses, "You do not have influence in Austria because you are an MP; but you are an MP because you are influential" (1985, 191).

3. The *media* may weaken, or at least reshape, parties and party government in two ways. First, by regular criticism of

government, they deprive opposition parties of their monopoly of the oversight/watchdog role. Second, television in particular tends to personalize politics around party leaders, giving them authority independent of their own parties (Katz 1986, 60–62). That is, national leaders often choose to speak directly to "the people," rather than to the legislature or to their own party caucuses.

4. *Direct democracy.* Some nation-states, such as Switzerland, France and Italy, have had frequent recourse to referenda, as have certain U.S. states such as California. (It is notable that there exists no federal or national power of referendum in the United States despite its frequent use at the state and local levels.) Indeed, in Switzerland any and all laws can be made subject to popular approval. In Italy, the referendum power is restricted to the repeal of existing laws and cannot be used for original legislation. Nevertheless, as the Italian Christian Democrats learned in the 1974 watershed vote on divorce, the referendum can prove risky for parties. Under such circumstances of direct democracy, political parties obviously cannot "take" decisions, even if they propose and/or take sides in these referenda (Spotts and Wieser 1986, 119; Pasquino 1987, 225–26).

French President Charles de Gaulle often made use of the referendum (under Article 11 of the Constitution) and of direct television appeals in order to bypass both parliament and the political parties. Under his successors the referendum instrument has largely fallen into disuse. But television remains an essential feature of French presidential politics. In general, referenda work against strong parties and strong party government.

Types of Democratic Systems

Our general framework is intended to identify those factors facilitating or limiting the relative strength and influence of parties. It has been noted that the specific functions and goals of any party are heavily shaped by its institutional context. Now this will be elaborated in terms of varying "types" of democracies. First of all, one can distinguish between direct or plebiscitary democracy (such as that of Switzerland) and representative democracy. Switzerland combines an intriguing mixture of consensual decision making, direct democracy and a highly decentralized federalism (Lehner 1989, 93–98). Moreover, the political parties themselves are both weak and heavily penetrated by interest groups (Katzenstein 1984, 127; Borner et al. 1990, 74).

Next, within representative systems, one can distinguish between those in which power is formally separated (presidential systems) and those in which it is concentrated in a parliamentary system (Lehner 1989, 55). It is no accident that plebiscitary modes are commonly associated with presidential or other nonparliamentary constitutional models. Parliamentary systems, in contrast, favour institutionalized representation.

Our focus here is on one of the key institutions relating to party government: the executive–legislative relationship (Pasquino 1986). For our purposes, it is useful to limit this discussion to parliamentary democracies, because these constitute, by definition, the regimes that facilitate party government. This should not imply that parties are unimportant or have no role in other systems. Obviously they remain crucial to understanding politics in the United States, Switzerland or various Latin American democracies, but these nations do not have the institutional basis for direct party governance that (potentially) applies under parliamentary systems (Lavaux 1990, 179). As the definitive "semi-presidential" system (Duverger 1980), France may be noted as a hybrid case in this context. Finland, in contrast, despite a powerful presidency, still seems essentially a parliamentary system (Pasquino 1986, 132).

In summary, there is a range of party government in democratic nations, from virtual nonexistence to the classic party-state, as listed in table 4.1. It is also interesting to note the overall correlation with voter turnout; that is to say, the more parties matter in government, the higher is public participation. Japan is exceptional because the results of its elections basically are a foregone conclusion and normally lack suspense. Moreover, Japan also has a district-based, and thus biased, electoral system. Nations with such systems have been shown to have lower turnouts than states using proportional representation (Blais and Carty 1990).

To identify the basic institutional dynamics of party government, a distinction must be made among three general types of parliamentary democracies: Westminster/Commonwealth, one-party dominance, as exemplified in Japan, and continental European. These three systems are outlined in table 4.2.

In the Westminster model of Commonwealth nations, parties are assumed to be purely competitive both electorally and in parliament (Dahl 1966, 336–39), with an "adversarial" pattern of government formation (Strom 1990, 90–91). Indeed, competition is the underlying sociopolitical value of Anglo-American nations. Elections thus determine governments by producing unambiguous, usually single-party, parliamentary majorities – even if intentionally "manufactured" by the

Table 4.1
Extent of party control and levels of participation
(percentage)

	Average turnout, 1970–89*
Nonparty rule	mean of 60
Switzerland	50
United States	55 (Presidential)
France	74
Basic party rule, normally by a single party in power	mean of 78
Japan	70
Spain	72
Ireland	73
Canada	73
United Kingdom	75
Portugal	79
Greece	81
New Zealand	87
Australia	92*
Party government, often including some form of a party-state	mean of 86
Finland	76
Norway	82
Luxembourg	83
Netherlands	84
Belgium	86*
Denmark	86
Italy	87*
West Germany	88
Iceland	88
Sweden	90
Austria	91

Source: Mackie and Rose (1982), updated by authors.

*Some form of compulsory voting in effect (Laundy 1989, 14).

electoral system (Lijphart 1984, 166–68). The pattern of political discourse is determined by the government–opposition relationship (including the institutionalization of the "leader of the opposition"), in which it is expected that one party will replace the other periodically as the result of elections. The Westminster version of party government does not require a perfect two-party system, but its plurality, single-member district system of voting normally concentrates competition between two broadly based parties, each capable of achieving a parliamentary majority. Such a pattern of competition between two – but only two – main parties thus characterizes the party systems of Commonwealth nations such as Great Britain, New Zealand, Malta and Jamaica.

Table 4.2
Patterns of party government: political regimes and cultures

Regime type	Socio-cultural context
Westminster	Commonwealth
one-party cabinet government; majoritarian electoral system; two major parties which alternate in power; elections central to government determination; powerful prime minister; weak legislature; clear and formal opposition with little effective input in policy process.	underlying values of competition and adversarial roles; clear distinction between the state and an autonomous society; conflictual labour relations; neutral civil service with a "hands-off" philosophy; pluralist policy-making, with a short-term outlook.
Hegemonic	Japanese
multi-party system, but with a "permanently" governing hegemonic party; elections do not produce a clear change, inasmuch as the same party (almost) always wins; opposition essentially has only negative power; strong probability of ruling party being factionalized with a very weak prime minister and influential, semi-autonomous deputies.	underlying values of conformity and concordance; dominance of ruling "system" or triad of a hegemonic party, civil service and business interests; civil service itself traditionally a powerful central actor; interchange of key élite personnel; society heavily penetrated by ruling "system" with resulting minimal autonomy; paternalistic labour relations.
Coalitional	Continental European
consensual party behaviour; multi-party system with proportional representation electoral system; elections alone are not determinant; post-election bargaining crucial to power-sharing among parties; one "hinge" party often plays a central role with quasi-permanence in government; legislatures usually strong, with influential committees.	underlying values of legalism and cooperation; interpenetration of a semi-sovereign state and a highly organized society; para-public bodies; politicized civil service; corporatist policy-making with a long-term outlook; a general intertwining of parliamentary politics with the bureaucracy, powerful interest associations, and the "party-state."

The relative endurance of three-party competition in Canada thus constitutes a significant deviation from this general pattern. In contrast, Australia is not really a three-party system in the Canadian sense since its preferential voting system facilitates two conservative parties which, however, are permanently allied against the Australian Labor Party.

This competitive Westminster model of party government first emerged within the British parliamentary system (hence the name) and was later exported throughout the British Empire (Powell 1982, 67–68). It has survived intact in Canada, despite the complexities of federalism and the frequency of third parties. Its essential element, one-party government, recently has been replicated in certain new democracies such as Greece and Spain.

In the Westminster model, while the government may be responsible to the assembly, system dynamics and party discipline ensure that individual deputies are constrained in their behaviour and have little policy influence. Parliament itself is primarily a "law-passing" rather than a "lawmaking" body, since the cabinet sets public policy (White 1990). The focus increasingly is on the personalities of the prime minister and the leader of the opposition (the latter a uniquely Westminster feature) rather than on party policies per se. The prime minister is a dominant figure, and indeed the power of the executive is extensive and essentially "unbridled," according to a New Zealand analyst and senior politician (Palmer 1987, 12). Federalism makes the situation less extreme in Canada and Australia, as compared with Great Britain and New Zealand. In all such Commonwealth nations, the opposition has little real power but is free to criticize. Above all, the opposition should provide an alternative "government in waiting."

Thus the expectation of government turnover is implicit in the Westminster model. Turnover is arguably facilitated by a first-past-the-post system of voting, which tends to multiply a small increase in the overall popular vote into a much larger gain in seats. Of course, one should not presume any even balance in governing between the two main parties. Indeed, there can be long periods between "swings of the pendulum" (Smith 1989b, 87), so that cumulatively one party will have governed much longer than its principal opponent. This is certainly true for the Liberals in Canada, the Conservatives in Great Britain, the Labour Party in Norway, Fianna Fail in the Irish Republic and the Liberal–Country (National) alliance in Australia. Even so, in each of these cases other parties have had several turns in power.

This is not so, however, in *one-party dominant* regimes (Pempel 1990c), of which Japan, and to a lesser extent Sweden and Italy, are the best examples. In Japan, the Liberal Democrats (LDP) have won every lower house election since their founding in 1955, with unbroken conservative rule dating from 1948. Normally the LDP wins a clear majority of the seats; when this has not been the case, independent conservatives can usually make up the difference. In Sweden, the Social Democrats (SAP) have been in power more or less continuously since 1932, the only long-term hiatus occurring from 1976 to 1982 when an unstable centre-right coalition took control. However, after the September 1991 elections, in which the Social Democratic vote dropped to its lowest level since 1928, four centre-right parties formed a governing coalition.

In both Japan and Sweden the dominant parties have used long periods in government to structure both society and political discourse in ways favourable to them, thus reinforcing their dominance. Pempel calls this a "virtuous cycle of dominance" (1990b, 16ff.). Of course, in both cases there has often been policy compromise with other parties. In Sweden the SAP has only rarely enjoyed an absolute majority. Yet importantly this has not normally led to coalition government, although the Social Democrats did govern in coalition with the Agrarians from 1936 to 1939 and again from 1951 to 1957. There was also a broad "grand coalition" government in (neutral) Sweden during the Second World War (Hadenius 1990). After the 1983 elections in Japan, the weakened Liberal Democrats conceded one cabinet post to a member of the New Liberal Club (itself an LDP-split-off), in return for a parliamentary alliance (Kishimoto 1988, 104). Aside from such exceptions, the Japanese LDP and the Swedish SAP have monopolized governing positions, and thus typify *one-party dominant* power.

Furthermore, in Japan there exist distinctive cultural values of deference and conformity rooted in history and Confucian beliefs which seem to provide great tolerance for "soft authoritarianism" and the anti-democratic reality of always retaining the same party in power. Such cultural traits are not shared by Western nations (including Sweden and Italy), but they *are* found in other East Asian "capitalist development states" such as South Korea, Taiwan and Singapore (Johnson 1987; Pye 1988). Singapore has had both competitive (if not fully fair) elections and one-party hegemony since its formation, but South Korea and Taiwan are only now becoming democratic regimes.

The influence of opposition parties in Japan (of which there are many) is basically limited to extracting modest policy concessions from the LDP, which does manage the Diet in line with the Japanese values of cooperation and conciliation. A united opposition can also exercise a veto over constitutional changes (which require a two-thirds majority). Generally, however, opposition parties have had minimal positive impact on policy-making. Of course, this is also true for opposition parties in Westminster systems, but these parties know they can "wait their turn" to implement their own agenda. Such an opportunity remains hypothetical in Japan, and indeed most of the opposition parties (the Communists excepted) have become essentially clientelistic and less concerned with offering "hard" alternative policies (Sato and Matsuzaki 1984, 32; Stockwin 1989, 104–106).

In Sweden, the opposition parties have acquired greater influence, and occasional control of the government, as the Social Democrats have become weaker in the past two decades. Indeed, to some extent Sweden appears to be shifting away from the pure one-party dominant model and becoming more like its continental European neighbours. Sweden thus is now a somewhat mixed case between the one-party dominant and the continental models.

Italy is also a mixed case, but one treated here as essentially continental – while recognizing that it has much in common with Japan. In particular, neither democracy has produced an alternation in power of the main parties. That is, in Italy the Christian Democrats (DC) have always been in government, whereas the Communists never have been. The DC, however, has rarely exercised power alone; it has usually had to govern with coalition partners. Indeed, the DC has shown a remarkable ability to adjust to permit new coalition possibilities. It is this coalitional aspect of Italian politics that, in our opinion, justifies its treatment primarily as a continental European case.

In summary then, the Swedish Social Democrats have almost always governed alone (but usually in a minority situation). The Italian Christian Democrats have always been in power, but have had to share power with other parties. Only the Japanese Liberal Democrats have since their formation remained continually and essentially always alone in power.

Within the *continental European* model, the assumptions and dynamics can be quite different, and there are a number of institutional variants. Typically, the continental party system is based on a pattern of multiple socio-economic cleavages, some of which are usually defined along ethnic, confessional or regional lines (see Lijphart 1984, chap. 8). As a consequence, a wide range of parties, multiple-party powersharing and sociopolitical cooperation is the norm. Elections rarely determine governments, which are instead the products of post-election bargaining. In many smaller nations, government formation will often involve specific individuals designated by the head of state to aid the process – an *informateur* or *formateur* who assesses and/or attempts various coalitional possibilities – a process that can take months to complete (Vis 1983; Maas 1986).

In many continental cases, Italy or the Netherlands for example, elections typically produce marginal shifts of coalitions but provide no clear choice between alternative government options, that is, between the "ins" and the "outs." (Indeed, certain parties always seem to remain "in.") Even where the partisan composition of government remains basically the same, the prime minister and/or cabinet may change – again, primarily as a result of élite bargaining. Usually, therefore, in such continental cases of low "electoral decisiveness" voters cannot meaningfully choose between pre-designated leaders for the top offices (Strom 1990, 72–75; see also Maas 1986; Steiner 1991, 122–26). In any case, the public focus emphasizes parties rather than leaders. The prime minister need not always be the formal or most powerful leader (chairperson) of the party.

Within this broad continental classification, there are perhaps five subtypes which reflect varying expectations about coalition formation. The first two of these are essentially historical phenomena, but still typically European. First of all, there is *consociational* democracy, that is, the balanced representation of subculture élites in government. Belgium and Switzerland remain the clearest examples (Lijphart 1984, chap. 2), but historically the concept also applies to the Netherlands and Austria. In the Swiss case, one still finds an essentially permanent governing coalition of the major parties, unchanged since 1959. Belgian cabinets must strike a linguistic balance as well as reflect coalitional shifts. The consociational feature of broad coalitions is also found in Finland, Israel and occasionally in Austria.

Standing in historical contrast to consociational democracy, where cleavages were overcome by cooperative behaviour among subcultural élites, we find *centrifugal* (Lijphart 1984) or *polarized* (Sartori 1976) democracies. Here hostility and suspicion shape élite behaviour, in large part due to the presence of various anti-system parties. This is noteworthy because parties, specifically the parties in parliament, tend to dominate political life (Dogan and Pelassy 1987, 164–65). Ultimately the centrifugal dynamics of such a system may contribute to the collapse of the entire regime, as in Weimar Germany, the first Austrian Republic and the French Fourth Republic. Italy has been considered by Sartori to belong to this category, although this argument is increasingly debatable and depends crucially on the assessment of the Communist Party (PCI) (van Loenen 1990), which in 1990 renamed itself the Democratic Party of the Left (PDS).

In any case, Italy corresponds to a third subtype of the continental system: *quasi-one-party dominance*. Unlike Japan or Sweden, this pattern involves centripetal coalition governments containing one dominant, centrist party that never enters the opposition. Here we are speaking in particular of the Italian Christian Democrats (Amyot 1988) and the Dutch Christian Democratic Appeal (CDA), both of which have always remained in office. (The Dutch Christen Democratisch Appèl (CDA) was only founded in 1977, but one of its predecessors, the Catholic Katholieke Volkspartij (KVP), belonged to every previous postwar government.) Near permanent governance has also been achieved by the Christian Democrats in both Belgium and Luxembourg.

These quasi-dominant parties must govern in coalition in large part because they normally receive no more than 35 percent of the vote. (The Italian DC previously won much more, but in the 1980s fell to this level.) Although such a level of support is below the strength of the dominant LDP in Japan, these parties remain the largest in their respective nations and are essential and central to governing. Such quasi-dominant parties, especially the Christian Democrats, are thus able to fulfil Pempel's four conditions of dominance: "In short, the dominant party must dominate the electorate, other political parties, the formation of governments, and the public policy agenda. Parties that combine these features fit most common-sense notions of a dominant party or of politics within a dominant party system" (Pempel 1990b, 4). In this sense effective domination can also occur in coalitional, continental systems. Moreover, in such fragmented multi-party systems domination by a centrally placed party is achievable with as little as a third of the popular vote. Such is obviously not the case in Westminster systems (Pempel 1990a, 336–39).

The Italian Christian Democrats provide the most striking example of such dominance (Leonardi and Wertman 1989, chap. 8). One can note in this regard the historic phrase attributed to Fiat President Gianni Agnelli: "The DC controlled 80 percent of the positions of power with 40 percent of the votes" (ibid., 248). Although the DC is now weaker in both votes and seats, the basic pattern and ratio remain.

In contrast to these aforementioned cases, there are other continental nations where governments clearly change; that is, major parties do alternate in power. For this reason such cases are more interesting and more applicable to the Canadian situation. In the *bipolar* cases of Scandinavia (our fourth subtype), there may be many parties but essentially only two "blocs" of left and right. Usually more votes change within each bloc than across them. Governments tend to be based on narrow majorities or even minorities, with alternation between blocs (although historically the leftist bloc has been in power more often). The corporatist and inclusive aspects of policy-making do, however, lead to cooperation across the centre, unlike behaviour in adversarial Westminster systems.

Lastly and centrally, we have a key fifth subtype: *two-party majority government*, which fits within the broad continental tradition but has certain crucial traits that bring it closer to the Westminster model. This system is exemplified by the Federal Republic of Germany, but Luxembourg and Austria also approximate the concept. The normal pattern in these nations is for two – but only two – parties to form a coalition government having a majority of seats (and votes). This pattern is thus different from multi-party coalitions, minority governments or single-party majorities.

Although single-party majority government has occurred at the state level in Germany and federally in Austria, it has never occurred federally in Germany. In this way Germany differs fundamentally from the Westminster model. Yet in other ways Germany does show parallels with Westminster nations (unlike most continental cases). The two main parties together get approximately 80 percent of the vote, a figure comparable to Britain or Canada. Both major parties – CDU/CSU and SPD – present candidates for the position of Chancellor, so that voters know that they are choosing between possible future chancellors. Moreover, the coalition alternatives are usually clear before elections are held, in large part because the pivot party FDP wishes to ensure its survival. German elections thus approach the decisiveness found in two-party systems (Strom 1990, 70).

The German pattern is discussed in detail in the section devoted to German party government. At this stage, it should be noted, however, that such coalitional patterns in Germany, Austria and Luxembourg arise out of a system with few parties in parliament, indeed for much of the postwar period only three (a large Christian democratic party, a large social democratic party and a smaller liberal party). These parties form a triangular party system in which each party has certain common ground (and certain differences) with each of the other two. Consequently, each of the three possible "pairings" or governing combinations is often feasible both numerically and ideologically. Each has in fact occurred historically in Germany.

Do Parties Govern?

Both the strength of specific parties and the types of democracy noted above lead to the general notion of "party government." This concept, however, has more than one meaning and application. At a very basic level, party government may be considered to involve the following four traits of unified or parliamentary democracy (Smith 1989b, 134–35):

- that the executive is elected directly from parliament without any separate mandate;
- that the executive is responsible to the legislature;
- that the government should be in the hands of the majority party (or a coalition having such a majority); and
- that the assembly itself does not decide; it only mirrors the decisions made by the electorate on the one hand, and by the party (or coalition) in power on the other.

These factors allow us to distinguish between regimes based on party government and those having presidential or collegial systems based on a clear separation of powers. Following our previous analysis, the latter model is of less relevance in the Canadian institutional context.

At the same time, it is important to stress that not all parliamentary democracies are equivalent in the extent of party government, as noted in table 4.1. One can thus distinguish between stronger and weaker versions of party government and party influence, in part related to the "party-state" discussion above. Indeed, the comparative scholarship on "party government" describes the ability both of political parties to shape the government agenda and of voters to choose clearly between two such parties. This literature, largely Anglo-American in origin, is normative in that it sees strong or "responsible" party government as a positive force for democratic politics and the endurance of the national polity.

Responsible party government was defined by the Committee on Political Parties of the American Political Science Association (APSA) back in 1950 as involving both programmatic choice and accountability. Specifically, "that the parties are able to bring forth programmes to which they can commit themselves and, second, that the parties possess sufficient internal cohesion to carry out these programmes ... The fundamental requirement for accountability is a two-party system in which the opposing party acts as a critic of the party in power, developing, defining and presenting the policy alternatives which are necessary for a true choice in reaching public decisions" (American Political Science Association 1950, 18; cf. Pulzer 1982, 10). The APSA Report argued that the United States lacked such party government. The United Kingdom, in contrast, was seen as possessing such features. This was not, however, the view of Richard Rose, who enumerated the following conditions for party government:

1. Parties must formulate policy intentions for enactment once in office.
2. A party's intentions must be supported by statements of "not unworkable" means to desired ends.
3. At least one party must exist, and after some form of contest, the party should become the government.
4. Nominees of the party should occupy the most important positions in a regime.
5. The number of partisans nominated for office should be large enough to permit partisans to become involved in many aspects of government.
6. Partisans given office must have the skills necessary to control large bureaucratic organizations.
7. Partisans given office must give high priority to carrying out party policies.

8. Party policies must be put into practice by the administration of government (Rose 1974, 381–83).

Using this framework, William Paterson (1982) has concluded that only the third condition is clearly met in Britain, with the power and/or inertia of the administration/civil service assuming most of the "blame" for Britain's lack of party government. In contrast, Paterson argued that most of Rose's factors (all but one and seven) are found in West Germany (ibid., 112).

A similar list of party government requirements has been developed by Richard Katz as part of a major international research project into party government. In adapted form, these requirements are as follows:

1. Decisions must be made by elected party officials or those under their control.
2. Policy is decided within parties which then act cohesively to enact it.
3. Officials are recruited and held accountable through party (Katz 1987a, 7; Sjöblum 1987, 156).

These conditions again speak to APSA's initial requirements that it be political parties which formulate, present and implement public policy and, concomitantly, that all key actors in policy-making be party politicians whom the electorate can identify and replace if so desired. Yet a clear change of government does not by itself fully achieve "party government," as alternations in power between presidencies in the United States attest.

From this analysis emerge two distinct comparative issues. The first one involves a measure (or continuum) of the increasing importance of political parties, shaped in part by the type of national democracy. Related to, but separate from, this concern is the notion of the relative power and effectiveness of parties, or of a given party. This latter is ultimately the more crucial dimension, and will be analysed in detail.

Types of Party Government
In terms of the first issue, the importance of parties is largely shaped by the type of democracy. Nations with regimes based on principles other than party government (Switzerland, the United States, France) tend to have relatively weak, less-dominant parties in a comparative context. Yet even within the spectrum of "party government" nations we still find sharp variations in intensity (cf. tables 4.1 and 4.2).

In Commonwealth nations, parties govern but only in a general supervisory sense. The Westminster model does guarantee a strong institutional basis for party government. In these systems, however, parties themselves are not organizationally strong, and lack deeper penetration into society. Political careers remain separate from bureaucratic ones. Consequently, the autonomous civil service retains a large impact on policy-making. Canada clearly falls within this category.

Generally speaking, the continental European parties tend to have broader social ties, but since government is normally coalitional, the power of any single party is constrained by the necessity of power sharing. Moreover, most of the nations in this group tend to exhibit some degree of neocorporatism in the policy process (Lijphart and Crepaz 1991). This suggests a reduced direct role for political parties aside from "big ticket" issues. Neocorporatism also implies a less autonomous bureaucracy, although the civil servants themselves may remain politically neutral.

This last point does not hold for those continental nations characterized by some version of the "party-state": West Germany (to be described in depth later), Austria, Italy and to a lesser extent Belgium. In these countries, powerful parties have succeeded in penetrating and dividing up positions in the bureaucracy and the (often numerous) state corporations and agencies. This extreme patronage is reflected in the national concepts of *Proporz* (Austria), *partitocrazia* (Italy) and *particratie* (Belgium). Although Austria has experienced alternation in government, and even single-party government, the overall balance of influence between the People's Party and the Social Democrats has been maintained – as has the general spirit of consensus and paradigmatic use of neocorporatist bodies.

For its part, Italy is a system characterized by quasi-one-party dominance in a dysfunctional atmosphere of partisan division, public mistrust, a weak executive facing strong parties (generally and within parliament) and a pluralist system of policy-making. In Italy the party-state encompasses most of the nation's social, economic and cultural life in a wide-ranging "subgovernment" (*sottogoverno*) (Spotts and Wieser 1986, 4ff.; Furlong 1990). Yet the parties themselves are not sufficiently autonomous and disciplined to govern coherently. The system is thus largely ineffective and "blocked." Pasquino has summarized Italy as a case of "party government by default" (1987, 212). Others question whether anyone really governs Italy.

West Germany is intriguing in this regard precisely because it combines strong parties in a system that is much more functional. Bureaucratic-partisan ties certainly exist at the highest level, but patronage does not permeate the whole polity. Elections do provide a quasi-Westminster choice, or at least a sense of being able to remove the government in power. Yet stronger parties mean that the German model is characterized by a much deeper and arguably more effective party government than is found in the classic Westminster systems.

Japan shares, on the surface, certain traits with continental European nations – above all, its underlying philosophy of cooperation and close ties between state and society. Whereas in Europe state and society essentially interpenetrate one another, Japanese civil society is weak and controlled or at least dominated by the ruling "system" of "insiders" which is broader than Western notions of a "state." This "system" is led by an interlocking triad of the bureaucracy, the Liberal Democratic Party (LDP), and organized business – but also takes in agriculture and the media – while normally excluding or co-opting other parties and actors. In Japan there is thus not so much a party-state, or even basic party government, as there is collective control by this dominant "system." Its three components generally share a common outlook, but conflicts and power struggles among them (and within them) do occur from time to time (van Wolferen 1989, especially chap. 2; Nester 1990, especially chap. 9).

More important for our purposes, the Liberal Democratic Party has become increasingly powerful and influential, compared to the early postwar years when the bureaucracy dominated the "system" (Nakamura 1990). Yet the LDP still lacks a strong central organization, and its individual parliamentarians retain autonomous influence.

THE ORGANIZATION AND BEHAVIOUR OF PARTIES

The extent to which politics is "all or nothing" affects strategies toward vote maximization and election outcomes. So does the self-perception of a party as a vehicle for narrow versus broadly-brokered interests. More generally, the role and importance – both perceived and actual – of political parties varies depending on the character of institutions or regime types. Historical factors, however, are also important. As Katz and Mair (1990, 5ff.) argue, specific historical periods can be associated with corresponding party types. The oligarchic era of limited suffrage democracy was characterized by élitist, cadre parties; the era of consolidated mass participation (ca. 1920 to ca. 1960) by mass parties of integration and encompassing ideologies; and the modern era of mass communications by rational-efficient, professional parties. Parties born within the "logic" of a given era tend to retain their original structure, style and purpose despite fundamental changes in society, economy and polity. Since most modern states contain parties that were founded (and shaped) in earlier periods, their party systems are likely to combine parties having distinctive self-images and styles.

This variation in self-definition leads to Panebianco's question of whether a party adopts an essentially "offensive" strategy of vote maximization or a "defensive" one of mobilizing and protecting an integrated subculture (Katz and Mair 1990, 10). The classic "milieu" or "pillar" party, common in many European systems prior to the Second World War (and in a few, such as the Netherlands, even as late as the 1960s), represents the proto-typical "defence of a subculture" party. Such pure milieu-parties no longer exist, although they have a legacy in modern-day successors.

Indeed, regardless of how tightly a party is organized, the leadership will always face potential trade-offs between loyalty to the organization/mass membership and the need to maximize a broad popular appeal; that is, a trade-off between internal and external legitimacy (Rose and McAllister 1990, 179–83). In general, the stronger and more deeply rooted the mass organization, the more difficult will be this trade-off for party leaders. A working hypothesis is that conflict over this trade-off will be greater in ideological mass parties than in pragmatic cadre or catch-all parties. Correspondingly, mass parties will experience considerable internal tensions in adapting both to the realities of social change and to competitive challenges from more flexible parties.

Party Strength and Weakness

Although our focus here is the internal organizational features of individual parties, the above distinctions regarding party government provide essential background to our more detailed consideration of the strengths and weaknesses of political parties. What then makes for a "strong" party? Angelo Panebianco, in his seminal work (1988), looks at the internal organization of political parties, noting five ways in which a party can be highly institutionalized:

- the development and bureaucratization of the central extra-parliamentary organization, which is "higher" (more formal and powerful) in more institutionalized parties;
- the homogeneity and coherence of organizational structures; for example, whether the local associations are organized the same way throughout the nation or are quite heterogeneous;
- the recognition, either by tradition or formally in the party constitution, of the effective "centre of power" in the party, such as the party leader for the British Conservatives;
- the organization and diversity of party funding: the level and regularity of contributions to the party, ideally from a *plurality* [Panebianco's italics] of sources so as to lessen dependence on any one particular (external) source; and

- the relationship between party and related or external allied organizations (trade unions, churches, etc.). A highly institutionalized party both has such organizations and controls them, whereas a weakly institutionalized party either lacks an external allied organization or is dependent on it (such as the dependence of the British Labour Party on the trade unions) (Panebianco 1988, 58–59).

These organizational factors speak to the autonomy of a political party and to its broader social networks. One should also note the potential competence of a political party; that is, the extent to which it can formulate detailed policy "in-house," and thus remain largely independent of the central bureaucracy. This requires that a party possess a certain expertise, normally within the central organization or affiliated to it.

In short, an ideal-typical "strong" party is well organized and well financed. It is disciplined and linked with other social actors but not dependent on them. It possesses policy expertise and often may possess its own media (party press). In contrast, a "weak" party will lack these traits. A strong party can thus fulfil King's stated functions of social aggregation, integration/mobilization, leadership recruitment and policy-formation. When in power a strong party can govern effectively. It might also be stressed that when in opposition a strong party is clearly superior to a weak party in its other potential functions and is better able to take control of government if and when the voters so decide.

Of course, few parties are consistently strong in all organizational respects. Typically, a national party organization will exhibit regional differences. For example, the German Christian Democrats manifest strong organizational traits in Baden–Württemberg and Bavaria but are much weaker in some of the northern Länder. The German Sozialdemokratische Partei Deutschlands (SPD) internalizes fundamental value differences between a traditional moderate wing and a post-materialist "new left," giving credence to its label as "two parties in one." In many instances, regional and ideological divisions may undercut the appearance of a solid national party organization. Other apparently strong organizations are riven by internal factionalism. This is certainly the case for the Italian DC, the Japanese LDP and to a lesser degree as well the French Socialists. Organization is thus largely a "within-party" matter, and must be distinguished from other measures of party performance – in particular, size and electoral success – which relate directly to a nation's party system. In terms of "size," for example, Gordon Smith (1989a, 158) defines what he calls catch-all parties in part by a cut-off of 30 percent of the total vote, which effectively limits a party system to no more than two such parties. Although this is probably a suitable electoral measure, our concern is with the organizational traits of the modern catch-all party or *Volkspartei*.

Moreover, the extent of influence or governmental "success" of a given party (regardless of size) is strongly affected by the type of democracy and electoral system in which it functions. In Westminster systems such as Britain and Canada, minor parties without regional strongholds are systematically disadvantaged and thus rarely gain any significant influence. Coalitional and consociational systems, however, enhance the role of key smaller parties, whose parliamentary representation is normally guaranteed by an electoral system based on proportional representation. Consequently, certain tiny but governmentally central parties, while organizationally weak, may manifest considerable influence due to their strategic placement in the national party system (for example, the Freie Demokratische Partei (FDP) in Germany and the Partito Socialista Italiano (PSI) or Partito Republicano Italiano (PRI) in Italy). This aspect of party politics must, however, remain beyond the scope of this report.

Such complications make it difficult to generalize about crossnational party organizations. One can note that the "membership ratio" – that is, the total number of members divided by the total party electorate – does vary across nations, being highest in central and northern Europe. Perhaps more striking are the high ratios generally found in agrarian and ethnic parties (Lane and Ersson 1987, 117–18).

Indeed, there are enormous within-nation variations in party organization. Japan provides a good example of this. Both the Japanese Communist Party and the *Komeito* (Clean Government Party) have mass features and centralized structures which make them similar to many European parties. Although small parties in terms of voting support, each has a devoted following – in the case of the *Komeito* through the Buddhist lay organization *Soka Gakkai* – and a well-developed and stable organization. Neither party is divided into factions, and in each the leadership keeps relatively tight control over its deputies. The Communists achieve this in part by requiring parliamentarians to turn over their salaries to the party, which then pays them an allowance. This practice previously applied to the *Komeito* as well (Curtis 1988, 157, 270–71).

These two parties, however, are exceptional within Japan. All other Japanese parties, including the dominant Liberal Democrats (LDP), the Socialists (JSP) and the (centrist) Democratic Socialists (DSP), more or less conform to a distinctive Japanese structure. Curtis notes that: "The dominant form of party organization in Japan, as applicable in basic respects to the JSP as to the LDP, is characterized by factional groupings, control by Diet members over the party's policy-making processes, and the absence of meaningful party organization at the local level. The critical role of forging linkages between parties and voters is performed by individual Diet members and their own personal support organizations, the *Koenkai*" (1988, 157). To a certain extent the *Komeito*, too, is adopting such traits, especially if one considers the *Soka Gakkai* as a de facto support organization. This thus leaves the Japanese Communist Party (JCP) as the nation's only true mass-organization party (Hrebenar 1986a, 26–27).

Party Types and Goals

Given such significant variance both across and within nations, how can we best summarize the range of parties in parliamentary systems? A classificatory scheme may be developed by combining the broader networks of a party with general estimates of the organizational and linkage traits described by Panebianco. From this, we arrive at the typology of political parties as shown in figure 4.1. The vertical axis measures differences in strength/weakness and centralization of control of the party organization.

**Figure 4.1
Types of political parties**

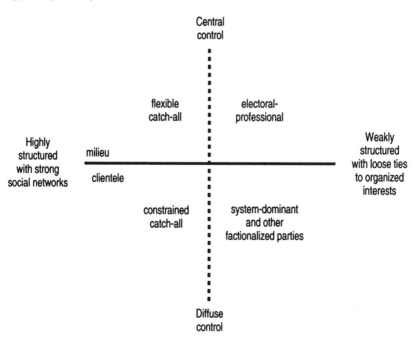

The horizontal axis measures the nature of a party's structure and relationship with allied actors. Here we distinguish among parties that correspond to a clear social "subculture" (to which they are tightly linked) and those parties having no formal ties (or only loose ties) to specific interests. This second category is distinct even if (as is invariably the case) the party has a specific socio-economic voting core.

The combination of factors shown in table 4.2 allows us to group parties into six distinct clusters of party type. First, there are the *milieu* parties, which are distinguished by their representation of specific sectors or groups and whose appeal is basically limited to such subcultures. As noted above, this is essentially a historical category, symbolized by the Communists, Social Democrats and Catholic *Zentrum* of Weimar Germany, or the Social Democrats and Social Christians of interwar Austria.

There remain, however, certain smaller parties, which although not tied tightly to a subculture, still intentionally appeal to a restricted segment of the electorate. We can refer to such parties as *clientele* parties. Such parties typically retain "cadre" features, such as the prominence of "notables" and a management style of semi-detached involvement. Most French parties tend to possess these organizational features.

We can identify five kinds of clientele party, based on the nature of appeal. First, there are linguistically based parties, such as the Swedish Peoples' Party in Finland. The second type includes confession-based parties, such as the smaller fundamentalist parties in the Netherlands or the aforementioned *Komeito* in Japan. Third, there are farmers' parties, most common in Nordic Europe, but which also existed prior to the Second World War in both Canada and the United States. Fourth, there are secular middle class parties such as the German FDP and the small Italian lay parties – PRI, Partito Socialista Democratico Italiano (PSDI), and Partito Liberale Italiano (PLI). These middle class parties tend to be less tightly linked to other actors than are most clientele parties. Lastly, there are "Green" parties, which strike a popular theme regarding the environment but often effectively appeal only to the core post-industrial subculture. In this category are the German Greens or the Italian Radicals, for example. Next, we have what various authors like to call *electoral-professional* parties. These lack a developed organization or affiliated interests, but the central party apparatus manifests a professional management style evident in modern techniques of media campaigning and financing (through direct mail using donor lists rather than a reliance on membership dues). Key party personnel are specialists in these funding techniques. Such parties often minimize ideology and specific programmatic commitments, focusing instead on the appeal of their leader. Even when electorally successful, however, they normally rely on other actors to help them govern, because they lack their own internal professional core of policy-making expertise.

A focus on leadership has of course also been central to "charismatic" parties such as the Gaullists or the National Front in France. Yet as Panebianco stresses, charismatic rule is unstable rule, and such parties must eventually develop some sort of organization, or else collapse (1988, 144, 161–62). It is usually the centrally controlled but loosely allied *electoral-professional* type into which charismatic parties will eventually develop. (The Nazis were an exception to the pattern, being a totalitarian rather than a democratic movement (ibid., 156).) A similar transformation can be noted with regard to protest parties, such as the Poujadists or the anti-tax parties of Denmark and Norway (Harmel and Svåsand 1989).

Additionally, and central to our analysis, there are two types of *catch-all* parties (in German, *Volksparteien*): constrained and flexible. We are using the notion of catch-all party not to refer to a party that has abandoned its roots, but rather one that has tried to reach out beyond them (in contrast to pure subculture parties). For example, Mintzel notes that the larger German parties (SPD and CDU) differ in terms of voting support, organization, ideology and policy output, so that in total they are clearly distinguishable, even if certain differences between them (especially on policy) are not huge (1989).

This being said, it is useful to distinguish between *constrained* catch-all parties, which are significantly shaped by their allied groups, if not indeed dependent on them, and *flexible* catch-all parties, which have a core group of supporters and interests, yet remain relatively autonomous from them. To some extent all parties rely on allied interests for financing, but for flexible catch-all parties money is given with very few strings attached in terms of internal party power or binding commitments. Constrained catch-all parties thus combine the flavour of a "movement" with a bureaucratic nature. Key personnel are often recruited from the allied networks, and the party leadership cannot stray too far from their concerns. Moreover, in continental systems such parties are often able to place representatives in various institutions, creating a reservoir of élite expertise not directly on the party payroll. In contrast, the management style of flexible catch-all parties is more modern and professional in the sense that senior administrators are valued primarily for their technical merit rather than for a loyalty to the party subculture (Panebianco 1988, 231–35).

The distinction between constrained and flexible catch-all parties roughly corresponds to that between social democratic and centre-right parties. This tendency is related to the powerful influence of trade unions in social democratic parties (Kitschelt 1990), an organizational feature without parallel in most conservative parties. Although most traditional social democratic and labour parties have tried to transform themselves into flexible catch-all parties, none has fully succeeded (Schmidt 1985). Typically, the weight of union and party-bureaucratic influence has made this transition difficult. The modernizing drive toward catch-all flexibility has endangered ingrained behaviour and organizational solidarity, both of which are typical of traditional mass parties. Large parties of the centre-right – while also having a mass membership – have been less burdened by such organizational and ideological baggage, and have found the transformation toward a modern, flexible party type a relatively easy task. Here we speak in particular of the British Conservatives and various (but not all) continental Christian Democratic movements. Thus, successful, broadly supported, catch-all parties are more often parties of the centre-right.

The Italian Christian Democratic Party (DC), however, having been permanently in power and having colonized much of the administration, is really of a different type. It constitutes a *system-dominant* party, whose permanence in government is a defining feature of the system (Amyot 1988). A similar situation exists in Japan with the Liberal Democratic Party (LDP). Moreover, some have argued that both of these parties could break up if ever forced into opposition.

Distinctions among these various types of parties are also reflected in their primary *goals*, as presented in figure 4.2. Historically, pure subculture parties existed essentially to defend the interests of their subculture. This was and is best done as part of government (for example, the *Zentrum* in Weimar Germany), which necessitates compromises with other coalition partners. On the other hand, electoral-professional parties seem largely concerned with vote maximization independent of an explicit purpose or programmatic agenda. All other party types have at least some interest in (strong) party government as defined above. Again, the fact should be underlined that the behaviour of a certain type of party combines with the type of democracy to shape the general character of party government in a nation.

For small clientele parties, party government and the implementation of key policies can be accomplished independent of major worries about "finishing first." For larger, would-be catch-all parties, this is obviously not the case. Flexible catch-all parties are sufficiently independent of their core groups, however, that they can concentrate, often successfully, on maximizing votes in the (policy) context of a general ideological tendency. Constrained catch-all parties must juggle all three

Figure 4.2
Political parties and their goals

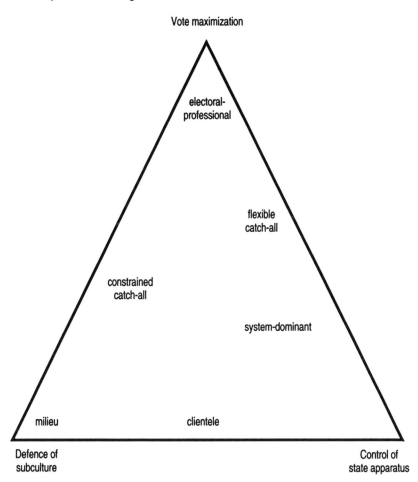

goals, but since there exists an inherent tension between subculture defence and vote maximization, they find this a much more difficult task. Lastly, system-dominant parties must by definition remain in government, which requires high but not necessarily maximal levels of support. Clientelism also provides them with a link between (certain) voting cores and the maintenance of power. Indeed, these successful (quasi-) dominant parties – such as the LDP and the DC – are in effect alliances of intraparty factions, which are virtually mini-party organizations under a large umbrella party structure.

Analysis of Relevant Larger Parties

The two principal parties in Great Britain, the Conservatives and Labour, provide a useful contrast in terms of both the strength-weakness and the constrained-flexible dimensions. The Conservative Party has traditionally had a massive membership, close to three million in 1948 and still around one and one-half million today. The steady revenue from membership sources, which is normally greater than business contributions, provides both strength and autonomy. Although one cannot ignore the significance of corporate donations, the fact remains that business associations lack any formal statutory influence inside the party. Financial stability has provided the wherewithal for an efficient party organization at central, intermediate and local levels.

Within this framework, the Conservative Central Office (the national headquarters) clearly dominates local party units. Through its regional agents, the Central Office is able to maintain a discreet but effective control over candidate selection. This Office is now divided into campaign, communications, research and a treasurer's department, the tasks of which are self-evident. However, the Office is itself subservient to the parliamentary party and especially to the party leader, where ultimate power lies. Whilst the party leadership is reinforced by a strong organization, it remains essentially autonomous from both the organization and key support groups (Panebianco 1988, 130–41; Ingle 1989, chap. 3; Pinto-Duschinsky 1990, 95).

Even so, the Conservative Party cannot be said to be strong in terms of its capacity to formulate coherent and detailed policy. Even though it has a research department and policy groups, the party headquarters' "basic role has traditionally been to give advice on how to achieve power when the party is in opposition and to provide loyal though largely uncritical support for the leadership when in office" (Ingle 1989, 70). Policy formation in Britain, even under Conservative governments, is still largely in the hands of a neutral, autonomous bureaucracy. This bureaucratic/political compartmentalization, which is characteristic of Commonwealth nations, sets limits on full party government – despite an otherwise strong governing party.

By contrast with the Conservatives, the British Labour Party is in many ways a much weaker organization. The party grew out of the trade union movement, and to this day union power manifests itself within the party in a variety of ways, of which five stand out. First, the unions still provide over half of all party income, and some 80–90 percent of the money available to Labour's Head Office (Pinto-Duschinsky 1990, 95). Second, the unions constitute one of the four divisions of the National Executive Committee that is central to the party organization, above all in policy matters. Third, the unions are able to cast "bloc votes" at the annual conferences. This is in large part to outweigh more radical elements in the constituency parties. Fourth, the electoral college, which since 1981 elects the party leader, assigns 40 percent of the weight to such union bloc votes. Fifth and finally, the unions have a strong say in candidate selection. About half of the current parliamentary party (including leader Neil Kinnock) are "sponsored," that is, endorsed and financially supported, by individual unions. The cumulative effect of all these union influences is to constrain the party leadership greatly, although this is mitigated somewhat by differences among the unions (or rather their leaderships), which often prevent a single "union voice" from being heard. Moreover, the unions tend to leave "political" issues, that is, nonindustrial ones, in the hands of the parliamentary party (Kavanagh 1990, 128).

In any case, the control exercised by the unions has also contributed to, or at least permitted, general organizational weakness in the Labour Party. Although trade-union affiliated members number over five million, the number of individual members remains under three hundred thousand. (These figures can be contrasted with those of the Swedish Social Democrats, whose individual members represent a full third of the affiliated total.) As a result, Labour can rely on only a comparatively limited membership income. The number of full-time constituency workers has declined from 296 in the mid-1950s to only 60 in 1987 (Ingle 1989, 140). Furthermore, the regional agents and especially the constituency parties are quite autonomous from party central control. Of course, it is often the case that disagreements between the Executive Committee and the parliamentary leadership preclude any effective central guidance for the lower levels (ibid., chap. 6; Panebianco 1988, 88–95).

Notwithstanding the experience of the British Labour Party, it is important to note that social democratic parties do not always correspond to constrained catch-all parties, or vice versa. Socialist parties fit this model depending on both how and when they were founded (as mass parties of a broader "movement"). Parties formed generations ago (usually the late 19th century) typically have a rich ideological heritage and deep social roots. Those which developed organizationally only recently are less encumbered by the past and have produced more flexible structures.

For example, the modern socialist parties in both France, Parti Socialiste (PS), and Spain, Partido Socialista Obrero Español (PSOE), both of which have been in power since the early 1980s, diverge from the more general model. Their current structures date only from the 1970s.

The leadership has centralized control, and the membership remains relatively limited in numbers and often dependent on public sector employees. In addition, their ties to a fractured and weak union movement are loose and informal, with leftist ideology having taken a back seat to policy pragmatism. All of this means that such party organizations, despite their socialist labels, are really closer to the electoral-professional type of party than we normally think. Of course, both the PS and especially the PSOE still constitute relatively well-organized parties within nations generally characterized by weak parties.

Conversely, not all centre-right parties have achieved flexibility, defined as freedom from affiliated interest groups. For example, the Austrian Peoples' Party, Österreichische Volkspartei (ÖVP), retains a quite rigid structure involving two decentralizing centres of power. The first of these centres consists of the provincial parties, whose influence has increased with greater electoral success at the provincial level than at the federal. The second is the six affiliated suborganizations or leagues of the party: employees, farmers, business, women, youth and pensioners. Party membership is effectively achieved through one (or more) of these leagues, and party leaders usually are recruited from one of the first three leagues. The league structure closely parallels Austria's neocorporatist Chambers (of Labour, Agriculture and Commerce). Yet the Socialist Party of Austria has a much less diffuse structure, in part because of the dominance of the Vienna party and the trade unions, which are themselves constraining in the traditional party-union way (Nick and Pelinka 1989, 58–62; Sully 1990, chap. 2 and 3). The electoral disaster of the ÖVP in the October 1990 federal elections (by far its lowest vote share ever) may be partially attributed to its inflexibility and antiquated image, both of which make modernizing changes difficult, if not unlikely.

The Japanese LDP and the Italian DC share many of the traits of flexible catch-all parties, especially their very broad range of voting support. Both parties are highly factionalized, however, with powerful deputies and very weak leaders. They are also very clientelistic (in the LDP at the deputy level). Most importantly, these two parties have remained permanently in power, and therefore represent unambiguous instances of *system-dominant* parties. Beyond such similarities, there are also significant differences between the two. DC factions not only reflect personalities and the internal struggle for power (as in the LDP), but also can be distinguished along a left–right continuum (Leonardi and Wertman 1989, chap. 4). More crucially, the LDP is clearly more dominant both within its party system and in its almost exclusive control of government. The DC must function within broad coalition governments (in which other parties, especially the PSI, share many of the same traits). As noted earlier, this places Italy somewhat uneasily between the continental and one-party dominant models of democracy.

The LDP is furthermore increasingly influential in terms of policy-making. The party organization contains a Policy Affairs Research Council (PARC) with 17 divisions, roughly paralleling the ministries of government. Every significant government initiative must receive approval from the relevant PARC division. Each division aims to achieve unanimous internal consensus. Afterwards, approval by the party as a whole and by the LDP-dominated parliament is normally a formality. The chairmanship of the PARC constitutes one of the four senior posts in the LDP, alongside the party president (usually also the prime minister), the secretary general and the chair of the General Council.

Moreover, each LDP deputy must belong to three PARC divisions, two of one's own choosing. Deputies tend to stay in the same divisions, and thus to specialize in certain precise areas. With this acquired substantive expertise, long-term PARC members and division chairs eventually become members of a *zoku* or policy "tribe," a smaller, less formal body with close ties to interest groups. The *zoku*, of which there are only eleven, are central to shaping and especially vetoing policies. This is especially so in "pork-barrel" areas rather than in, say, industrial policy, where the Ministry of International Trade and Industry (MITI) remains relatively autonomous.

Although parallels may be drawn between these policy "tribes" and U.S. congressional committees, three important distinctions should be made. First of all, only (certain) members of the ruling LDP have *zoku* influence; the opposition is totally excluded. Secondly, both the PARC divisions and the *zoku* lack support staff. They both (especially the divisions) must rely on the bureaucracy for expertise, and both wish to ensure good, long-term relations with senior bureaucrats. Finally, it is the PARC leaders who forge compromises among competing *zoku*. Those cases too sensitive for a PARC division are dealt with at the party's senior levels, at which point LDP central control reappears. One must always be mindful, however, of the mitigating effects of party factions (Kishimoto 1988, 105–107; Curtis 1988, 106–16; Campbell 1989, 130–33; Koh 1989, 212–13; Nakamura 1990).

The many facets of party organizational life cannot of course be fully elucidated by these various examples of quite different parties operating within different institutional contexts. Nevertheless, collectively they serve to illustrate basic features of party organization that impinge upon the most basic functions of parties within modern democracies.

COMPARATIVE PARTY FINANCE

The preceding discussion has demonstrated how differences in parliamentary models of governing may have implications for party structure. Variations in the nature of party organization and the centrality of parties in the governmental process are also shaped by legal/regulatory conditions. Among the most important of these are systems of party financing. There exist some overlaps between regime types and modes of party financing but certainly no precise fit. Consistent with our emphasis on continental versions of party government, the analysis in this section also concentrates on these regimes, with special reference given to the German experience, followed by some brief comparisons drawn from Austria. Considered next are some aspects of party finance evident in the Japanese and Anglo-American traditions that carry with them implications for party management.

There are various democratic rationales for public support and control over elections and party activities. In general these involve protection of the integrity of the democratic process, particularly the principle of equal opportunity in electoral competition through control of private lobbying and corruption. Fairness, accountability and transparency are recurrent themes in discussions of party finance. As Alexander has noted, less obvious but more important is the problem of what effects systems of public support for parties have on the operation of the political system in general and political parties in particular (1989, 10). We are especially interested in how various modes of public finance may alter party management capacities.

Without doubt public financing enhances the organizational infrastructure of parties and leads them into new activities. It may also lead to a professionalization of party careers and a modified role for amateur activists. All of this may generate a vicious cycle of reinforcing effects, in which public money stimulates organizational development. This then encourages parties to extend and expand their tasks, which in turn leads them into a new indebtedness requiring an expansion of public funding. This cycle may be further accentuated where public financing reduces the traditional reliance on membership dues and voluntary contributions. Thus we find parties adopting a "help yourself" approach to public funds (Nassmacher 1989b, 249). This tendency would appear to be more likely in those systems where the scope of public subsidy is undefined and where aid is distributed with no strings attached, as opposed to those systems where support is restricted to electoral campaigns. In some systems, such as the U.S., the public role has been defined narrowly to mean the regulation of campaigns and electoral procedures. In Britain only public support-in-kind is permitted. In other cases, including Germany, Austria and a number of other European states, the scope of public involvement has developed within a broader conceptual framework and corresponds to a general system of "political finance" (ibid., 237).

For all advanced democracies, the development of legislation covering public financing of parties is relatively recent. The Government of Canada's involvement in this policy domain dates only from 1974, although at the provincial level Quebec led the way with innovative legislation as early as 1963.

German Party Finance

Among European states West Germany in 1959 pioneered the public funding of parties, but no comprehensive law on party finance was adopted until 1967. Over the past three decades, German party finance has certainly been characterized by rapid expansion of public funding and major problems of indebtedness. These trends gave rise to a series of scandals that came to the surface in the early 1980s, which in turn led to significant reforms (Jesse 1986, 125–30: Rudzio 1987, 135–45; Padgett and Burkett 1986, 291–93).

Both in reaction to the historical precedent of secret financial support provided by industrialists for the Nazis and in order to protect against undue influence, Article 21 of the 1949 Basic Law required parties to publish the sources of their income. The implementation of these goals was to be assured through federal law, but for the first decade of the Federal Republic, no implementing policy was forthcoming. Tax laws (between 1954 and 1958) did permit generous tax deductions for contributions to political groups. In 1958, however, the Federal Constitutional Court ruled such deductions to be unconstitutional violations of the principle of equality of opportunity. This decision initiated a pattern of legislative-judicial interaction in which actions by one branch were stopped or modified by the other, producing a period of trial-and-error innovation in the realm of party finance. The 1958 ruling also threatened the income of parties, especially that of the Christian Democrats and Free Democrats who were most dependent on contributions, primarily from corporations. This no doubt encouraged the parties to consider new approaches to public financing. Starting in 1959 the federal budget allowed for flat grants but only to those parties having representation in the Bundestag.

A subsequent court decision in 1966 ruled this restriction, as well as the principle of subsidization of party work for education and other activities, to be unconstitutional. At the same time, however, the Court declared that a limited reimbursement of necessary expenses for election campaigns was permissible as long as the principle of equal opportunity was observed. Once again the parties responded to this new judicial challenge, and in 1967 the Bundestag enacted the first comprehensive legislation corresponding to the principles laid down in Article 21. This law required an accounting of party income. It also granted to each party winning 2.5 percent of the vote an amount of DM2.5 per vote for each electoral period. In 1968, after another court ruling, the threshold for eligibility was reduced to 0.5 percent of the vote and by 1983 the rate per vote was set at DM5. An equal amount for European elections was added in 1979. Separate laws in the Länder also initiated support at DM1.5 per vote, with these rates by now being DM5 in most cases.

The revised system of party funding provided for three sources: tax benefits for donations of up to DM1 200 per couple, grants by the federation and by the Länder for "reimbursement" (in reality a flat grant) of election expenses, and allowances to the political foundations. As well, there was established a special allocation to party caucuses at both levels, in addition to the standard funding for regular parliamentary activities and members' privileges (Nassmacher 1989b, 246–47).

The beginning of the 1980s was a time of political change – including notably the collapse of the SPD/FDP coalition and Helmut Kohl's election as chancellor by the procedure of a constructive vote of no-confidence. Coalition change was followed by early elections in March of 1983, which confirmed the new CDU/CSU-FDP majority but also led to the entry of the Greens into the Bundestag. By this time many dubious financial arrangements had come under substantial criticism, and the pressure for change intensified. By 1982, at the height of political scandals, party finance had emerged as a public controversy requiring policy response. The 1967 law had imposed rather restrictive limits on tax deductibility (to a maximum of DM600 per person) and required disclosure of major donations (DM20 000 and up) from private sources. In the course of the next decade parties expanded their activities and also incurred massive debts. As parties increasingly found themselves strapped for money, they were tempted to engage in legally dubious practices. This led them to resort to secret, often illicit modes of support. These *Umwegfinanzierungen* became increasingly widespread and eventually became the object of public scrutiny and legal action, once scandals exposed these problems.

The Flick affair, as the most notorious instance of contributions to parties in exchange for very favourable tax exemption treatment, had the effect of exposing the vast extent of secret payments (Gunlicks 1989, 240–44). Peter Lösche has argued that the real scandal was the law itself, which allowed too much discretion to the ministries concerned. Furthermore, the significance of the Flick affair was really to be found in what it said about the degree to which politicians appeared to be "buyable" by private interests. In this sense the problem went to the heart of the democratic process (Lösche 1986, 84).

Many argued that parties had become too distant from the citizenry and too institutionalized as quasi-state organs (*Staatsparteien*). This negative climate induced the parties themselves to request an independent commission of inquiry. This was established by Federal President Carstens in 1982. The Commission was charged with the task of proposing a new set of arrangements that would avoid the pitfalls of past practice.

One of the commissioners, Hans-Peter Schneider, has provided a detailed account of the proposed reforms, many of which were enacted in the 1983 law. The most important proposals concerned: the reporting not only of party income but also of expenditures as well as an account of debts and assets, the elimination of "special contributions" deductions from the salary of elected officials, and the preferential treatment of parties for tax purposes. A tax credit of 50 percent for small donations (up to DM2 400 per couple annually) was proposed. The Commission also recommended that up to 5 percent of personal income be eligible for tax deduction, with a complex provision for equalization.

Among the most important changes enacted were:

1. Reimbursement per voter was increased to DM5.
2. Parties were now to report not only income but expenditures, debts and assets.
3. Salary contributions from elected officials were made illegal. They were not, however, effectively eliminated. Instead contributions were hidden under donations or membership fees.
4. Parties were now explicitly allowed to accept donations, with some important exclusions. To protect against "laundered" money, donations were prohibited from foreign and unidentified sources, as well as from party foundations, charitable organizations and churches.
5. A formula for the equalization of tax benefits among the competing parties was adopted in order to assure the equality of opportunity principle.
6. The sum of campaign reimbursements for any year was not to exceed the total income from other sources.
7. If a party received funds illegally or if funds were not expended in conformity with law, or not listed in the annual report

(DM20 000 or more), the party would forfeit double the amount (Schneider 1989; Gunlicks 1989, 235–36).

Relevant tax laws were also changed to encourage contributions to parties, making the treatment of parties similar to charitable organizations. This was the most controversial aspect of the reforms (Gunlicks 1989, 237).

In response to a complaint from the Greens, the Federal Constitutional Court in 1986 ruled on the constitutionality of the new provisions in the party law and the income tax laws as amended in 1983. The Court rejected the allegation that the financing of the party foundations was merely a disguised form of support for the established parties. It also set controls on the generous system of donations by restricting total tax deductibility to DM100 000. In general, the Court upheld the major reforms as compatible with Article 21 of the Basic Law (Hübner and Rohlfs 1987, 250–51). There is little doubt that the 1983 reforms greatly enhanced the transparency of party finance (Nassmacher 1989a, 32). The 1986 court ruling led directly to new reforms adopted in 1988, including a reduction in the maximum amount eligible for tax deductibility to DM60 000 (or DM120 000 for couples).

The persisting features of party finance in the 1980s are evident in the patterns of income and expenditure associated with the parties (table 4.3). The three most important sources of income were membership dues, contributions and public campaign reimbursements. For both major parties, membership was the single largest source, about 50 percent of income for the SPD and about 45 percent for the CDU. The three smaller parties were all more reliant on contributions, often gaining 30 percent or more of their income in this way while the major parties were only 10 to 15 percent dependent. For this reason, the likely impact of private contributions should not be exaggerated. We did not observe an increase in this source in the course of the 1980s, except for the Greens, who, to conform with the 1983 prohibition against party taxes on elected officials, have treated funds from this source as contributions. Other parties have achieved similar effects by treating such income as membership contributions. Reimbursements for campaign costs generally account for approximately 30 percent of party income, and this has remained fairly constant over the past 20 years. It is worth noting that the source of party income varies considerably depending on the level of party organization. At the local level (*Kreis* or district) membership and private donations account for almost all income. The share of public funds increases sharply at the higher levels with federal

Table 4.3
Income and expenditures by party and organizational level
(DM millions)

	CDU/CSU					SPD					FDP					Grüne				
	Federal	Land	Local	Total	%	Federal	Land	Local	Total	%	Federal	Land	Local	Total	%	Federal	Land	Local	Total	%
Income																				
Membership dues	24.8	40.4	139.3	204.5	41.4*	36.0	92.6	90.8	219.4	53.0	1.6	5.6	9.7	16.9	21.8	2.3	3.4	5.2	10.9	13.9
Private contribution	19.7	29.1	85.9	134.7	27.2	40.9	12.4	47.1	100.4	16.1	4.0	10.2	15.5	29.7	38.2	2.8	7.6	19.8	30.2	38.5
Public sources	94.0	60.4	0.0	154.4	31.2	78.0	49.1	0.0	127.1	30.8	23.2	7.9	0.0	31.1	40.0	27.1	10.2	0.0	37.3	47.6
Expenditures																				
Personnel	46.9	56.0	43.6	146.5	27.3	32.7	85.2	6.6	124.5	29.8	4.6	6.3	1.6	12.5	18.2	2.4	4.7	2.5	9.6	15.6
Administration	41.9	29.7	86.2	157.8	29.5	23.8	23.0	55.5	102.3	24.5	9.0	6.5	10.4	25.9	37.6	4.3	8.4	15.0	27.7	44.9
Campaigns, public relations	90.2	51.2	90.0	231.4	43.2	70.8	49.1	71.0	190.9	45.7	7.4	10.0	13.0	30.4	44.2	3.8	8.8	11.8	24.4	39.5

Source: Adapted from K.-H. Nassmacher (1990).

*Percentages may not add to 100.0 because of rounding.

party headquarters heavily dependent on this source (K.-H. Nassmacher 1990, 146; Mintzel and Oberreuter 1990, 410–32).

One finds, as well, relative stability in spending patterns since 1984. Personnel costs are more important for both the SPD and CDU than for the smaller parties. Administrative costs represent roughly 20 percent of party spending. Political functions occupy the most important place for all, usually 50 percent or more. The Greens as a new party with a relatively limited organizational infrastructure have tended to spend more on the latter category. Again, it is important to note that spending patterns, like income, vary by level of party organization. Although total spending levels are close across federal, Land and local levels, the middle level spends disproportionately on personnel and the local on general administration (K.-H. Nassmacher 1990, 152).

In all parliamentary systems, but particularly in Germany, the regulation and subsidization of political parties have raised broader concerns about democratic performance. In consequence, the funding of parties has been the subject of continuing debate (Heidenheimer 1989, 225). The regular involvement of both the judiciary and the media in matters concerning party finance is reflective of the political sensitivity of such issues. Two persisting problems very evident in, but hardly unique to, the German experience are manifested in an ambivalence about the public-private balance in party function and status, and an anxiety over the possibility of unfair influence.

Parties are private organizations, but with a constitutionally defined public role. There is always the danger that they may become isolated from the public they are supposed to serve. All legislation regarding public funds has assumed that donations or subsidies are given primarily to parties themselves and not to candidates (which has been extremely rare). As the system of support has expanded over time, the federal parties have become increasingly dependent on public funding. This has fueled concern that parties have grown distant from the public and have become too much state institutions. The resultant profusion of funds also may have encouraged the parties to be spendthrift, according to the vicious cycle hypothesized above (Padgett and Burkett 1986, 292).

The problem of unfair influence was illustrated through the pervasiveness of illicit support from corporations, which had been made necessary by the chronic indebtedness of parties. The Flick affair stands as the most obvious but certainly not the only incident of misuse of influence. Framing both these concerns is the special historically justified German sensitivity to the workings and health of the democratic order.

Austrian Party Finance

Although both Austrian and German procedures share much in common when compared to typical Anglo-American practices, the Austrian experience demonstrates some informative variations on the general theme of public financing. The Austrian model, like the German, certainly can be described as a generous approach to party finance. Indeed, as Nassmacher (1989b, 242) reports, total subsidies in Austria amount to U.S.$1.75 ($ per capita, 1985) and are considerably higher than in Germany, Sweden or Italy (all under U.S.$1.60).

In other respects Austrian party funding is less restrictive than is the German. Public monies are not confined to campaign reimbursements; they take the form of generalized grants to cover all forms of party activity. Austrian parties also receive free radio time outside of campaign periods, and there are subsidies for the party presses. In addition, there is an automatic inflation protection adjustment which eliminates a chronic impediment found in many other systems. Furthermore, the practice of a party tax on officials remains legal in Austria. The most significant item missing here but present under German tax law is the tax credit system for contributions (Nassmacher 1989b, 239–46).

The major Austrian parties, Sozialistische Partei Österreichs (SPO) and ÖVP, enjoy very high member to-voter ratios and can draw upon multiple financial sources. In 1989 (a non-election year) these two parties each took in some AS420 million from dues, party taxes, provincial branches and affiliated organizations. When supplemented by state subsidies, total revenue for each party amounted to about AS850 million, or about Cdn.$90 million (Nick and Sickinger 1990, 130–31).

A Note on the Financing of Party Foundations

The German foundations run civic/political education programs and support various research projects. They also provide considerable support for international aid programs. Their financing depends on governmental grants from several ministries (including a global subsidy from the Ministry of the Interior, as well as specific grants from various other ministries, e.g., Economic Cooperation (Development), Education and Science, and Foreign Affairs). Interparty agreements determine ministerial allocations. Governments of the Länder provide similar funding to foundations at that level. In addition, foundations receive some limited donations from individuals, corporations, unions and party-controlled enterprises. They also gain support through research grants. All such foundation funding is independent of the public financing of political parties.

Over time the financial resources and budgets of the foundations have expanded very substantially. In 1968 governmental grants accounted for a total of DM9 million. By 1988 this figure was DM142.1 million, an increase by a factor of 15. Correspondingly, total public funds for parties increased over the same 20 years by a factor of 6.5. Thus the public funding for foundations increased at a much higher rate (Nassmacher 1989a, 31). The total budget for each foundation includes other sources of income and is therefore considerably larger than public funding alone would indicate. For example, in 1988 the Ebert Foundation budget totaled DM185 million while the Adenauer Foundation's was DM160 million.

As with the German foundations, there is significant public support for the equivalent Austrian academies. It is worth noting that these academies are much more directly linked to party organizations and serve as important service institutions for them.

Japanese Party Finance

The first section of this study referred to some of the distinctive features of party government and party organization found in Japan. Some of these traits carry over into questions of party finance.

The most striking aspect of Japanese party finance involves the dominant Liberal Democrats. Officially in 1984 the party received ¥13.2 billion (then Cdn.$72 million). Most of this amount (72 percent) came from the corporate sector. Indeed, every year LDP leaders provide business with a "target figure" for donations, in the range of ¥10 billion (approximately $85 million in 1991 Canadian dollars). Business leaders consult among themselves on how this amount is to be divided, taking into account industrial size and recent profitability. Through the 1970s the major supporters were the steel, automobile, electric power and banking sectors. Recently, the consumer electronics and financial associations have also emerged as significant donors. In any case, a wide range of industrial associations provides financial support to the LDP to an annual amount of about ¥1.2 billion each (van Wolferen 1989, 133; Curtis 1988, 183–84; Fukui and Fukai 1990, 5).

This level of publicly acknowledged support appears to be close to reality for other Japanese parties, but it is only the tip of the iceberg for the LDP. The various factions of the LDP, as well as senior party leaders, together receive, at a minimum, an additional ¥5 billion per year. Moreover, the actual amount taken in by the party and its factions may be as much as five times these stated amounts (Fukui and Fukai 1990, 5; Hrebenar 1986b, 58).

These totals do not include financial support to individual LDP Diet members. Although deputies are granted some funds from LDP headquarters at election time, the weak party organization and the factional nature of the party (in which the real political battle is often among competing LDP candidates) mean that each member needs a personal support organization, or *koenkai*. The *koenkai* is built around a core of friends and relatives (analogous to the Italian *parentela*), but it also functions as a large clientelistic network within the district, providing in particular aid in legal matters. LDP members also personally reward their constituents with gifts and holidays (Fukui and Fukai 1990, 6–7).

All of this entails high costs, in the order of an estimated annual ¥160 million per deputy. With about 400 LDP deputies in both houses, this works out to approximately ¥64 billion (Cdn.$576 million) per year spent by LDP Diet members. This figure, and LDP spending in general, must be doubled in election years, expanding the discrepancy between the LDP and all other parties whose election year spending remains essentially the same as in non-election years (Fukui and Fukai 1990, 5; Hrebenar 1986b, 58).

LDP politicians thus employ a range of instruments to attract vast revenues. For example, fund-raising parties for which businesses buy large blocks of tickets, contributions to (multiple) personal funding organizations, and even brown paper bags stuffed with millions of yen by a firm in one's constituency provide means for direct contributions to the *koenkai*. Some of these practices suggest parallels with the role of political action committees (PAC) in American politics. Although legal limitations on such behaviour do exist, these are widely ignored and easily circumvented. For example, the limitation on contributions to a personal funding organization has simply encouraged each LDP politician to create perhaps dozens of such funding units (Curtis 1988, 180–87; van Wolferen 1989, 132–34).

The Socialists (JSP) and Democratic Socialists (DSP), for their part, have relied traditionally on their affiliated union confederations, respectively *Sohyo* and *Domei*, for financial support. This is especially the case at election time, when each confederation has normally donated the equivalent of Cdn.$3 million to 4 million to its party. (Because these confederations have recently largely merged, and because the Japanese labour movement is currently in considerable flux, we can expect some consequences for the parties.) In addition, the middle-of-the-road DSP also receives donations from corporate Japan. The JSP, in contrast, is the party most dependent on dues (about 32 percent of total revenue in 1984), despite a comparatively small membership (Hrebenar 1986b, 58). In total the JSP received some ¥6 billion and the DSP ¥1.6 billion in 1984.

Finally and atypically, the Communists (with revenues of ¥22 billion in 1984) and the *Komeito* (¥10 billion) raise most of their money "in-house" through party businesses and especially through the sale of party publications (Hrebenar 1986b, 58). Each party pays all campaign expenses for its own candidates in both parliamentary and local elections, obviating any need for independent candidate revenue (Fukui and Fukai 1990, 5).

Anglo-American Party Finance

In this subgroup we find great variation in both law and practice. Despite a common heritage, Britain and Canada, for example, share little when it comes to party financing. Indeed, there can be said to be no consistent pattern across Westminster regimes to describe how party financing should work. Moreover, the American experience, for reasons that we cannot pursue here, is quite idiosyncratic and not amenable to easy comparison. If there is a common pattern at all, these Anglo-American cases generally are characterized by a candidate-centred approach and by contradictions with the ideal of strong party government. By contrast the continental systems tend to exemplify relatively comprehensive and explicitly developed financing arrangements. In the Anglo-American cases, as in Japan, ad hoc arrangements appear common.

Public campaign funding in the United States is very candidate-oriented and therefore shares something in common with Japanese practice. The American pattern reinforces existing institutional barriers that effectively block any prospect for the development of strong parties or any semblance of party government.

Among Western democracies, Britain is the most restrictive in this domain. Parties remain on their own where financing is concerned. The absence of public support has left in place traditional organizational disparities. The Conservative party has enjoyed a much larger individual membership and thus a far stronger base for contributions than has Labour, which relies on the trade unions for half of its (smaller) total income. Importantly, the Conservative party headquarters and constituency candidates are relatively autonomous of their sources of support. For Labour, however, party rules allow trade unions to provide up to 80 percent of the election expenses of constituency candidates. This obviously creates a situation of considerable influence (Kavanagh 1990, 72).

In the eleven election campaigns from 1951 through 1987, the Conservatives at the national level outspent Labour by an average ratio of 1.8 to 1. For its part, Liberal election spending has been usually one-fifth or less of Conservative spending. And in nonelection years the Conservatives always raise more money than Labour (Pinto-Duschinsky 1990, 98–100). Conservatives have more money and also spend more both during and between election campaigns in part because the equalizing and homogenizing effects of public finance are absent.

Unlike U.S. and Canadian parties, however, British parties cannot buy commercial television time, which provides a built-in limit on campaign spending. Indeed, the standard – and equal – provision of 50 minutes of free air time on all channels to each of the Conservatives and Labour parties (somewhat less to the Liberals) has been a great equalizer among them. British parties in fact receive total benefits-in-kind (television and radio time, postage, halls for election meetings, etc.) greater than their individual direct spending (Pinto-Duschinsky 1990, 101).

Although in Canada we find strong candidate-targeting of public subsidies, in general the broad features of public financing differ considerably from the British and American cases and look rather more continental European in their application. Canadian party finance is more comprehensive, with its principal components including the doctrine of agency for parties and candidates, a set of regulations governing the reporting and disclosure of funding sources and campaign expenditures, a system of campaign reimbursements, and in some jurisdictions support through tax credits (Paltiel 1985, 1989; Stanbury 1989).

Australia, a late-comer to public financing, developed in the 1980s a system of support that strikes a balance in funding among central party organizations according to their share of the vote and individual candidates (Chaples 1989, 78–89).

A Note on Independent Candidates

In U.S. politics it is not uncommon to observe "independents" as significant players in electoral politics. For example, in the 1990 elections, a former Republican running as an independent won the governorship in Connecticut. Another independent (formerly a socialist in local politics) won Vermont's only congressional seat. There are as well several examples of prominent independents or "third party" candidates in presidential elections.

Such independent candidates are the product of three conditions. The first is a single-member district plurality electoral system that gives prominence to political personalities and local notables. The second is the general weakness of party organizations, which are often overshadowed by the candidate's own organization and candidate-controlled funds. The third factor is the unpredictable character of primary elections, which deprives parties of control over the nomination process. Well-known and experienced public personalities may, after losing a primary, still present credible candidatures. In other words, "independent" becomes a surrogate for mainstream contenders who are nevertheless outsiders within their own party. By contrast, in systems based on strong parties and some version of party government, independents, if they exist at all, will tend to be fringe, often extremist candidates. In German politics the concept of an independent candidate has virtually no counterpart to the American experience. Given the German proportional, two-ballot system, the best prospect for any small independent force is to win representation by surpassing the 5 percent hurdle on the second ballot. This provides strong incentive for individual would-be candidates to develop the facade of a minor party. The fact that party financing is granted to parties winning as little as 0.5 percent of the total vote reinforces this tendency. It is also possible under the German party law, however, for an individual running as a district candidate to qualify for financial support by winning at least 10 percent of the first ballot votes. In practice this option has remained without significance.

Comparative Perspectives and Implications

In the past thirty years, public policies designed to address the problem of funding political parties have matured. Karl-Heinz Nassmacher has proposed three phases in the development of public financing: an experimental stage in which new objectives/types of expenditure are defined, followed by a stage of enlargement, in which parties expand their claim for public money through various new objects of subsidization, and finally a period of adjustment, in which the problem of inflation protection becomes paramount (1989b, 238–39).

Not all systems, however, have followed the same course or proceeded at the same rate. The British and West German experiences with public party finance stand out as unmistakable opposites. British parties, which receive only support-in-kind, must be financially self-reliant (Pinto-Duschinsky 1990, 95–98). Moreover, there are strict limits on campaign expenses. By contrast, the German model is one of expansive public financing of parties. The development of generous systems of support is of course to be found in many other countries, but comparative research shows that German party incomes rose at a higher per capita rate than did those in Sweden, Austria or Italy (Nassmacher 1989b). Again unlike Britain but in common with most other systems of public funding, in Germany it is generally campaign costs that represent the major item of spending. There can be little doubt that the German approach to party finance not only has had significant effects on party politics but has been a recurrent object of political contention and policy reform (Gunlicks 1989, 240).

In his comprehensive comparative survey of party finance laws and practice, Paltiel (1981) argued that there appear to be two over-riding concerns about party finance in all modern democracies: fairness and costs. Efforts to improve the fairness or purity of the electoral process have often been provoked by evidence of scandals and corruption and have resulted in various measures designed to regulate and make financing practices more visible. Perhaps the most significant step in this regard has been the move toward effective disclosure of sources and expenditures. In the case of Germany, the 1983 reforms represent the most dramatic advance toward transparency. The concern for costs has often been reflected in attempts to limit expenditure, but many times such efforts have also provoked a new round of evasion. Generally, enforcement has been partial or inadequate.

Paltiel was less than optimistic about the overall impacts of efforts to control public financing. He contended that these measures have tended to advantage established parties and incumbents. They have too often fostered professional paid staff and led to a reliance on specialized expertise in campaigning that has eroded the role of traditional, often amateur, activists. Furthermore, central party organs have assumed an increased control over party affairs. The total package of negative effects was in his view, "to stabilize the party system and entrench the electoral position of established groups. The result has been the crystallization of external as well as internal party relationships, growing rigidity in the party system, and lessened responsiveness to emerging social groups and changed political demands. The consequence may very well be the very alienation from the virtues of the electoral process that the reforms purportedly were designed to avoid" (Paltiel 1981, 170). In light of the past decade this judgement seems too harsh. The bias in favour of established élites is hardly new. Signs of de-alignment and voter volatility in many systems cast doubt on any systematic shift toward stability due to public funding arrangements. The 1980s success of the Greens in Germany, and of "new politics" movements elsewhere, is testimony to the limited capacity of any such measures to change decisively, by themselves, the dynamics of party competition.

PARTIES AND PARTY GOVERNMENT: THE GERMAN CASE

The Federal Republic of Germany provides a particularly useful case for comparison precisely because its parliamentary system rests on the practice of strong party government but does not depend on other traits usually associated with the Westminster model. In addition, compared to many multi-party parliamentary systems, party government in the Federal Republic over the past forty years has reached a high degree of electoral decisiveness (Strom 1990, 70). Voters generally have a clear choice between two alternative governing majorities, each represented by a chancellor-candidate. Nevertheless, coalitional governments remain the norm, with one minor party (in particular the FDP) playing a pivotal role. These conditions provide good reason for viewing Germany as occupying a middle ground between classic competitive party politics, typical of Anglo-American systems, and coalitional power-sharing, typical of continental democracies.

Postwar German politics has also generated special comparative interest due to the constitutional recognition it provides for the role and character of political parties. As well, there exists since 1967 an elaborate Party Law that both implements such constitutional provisions and provides for a generous system of public funding (as discussed in the preceding section). These circumstances are conducive to making the German system one of strong party organizations operating within a governing system characterized by high party centrality and control – but without the drawback of non-alternation in power that is symptomatic of hegemonic party-rule systems.

The Institutional Contexts of German Parties

The polarized, ideological partisanship that characterized much of the Weimar years, 1919–33 (as was also true for the interwar years in Austria and Third Republic France), has often been seen as a major factor in the demise of parliamentary democracy. In sharp contrast to this era, political parties in the postwar Federal Republic were "constitutionalized," which helped to ensure the legitimacy of the democratic rules of the game (Johnson 1982, 155). The German Basic Law ascribes to parties a constitutional status and sets conditions for their organization. The intent of Article 21 was to avoid the earlier institutional flaws that had permitted the rise of anti-democratic extremism and led to the downfall of the Weimar Republic. This article is probably best known for the requirement that parties maintain internal democratic procedures and the provision for the prohibition of anti-democratic parties, which led to the outlawing of both the neo-Nazi Sozialistische Reichspartei (SRP) and the communist Kommunistische Partei Deutschlands (KPD) in the 1950s. Perhaps more important are the positive functions that Article 21 assigns to parties, especially the participatory role in forming the political will of the people.

The Electoral System

Another institutional framework essential for understanding German political parties is the Electoral Law. This unique and innovative solution to the problem of representation is often called personalized proportionality. One half of the Bundestag members is chosen on a plurality basis within single-member districts. The other half is selected according to the shares of the popular vote won by each party. This procedure is not a mixed system, since the outcome is directly proportional and based on the second, party-list ballot. Furthermore, there is the important proviso that, in order to benefit from this proportional allocation of seats, a party must win 5 percent of the national vote or win a minimum of three plurality seats. This rule has effectively blocked fringe parties from winning parliamentary seats without destroying the essence of proportional representation.

For the voting public, this system is relatively complex. Each voter may vote twice; on the first ballot one votes for a constituency candidate, on the second for a party list. Survey evidence over the years has shown that many German voters do not understand the implications of the two-ballot procedure. For example, a 1983 *Infas* poll four weeks prior to the vote indicated that only 40 percent of respondents identified the second ballot as the more important. As election day nears, popular comprehension increases substantially. Nevertheless, there seems little doubt that many citizens remain ignorant of the meaning of the balloting system.

The two-ballot procedure also allows for the "loaning" of votes. Smaller parties, like the FDP and the Greens, must worry about the dangers posed by the 5 percent rule. It is often the case that in order to protect a minor coalition partner, supporters of a major party may vote for the minor party on the second ballot. Such ticket-splitting is widespread and has important consequences for the shape of the party system (Conradt 1989, 117–22).

Party and State Bureaucracy

Beyond these institutional features, the relationship between party and state bureaucracy provides vital clues to the character of German parties. West Germany has often been referred to as a party-state (*Parteienstaat*), a term which describes the overall pattern of mutual penetration and the symbiotic relationship existing between parties and state bureaucracy. The concept originated with Gerhard Leibholz, a constitutional theorist and long-time justice of the Federal Constitutional Court. According to Dyson, "*Parteienstaat* refers to the presence of partisans in the key offices of the state apparatus, a presence which is legitimated by the idea that parties must occupy the commanding heights of public authority if the democratic character of rule is to be safeguarded" (1982, 90). This suggests a very broad definition of the role of parties, which goes far beyond the assumptions of Anglo-American traditions.

In the Weimar Republic, *Parteienstaat* "was primarily a pejorative term which offered an explanation of political crisis" (Dyson 1982, 78; 1977). With the destruction of the Third Reich and military occupation, however, there existed a power vacuum to be filled. Political parties, untainted by the Nazi regime, because they had been abolished, were in a position to fill a need in the process of political reconstruction. The occupation authorities re-established parties under licence in order to recruit a new democratic leadership. Party affiliation became a test of loyalty to the new state and a safeguard against the return of ex-Nazi élites. The claim to be nonpartisan or independent was often perceived as a sign of a lack of commitment to democratic principles. Therefore, party patronage took on an unusual democratic legitimacy. It also became obvious that there were immediate material incentives to be had from belonging to a party. For the first time in German history, parties were accorded an unchallenged primacy in the governmental process and became pre-eminent in postwar political reconstruction. This party role as defenders of democracy was soon entrenched in Article 21 of the Basic Law.

In addition, party loyalty is a factor in bureaucratic career advancement, not only at the highest levels of state secretary (deputy minister) and *Ministerialdirigent* (division head), where positions are explicitly designated as political, but also throughout regional and local officialdom. There appears to be some incentive for bureaucrats to establish a partisan connection. B. Steinkemper found in his 1974 study that over 50 percent of senior officials were party members and that career advancement was faster for party members than for nonparty members. The majority of civil servants have partisan affiliations, but this does not mean that the system works on pure patronage. While the merit principle remains primordial, when choosing between qualified candidates, party affiliation can be decisive. This leads to an extensive politicization of the bureaucracy and of other public sector institutions such as broadcasting and education. Derlien has documented the high incidence of political turnover within the higher civil service following each of the two postwar transfers of power between the two major parties, in 1969 and 1982. The practices of "temporary retirement" and lateral reshuffling of positions permit new governments to replace a large share of incumbent civil servants. Derlien also notes that this transfer occurs fairly quickly, usually within six or nine months of the government taking office (1988, 58). The close relationship between party and civil service has meant that as parties have extended outward, "appointments to a huge penumbra of governmental and non-governmental organizations have a partisan colouring" (Paterson 1982, 106).

Much of the empirical research on this aspect of German politics has originated from the perspective of public administration and has naturally focused on the effects of partisan politicization on the public service. We are here also interested in the reverse effect: how bureaucratic involvement in parties may affect their character and functioning. Public servants are very active in party organizations at all levels and represent a disproportionate share of total party members; approximately one out of five party members has the status of *Beamte* (Pulzer 1982, 29), although there is considerable variation across the parties in this regard. Civil servants represent a high proportion of party members and an even higher proportion of elected officials.

Certainly, bureaucrats can be seen as a source of expertise for party management, especially at the local level. Paterson observes that "administrative expertise carries a great deal of influence in the councils of all the main parties" (1982, 104). At the level of ministers there is also a strong emphasis on expertise. The rate of turnover compared to Britain or Canada is low. Generalist ministers, i.e., those who serve in multiple portfolios, are rare, although a number of important exceptions to this can be found (e.g., Helmut Schmidt, Hans Apel, Gerhard Stoltenberg, Friedrich Zimmermann, Wolfgang Schäuble, Hans-Dietrich Genscher).

The German public service enjoys prominence and prestige. It comprises not only bureaucrats but a number of other professions, including professors and teachers. Hence it is a more inclusive category than is the case in Canada or in many other Western systems. Even more relevant to this research is the fact that there is extensive interpenetration of party and state bureaucracy, operating in both directions. Civil servants (*Beamten*) have extensive political rights, which they exercise freely and frequently. There are no barriers to seeking a legislative mandate. The Bundestag and legislatures at provincial and local levels always include many members who are career civil servants. Once their legislative tenure ends, such bureaucrats may return to their administrative jobs without penalty. There is, in short, no incompatibility in the two careers.

The Organizational Character of Individual Parties

The Christian Democrats

The CDU and CSU emerged after the war as essentially new entities. The organizational character of the Union parties was at the outset uncertain. Parties were first licensed at the local and regional levels, so that the CDU started off as a loose confederal organization made up of autonomous organizations dominated by regional notables. In its formative years, the CDU lacked a cohesive organization and had little policy-making capacity. Because Konrad Adenauer assumed power at the birth of the Federal Republic, chancellorship preceded party leadership. Similarly, the imperatives of governing preceded a national party organization. Chancellor Adenauer's party quickly became an electoral machine (*Kanzlerwahlverein*) dedicated to supporting him and his government. This resulted in a weak party apparatus. Its organizational pattern crystallized within a decentralized and underdeveloped mould. It remained atrophied during the twenty years of CDU/CSU governance, but its electoral success made this condition tenable. As long as the Christian Democrats governed, they could maintain their role as a state-party, without any revamping of an old-fashioned cadre party style based on the combined power of regional notables and the chancellorship in Bonn (Schönbohm 1985, 31–48). Correspondingly, during these years membership stagnated. At the same time, the CDU/CSU succeeded in becoming Germany's first true catch-all party electorally.

It was the shock of opposition, beginning in 1969, that provoked the first serious consideration of organizational reform for the CDU. (The CSU had undergone its own shock of opposition in the 1950s and had modernized its apparatus well ahead of the CDU.) Substantial renewal started in earnest only after another defeat in 1972 and a change in the top leadership. The 1970s corresponded to a period of rapid modernization for the CDU. As part of this process power began to shift from the party organizations of the Länder to the national headquarters. From a weak confederation, the CDU developed a strong federal structure with the centre increasingly able to set priorities and design strategies. Over the decade of the 1970s, one observes a phenomenal explosion in membership from about 300 000 in 1969 to almost 700 000 in 1980 (not including the CSU). This change also meant an increase in previously underrepresented groups – women, youth and Protestants. By the 1980s the membership was distinctly more modern, i.e., more representative of the population as a whole.

An important part of the CDU's organizational depth depends on its network of affiliated associations. By party statute, the party has a set of associations (*Vereinigungen*) with official links and overlapping memberships. These include, for example, a youth organization, a women's association, employees' groups, a small business association, a local government association and an organization representing refugees and expellees. Such affiliated associations provide bonds to key support groups and are carefully integrated into the party by the proportional sharing of offices and the allocation of candidate positions on the all-important party lists. The delicate balance of various client groupings in internal party representation gives to the CDU a consensus-building style that reinforces its programmatic fluidity and its catch-all electoral strategy (Chandler 1989, 302–306; Haungs 1983, 51–64; Schönbohm 1985, 219–29).

Finally, we should note that organizational strength and depth is far from uniform across the country. The CDU/CSU is organizationally powerful in the two southern Länder, but often considerably weaker elsewhere. Even in North–Rhine Westphalia which accounts for one-third of all CDU members, the party in organizational terms is not strong, in part because it has not been able to dominate local governments and control patronage. Of course, intraparty distinctiveness is likely to be accentuated by German unification.

The Social Democrats

The SPD, Europe's oldest social democracy, has often been taken as the classic example of a mass party of integration. For much of its early history, up to its banning by the Nazis in 1933, the model of a "solidarity community" remained essentially valid. The SPD established deep social roots among skilled workers and their unions. In a politically hostile environment, the party's complex organizational network performed a defensive/protective function (Lösche 1990, 46–47).

After the war, the SPD was re-established, but in fact the party could not be cloned exactly from its pre-1933 existence. The traumas of war, including massive population shifts, meant that the organizational networks of the solidarity community could never be fully restored. Furthermore, economic reconstruction and recovery led to a shift in class structure, which for the party would mean a steady increase in new middle class members.

Such trends, combined with the electoral stagnation of the SPD in the 1950s, led to programmatic reform (in the 1959 Godesberg Program) and organizational reform (in the 1958 Stuttgart party congress). These changes confirmed the fact that the mass integration party was a thing of the past and that in adopting a catch-all electoral strategy, the SPD was irreversibly on the road to becoming a modern *Volkspartei* (Paterson 1986, 128–29).

The late 1960s and the 1970s were years of rapid internal change. They did not produce an increase in total membership on the scale that occurred in the CDU at about this time, but they did change fundamentally the internal composition of the party. The influx of youth associated with the popularity of Willy Brandt was particularly remarkable. The education explosion also contributed to a better educated and younger membership. The increasing weight of "new middle class" activists and leaders corresponded to a steady decline in the blue collar core and produced an enduring tension between the old and the new conceptions of what the SPD should be. In the early 80s, Helmut Schmidt's policy directions and leadership style provoked intense and bitter struggles within the party. Since then there have been continuing tensions in which trade union–based traditionalists have been at odds with a "new politics"–inspired younger generation of activists. At stake in this struggle has been the question of the transformation of the SPD itself. The old labels of right and left seem of little use in understanding these tensions (Paterson 1986, 129–30; Braunthal 1983, 37–60).

Lösche has convincingly shown that today's SPD is far from the traditional "milieu" party model. The cohesion of the past has been displaced by a fluid pluralism. Dispersion rather than centralization of power is now the norm. The central party headquarters in Bonn is primarily oriented toward parliamentary and governmental concerns. It does not control the rest of the party, and its functions appear to be primarily those of a service/communications centre.

Generally, the party organization is no longer responsible for national elections. Campaigns are largely handled by the chancellor-candidate and managed by professional strategists and media specialists. Electorally the SPD is a very broad coalition of diverse interests. Especially since the rise of the Greens, holding this intraparty coalition together has become one of the party's most compelling tasks.

Like the CDU, there is considerable variation in organizational strength regionally, which makes the SPD something of a patchwork (Lösche 1990, 56). For example, the SPD is organizationally very strong in North–Rhine Westphalia, Hamburg and Bremen but decrepit in Baden–Württemberg and Bavaria. Generally the grassroots organizations are active. They are typically concerned with local issues and usually are financially self-sufficient through dues and small contributions.

The Free Democrats

The FDP stands out as distinctive from the two larger parties, for it does not fit the model of a modern catch-all/*Volkspartei*, either in electoral base or organizational depth. The crucial aspect of this party is that its organization reflects the fact that it is above all a party in and of government. Through patronage the FDP has the leverage to attract members primarily for reasons of career advancement. Thus many join for personal reasons, not out of ideological or social solidarity. This means that members are not particularly interested in the workings of the party. It is this fact rather than the absolute number of members which accounts for the FDP's "organizational anemia" (Søe 1989, 329). In some respects the FDP looks like a traditional cadre-type party with a strong élite presence but weak grass roots. Its membership is well educated and well-off, with a high proportion of self-employed professionals. It is best seen as a modern version of the party of notables. Finally, one should note that in socio-economic terms the memberships of the FDP and the Greens are remarkably similar. Both are urban, well educated and secular. The difference is that while the typical FDP member is career-oriented and has opted in to the system, the typical Green is more likely to have opted out (Schiller 1990).

Common Features and Trends in the Major Parties

Traditionally, the linkage of the mass public to political élites was advanced through the organizational networks of parties. As once solid loyalties have loosened and as parties have had to adapt to new media technology, the impact of social networks appears to have declined. In particular, television has provided the primary alternative linkage between citizens and leaders. Related to this trend are the effects of public finance that allow parties a source of support other than membership. This public payment may distance them from their own members and from the citizenry.

The trend toward professionalism and expertise in party organization has altered the significance of mass membership. Total membership figures are of decreasing significance. Although the modern *Volkspartei* typically does have a substantial membership base, the modern party organization no longer relies on this base to the same extent as did its predecessors, the traditional mass or milieu parties. Certainly since the 1980s, the evolution of party organization is seen in the professionalization of much party work, especially election campaigns and fund-raising, through a reliance on modern techniques of donor-lists and direct mailing. Effective internal communications systems and use of the electronic media to mobilize support have emerged as basic to modern party activity. All these trends have been facilitated by public funding.

Both major German parties have evolved from traditional forms (a party of mass integration in the case of the SPD and a party of notables in the case of the CDU) to become modern *Volksparteien* (Smith 1982; Kirchheimer 1966). This concept involves more than a catch-all electoral strategy. It also has meant a transformation away from ideological orthodoxies and away from defensive protection of a socio-economic or cultural milieu. Yet they have retained certain legacies, including well-developed organizational patterns and distinctive core support groups. This has meant that the converging trend in party development has not produced two identical pure types of the *Volkspartei* phenomenon. In fact, each is a complex organizational mix.

The permanence of organizations represents a feature common to both parties. Party staffs consist of career employees who are stable and bureaucratized. Unlike Canadian and American party personnel, staff is not hired just for a few months, i.e., for the intense period of campaign activity. In Germany party employees become, in effect, professionals and for this reason take on similarities to civil servants. Party organizations are correspondingly not skeletal; they have a physical presence that makes them look rather like private sector corporations or public sector agencies.

In terms of competence within parties, it is useful to distinguish between parliamentarians and members of the party apparatus. In the German case, there is no evidence of any trend toward greater expertise among elected officials. Indeed, the bottom-up emphasis in candidate selection to party lists has often meant that local candidates can win out over nonlocal experts. Where nonelected expertise is concerned, however, governing parties can call upon networks of expertise within the ministries (in which the top positions are designated as political appointments). All parliamentary parties also hire their own professional staffs, and within the party apparatus (e.g., the CDU Adenauer-Haus and the SPD Ollenhauer-Haus) there is considerable career expertise available. In addition, but less importantly, there are the party foundations with their own substantial staffs and resources. For all these professional channels, there is an ongoing process of recruitment from the universities and public service.

In both major parties professionalism and flexibility have been enhanced over the past four decades. Both have evolved structurally in the direction of internal pluralism with broad membership bases. The prevailing style is integrative yet flexible. This transition to a modern organizational form has been easier for the CDU/CSU. For the Social Democrats, the change has been arduous and has generated considerable internal strife. Although the SPD may be said to possess most of the attributes of a strong organization, its own bureaucratic tradition combined with ideological divisions has severely constrained the party's transition to becoming a flexible and professionalized party. As was hypothesized above, parties such as the SPD, which built a mass membership based on deep social roots and an organizational density with bureaucratic structure, may have become organizationally frozen. In the face of socio-economic modernization, such parties become weighted down by what previously made them strong (mass membership, ideological solidarity, client groups). This makes for a difficult and painfully slow transition toward a professionalized, modern *Volkspartei*.

For the CDU similar internal conflicts between modernists and traditionalists are also to be found, but rarely have they divided the party so fundamentally as has been the case for the SPD. The Bavarian CSU has achieved a remarkable coexistence of traditional conservative ideology with a cohesive modern party organization that is deeply entrenched at the grass roots. Since the death of Franz Josef Strauss in 1988, however, there is growing doubt that the CSU will be able to hold on to its effective monopoly of power in Bavaria.

Although we see mixed forms of organization emerging (Mintzel 1989; Katz and Mair 1990), the modern *Volkspartei* should not be thought of as a simple blend of the traditional mass and cadre models. The two major German parties are among the best examples of this trend, but they are hardly pure types. Each has maintained its own distinctiveness. They are, in short, organizational mixes that do not correspond perfectly to any pure form of ideal-type catch-all or *Volkspartei* model.

Both German parties have sought both formally and informally to assure the representation of diverse core support groups under the principle of proportionality (*Proporz*). This is most prominent within the CDU where there is a careful balancing in the selection of candidate lists. Internally this gives to the Christian Democrats a quasi-corporatist pattern of social integration and representation reflected in the formalized status of certain auxiliary or affiliated groups. In the SPD, this sharing of representation, especially in the composition of candidate lists, is primarily regional in character. Proportionality also spills over into governmental and parliamentary practice where there is great concern for broad coalitions of support and interparty cooperation.

Related to this tendency is the fact that both *Volksparteien* also have a number of affiliated groups (*Vereinigungen* for the CDU, *Arbeitsgemeinschaften* in the SPD and CSU) integrated into the party structure. The FDP has a corresponding group for youth, but it lacks a strong grassroots basis or social network.

Other traditional cadre parties have also moved toward professionalism in organization but without the baggage of a mass organization. The U.S. Republicans are often cited for their innovations in building a professional party, sustained by donor lists and an effective communications network. This model has recently been imitated by the Progressive Conservatives in Canada.

Party Foundations *(Stiftungen)*

The German party foundations have provoked considerable curiosity among outside observers. It is therefore useful to comment on their status and role.

The foundations were given new political importance in the wake of the Federal Constitutional Court's 1966 ruling that parties could not be subsidized for "political education" but that they could be reimbursed for campaign expenses. The Party Law of 1967 did not provide for the establishment of foundations, but the already existing budgetary allocations for political education provided an occasion for (until then) letterhead organizations to flourish with public funding in the areas of political education, international aid and research. With the support of the parties represented in the Bundestag, the foundations started to establish themselves during the Grand Coalition years in the late 1960s. Since then, with generous funding increases, they have flourished to become extensive operations. Interparty agreements have allocated ministry funds proportionally based on vote shares in the preceding election.

The autonomy of the foundations is protected by a separate system of funding. They coexist alongside the parties; they are party-friendly, but not part of formal party organization. Just as it is erroneous to think that they are creatures of parties, it is also misleading to assume that their autonomy is complete. Through political education, training and research activities, foundations can lend indirect but significant support to parties. From time to time foundations, using public funds, may also conduct publicity campaigns in support of specific policy goals. In practical terms foundations have reinforced parties by providing a substantial corps of expertise. They provide a speakers' bureau and offer an opportunity for retired politicians to play an active role. The bonds between party and foundation are reflected in leadership positions. For both the SPD-related Ebert-Stiftung and the CDU's Adenauer-Stiftung, the current chairs are former provincial premiers (Holger Börner and Bernhard Vogel, respectively). It is also important to note, however, that the greatest share of foundation spending goes to international projects and to research programs that do not provide any direct help to political party activities.

In the 1980s the Greens challenged the constitutionality of party foundations on the grounds that the funding of foundations was an unfair way of financing parties through the back door. The Federal Constitutional Court in 1986 upheld the organization and functions of the foundations. Thereafter the Greens decided that they, too, would establish their own foundation. To accommodate the uneasy ideological/factional tendencies within the diverse Green movement, three foundations were set up: one for the ecologists, one for the feminists, and one for the left-wing. All three operate under a single umbrella foundation (the *Stiftungsverband Regenbogen*) which is the recipient of all public funding.

The organizational structure of the CDU and FDP foundations is regionalized, with separate provincial organizations often having their own names. The structure of the SPD-related foundation is more centralized. The CSU-friendly Hanns-Seidel-Stiftung is limited to Bavaria, although it, too, receives federal funds.

CONCLUSIONS

Our panoramic investigation of alternative forms of party government and party organization in "comparable" parliamentary systems has up to this point reserved the question of the applicability to Canada. Nevertheless, the practice of party government elsewhere does have substantial relevance for the dilemmas confronting Canadian politics. At the same time it is necessary to recognize that if Canadian parties are to be strengthened, this must occur within the context of the Westminster parliamentary tradition. Our working assumption has been that any revisions or additions to existing laws governing the role of parties should reinforce rather than impair that governing model.

Given the goal of maximizing strong party government, the question may be asked: what strengthens or weakens it? Recommendations may take the form both of hazards to be avoided and reforms to be implemented. Before commenting on possible areas of change, it is essential to recall some basic comparative perspectives that must shape such considerations.

Problems of Comparison

It is always tempting to idealize other systems and believe that they are problem-free, but where parties are concerned, this would be risky to say the least. In all modern democracies, the public's perception of parties and political leadership mixes loyalty/support with significant degrees of cynicism/distrust. Disenchantment with parties in a number of European states has fostered de-alignment and has facilitated the rise of protest movements. In Germany, for example, parties have frequently been accused of being oligarchic, unresponsive and, consequently, unable to deal with new issues. The 1980s emergence of the Greens as an "anti-party" party provided evidence that substantial numbers of voters had come to believe that the established parties were out of touch with citizen concerns. Such criticism, however, has not led to a diminution in the centrality of political parties for the governing process. Parties retain their pre-eminence, and German parliamentary institutions enjoy diffuse public support. Part of the reason for this is to be found in the organizational capacities of parties.

We have also stressed in our analysis that variation between strong and weak party structures is very much linked to national traditions and institutional constraints. These conditions cannot be replicated easily. Parties themselves often have social roots deeply embedded within a political culture. They are therefore normally very resistant to restructuring even within their own environment. Undoubtedly there are basic differences between the Westminster/Commonwealth and continental traditions of parliamentary governance, which are not subject to revision. Any suggestion that the continental European models of party management are likely to find easy acceptance in Canada must be discounted at the outset. Even if the transplanting of institutions, including parties, may encounter difficulties analogous to those of an organ transplant, many of the organizational principles found elsewhere may be adaptable to different institutional or cultural contexts. In this respect, there are important lessons available from comparative evidence that might facilitate a renewal of political parties in Canada.

In comparing Canadian and German parties specifically, it is essential to recognize that within German parliamentary democracy we find a different approach, or governing style, to the task of conflict resolution. A system of complex and stable policy networks fosters consultation and collaboration within and among parliamentarians, parties, interest groups and ministries. This generates a fundamentally integrative dynamic in both the policy process and intergovernmental relations. Importantly, German parties reinforce this dynamic by virtue of their organizational depth and permanence. By contrast, the governing style in Canada is at base confrontational. This trait is solidly entrenched within the government-versus-opposition model of political discourse. Such an adversarial starting point allows neither opportunity nor incentive for interparty collaboration. Outside the parliamentary arena, a similar pattern is often evident in Canadian intergovernmental relations.

Hazards for Party Government

Before turning to specific recommendations for enhancing party government in Canada, it is first useful to comment briefly on some general conditions that may inhibit this form of governance. These imply recommendations for avoidance rather than new policies. It is important to note that these concerns could apply to any parliamentary democracy, not only to Canada.

Negative factors include most generally all those institutions and practices that serve to block or diminish party government, i.e., conditions that may weaken and impede the functioning of parties:

1. Party government versus interest group power. The influence of private interest lobbying in the policy process represents the most pervasive source of competing influence that is capable of pre-empting the role of parties. In the extreme case lobbying or other modes of private influence can endanger the principles of representation and accountability that are the cornerstones of party government. Interest group politics emphasizes private goals rather than the more encompassing, collective priorities. Parties, as the primary aggregators of the public will, normally are better able to articulate such public interest goals. To the extent that parties lack the capacity to engage in systematic policy formulation, however, private interest organizations find an opportunity to enlarge their role in the policy process. To the degree that there exists a fundamental incompatibility that challenges the role of parties and the workability of party government, institutional safeguards against the excesses of lobbying inside parties and within the parliamentary process are both desirable and necessary. A strengthening of party structure to incorporate a greater policy competence constitutes a significant limit on the power of lobbies.

2. Conditions that allow personality factors to dominate the role of parties. Some regime forms normally encourage structures and practices in which political organizations are built around personality rather than program. Weak party organizations are a natural by-product of such regimes. Certain institutional options (especially presidential systems, winner-take-all electoral competition and the power of referendum) may enhance this tendency.

In this regard the German case may be seen as a balanced system that permits effective leadership compatible with strong party government. For example, the chancellor can be seen as primarily a party leader, not a first minister above party. (Historically it is true that Konrad Adenauer used his party as a chancellor-support organization, but this occurred during a formative period when parties were yet to emerge as modern, effective organizations.) In general the primacy of parties has been fully institutionalized in the postwar Federal Republic and has effectively constrained potentially strong personalities.

3. There is some danger to strong party government to be found in extreme forms of candidate orientation fostered by the structure of competition and by party finance laws. Continental systems typically stress party over individual candidates, while Anglo-American parties give greater weight to candidates, a tendency taken to an extreme in the U.S. where candidates often pre-empt party. In Canada, too, candidates are quite visible and are the object of considerable financing support, within the context of a single-member district, plurality electoral system.

Of course, if the single-member district, plurality electoral system is not to be altered, a considerable degree of candidate focus in party politics must be accepted as normal. Nevertheless, a balance must be struck between the role of individual candidates and constituency representatives and the broader collective representative role of parties.

4. Institutions that by-pass parties include various forms of direct democracy, especially referenda, primary elections and recall laws. Most forms of direct democracy are pernicious to party government and should be avoided where possible. Of course, measures to enhance citizen participation and a sense of involvement in the electoral process must be encouraged.

Proposals for Reform

Beyond such pitfalls, there exists a variety of positive initiatives that can enhance the role of parties and thereby encourage the workability of parliamentary party government. These include:

1. Enhancement of the organizational strength of parties within the boundaries of constitutional and customary practice. Effective parties reinforce the basic mechanisms of the democratic process and maximize representation and accountability. Of course, for party government to work well there must always be the possibility that the voters can vote one majority out of power and choose another. This requires that there be an opposition available playing the role of "shadow government." This in turn requires a competitive party system in which voters perceive that a viable choice exists. The failure to achieve this condition is manifest in one-party dominant regimes such as Japan and, with some qualifications, Sweden and Italy.

The difficulty in Canada is that party organizations are fundamentally skeletal but must perform within a parliamentary system of party government. They lack the organizational depth that is a source of professionalism and expertise in the policy process and that encourages stable patterns of policy cooperation across party lines or among party officials, bureaucrats and interest groups. Canadian parties remain essentially oriented to electoral competition; they have little or no organizational capacity to engage on a regular basis and over the long haul as stable participants in the policy process.

Therefore it is essential to identify reforms that could enhance the role and capacity of parties without endangering the model of Westminster governance that is at the heart of Canadian politics. Our analysis of German party management suggests that the presence of expertise and professionalism is conducive to the roles of parties in political representation and conflict resolution. Canadian parties could perform better if they had this capacity. Some version of the party foundation model would provide one means of achieving this.

2. Professional skills of governance should be integrated into party management on a regular basis. Canadian party activists are normally amateurs who have little or no experience in the workings of government. Nor do they have any direct interest in addressing intractable policy problems or long-term concerns. Winning elections should not be everything as far as party organization is concerned.

Political foundations could enhance the research capacity and the policy analysis components of party life. If the idea of party foundations is to be pursued, however, great care must be taken about how foundations are established. It is crucial that party foundations, once established, be able to pursue research and educational functions free of partisan control. That is, foundations should be seen as resources for enhancing the virtues of reflection and education, free from the pressures of electoral competition. Most importantly, they must be financially and legally autonomous from the parties to which they are linked. They must be party-friendly, but not party-dependent. Otherwise they will be in danger of becoming nothing more than another source of traditional patronage. Their policy, information and research functions must remain in the forefront.

3. Party financing. A first principle is that a suitable system of party financing must be compatible with the system of government in which it operates. It should ensure the basic aims of fairness, equality of opportunity and transparency. Party finance laws

should be comprehensive in the sense of providing a level playing field for party activity. Public funding, like related legal restrictions, provides a common base for all competing parties. The more inclusive and standardizing the system is, the greater will be the homogenizing effect on party structure because all parties tend to develop expertise and infrastructure commensurate with their financial resources. In addition, there should be a reasonable balance between public and private sources of funds. Multiple sources, fully disclosed, help to preclude undue influence for select interest groups or individuals and also help to guarantee the autonomy of parties. There should also be a balance in distribution and expenditure between central party organizations and constituency organizations or individual candidates.

Concluding Thoughts

On the basis of our comparative survey of party organizations and their institutional contexts, we have sought to explain how key organizational features, alone or together, allow parties to perform their democratic functions. Our investigation has been designed to develop a comparative vantage point as the basis for an informed reconsideration of management factors within parties.

This research study has addressed the nature of internal party organization comparatively with a view to suggesting how various national experiences might provide insights for understanding the role of parties in democratic systems. Its policy implications are therefore broadly applicable. In general, there appear to be significant aspects of party organization that could generate integrative effects within the larger political system. It is certainly plausible to argue that the functions of parties will be enhanced or diminished by their own structures and that performance of basic party functions will have significant ripple effects for the system in which parties operate. Of course, the problems of democratic government and national integration do not depend on party politics alone. Nevertheless, because parties are the primary mediators between the public and government, how they operate will have important systemic effects.

Parties are essential to harnessing the major social and economic challenges facing the modern nation-state, but they must have the organizational capacity to do their job. For this reason party-building is a goal aimed at maximizing parliamentary democracy.

APPENDIX

CDA	Christen Democratisch Appèl (Netherlands)
CDU	Christlich-Demokratische Union (Germany)
CSU	Christlich-Soziale Union (Germany)
DC	Democrazia Cristiana (Italy)
DSP	Democratic Socialist Party (Japan)
FDP	Freie Demokratische Partei (Germany)
JCP	Japan Communist Party (Japan)
JSP	Japan Socialist Party (Japan)
KPD	Kommunistische Partei Deutschlands (Germany)
KVP	Katholieke Volkspartij (Netherlands)
LDP	Liberal Democratic Party (Japan)
ÖVP	Österreichische Volkspartei (Austria)
PCI	Partito Comunista Italiano (Italy)
PDS	Partito Democratica della Sinistra (Italy)
PLI	Partito Liberale Italiano (Italy)
PRI	Partito Republicano Italiano (Italy)
PS	Parti Socialiste (France)
PSDI	Partito Socialista Democratico Italiano (Italy)
PSI	Partito Socialista Italiano (Italy)
PSOE	Partido Socialista Obrero Español (Spain)
SAP	Sveriges Socialdemokratiska Arbetarepartiet (Sweden)
SPD	Sozialdemokratische Partei Deutschlands (Germany)
SPÖ	Sozialistische Partei Österreichs (Austria)
SRP	Sozialistische Reichspartei (Germany)

BIBLIOGRAPHY

Alexander, Herbert, ed. 1989. *Comparative Political Finance in the 1980s.* Cambridge: Cambridge University Press.

American Political Science Association. 1950. *Towards a More Responsible Two-Party System: A Report of the Committee on Political Parties.* Washington, DC: American Political Science Association.

Amyot, G. Grant. 1988. "Italy: The Long Twilight of the DC Regime." In *Parties and Party Systems in Liberal Democracies*, ed. Steven B. Wolinetz. London: Routledge.

Blais, André, and R.K. Carty. 1990. "Does Proportional Representation Foster Voter Turnout?" *European Journal of Political Research* 18:167–81.

Bogdanor, Vernon, ed. 1983. *Coalition Government in Western Europe.* London: Heinemann.

———. 1985. *Representatives of the People? Parliamentarians and Constituents in Western Democracies.* Aldershot: Gower.

Borner, Silvio, Aymo Brunetti, and Thomas Straubhaar. 1990. *Schweiz AG: Vom Sonderfall zum Sanierungsfall?* Zurich: Verlag Neue Zürcher Zeitung.

Braunthal, Gerard. 1983. *The West German Social Democrats, 1969–1982: Profile of a Party in Power.* Boulder: Westview.

Campbell, John Creighton. 1989. "Democracy and Bureaucracy in Japan." In *Democracy in Japan,* ed. Takeshi Ishida and Ellis S. Krauss. Pittsburgh: University of Pittsburgh Press.

Castles, Francis G., and Rudolf Wildenmann, eds. 1986. *Visions and Realities of Party Government.* Vol. 1 of *The Future of Party Government.* Berlin: de Gruyter.

Chandler, William M. 1989. "The Christian Democrats." In *The Federal Republic of Germany at Forty,* ed. Peter Merkl. New York: New York University Press.

Chaples, Ernest A. 1989. "Public Funding of Elections in Australia." In *Comparative Political Finance in the 1980s,* ed. Herbert Alexander. Cambridge: Cambridge University Press.

Conradt, David. 1989. *The German Polity.* 4th ed. New York: Longman.

Curtis, Gerald L. 1988. *The Japanese Way of Politics.* New York: Columbia University Press.

Daalder, Hans. 1966. "Parties, Élites, and Political Developments in Western Europe." In *Political Parties and Political Development,* ed. Joseph LaPalombara and Myron Weiner. Princeton: Princeton University Press.

Dahl, Robert A. 1966. "Patterns of Opposition." In *Political Opposition in Western Democracies,* ed. R.A. Dahl. New Haven: Yale University Press.

Derlien, Hans-Ulrich. 1988. "Repercussions of Government Change on the Career Civil Service in West Germany: The Cases of 1969 and 1982." *Governance* 1 (1): 50–78.

Dewachter, Wilfried. 1987. "Changes in a Particratie: The Belgian Party System from 1944 to 1986." In *Party Systems In Denmark, Austria, Switzerland, the Netherlands, and Belgium,* ed. Hans Daalder. London: Frances Pinter.

Döring, Herbert, and Gordon Smith, eds. 1982. *Party Government and Political Culture in Western Germany.* New York: St. Martin's.

Dogan, Mattei, and Dominique Pelassy. 1987. *Le Moloch en Europe: Étatisation et corporatisation*. Paris: Economica.

Duverger, Maurice. 1980. "A New Political System Model: Semi-presidential Government." *European Journal of Political Research* 8:165–87.

Dyson, Kenneth. 1977. *Party, State and Bureaucracy in Western Germany*. London: Sage Publications.

————. 1982. "Party Government and Party State." In *Party Government and Political Culture in Western Germany*, ed. Herbert Döring and Gordon Smith. New York: St. Martin's.

Fukui, Haruhiro, and Shigeko N. Fukai. 1990. "Informal Politics and One-Party Dominance in Japan." Paper presented at the annual meeting of the American Political Science Association. San Francisco.

Furlong, Paul. 1990. "Parliament in Italian Politics." *West European Politics* 13 (3): 52–67.

Gunlicks, A. 1989. "The Financing of German Political Parties." In *The Federal Republic of Germany at Forty*, ed. Peter Merkl. New York: New York University Press.

Hadenius, Stig. 1990. *Swedish Politics during the 20th Century*. 3d ed. Stockholm: Swedish Institute.

Harmel, Robert, and Lars Svåsand. 1989. "From Protest to Party: Progress on the Right in Denmark and Norway." Paper presented at the annual meeting of the American Political Science Association. Atlanta.

Haungs, Peter. 1983. "Die Christlich-Demokratische Union Deutschlands CDU und die Christlich Soziale Union in Bayern CSU." In *Christlichdemokratische und konservative Parteien in Westeuropa, I*, ed. H.-J. Veen. Paderborn: Schoningh.

————. 1990. "Die CDU: Krise einer modernisierten Volkspartei?" In *Parteien in der Bundesrepublik Deutschland*, ed. Hans-Georg Wehling. Stuttgart: Kohlhammer.

Heidenheimer, A.J. 1989. "Adenauer's Legacies: Party Finance and the Decline of Chancellor Democracy." In *The Federal Republic of Germany at Forty*, ed. Peter Merkl. New York: New York University Press.

Hrebenar, Ronald J. 1986a. "The Changing Postwar Party System." In *The Japanese Party System*, ed. R.J. Hrebenar. Boulder: Westview.

————. 1986b. "The Money Base of Japanese Politics." In *The Japanese Party System*, ed. R.J. Hrebenar. Boulder: Westview.

————, ed. 1986c. *The Japanese Party System*. Boulder: Westview.

Hübner, Emil, and H.-H. Rohlfs. 1987. *Jahrbuch der Bundesrepublik Deutschland*. Munich: DTV.

Ingle, Stephen. 1989. *The British Party System.* 2d ed. Oxford: Basil Blackwell.

Ishida, Takeshi, and Ellis S. Krauss, eds. 1989. *Democracy in Japan.* Pittsburgh: University of Pittsburgh Press.

Jesse, Eckhard. 1986. *Die Demokratie der Bundesrepublik Deutschland.* 7th ed. Berlin: Colloquium Verlag.

Johnson, Chalmers. 1987. "Political Institutions and Economic Performance: The Government–Business Relationship in Japan, South Korea, and Taiwan." In *The Political Economy of the New Asian Industrialism,* ed. Frederic C. Deyo. Ithaca: Cornell University Press.

Johnson, Nevil. 1982. "Parties and the Conditions of Leadership." In *Party Government and Political Culture in Western Germany,* ed. Herbert Döring and Gordon Smith. New York: St. Martin's.

Katz, Richard S. 1986. "Party Government: A Rationalistic Conception." In *Visions and Realities of Party Government.* Vol. 1 of *The Future of Party Government,* ed. Francis G. Castles and Rudolf Wildenmann. Berlin: de Gruyter.

———. 1987a. "Party Government and Its Alternatives." In *Party Governments: European and American Experiences.* Vol. 2 of *The Future of Party Government,* ed. R.S. Katz. Berlin: de Gruyter.

———, ed. 1987b. *Party Governments: European and American Experiences.* Vol. 2 of *The Future of Party Government.* Berlin: de Gruyter.

Katz, Richard S., and Peter Mair. 1990. "The Official Story: A Framework for the Comparative Study of Party Organization and Organizational Change." Paper presented at the annual meeting of the American Political Science Association. San Francisco.

Katzenstein, Peter J. 1984. *Corporatism and Change: Austria, Switzerland and the Politics of Industry.* Ithaca: Cornell University Press.

Kavanagh, Dennis. 1990. *British Politics: Continuities and Change.* 2d ed. Oxford: Oxford University Press.

King, Anthony. 1969. "Political Parties in Western Democracies: Some Sceptical Reflections." *Polity* 1:111–41.

Kirchheimer, Otto. 1966. "The Transformation of Western European Party Systems." In *Political Parties and Political Development,* ed. Joseph LaPalombara and Myron Weiner. Princeton: Princeton University Press.

Kishimoto, Koichi. 1988. *Politics in Modern Japan: Development and Organization.* 3d ed. Tokyo: Japan Echo.

Kitschelt, Herbert. 1990. "The Strategy and Performance of Socialist Parties in the 1980s: A Comparative Analysis." Paper presented at the conference of the Council of European Studies. Washington, DC.

Koh, B.C. 1989. *Japan's Administrative Élite*. Berkeley: University of California Press.

Lane, Jan-Erik, and Svante O. Ersson. 1987. *Politics and Society in Western Europe*. Beverly Hills: Sage Publications.

Laundy, Philip. 1989. *Parliaments in the Modern World*. Aldershot: Dartmouth.

Lavaux, Philippe. 1990. *Les grandes démocraties contemporaines*. Paris: Presses universitaires de France.

The Law on Political Parties. 1987. Bonn: Inter Nationes.

Lehner, Franz. 1989. *Vergleichende Regierungslehre Grundwissen Politik 4*. Opladen: Leske and Budrich.

Leonardi, Robert, and Douglas A. Wertman. 1989. *Italian Christian Democracy: The Politics of Dominance*. London: Macmillan.

Lijphart, Arend. 1984. *Democracies*. New Haven: Yale University Press.

Lijphart, Arend, and Markus M.L. Crepaz. 1991. "Corporatism and Consensus Democracy in Eighteen Countries: Conceptual and Empirical Linkages." *British Journal of Political Science* 21:235–46.

Lösche, Peter. 1986. "Über das Geld in der Politik." In *Parteien in der Krise*, ed. Christian Graf von Krockow and Peter Lösche. Munich: Beck.

———. 1990. "Organisationspolitischer Traditionalismus? Die SPD: vom Kampfverband zur Interessenkoalition." In *Parteien in der Bundesrepublik Deutschland*, ed. Hans-Georg Wehling. Stuttgart: Kohlhammer.

Maas, P.F. 1986. "Coalition Negotiations in the Dutch Multi-Party System." *Parliamentary Affairs* 39 (April): 214–29.

Mackie, Thomas T., and Richard Rose. 1982. *The International Almanac of Electoral History*. 2d ed. New York: Facts on File.

Merkl, Peter, ed. 1989. *The Federal Republic of Germany at Forty*. New York: New York University Press.

Mintzel, Alf. 1989. "Grossparteien im Parteienstaat der Bundesrepublik." *Aus Politik und Zeitgeschichte*, 10 March.

Mintzel, Alf, and Heinrich Oberreuter, eds. 1990. *Parteien in der Bundesrepublik Deutschland*. Bonn: Bundeszentrale für politische Bildung.

Nakamura, Akira. 1990. "The Transformation of the Japanese Policy-Making Process: The LDP Governance at the Crossroads." *Governance* 3 (2): 219–33.

Nassmacher, Hiltrud. 1990. "Die Parteien der Bundesrepublik im Umbau." In *Parteien in der Bundesrepublik Deutschland*, ed. Hans-Georg Wehling. Stuttgart: Kohlhammer.

Nassmacher, Karl-Heinz. 1982. "Parteifinanzierung in Kanada – ein Modell für Deutschland?" *Zeitschrift für Parlamentsfragen* 3/82: 338–59.

———. 1989a. "Parteienfinanzierung als verfassungspolitisches Problem."
Aus Politik und Zeitgeschichte 11/89: 27–38.

———. 1989b. "Structure and Impact of Public Subsidies to Political Parties
in Europe: The Examples of Austria, Italy, Sweden and West Germany."
In *Comparative Political Finance in the 1980s,* ed. Herbert Alexander.
Cambridge: Cambridge University Press.

———. 1990. "Parteifinanzierung im Wandel." In *Parteien in der Bundesrepublik Deutschland,* ed. Hans-Georg Wehling. Stuttgart: Kohlhammer.

Nester, William R. 1990. *The Foundation of Japanese Power: Continuities,
Changes, Challenges.* London: Macmillan.

Nick, Rainer, and Anton Pelinka. 1989. *Politische Landeskunde der Republik
Österreich* (Beiträge zur Zeitgeschichte 20). Berlin: Colloquium Verlag.

Nick, Rainer, and Hubert Sickinger. 1990. *Politisches Geld:
Parteienfinanzierung in Österreich.* Thaur: Kulturverlag.

Padgett, S., and T. Burkett. 1986. *Political Parties and Elections in West
Germany.* London: Hurst.

Palmer, Geoffrey. 1987. *Unbridled Power: An Interpretation of New Zealand's
Constitution and Government.* 2d ed. Auckland: Oxford University Press.

Paltiel, K.Z. 1981. "Campaign Finance: Contrasting Practices and Reforms."
In *Democracy at the Polls: A Comparative Study of Competitive National
Elections,* ed. David Butler, Howard Penniman, and Austin Ranney.
Washington, DC: American Enterprise Institute for Public Policy Research.

———. 1985. "The Control of Campaign Finance in Canada: A Summary
and Overview." In *Party Politics in Canada.* 5th ed., ed. Hugh Thorburn.
Scarborough: Prentice-Hall.

———. 1989. "Canadian Election Expense Legislation, 1963–85: As Critical
Appraisal or Was the Effort Worth It?" In *Comparative Political Finance
in the 1980s,* ed. Herbert Alexander. Cambridge: Cambridge University Press.

Panebianco, Angelo. 1988. *Political Parties: Organization and Power.*
Cambridge: Cambridge University Press.

Pasquino, Gianfranco. 1986. "The Impact of Institutions on Party
Government: Tentative Hypotheses." In *Visions and Realities of Party
Government.* Vol. 1 of *The Future of Party Government,* ed. Francis G.
Castles and Rudolf Wildenmann. Berlin: de Gruyter.

———. 1987. "Party Government in Italy: Achievements and Prospects."
In *Party Governments: European and American Experiences.* Vol. 2 of *The
Future of Party Government,* ed. R.S. Katz. Berlin: de Gruyter.

Paterson, William E. 1982. "Problems of Party Government in West
Germany – A British Perspective." In *Party Government and Political
Culture in Western Germany,* ed. Herbert Döring and Gordon Smith.
New York: St. Martin's.

————. 1986. "The German Social Democratic Party." In *The Future of Social Democracy*, ed. William E. Paterson and Alastair H. Thomas. Oxford: Clarendon Press.

Pelinka, Anton. 1985. "The Case of Austria: Neo-Corporatism and Social Partnership." In *Representatives of the People? Parliamentarians and Constituents in Western Democracies*, ed. Vernon Bogdanor. Aldershot: Gower.

Pempel, T.J. 1990a. "Conclusion: One-Party Dominance and the Creation of Regimes." In *Uncommon Democracies: The One-Party Dominant Regimes*, ed. T.J. Pempel. Ithaca: Cornell University Press.

————. 1990b. "Introduction." In *Uncommon Democracies: The One-Party Dominant Regimes*, ed. T.J. Pempel. Ithaca: Cornell University Press.

————, ed. 1990c. *Uncommon Democracies: The One-Party Dominant Regimes*. Ithaca: Cornell University Press.

Pinto-Duschinsky, Michael. 1990. "Funding of Political Parties Since 1945." In *UK Political Parties Since 1945*, ed. Anthony Seldon. London: Philip Allan.

Powell, G. Bingham, Jr. 1982. *Contemporary Democracies: Participation, Stability and Violence*. Cambridge: Harvard University Press.

————. 1990. "Holding Governments Accountable." Paper presented at the annual meeting of the American Political Science Association. San Francisco.

Pulzer, Peter. 1982. "Responsible Party Government in the German Political System." In *Party Government and Political Culture in Western Germany*, ed. Herbert Döring and Gordon Smith. New York: St. Martin's.

Pye, Lucian W. 1988. "The New Asian Capitalism: A Political Portrait." In *In Search of an East Asian Development Model*, ed. Peter L. Berger and Hsin-Huang Michael Hsiao. New Brunswick: Transaction Books.

Rose, Richard. 1974. *The Problem of Party Government*. London: Macmillan.

Rose, Richard, and Ian McAllister. 1990. *The Loyalties of Voters: A Lifetime Learning Model*. London: Sage Publications.

Rudzio, W. 1987. *Das politische System der Bundesrepublik Deutschland*. 2d ed. Opladen: Leske.

Sartori, Giovanni. 1976. *Parties and Party Systems: A Framework for Analysis*. Cambridge: Cambridge University Press.

Sato, Seizaburo, and Tetsuhisa Matsuzaki. 1984. "Policy Leadership by the Liberal Democrats." *Economic Eye* (December): 25–32.

Schiller, Theo. 1990. "Die FDP: Partei der wechselden Wechselwähler." In *Parteien in der Bundesrepublik Deutschland*, ed. Hans-Georg Wehling. Stuttgart: Kohlhammer.

Schmidt, Manfred G. 1985. "Allerweltsparteien in Westeuropa? Ein Beitrag zu Kirchheimers These vom Wandel des westeuropäischen Parteiensystems." *Leviathan* 13 (3): 376–97.

Schneider, Hans-Peter. 1989. "The New German System of Party Funding: The Presidential Committee Report of 1983 and Its Realization." In *Comparative Political Finance in the 1980s*, ed. Herbert Alexander. Cambridge: Cambridge University Press.

Schönbohm, Wulf. 1985. *Die CSU wird moderne Volkspartei*. Stuttgart: Klett-Cotta.

Seldon, Anthony, ed. 1990. *UK Political Parties Since 1945*. London: Philip Allan.

Sjöblum, Gunnar. 1987. "The Role of Political Parties in Denmark and Sweden." In *Party Governments: European and American Experiences*. Vol. 2 of *The Future of Party Government*, ed. R.S. Katz. Berlin: de Gruyter.

Smith, Gordon. 1982. "The German *Volkspartei* and the Career of the Catch-All Concept." In *Party Government and Political Culture in Western Germany*, ed. Herbert Döring and Gordon Smith. New York: St. Martin's.

———. 1986. *Democracy In Western Germany*. 3d ed. New York: Holmes and Meier.

———. 1989a. "Core Persistence: Change and the 'People's Party.' " *West European Politics* 12 (4): 157–68.

———. 1989b. *Politics in Western Europe*. 5th ed. New York: Holmes and Meier.

Søe, Christian. 1989. "Not without Us! The FDP's Survival, Position and Influence." In *The Federal Republic of Germany at Forty*, ed. Peter Merkl. New York: New York University Press.

Spotts, Frederic, and Theodor Wieser. 1986. *Italy: A Difficult Democracy*. Cambridge: Cambridge University Press.

Stanbury, W.T. 1986. "The Mother's Milk of Politics: Political Contributions to Federal Parties in Canada 1974–1984." *Canadian Journal of Political Science* 19:795–821.

———. 1989. "Financing Federal Political Parties in Canada, 1974–1986." In *Canadian Parties in Transition*, ed. Alain G. Gagnon and Brian Tanguay. Scarborough: Nelson Canada.

Steiner, Jürg. 1991. *European Democracies*. 2d ed. New York: Longman.

Steinkemper, B. 1974. *Klassische und Politische Bürokraten in der Ministerialverwaltung der Bundesrepublik Deutschland*. Cologne: Carl Haymanns.

Stockwin, J.A.A. 1989. "Political Parties and Political Opposition." In *Democracy in Japan*, ed. Takeshi Ishida and Ellis S. Krauss. Pittsburgh: University of Pittsburgh Press.

Strom, Kaare. 1990. *Minority Government and Majority Rule*. Cambridge: Cambridge University Press.

Sully, Melanie. 1990. *A Contemporary History of Austria*. London: Routledge.

Thorburn, Hugh, ed. 1985. *Party Politics in Canada*. 5th ed. Scarborough: Prentice-Hall.

van Loenen, Gerbert. 1990. "Weimar or Byzantium: Two Opposing Approaches to the Italian Party System." *European Journal of Political Research* 18:241–56.

van Wolferen, Karel. 1989. *The Enigma of Japanese Power: People and Politics in a Stateless Nation*. London: Macmillan.

Vis, Jan. 1983. "Coalition Government in a Constitutional Monarchy: The Dutch Experience." In *Coalition Government in Western Europe*, ed. Vernon Bogdanor. London: Heinemann.

Ware, Alan. 1987. *Citizens, Parties and the State: A Reappraisal*. Princeton: Princeton University Press.

Wehling, Hans-Georg, ed. 1990. *Parteien in der Bundesrepublik Deutschland*. Stuttgart: Kohlhammer.

Wewer, Göttrik, ed. 1990. *Parteifinanzierung und politischer Wettbewerb*. Opladen: Westdeutscher Verlag.

White, Graham. 1990. "The Legislature: Influence not Power." In *The Government and Politics of Ontario*. 4th ed., ed. Graham White. Scarborough: Nelson Canada.

5

THE STRUCTURES OF CANADIAN POLITICAL PARTIES
How They Operate

Réjean Pelletier
with the collaboration of
François Bundock and
Michel Sarra-Bournet

POLITICAL PARTIES ARE usually considered as being organizations that seek to gain power. More specifically, LaPalombara and Weiner (1966) chose four criteria that define modern political parties. According to them, a party is characterized by a comprehensive and enduring organization as well as by a desire to exercise power directly through the support of activists and voters.

Sartori (1976) put more emphasis on the electoral criterion and the organizational character of a political organization when he defined a party as being any officially labelled political group that takes part in elections and is capable of placing candidates in public office by means of elections, free or not. In short, political parties can be defined as organizations that bring together individuals seeking to act in common within a more or less structured framework, who strive for common objectives by exercising power with the support of voters and activists.

It is not our purpose here to undertake an exhaustive analysis of the various problems that such organizations face or to choose from the variety of theoretical models available in the study of political parties as organizations. Thus, the "rational model," which holds that organizations, including parties, are instruments for realizing or putting specific, well-identified objectives into practice, is usually contrasted with the "natural-system model," which posits that the official goals of an organization are in reality a mere façade, and the only goal uniting all the members of an organization is the survival of the organization itself (Etzioni 1960). In the case of volunteer associations and organizations, a theory of collective benefits or incentives was also opposed to a theory of selective benefits. Most often, both these models should be taken into account when studying a single organization. Solidarity-producing or ideological incentives could then be considered as benefits distributed equally among all participants, and other incentives or benefits as more selective in nature, profiting only some.

A third problem, which will not be addressed in this study, is that of whether a party adapts to or dominates its environment. The systems analysis literature of the 1960s defined parties as intermediaries between voters and rulers of the government apparatus. As mediating agents, they were responsible for transmitting the public's demands and requirements to political authorities after filtering and consolidating them. This concept produced a theory that became standard in the study of parties: the "brokerage theory," in which the party is an intermediary and representative, an instrument of consensus that seeks to rally and satisfy the most diverse interests of society. Applied to Canada, this theory made it possible to measure the extent and effectiveness of national parties' ability to accommodate the range of opinions and interests that are expressed in the country. Parties' success or failure was measured by their electoral support at the national level and, more particularly, at the regional level. This led to the conclusion that for a quarter of a century our national parties failed as agents of consolidation and instruments of consensus: they became regionalized political forces rather than true national parties (Clarke et al. 1984).

Elsewhere, we put forward an argument that in part runs counter to this theory, which is widely held in Canada (Pelletier 1989). Our argument was that Canadian political parties do not seek solely to meet citizens' demands and claims and cannot be seen as primarily dependent on the economic and social forces that dominate society. We defined parties, especially governing parties, as tools in the hands of their officers and in particular of their leaders, their purpose being to formulate and carry out policies that shape society in accordance with their beliefs. In this sense, parties enjoy a real autonomy that enables their officers to respond to and integrate the most contradictory pressures from individuals and groups as they see fit, as well as integrate the internal and external influences that weigh on them. In this sense, party officers do not seek only to conciliate diverse interests: they are also developing and imposing on their parties political orientations that influence society as a whole, especially when the party is in power.

The purpose of this study is not to test the truth of the doctrine of the party as an intermediary, as the brokerage theory suggests, or of the doctrines of party autonomy and of party officers' influence. Our intent is to analyse how the structures of Canadian political parties operate.

A recent study by Panebianco (1988) dealt primarily with what he calls organizational power, explaining the operation and activities of organizations in terms of alliances and the struggle for power among the various players. The key to understanding the operation of an organization, he added, lies in the dynamics of the struggle for power within the organization. Such a study may be interesting, but would lead us down a path that is different from the one we will be exploring here.

First and foremost, the problems of relationships between the various echelons of a political party and the powers that each may hold are at the very heart of our research. More specifically, from the formal structures defined by the constitutions of the three major Canadian political parties, we will study the actual operation of various levels of authority within each party. In other words, what levels of authority – for instance, the party leader, members of Parliament and elected officers – are involved in developing each party's characteristic policies, internal decision making and the conduct of election campaigns? In addition, given current financing methods, we will also consider their implications for party operations.

Our perspective is *how* the structures operating within a partisan organization work, rather than *what* the nature of the organization is: centralized or decentralized, an organization of party officers or a grassroots organization, or *why* people join the party, what its objectives and its program for action are. Clearly, answering the "how" will sometimes lead us to the problem of centralization or decentralization or to the idea of a party of officers or a grassroots party, but this will be implicit or deduced from preceding discussion and not from systematic study of centralization.

From this point of view, Wilson's classic work on political organizations (1973) is not immediately interesting to us. According to Wilson, the behaviour of people who occupy positions within organizations is determined mainly by the need to maintain and strengthen the organization. This in turn implies that people need tangible and intangible incentives to induce them to become or remain members of organizations and to carry out certain tasks. Beyond certain references to social and political structures, this theory is based primarily on Wilson's idea of incentives. This theory would produce a better answer to the question of why people join organizations or continue to work within them than to the question of how the structures operate.

Similarly, Gibson et al. (1983) sought to establish a relationship between electoral behaviour and partisan organizations. More specifically, they asked whether changes in party identification and the vote have an effect on conditions within a partisan organization. To determine these conditions, they developed a concept of a party's organizational strength based on both the organization's complexity (accessibility of the national office, division of labour, party budget, professionalization of positions) and its programmatic capabilities (institutional support and candidate-centred activities). They concluded that U.S. parties had greater organizational strength – especially during the 1960s with a slight decline during the 1970s – which was not determined by different degrees of identification with parties.

Given the perspective adopted here, this study cannot guide our research either. On the contrary, we start from the idea that Canadian political parties already possess a certain organizational strength, although this strength varies according to a party's electoral fortunes and popular support.

Lemieux (1985) based his systemic approach to parties on the work of Sorauf (1964, 1968). He distinguishes three components – internal, public and governmental – and establishes functional relationships between them. Analysing the internal component, he opts to characterize this component, as did Michels (1971) and others, by opposition between the centralization and decentralization of controls. He established this opposition on three criteria borrowed from Janda's model (1980): selection of the leader and other officers, selection of candidates and concentration of leadership.

This study is closer to the goal we are pursuing here. But as we pointed out above, it is not first and foremost a question of measuring centralization and decentralization in Canadian political parties, but of seeing how the structures of these organizations operate. We can deduce a certain form of centralization or decentralization from it only implicitly.

From this perspective, Janda's model (1980) seems more appropriate to our initial question. We will take five key variables from his model to guide our study:

1. Nationalization of structures: What is the importance of local and regional levels in relation to the national level?
2. Concentration of leadership: What is the extent of the power of the leader and his or her principal lieutenants?
3. Formulation of policies: Who formulates policies and who makes the final decision on whether a party adopts a policy?

4. Selection of candidates: What roles and powers do various party echelons have in this respect? What roles do local associations and the rank and file play?
5. Allocation of funds: Who controls finances? How are funds allocated and what are the consequences of allocation?

To answer these questions, first we consider the most relevant Canadian studies, so we can glean several historical perspectives to give us a better grasp of the various aspects of the problems connected with the actual, concrete operation of political parties. We then go on to a brief analysis of the official constitutions of Canadian parties to isolate their formal structures. Finally, we compare these formal structures with actual party operations, based on 13 interviews, mainly with national officers – five from the Liberal Party of Canada, four from the Progressive Conservative party and four from the New Democratic Party (NDP) (see the "Interviews" section for a list of officers interviewed).

WHAT OTHER AUTHORS HAVE TO SAY

Unlike the Quebec Liberal party, which has not been the subject of many studies, most major Canadian political parties, both federal and provincial, have been studied from various angles. Literature on the Conservatives is dominated by study of the party's problems. The historian LaTerreur (1973) analysed the tribulations of the Quebec Conservatives at length from the Bennett to the Diefenbaker administrations. He pointed out the Conservatives' continual problems at both the federal and provincial levels in Quebec with respect to organization, financing and maintenance of central organization and constituency associations.

The most trenchant study of the Conservatives is probably that of Perlin (1980). Perlin recounted the conflicts surrounding the party leadership between 1956 and 1976, analysing delegates' behaviour at the 1967 and 1976 conventions, which he thought was based primarily on emotion rather than policy or patronage. He found few ideological splits in the party except over English–French relations. He also analysed the Progressive Conservative party at the national level as a leader-dominated institution in which the leader must retain the confidence of both the caucus and the party membership, including activists and the party establishment, which may have different interests and points of view. This led him to conclude that the Tory syndrome, the development of an opposition mentality in a minority party, caused continuous formation of factions and sparked almost constant conflict, which made it difficult for the party to attract the best leaders, the best candidates and the best organizers. The repercussions of these internal problems on the party's electoral vitality were that it could not regain power, which stirred up more internal conflict centred on the leadership problem.

This brief summary does not convey all the substance and richness of this work. Perlin (1980) analyses in depth the leader's role in the party, his authority in policy formulation, the scope of his prerogatives with respect to nominations and the control he exercises over party resources. Perlin also analyses Conservative organizations on the provincial and riding levels, observing that the strength of these organizations varies from province to province and from riding to riding. In this study we will return to some of the points raised in Perlin's book, in particular with respect to the scope of the leader's powers and his involvement in policy formulation.

Wearing (1981) was interested in the Liberal Party of Canada between 1958 and 1980. He concentrated his research on two main issues: party organization and financing; and policy formulation and development. More generally, he studied the relationship between the parliamentary and non-parliamentary wings, specifically, the place of the party membership. This led him to ask the following question: When in power, will the parliamentary wing (particularly the Cabinet) dominate the party? This in turn led to the questions of how to maintain a strong organization between elections and how to ensure that cabinet ministers do not control the whole organization. More generally, he considered the question of democratizing the party structure, because the party had to rebuild after the 1957 defeat and at the same time try to redefine its policies. The notion of party democratization is basic, because he dwells on the need to integrate the grass roots into party organization and into financing and policy development to prevent decline in the party organization. He also describes cycles of decline and renewal – decline after several years in power, then renewal after an election defeat or near defeat, as in the case of a minority government.

He also underlines the difficulty Prime Minister Trudeau had in adapting to his role as leader and to the needs of party members, as well as in bringing new blood into the party and the Cabinet, trusting as he did the bureaucracy more than the party itself. In this study we deal with various problems raised in Wearing's book (1981). Policy development within a party and members' participation in the internal life of the party come to mind. The same may be said about the central role a leader plays in a political party.

In his monumental study of the Liberal party, Whitaker (1977) analyses the problems of financing and organization, including one of its important aspects, federal–provincial relations within the party.

Beginning with the weakness of Liberal organization at the beginning of the 1930s, he details how it reorganized with an eye to the 1935 victory, making the National Liberal Federation an effective body and improving the party's precarious financial situation. Whitaker shows that when the party was in power, the Federation was a rather amorphous body that, as Mackenzie King preferred, did not favour participation although the financial situation improved.

The National Liberal Federation attempted another revitalization so that members could both express their reformist ideas and support the ideas of certain cabinet ministers. The Federation became dormant again, while the caucus rose to dominance. This eclipse of the party continued under the leadership of both Mackenzie King and St. Laurent. After the Second World War, however, finances improved again, particularly with the more active participation of Montreal-based groups. Whitaker (1977) concluded that when the party was in power, and it governed for a remarkably long time, it forgot its specifically political roles in favour of administrative and bureaucratic roles. In short, here again cycles can be seen in the life of the party. When it is in power, it tends to put its activist wing on ice. In opposition, party activists again come to prominence and a greater desire for reform is also expressed.

Our investigation also revealed cycles. It may seem paradoxical, but ascent to power is often marked by decline in the party's internal life. Activists who have worked hard to gain power feel "less useful" once their party has finally reached this objective: the leader, the Cabinet and the caucus (in short, the parliamentary wing), supported by the Prime Minister's Office (PMO), come to embody the whole party, leaving only a little room for the rank and file.

Unlike the Conservative and Liberal parties, the NDP and its predecessor, the Co-operative Commonwealth Federation (CCF), always wanted to base themselves, at least officially, on active participation by their members. According to Morton (1986), the farmers' movement – one of the essential elements in the founding of the CCF – brought two major contributions to the Canadian left-wing tradition: co-operatives (referred to in the name of the CCF); and the importance given to democratic control and very broad-based financial support. He added that these two contributions produced a model centred on democracy exercised by members and delegates at various levels, regular consultation and the strict responsibility of leaders to their activists: this model, which prevailed in the CCF, was also adopted by the NDP.

However, the national NDP is a federation of semi-autonomous provincial parties. This presents operating problems for the national organization, which scarcely exists between federal elections. In other words, the tendency – also found in the other parties – toward a low level of partisan activity between elections is also found in the NDP, although the NDP strongly encourages members to participate actively in party life. The very structure of the organization may accentuate this problem, as former leader Ed Broadbent has already acknowledged. Without denying these operational problems, we can say that we found the NDP still stresses democratic operation, members' participation in party life, and exercise of control over party officers by activists. In these areas, the NDP seems to differ from the other two parties, although its formal participatory structures and declarations of officers' principles do not prevent genuine operational problems.

Wearing (1988) demonstrated this in a recent book. Comparing Canadian political parties, he analyses the "party in Ottawa" and the "grassroots party" and points out the differences between them. For example, the NDP caucus differs from those of other parties. The NDP caucus distributes written agendas and votes on party policy. The other two parties do not use written agendas or formal votes. Instead, the leader consults and "takes the pulse" of members of Parliament to establish better positions for the party. Also, the leaders of the Liberal and Conservative parties choose the whips, who are responsible for party discipline; in the NDP, the caucus chooses the whips. This is also the case with national conventions – the leader of the NDP, but not the leaders of the Conservative or Liberal parties, is bound by resolutions adopted there.

The differences that Wearing revealed were noted in our interviews with party officers: the NDP is distinguished from the other two political parties in many ways, especially in concentration of leadership. This does not prevent party officers from intervening to exercise control over internal party life, however.

WHAT THE PARTY CONSTITUTIONS REVEAL

It is not our purpose here to analyse in detail the parties' formal structures as described in their constitutions. Instead, we would like to present and comment briefly on three simplified organization charts that not only show the overall structure of each party (essentially its top level) and the relations between its various echelons but also amplify the findings set out in the following section. In general, the organization charts look similar from party to party; political parties are in fact distinguished by their actual operations at various levels of authority.

In the Progressive Conservative Party of Canada, the general meeting of the association elects the party leaders, amends the constitution and defines general political orientations (see figure 5.1). The biennial general meeting is different from a leadership convention, which can be called at any time (Progressive Conservative Association of Canada 1989, Art. 12). Between general meetings, the National Executive directs, manages and controls the affairs of the association. What the Conservative party calls its executive is really equivalent to the NDP's Federal Council, since it has about 150 members. The 40-member Executive Committee should really be considered the important body, because although its decisions are subject to review by the National Executive (ibid., Art. 7), it assumes all the powers of the National Executive and adopts the annual budget for financing the party's activities.

On another level, the Steering Committee has about 15 members and is responsible, among other things, for recognizing affiliated organizations. In its turn, the Steering Committee assumes all the powers of the Executive Committee, which can review its decisions. From one level to the next, therefore, power is delegated. All decisions can be reviewed at the next higher level.

Finally, the permanence of the party is assured by national headquarters, which is also responsible for recognizing constituency associations. Headquarters serves as the organizational, administrative and coordinating centre for all branches of the party. The Steering Committee appoints its national director on the leader's recommendation.

Figure 5.1
Schematic organization chart, Progressive Conservative Party of Canada (1989 constitution)

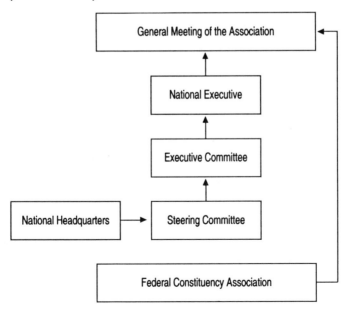

In short, this is a more or less classic structure with a general meeting at one end and a smaller group at the other, although its other two levels (Executive Committee and Steering Committee) could make it a special case. The small Steering Committee is obviously easier to convoke than the large Executive Committee. This overall structure has remained essentially the same for 10 years. If we compare the 1989 constitution with that of 1981, we find additions and clarifications rather than substantial changes: for example, it contains more precise information about the makeup of the different committees and the General Meeting of the Association. What is more, the four major principles or objectives defined at the 1956 national convention, which were retained in the 1981 constitution, were retained in the 1989 constitution with two additions: quality of the environment and equality of the sexes.

The four principles adopted in 1956 are:

1. We believe in freedom of worship, speech and assembly; loyalty to the Queen of Canada; and the rule of law. Believing these things, we hold, with history, that vigilance over such parliamentary institutions is the best guarantee of such traditional freedoms.
2. We believe that the state should be the servant of the people and that our national progress depends on a competitive economy, which, accepting its social responsibilities, allows to every individual freedom of opportunity and initiative and the peaceful enjoyment of the fruits of his labour.
3. We believe that progress and stability can best be achieved by building on the firm foundation of those things proved good by experience.
4. We believe in Canada, founded on these principles, a nation of many creeds and many cultures, united in its aims and accepting its obligations among the nations of the world.

Of the three parties under study here, the Liberal party certainly has the most detailed constitution. It describes, in detail, the responsibilities and composition of the party's various committees and commissions: the Standing Committee on Policy Development, the Standing Committee on Organization, the Standing Committee on the Constitution and Legal Affairs, the Standing Committee on Communications and Publicity, the Standing Committee on Multiculturalism (since 1990), the Financial Management Committee, the National Platform Committee, and the National Campaign Committee. There are also the Commission of Young Liberals of Canada, the National Women's Liberal Commission and the Aboriginal Peoples' Commission, which represent and promote the interests of these groups within the party and encourage participation in party activities at all levels (Liberal Party of Canada 1990, Art. 4).

When we compare the structures of the Liberal and Conservative parties, we see that one national level no longer exists in the Liberal party (see figure 5.2). The National Executive of the Liberal party, which has about 50 voting members and 15 non-voting members, is about the same size as the Conservatives' Executive Committee, and the Liberals' Management Committee is equivalent to the Conservatives' Steering Committee. The larger Conservative National Executive, which may be compared to the Council of the Federal Party of the NDP, has no equivalent in the Liberal party.

The Liberal party constitution also sets out that the National Convention, which elects national officers and establishes basic party policies, is the party's highest authority (1990, Art. 15). This demonstrates an intention to emphasize the importance of this body, as do the constitutions of the NDP and the Parti québécois (PQ), which emphasize participation and members' responsibilities in party life. As with the Conservatives, Liberal national conventions are distinct from leadership conventions held after the death or resignation of the leader and, if the members so wish, after a federal general election (ibid., Art. 16).

The National Executive is generally responsible for party affairs between national conventions (ibid., Art. 5). It must meet at least three

Figure 5.2
Schematic organization chart, Liberal Party of Canada (1990 constitution)

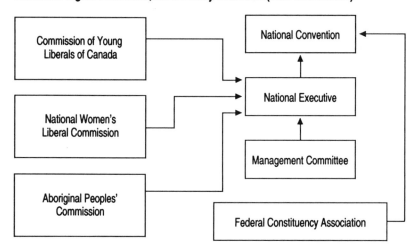

times a year, and all commissions and standing committees are accountable to it. The Management Committee, which meets every two months,
is the "nerve centre" of the Liberal party, although it must report to the
executive. It considers continuing business matters, develops the two-
year plan for directing party operations and manages Liberal party
affairs between meetings of the National Executive (ibid., Art. 6).

In short, although the overall structure appears simple enough, the
addition of commissions for young people, women and Aboriginal
people to the five standing committees and three other committees
makes the structure considerably more elaborate. This increases the
importance of the National Executive and in particular the Management
Committee, which coordinate all these commissions and committees.
At the same time, however, this proliferation is evidence of the Liberal
party's desire to reach out to different groups within the general public,
for example, young people, women, Aboriginal people and ethnic groups.

Finally, we might point out the intent to set up twin structures, one
concerning programs and the other concerning organization. As often
happens with political parties, organization has a tendency to take
precedence over activity. We have only to recall the well-known debate
between "participationists" and "electoralists" within the PQ when it was
still in opposition in the early 1970s (Murray 1976). The electoralists
won out over the participationists because of a concern for "political
realism," thereby demonstrating that a political party, as we have said,
is an organization concerned with electing candidates and gaining
power. The desire to motivate its members and educate the public gradually gave way to the need to build a solid organization to win elections.

The NDP, however, wished to set itself apart from tendencies exhib-
ited by the other two major Canadian parties, although it could not
always surmount obstacles to internal democracy, participation by
members and control of officers. In this respect the NDP can be compared
to the PQ: the importance of the members' role in party life is defined
in the constitution, and this role seems to be even more effective in the
actual operation of the party.

Therefore, as in the other parties, the convention elects the officers
and is the party's supreme governing body (see figure 5.3). This is also
written into the constitution of the Liberal party. The New Democrats,
however, also make clear – and no such article is found in the constitutions of the other parties – that the convention "shall have final
authority in all matters of federal policy, program and constitution"
(New Democratic Party of Canada 1989, Art. V).

Between conventions, the Council of the Federal Party adminis-
ters the party's affairs. It can issue "policy statements" and "election

statements" consistent with the decisions made at the conventions. It can even initiate policy statements, following party philosophy, in matters not yet considered by convention (ibid., Art. VIII). This means that, although the Federal Council – like the National Council of the PQ – is an important, powerful branch of the decision-making structure of the party, it remains subject to resolutions adopted by convention. Federal Council decisions have to agree with the NDP program or philosophy.

With about 30 members, 14 of whom are elected by the Federal Council from among its members, the NDP Executive of the Federal Party has authority, as in the other political parties, to conduct and administer party affairs and business between Council meetings. It also has the power to issue statements in the name of the party, subject to confirmation by the Council (ibid., Art. IX).

In short, although the Executive remains subject to the Federal Council, the Council must comply with the resolutions adopted in convention, which also bind party officers. One must therefore recognize the importance of conventions, which assemble both individual and affiliated members. Affiliated membership is another feature peculiar to the NDP, which welcomes "trade unions, farm groups, co-operatives, women's organizations and other groups and organizations which, by

Figure 5.3
Schematic organization chart, New Democratic Party of Canada (1989 constitution)

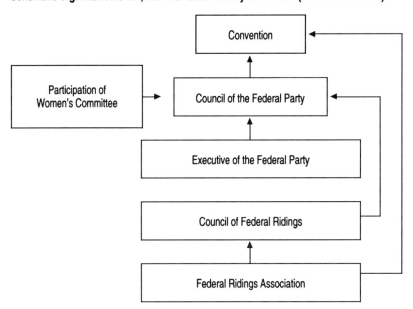

official act, undertake to accept and abide by the constitution and principles of the Party, and are not associated or identified with any other political party" (ibid., Art. III).

Another feature peculiar to the NDP, provided for in the 1989 constitution, is the creation of councils of federal ridings to promote federal party activities and policies in each province or territory and to elect federal riding delegates to the Federal Council (ibid., Art. X). This is how the NDP clearly highlights its federal nature – it is made up of largely autonomous provincial parties – and ensures that the provinces and territories are represented in the body that is most important between elections, the Council of the Federal Party.

In short, since its foundation, the NDP has always wished to underscore members' active participation in party life. This makes the convention very important, for it is there that policies and programs are decided on, officers selected and the constitution amended. What is more, all other party authorities, including the leader, must comply with resolutions adopted at the convention. In this way, the NDP ensures more participation by members and more control over officers than the other parties, although it should be recognized that operational difficulties still exist despite these formal structures, as we shall see in the following section.

WHAT PARTY OFFICERS THINK

This section, the most important part of this study, is based on 13 interviews, most with officers of the three major Canadian political parties. It therefore represents a partial vision of reality: the people we interviewed are not necessarily representative of party officers; even less are they representative of the membership as a whole.

However, since these are people who hold important party positions (see the "Interviews" section for a list of officers), it can be argued that their points of view not only permit an excellent overview of the actual operations of different bodies within the parties, but also convey the prevailing situation in their parties better than rank-and-file activists could. We do not wish to imply that activists could not have provided solid information, but we did not have enough time to consult party members. Besides, officers are in a better position to grasp the situation as a whole, not just as it applies in a given sector, riding or region.

Here we will consider their answers to five questions referred to above concerning nationalization of structures, concentration of leadership, policy development, candidate selection and local associations, and allocation of funds (see the Appendix, which reproduces the questionnaire).

Nationalization of Structures

The constitutions of all the political parties acknowledge the importance of the general membership meeting or general convention as the supreme party authority: "The national convention shall be the highest authority of the Liberal party, subject to the provisions of this Constitution. The basic policies of the Liberal party shall be established by the Party assembled in national convention" (Liberal Party of Canada 1990, Art. 15(1)); "the Convention shall be the supreme governing body of the Party and shall have final authority in all matters of federal policy, program and constitution" (New Democratic Party of Canada 1989, Art. V(2)).

Our respondents also acknowledged the importance of national conventions. However, the actual function of these conventions varies from party to party. In the Progressive Conservative party and the Liberal party, conventions elect the principal officers or national party executive and define the party's major orientations or "general philosophy." The Liberal party constitution is more explicit about this than the Conservative constitution, which states simply that the general meeting of the association will take place every other year. A Conservative officer observed that:

> When the party wa⌣ in opposition, conventions were much more centred on the adoption of political resolutions. Now that it is in power, conventions are often structured in advance. It is normal for there be some "direction from the top," since to allow just any activist to take the mike could lead to the convention "holding together or falling apart." But in the final analysis the general meeting is supreme. However, the party hopes to have some "influence" over the government's philosophy, not necessarily over the details of legislation.

In the New Democratic Party, however, the convention really has final authority over policy, programs, the constitution and selection of officers. All NDP conventions are policy conventions (in the sense that party policies are defined there) as well as leadership conventions, because the party leader must submit to the vote of all delegates. The leader is usually acclaimed, however.

Aside from fulfilling these well-defined functions, conventions are also symbolic. They maintain group solidarity because they give activists who identify with the party the opportunity to meet and form alliances to defend policies or a certain concept of party philosophy. A convention can also improve the sense of participation in the party by transforming activists into defenders and propagandists for party policies. In other words, activists are encouraged to spread the "good news" around the country. Finally, it should be observed that a convention is always an important media event, particularly when major issues are raised. The party then benefits from media coverage that can bring positive publicity.

Conventions happen only occasionally, however, usually every other year. In the meantime, regular party operations are carried out by other bodies. All these national organizations have essential functions: this is the case with the Council of the Federal Party of the NDP and the national executives of the Progressive Conservative and Liberal parties, as well as smaller groups such as executive committees and steering committees.

The national executives of both the Liberal and Conservative parties administer their parties, allocate budgets for the various party organizations, appoint almost all non-elected officers, establish parameters such as dates, schedules and rules of procedure for policy or leadership conventions, maintain close communication with the rank and file, implement current party lines and even influence party orientation and philosophy. A national executive, therefore, does much more than simply carry out policies: it is a real board of directors that makes decisions likely to affect the internal life of the party. In the NDP, this function belongs to the Council of the Federal Party, but the Council must follow policies adopted in convention.

In short, these bodies are influential because they meet regularly, usually three or four times a year; the principal party officers – the leader, the president, the vice-presidents – attend; they are consulted more or less regularly to explain or define policies; they run the party; and in particular, they are usually federative in nature and represent the various regions of the country. This enables members of the national executives to introduce concerns from the regions they represent. As one NDP officer pointed out, "the leader attends all meetings of the Executive, not simply to make a speech but to participate in the discussion. For her it is a real tour of the political landscape."

What applies to organizations of the major national parties is also true of their smaller executive committees and steering committees, which have the advantage of fewer members and can meet even more regularly. Their composition nevertheless reflects the federal principle of national bodies, so they are true microcosms of their parties. In this sense, the national levels of each party are important in regular operations and internal party life, more important than regional and local structures, which cannot claim to act for the whole party.

Concentration of Leadership

The democratic, participatory structures that all these political parties have in place do not always withstand the double phenomenon of personalization and concentration of power. In all three parties, it is the leader who has been identified as the person with the most power. "He is unquestionably the big boss. He personifies success or failure," a Liberal officer pointed out. "In Canada, it is the leader who wins or loses elections," added a Conservative officer.

Nevertheless, this power is not absolute: the leader is usually called upon to share it with others, even when everything contributes to concentration of leadership in the hands of a single person. When a party is in power, therefore, ministers have an important function. The same is true for the caucus, which meets regularly so the leader can consult his or her parliamentary wing. In this we see a concentration of leadership phenomena, which is focused on Parliament Hill: when a party is in power, this concentration benefits the prime minister and the Cabinet; when the party is in opposition, it benefits the party leader and the parliamentary wing. By focusing on Parliament, the media magnify the concentration of power and at the same time confer upon it a certain legitimacy.

The Prime Minister's Office (PMO) is important in the concentration of power. In constant contact with the prime minister, its officials intervene in both party administration and policy development, according to Liberal and Conservative officers. "It is an unequal battle between two structures," a former Liberal officer pointed out. "It is then that the party takes a back seat," added another. The PMO becomes even more important when it is run by someone totally dedicated to the party, who participates actively in conventions, general meetings or steering committees and who exercises much influence. This was the case with Marc Lalonde when Pierre Elliott Trudeau was prime minister.

The influence of the PMO is tempered, however, by the prime minister's own regular consultations with the caucus, which establish a kind of balance between the PMO and the parliamentary wing: the more divided the caucus is, the stronger the PMO will be. But the exchange of information between the prime minister, the caucus and the party counts most of all. "Honestly," a Conservative officer pointed out, "I can tell you that there is continual consultation to discover what the rank and file and the caucus are thinking."

The NDP has not yet taken power at the national level, so questions concerning its PMO could only be hypothetical. However, the answers we received revealed the major party orientations. NDP officers considered that their PMO would play an important role if the party were in power, but "this role would be contained through the vigilance of activists." One NDP officer pointed out:

To be realistic, I believe that it would also be the prerogative of the Cabinet to decide what policies would in fact be implemented. Our government would not be different from the others in this respect. The difference would be that our government would not go against party policy.

Another added: "I believe that, in addition to the technical bureaucracy that constitutes the Prime Minister's Office, the party should set up, within the PMO, a kind of people's component." In short, the NDP believes that the party and its activists will have to show vigilance when confronted with other structures that could counterbalance, if not completely overshadow, members' influence over the leader and principal officers. These remarks clearly convey that the NDP, like the other two parties, which have been in power, might also be subject to the phenomenon of concentration of power in the hands of the prime minister and the PMO, despite the NDP's structures governing participation and control.

When it came to identifying their parties' major decision-making persons or groups, Liberal and Conservative officers unanimously identified the leader and his or her main advisers, including the party president. They also acknowledged that the president and national executive are responsible for party administration and that the caucus has little influence, although it is consulted regularly. In the NDP, although its leader makes the daily decisions, major party decisions are developed by party activists meeting in convention. In the NDP, the democratic model of member participation still appears to prevail, while concentration of power in the hands of the leader and main advisers is the rule in the other two parties.

This rather disillusioned Liberal officer summarized the situation in the two traditional leading parties quite well:

When the party is in power, the [party] bureaucracy is not of much importance. Everything seems to happen on the Hill, originating with the Prime Minister's Office and the regional ministers. When in opposition, none of this is the case and the party becomes more important again. Why has the party been in difficulty since 1984? Because we had been in power since 1968. The party was neglected during all that time. It has atrophied considerably.

These remarks are similar to the conclusions of a 1984 committee report on reform of Liberal party structures and operations requested by the party's National Executive. That report recognizes the importance of the PMO and other central agencies that replace the party itself when the party is in power:

The growth of central agencies (such as the Prime Minister's Office and the Privy Council Office) had a radical effect on the role of the Liberal party. The development of powerful resources around the leader meant that a number of "political" functions – in the partisan sense of the term – were entrusted to civil servants paid out of the public purse. Much of what might have been the role of the party thus disappeared or was at least much reduced. (*Le Soleil* 1984)

Responses were more qualified when it came to identifying not the holders of power but rather those who control the political parties. In the Progressive Conservative and Liberal parties, the leader exercises this control but shares it with a small group including the PMO and the party establishment. Some of those interviewed, especially Liberals, even commented that small power groups were developing within the party. Groups can control individual sectors, but not necessarily the party as a whole. Borne out in real life, this model would make the Liberal party more like the American parties described by Eldersveld (1964). He defined them not as oligarchies but as "stratarchies," in the sense that power is shared among several subgroups that make up a party and that each can take as much power as it likes. There is thus a stratification of power, with minimal control from the centre.

In general, Canadian political parties are closer to the oligarchic model described by Michels (1971). Power is concentrated at the top, in the hands of the principal officers. It should be emphasized, however, that within the NDP, the rank and file has more control than in any other party. Activists thus retain all their power because they exert extensive control at conventions and through national party organizations.

The phenomenon of the concentration of power is, first, connected with the British parliamentary system, in which the powers of the monarch are transferred, not to the elected assembly that sought to limit them, but to one of its members, the prime minister, who became a new monarch, invested with considerable powers. The prime minister is, however, subject to control by opposition parties, which are usually a minority in the House, by external groups and, at election time, by the voters.

Some analysts have also linked this phenomenon to new marketing techniques, which make style and image more important than the message (Sabato 1981). These techniques are designed to forge personal links between a leader and voters, not to stress policies or differences between different parties' programs. They therefore tend to consolidate the leader's position in the organization and reinforce the traditional leadership-centred orientation of Canadian politics (Amyot 1986), unlike U.S. politics, which is more centred on local candidates.

Carty (1988) came to the same conclusion in his interpretation of the development of Canadian national politics since 1867. Patronage politics, which operated until 1917, was succeeded by brokerage politics, which lasted until the early 1960s. Since then, technology has dominated the Canadian political landscape: politics has been personalized by growing dependence on new technology during election campaigns, and in practice parties have become extensions of the leaders. Carty concludes that the considerable importance accorded the leader gives these three periods a common backdrop.

However, it is important to point out that the three parties instituted leadership reviews, which constitute a form of control over the leader. The NDP has practised leadership review for a long time; each NDP convention is both a policy and a leadership convention in which the leader submits to a delegates' vote – often a formality, since the leader is usually re-elected by acclamation.

In the Liberal party, a nomination convention is called after a leader's death or resignation. In addition, a "resolution calling for a leadership convention shall be placed automatically on the agenda of the convention next following a federal general election" (Liberal Party of Canada 1990, Art. 16(4)). If the convention adopts this resolution, the national executive must call the leadership convention within a year. Former Liberal leader Pierre Elliott Trudeau had to submit to this procedure four times when he was prime minister. He won decisively each time, although in 1972, when he headed a minority government, the PMO had to work hard to reaffirm his position as party leader (Wearing 1989).

By 1974, the Progressive Conservative party constitution also included this review procedure – former party leader Joe Clark, after losing the 1980 federal election, was subjected to it. Even with two-thirds of the 1983 vote, he preferred to resign. In 1989, delegates to the convention of the association changed the wording of the constitution to make it less binding, at least on a prime minister. Henceforth, the leadership question will no longer be raised at each general meeting of the association, but rather only at the first meeting following "a federal general election in which the Party did not form the government" (Progressive Conservative Association of Canada 1989, Art. 12.2). This means that the Conservatives have diluted their initial position considerably, reducing control exercised by the activist rank and file over the leader. Of the three major Canadian parties, the Conservative party now puts the least emphasis on leadership review.

Despite leadership review, we can conclude that leaders concentrate power in their hands and exercise, with the help of small groups, real control over their parties, although NDP activists can exercise their rights to a greater extent. A Liberal officer very pertinently observed that "the Canadian prime minister of a majority government has a great deal more power than the U.S. president. He leads the country as he likes. There are power struggles that do not disappear, but as far as his party is concerned he makes the law."

The authors of the report of the Liberal party reform committee (quoted above) see things the same way. They wrote the following:

> The leader has acquired immense political stature and is truly at the centre of party life. He is not only the pivot of modern government, the nucleus around which the resources of the central bodies orbit; he has also become a central *political* entity beyond anything we have known thus far. All Liberal activists acknowledge the leader's importance. He is the prime symbol of the party in campaigns and in terms of communication and is the main if not the only person responsible for the development and publicizing of party policy. The party well knows that it is the leader who legitimizes its activities by approving them and that it is he (or his officers) who is responsible for many appointments to essential positions in the party. (*Le Soleil* 1984, A13)

The authors concluded: "A strong and enduring party requires balance between the authority invested in the leader and his responsibility to the party."

In short, the oligarchic model, in which power is concentrated in the hands of a few party officers, seems to prevail generally over the "stratarchic" model, in which power is shared within the party. The NDP is distinguished from the other two parties by its desire to encourage members to participate in party life and exert control over officers, although activists are not always successful in this.

Policy Development

All our respondents stressed that national conventions, where party activists meet, are important to policy development, but there are major differences between the parties. In the NDP, this is essentially the function of activists, although they acknowledged that the leader and her advisers may exercise a certain influence. The NDP tradition is that the party – its members meeting in convention – develops policy, and that the party – its Executive or, sometimes, its Federal Council – is generally consulted on major positions to be taken between conventions. More specifically, they emphasized that when a decision could deviate from the party line, the leader would have to consult with the caucus and party authorities. "We work together on policy issues," added an NDP officer, "in a more integrated way than the two other parties."

Therefore, the leader and the party secretary consulted the National Executive and principal party officers, about 30 people, on the decision to support the Liberal senators' attempt to kill the Goods and Services Tax (GST). Abolition of the Senate is still a plank of the NDP platform, however. Faced with this dilemma, the party resolved, after consultation, to support the Liberal senators because abolition of the GST was more important in the circumstances than abolition of the Senate.

On the other hand, the decision to support the Meech Lake Accord was apparently made without consultation. And according to some it was this lack of consultation more than the decision itself that caused a rift in the party. When the Federal Council met, a New Democratic officer said, "it was terrible: people in our party want to be consulted!"

All NDP conventions are policy conventions, and activists value this. The leader has the same status in policy setting as any rank-and-file activist and has the same rights they do to submit political resolutions. What is more, "the leader and the caucus are bound, in principle, by the policies adopted by the convention." They must, therefore, take these policies into account when establishing their positions.

This idyllic picture hides a few operational problems, however. Although activists' participation in conventions is ensured, this does not mean that members will vote on or even debate all resolutions. As one New Democratic Party officer remarked, "activists send resolutions, but the resolutions are prioritized by those on the resolutions committee ... If a policy ventures too far to the left, it will never be examined." Thus, party management – in particular the Federal Council – controls resolutions so it can manage or direct the deliberations of the convention. In addition, the NDP Federal Council is more active in policy development than the national executives of the other two parties. Program development by activists is therefore subject to closer scrutiny by party authorities precisely because party officers are bound by resolutions adopted at conventions, a situation that does not prevail in the other two political parties.

In the same vein, this officer added:

> I think that NDP policies have become more realistic as the party has grown in legitimacy: we came to realize that we could form the government one day.
>
> We don't have to adopt policies so strange that they could never be implemented. For example: the nationalization of banks. At the convention before last or the one previous to that, this policy was changed: only one bank would be nationalized. People told themselves: if we form the government, we'll have thousands of activists screaming for the nationalization of banks. We should have a more

reasonable policy on our books. People at the top therefore influenced the policy.

Already, as the party thinks it is approaching power, it is becoming more "realistic." This tendency could become more marked if the party does come to power. This is the conclusion Edwards (1985) reached. According to Edwards, NDP governments tend to become more conservative once they are in power. This is not to say that they completely abandon their social-democratic ideals. It simply means that socialist parties must compromise to obtain the acceptance and support of as many sectors in society as possible. This is how they come to terms with the realities of Canadian brokerage politics.

This "realism" is also borne out in government spending. Comparing the performance of Manitoba's NDP government between 1969 and 1977 with that of its Conservative predecessor and of other provincial governments of the time, McAllister (1980) concluded that total government growth (revenues and expenditures, public service) does not seem to be influenced by partisan ideology, even if the revenue base and spending priorities change a little. In short, NDP government practice was comparable to that of other Canadian provinces and not fundamentally different from that of the preceding government.

This view of NDP governments contrasts sharply with what Young had to say about CCF ideological purity:

> The militants opposed the development of the CCF as a political party and made a fetish of their opposition to making ideological sacrifices in order to win office. Success, they feared, would transform the CCF from a vehicle of protest into a disciplined party in which there would be little room for the rebel. They preferred to see the CCF remain as a perpetual gad-fly that bit the hide of the establishment and goaded the "old line" parties into reform while providing the outsiders of Canadian society with a platform and a haven. (1969, 291–92)

However, it should be noted that Ontario's 1991 NDP budget adopted a position totally different from that of the federal government and other provincial governments. Preferring to increase the deficit rather than reduce the budget and slash jobs in the public service, the Ontario government increased the deficit to a level that had until then been unknown in the province.

In short, we may conclude that even parties that favour members' participation in policy development must show a certain amount of realism and submit at times to their officers' influence. On the other hand, the very essence of partisan democratic life seems most often

protected by activists and by the officers themselves. It was acknowledged that once the NDP was in power, it would not always find it easy
to operate its participatory structures properly. The party would then
have to set up clear means of communicating with the government. At
the same time, ministerial statements would have to be compatible
with party policies. As one New Democratic Party officer said:

> Those at the head of the party will be very accommodating toward the
> government and the party, but the rank and file should know that
> decisions are made within the parameters of party policies and the
> limits of the government's powers. If the government begins to act
> against party principles, it is going to lose members.

In the other two Canadian parties, resolutions adopted in conventions express the general position of the party, its orientation and its
political philosophy and do not necessarily bind party authorities. The
Progressive Conservative party, therefore, develops general policy from
a biennial process of reflection. To arrive at policy, the party organizes
regional meetings where activists can express their views. Likewise,
the National Executive informs and encourages people in the field who
have to explain party policies. The parliamentary wing is more
concerned with selling party and government policies in the regions
and drawing party and government attention to the policies that the
regions want on the agenda.

Although various Progressive Conservative party organizations
participate in policy development, it is the leader – particularly a prime
minister – who plays the central role. "The influence of the party structure is one of awareness," one Conservative officer said. To highlight
the central role of the leader even more, he added: "Most initiatives
having to do with policy are submitted for the leader's attention very
early on. I would be surprised if in our party there were policies that
surprised the leader."

In the Liberal party, in accordance with its constitution, proposed
resolutions come from the Policy Committee, riding associations, provincial associations, the Women's, Young Liberals', and Aboriginal People's
commissions, and sometimes individuals. These resolutions appear in
a register that is sent to the general meeting of members, where they
are voted upon. The adopted resolutions then constitute the party's
general policies.

We should mention here the significance of the Standing Committee
on Policy Development. It is responsible, among other things, for policy
development between conventions. The constitution stipulates also

that it "prepare, maintain and publish a consolidation of resolutions approved at national conventions" and "strive to ensure that the policy document is respected by the parliamentary wing and shall report thereon to the national convention" (Liberal Party of Canada 1990, Art. 7(4)). In a way, it guards the party program while participating in policy development. A party leader who repudiated resolutions would probably cause more problems for the Liberals than for the Conservatives, who define few policies at conventions.

It is acknowledged, however, that the Liberal leader has the most important function in the entire process, since he can ultimately accept or reject policies adopted at conventions, whatever problems that could cause. Party policies crystallize around the leader, who undeniably inspires the party and its various bodies at all levels of responsibility, especially the parliamentary wing – in short, the leader is the key to party vitality. As a Liberal officer pointed out:

> In our party, we have always considered that with regard to policy, even when adopted by party resolution, in the final analysis it is the prime minister or the party leader who had the right – and I think that this is still the case – to say "I accept it" or "I do not accept it."

And from still another Liberal officer:

> The leader is the supreme authority. He has the last word in almost all circumstances. If there were a policy that ran counter to the leader's ideas, I would tend to think either that the policy would not be adopted, or that it would be put aside... Within the Liberal party, there are no resolutions that bind the leader or the caucus. There is no right of veto, but in fact he has the last word.

But the leader does not act alone. He is usually required to compromise with the parliamentary wing as new situations develop. The leader may consult the Policy Committee or the National Executive, but it was admitted that, unlike the NDP, the Liberal party does this rarely; it is also rare for these two bodies to intervene.

The Liberal caucus, on the other hand, is important because its members are critics of government departments. When policy issues are raised, it is understood that the critics will help define party policies. On the Free Trade question, for instance, the caucus had decided on a position; it refused to negotiate at all on the subject. Party activists wanted to negotiate, even if the agreement was not to be signed. The caucus finally succeeded in selling its position to the activists after heated discussion on the convention floor, and the party then rallied behind the caucus.

According to a Liberal officer, the parliamentary wing is crucial for three main reasons:

1. It has research facilities, an office with a staff of about 15 to prepare the documentation critics need to formulate policies.
2. Attention must be paid to the opposition critics who follow government policy on various issues.
3. Members of Parliament are often looking for experts to inform them on one or another aspect of policy.

In short, although activists take part in policy development through their participation in conventions and party committees, it may be observed that the leader, with the help of the parliamentary wing, forms the essential nucleus that orients the party. This is shown in figure 5.4, prepared by the Liberal party itself. It can be seen that the leader really does form the nucleus of policy development, although the caucus, the Platform Committee, the Policy Committee and policy advisers can assist. In the NDP, on the contrary, members define party policies, under supervision by party authorities if necessary; depending on circumstances between conventions, the leader may act, but only after consulting party authorities. The NDP intends thus to preserve democratic life within the party, although such a democracy does have its limits.

Everywhere, we see a media phenomenon that personalizes power and an organizational phenomenon that concentrates power, and both are enhanced by new technology. Until now, the NDP has done better than the other two parties in preserving its activists' essential role, according greater importance to its national conventions and more significance in policy development to its other national bodies rather than entrusting it solely to party administration. Similarly, in contrast to the Progressive Conservative party, the Liberal party has developed a longer tradition of member participation in party life.

Be that as it may, we should recall what Pross wrote about the parties' function in policy development:

> If parliamentarians are seen to play a meaningful role in policy formation, the party should attract strong candidates, and community leaders should once again wish to be associated with party organizations. To capitalize on these trends, however, Canada's political parties will have to transform their grassroots organizations from electoral machines chugging away on the fuel of minor patronage into bodies with a genuine capacity to assist in policy formation. If parties succeed in restoring a policy capability to the grass roots, there is reason to hope that the competition of parties and pressure groups will turn into something more productive, not only for the organizations themselves, but for the general public. (1986, 260)

Figure 5.4
Policy development

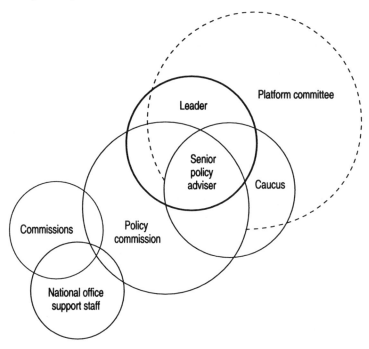

Source: Liberal Party of Canada.

Candidate Selection and Local Associations

All three parties select candidates for upcoming elections similarly. This is the ideal moment for the party rank and file to express itself at local association meetings, and members remain deeply attached to this procedure, guarding the prerogative jealously. As a Conservative officer pointed out, the party activists' position is all the more secure because they have the advantage of a solid organization in the ridings: they can thus counteract the plans of organizers who might want to nominate a candidate the activists do not like.

Some of our respondents also commented that the number of activists in any given association is not fixed, and it can vary enormously just before a nomination meeting. Membership in associations sometimes rockets from 200 to 3 000, particularly in urban areas like Toronto and Montreal. Such a change can give a false impression of activism in the party. Despite all this, the final decision always rests with the membership of constituency associations.

Constituency associations do not usually accept with good grace too-obvious intervention by top party management. Sometimes members will reluctantly agree to support a parachuted-in candidate, especially if the candidate is likely to become a minister. Such intervention usually follows consultation with the executive of a local association, and ridings are usually offered freely, without deep conflict between high-level organizers and the local association. Sometimes the party's directors, even the leader, can exercise the veto. The constitution of the NDP clearly stipulates, however, that the "Council of the Federal Party shall have authority to intervene with respect to a federal nomination if the interests of the Federal Party are involved and if the provincial party concerned had failed to take appropriate action" (New Democratic Party of Canada 1989, Art. XV). The same article also sets out procedures to be followed in these rather exceptional circumstances.

At the provincial and national levels of the NDP, there are candidate search committees to recruit candidates who meet specific criteria such as gender parity, party experience and community involvement. The organization can also try to guide members without imposing a choice on them. It was acknowledged, however, that one New Democratic Party directive does constitute interference by the central party authority in the selection process, but this directive has been adopted by the party: the achievement of gender parity in the selection of candidates. This can raise problems in certain regions, as is the case in Saskatchewan, where in the 1988 election, the NDP won 10 of 14 ridings, all with male candidates. "It's minor interference by the central party authority," acknowledged one New Democratic Party officer. "There will be discontent, but the benefits of this policy outweigh local resistance," he concluded.

The parties' national executives are seen as police who supervise the observation of selection rules and procedures, not as authorities that impose their choices. Certainly, a national executive will sometimes intervene to boost the candidacy of someone prominent in a certain milieu, but this does not mean the national executive can impose its choice. If a candidate has not been chosen by the rank and file, as a Liberal officer pointed out, this could cause problems on an organizational level.

Our respondents said that a candidate must have the leader's approval, not least because the leader signs the candidate's nomination form. Likewise, the leader encourages people to come forward as candidates. The leader's power, however, really lies in positive or negative moral persuasion; above all, the leader can refuse a candidacy. If the leader does refuse a candidate, it is often at the urging of close advisers. This is rare, but such intervention by a leader is clear – and final.

In general, then, the final decision belongs to the meeting of constituency members, and if the leader has to intervene, he or she usually contacts the potential candidate last. This Liberal officer's remarks sum up the situation well:

> All the party, or the leader, can do is to give the impression that one would like to have that person by letting it be understood that the constituency will be represented in the Cabinet ... The constituency people cannot be forced. They are jealous. There are activists who have worked for years and consider candidate selection their most important act.

The three criteria Ranney (1981) developed in his study of candidate selection in 24 democracies lead us to point out first that members of Canadian political parties participate *directly* in candidate selection by voting for the candidates of their choice in their ridings. At a higher level, on the other hand, their participation has until now been indirect: they elect delegates to the conventions that choose the candidates.

It should be pointed out, however, that parties tend to increase the number of delegates to national conventions. As Wearing (1989, 279) has remarked, the Liberal party has increased the number of elected delegates per riding from three, in 1958, to six in 1968, then to seven and now to twelve. At the same time, the Liberals were working to limit the number of ex officio delegates so they do not make up more than 15 percent of the total number of delegates; previously, up to 30 percent of the group were ex officio delegates.

On the other hand, participation in candidate selection is not governed by very restrictive criteria. Clearly, only party *members* may participate, but each party's membership criteria are rather flexible: pay a nominal fee, be accepted by the party, abide by party principles (although it is really for the member to decide whether he or she meets this test) and refrain from membership in other federal political parties. Obviously, these criteria seem more restrictive than American requirements; their system of open primaries includes all voters.

The third criterion is *centralization* of the process. In Canada, although party members in good standing select candidates in the ridings, they usually act under the supervision of a regional or central party authority. As we made clear above, these authorities intervene in the process very rarely. They do have veto power over rank-and-file selection, but they rarely use it. It is therefore at this level that rank-and-file autonomy is most apparent and decentralization most evident.

If candidate selection is most important to many activists, they nevertheless have other functions in the party. Our respondents generally agreed that these functions are different depending on whether or not an election campaign is in progress. Between elections, constituency associations:

- promote and publicize party principles, defend the organization's policies and help people understand party policies;
- organize political discussions or study days and participate in policy formulation;
- organize fund-raising activities to cover current and election expenses;
- recruit;
- select convention delegates; and
- collect information by taking the pulse of the general public.

In short, a team must be kept in place between elections, but all our respondents asserted that this was not easy. "Excuses have to be found for existing," stated a Conservative officer.

"Between elections, we don't have the structures for integrating all these people," added a Liberal interviewee. "If everyone who works on an election arrived on our doorstep tomorrow morning, three years away from an election ... we wouldn't know what to do with them."

"Election campaigns should be continuous," concluded a New Democratic Party officer, acknowledging that constituency associations fall into a state of lethargy for two or three years only to revive approximately a year before a federal election.

Constituency associations are more active during election campaigns. Responsible for finding candidates, recruiting members, collecting funds, managing the nomination convention, and ensuring that the campaign is being run "efficiently and honestly," activists get involved to lead their candidate to victory. However, this special time in party life can also be inconvenient for members. Some candidates choose their own teams and set up their own organizations at the expense of the regular constituency association members, especially if the association is more or less efficient. A candidate's team might include a few members of the constituency executive, certainly the association president. There is a great temptation to set up two parallel organizations or put the local association on ice. Such a situation does not encourage members to participate.

Some of our respondents also pointed out that participation depends on whether or not a party is in power. Activists carry less weight when a party is in power. Since decisions are made by the prime minister, the PMO or the Cabinet, members feel left on the sidelines. The parliamentary wing often stagnates because it is comfortable in power. In opposition, a party has to depend more on its members because it lacks the resources that power confers. Constituency associations then become more important because the parliamentary wing is less able to intervene and organize. The NDP, on the other hand, believes that activists will be even more enthusiastic when the party is in power, because each local association will then have to work on the re-election of its member and party.

In general, we can conclude that activists find it easier to participate when their party is in opposition than when it is in power, although some acknowledged that power can heighten their enthusiasm. Everyone also pointed out that it is difficult to keep local associations active between elections. At the same time, it was observed that during election campaigns, nominated candidates surround themselves with teams of organizers that do not always include long-service activists, which actually erodes rank-and-file participation. All these factors can only work toward strengthening the power of leaders and their principal party advisers. "An association," concluded a Liberal officer, "should always be vigilant and active: this is the force of the party. Unfortunately, this is not always the case."

Financial Resources

This is a crucial problem for all political groups that depend on diverse sources of financing. These usually take the form of fund-raising dinners, direct-mail campaigns aimed at individuals, and political clubs.

For the Progressive Conservative and Liberal parties, fund-raising dinners are an important source of revenue. In the Liberal party, for example, affairs such as Toronto's Confederation Dinner, Ottawa's Maple Leaf Dinner and Montreal's benefit brunch are practically institutions. These get-togethers are important because not only particular individuals, but also representatives of the business community are invited and attend regularly. The Progressive Conservatives do the same, and they have the advantage of organizing dinners, brunches or cocktails within the framework of the prime minister's schedule; he is quite successful at attracting crowds.

These activities are not limited to the national level, although they are much more visible there. Local associations organize them around the participation of the constituency MP or a special guest such as a cabinet minister. Activists and permanent staff always have to work hard to make a success of these events.

Direct-mail campaigns seem to be increasing in importance as a source of revenue, as both Liberal and Conservative officers confirmed.

Both parties carry out national direct-mail campaigns from lists of people who have been asked to contribute to the party. This form of solicitation seems more popular among English-speaking than French-speaking people and does not always meet officers' expectations; it must be acknowledged, too, that such a system is costly to establish and has to be constantly improved. As a Liberal officer noted: "When the financial situation is tight, there is a tendency not to go too far with prospecting. We stay with the lists of people who have already contributed, so it's a vicious circle."

The NDP has enjoyed a longer tradition of "popular" financing. The Progressive Conservative party has already had great success with this method: more than half its funding, according to Paltiel (1989, 343) comes from individuals. The Liberal party, on the other hand, has not done as well in fund-raising because it was not able to modify its financing methods during its long years in power. It should also be pointed out that all parties have benefited from the tax credit introduced in the 1974 reform of the *Canada Elections Act*.

The main function of political clubs is to solicit the business community; they are found mainly in the two traditional leading Canadian parties. For $1 000 and $500 a year, the Liberals' Laurier Club and the Conservatives' 500 Club give business people opportunities to meet the prime minister, party leader and important ministers from time to time to promote networking with them.

It goes without saying that direct solicitation of companies is still a major source of revenue for the two major parties, which make annual requests for contributions and special requests during election periods. But as some Liberals commented, this source tends to dry up: contributions are fixed and, in comparison with company sales figures, very small. Also, more and more companies refuse to contribute to political parties. These circumstances help explain the words of a Liberal officer who would like to change the system:

> I myself don't like the image of the Liberal party to be too closely linked to those circles (the large corporations). Secondly, when there is a recession and budgets are tighter, it becomes more and more difficult to solicit them. And also for the health of the party it is necessary to increase the rank and file, not just with members but also with contributors. Because members who contribute are really interested. That makes for a stronger party.

Where the Progressive Conservative and Liberal parties still use business circles as a financial resource, the NDP turns instead to the trade unions. Union contributions are as important during the periods between elections as they are during election periods, since affiliated members are required to pay a monthly per capita fee based precisely, as its name indicates, on the number of members in the affiliated organization, unless the organization declines to make the payment (New Democratic Party of Canada 1989, Art. IV). Trade unions become even more involved during elections by providing workers, as some companies do for the other parties. A New Democratic Party officer pointed out that several election campaigns have been managed by union organizers. But we were assured that all this is entered in the books.

The sale of membership cards is not a major source of revenue for the Progressive Conservative and Liberal parties; it is more important for the NDP, but mainly on the provincial level. The NDP attaches more value to party membership than the other parties do because its constitution confers major powers on its activists and it has developed procedures for consulting the rank and file. "Instant" or last-minute memberships more often appear in the two other parties, especially in major urban centres when a candidate is to be selected in a given riding.

With a better-identified and more constant membership, the NDP has been able to set up truly popular fund-raising campaigns similar to Quebec practice since the appearance of the Parti québécois on the political scene and the enactment of the *Act to govern the financing of political parties*. NDP campaigns usually take the form of direct-mail solicitation, like those conducted by the other two parties. The NDP first works systematically through its membership list, and then through lists of potential donors. Potential donors could be subscribers to magazines whose mailing lists the NDP has rented – magazines like *Canadian Forum*, *Saturday Night* and *L'actualité*. The systematic use of the membership list, which is kept as up to date as possible, contributes to more active involvement by members in party life.

Our respondents also pointed out that state reimbursement of candidates' election expenses is another source of party financing in cases such as the Liberal party, in which half of candidates' reimbursements are paid to the party. Above all, our respondents dwelt on the federal tax credit, which encourages broadening of the sources of party financing. As a Liberal officer pointed out, "it is a good marketing technique" that makes it possible to reach more contributors ready to donate smaller amounts.

In general, all the parties tend to broaden sources of financing by increasing emphasis on individual contributions, especially through direct-mail campaigns. As a Liberal officer noted:

> Our weakness lies in having been in power too long. When you're in power, money is easy, everything is the leader's responsibility. The

same thing happened to Laurier in 1912 ... Now we're trying to do something that has a certain stability, a broader base for financing ourselves.

These comments are very similar to remarks made by the presidents of the Progressive Conservative party and the PC Canada Fund in their brief of 21 September 1990 to the Royal Commission on Electoral Reform and Party Financing. The brief points out that since 1974 (when the *Election Expenses Act* came into force), the Progressive Conservative party has increased its sources of financing considerably by increasing its emphasis on small contributions from individual Canadians, adding that since that date the number of contributors has increased considerably: from 1974 to 1978, individual contributors increased ninefold and corporate donors sevenfold.

It would therefore be advantageous to go on encouraging the broadening of sources of financing, especially by relying more on individual contributions – if necessary by increasing the tax credit – and by imposing more severe restrictions on the contributions from companies and trade unions, which in any case do not have the right to vote.

Our respondents also pointed out that organizers are important fund-raisers, both between elections and during election campaigns, whether their party is in or out of power. One way the organizers are active, for example, is as planners of fund-raising dinners. The NDP, on the other hand, emphasized that activists should do this work, in accordance with their role in the party. All, however, acknowledged the importance of the leader, who projects the party's image and attracts crowds to certain events.

In addition, official structures such as the Liberal party's Financial Management Committee, which has a subcommittee responsible for annual corporate fund-raising, and the PC Canada Fund, which acts as the party's official agent and issues income tax receipts, are required to intervene in financing. Because they are involved in preparing annual budgets that are then approved by other party authorities, the Liberal party's Financial Management Committee and the NDP's Finance Committee play an important part in the allocation of resources.

During election campaigns, when a great deal of money is needed and the party must act quickly, the usual sources of financing are not always reliable. This is not the time to organize fund-raising dinners, run direct-mail campaigns or set up political clubs; consequently, the importance of official structures tends to diminish. As a Conservative officer said:

Then we become interested in the large corporations and in members, to whom we point out that if it costs $5 to be a member, it costs a great deal to win an election. Give us $25 and we will give you a tax credit so that it will cost you only $7 or $8. However, this doesn't impress them and they prefer to give us $5. I can't give them a receipt.

These comments give us a good idea of the difficulties involved in popular financing, even with tax credits, for a party that was and still is used to other financing methods. The Liberal party has the same problem – one Liberal officer says it has about 17 financing programs but it cannot count on popular financing alone to ensure its survival. These comments also apply to the NDP, which counts on union contributions to fill out its financing campaigns.

The control of finances is always the responsibility of official organizations like the PC Canada Fund, which exercises effective control because it has the legal power to do it, while in principle, some pointed out, the National Executive should exercise that control. It goes without saying that at the local level, constituency associations have to control finances in their areas of activity.

In the Liberal party, the Federal Liberal Agency issues receipts for donations received at all levels of the party and fulfils the party's legal responsibilities under the *Canada Elections Act*. Moreover, as in the case of the Progressive Conservative party, another structure, the Financial Management Committee, must intervene. Responsible for Liberal party finances and accountable directly to the party leader, this committee prepares and implements long-range financial plans and operating budgets for all national-level activities, raises funds and allocates funds among the various elements of the national party (Liberal Party of Canada 1990, Art. 12).

Although it is not always clear, it is possible to establish the division of responsibility among the various party organizations:

- The Revenue Committee raises funds and finds money.
- The Financial Management Committee prepares budgets, allocates funds and negotiates the budgets with the various elements of the party.
- The chief financial officer oversees expenditures and controls finances.
- The Federal Liberal Agency issues receipts for donations.

In the NDP, party treasurers at the federal and provincial levels control finances, whereas the Finance Committee establishes the annual budget. The federal secretary is also involved in financing. According to a New Democratic Party officer, the federal secretary and treasurer are the decision makers and are responsible to the national executive for expenditures.

In all parties it is always ultimately a higher authority – the Executive Committee, the National Executive or the Federal Council – that gives official approval on budgets and thereby controls the organization's finances.

In general, it is the responsibility of the national party to allocate funds; however, most money collected at the local level remains there. This is also the case in the NDP, but it should be pointed out that some of what the provincial sections collect (15 percent according to one of our respondents) should normally be paid to the party's national organization. Several New Democratic Party officers said that the provincial sections do not always send the amounts due. Furthermore, our study shows that it is sometimes difficult to determine clearly what party funds belong to the local, provincial and national levels, although fund-raising is usually centralized in order to issue tax receipts.

All in all, it should be remembered that although groups or legal persons such as corporations and trade unions are still relied upon to finance Canadian political parties, the parties seem to want to broaden their sources of financing by refining direct-mail campaigns addressed to individuals. They are thus approaching a popular financing technique already widely used in Quebec, which has also been tested by the NDP. To achieve this, parties will have to rely not only on their usual organizers and marketing specialists, but also on their activists. They will therefore have to get into the habit of establishing up-to-date lists of members and inviting these members to participate actively in party life, even outside election periods. Moreover, according to Paltiel (1989), modern marketing techniques have not fragmented Canadian parties but have, rather, combined to reinforce the national leaders' and central organizations' position. This obliges the parties, with the advent of pollsters and advertising and fund-raising specialists, to transform themselves. As for other aspects of financing, parties have already developed structures to enable them to establish budgets and control finances while complying with the *Canada Elections Act* in issuing income tax receipts.

CONCLUSION

In conclusion, we will make a brief review before discussing the impact that electoral legislation could have on political parties and suggesting a few desirable reforms.

The authors reviewed at the beginning of this report dealt with questions or problems concerning party structure. Although leadership problems in the Progressive Conservative party were emphasized, organization and financing, which are so important in the life of a political party, were nevertheless not forgotten. These topics were also very ably analysed in connection with the Liberal party. Parties seem to develop in cycles: in power, they tend to neglect their activists; in opposition, they turn back to their members when demand for reform increases. Financing is usually more secure when a party is in power, and the organization then tends to leave matters to the parliamentary wing, especially the prime minister. But when a party finds itself in opposition, financing is harder to come by and activists have to get busy rebuilding the organization and finding sources of financing.

The federal New Democratic Party, which has never been in power, is not as marked by these cycles, especially since its activist tradition is stronger than that of the other two parties, as Morton (1986) has already pointed out. Nevertheless, like the other two political parties, the NDP finds it very difficult to maintain the activities of its local associations and even its national organization between elections. The New Democrats are strongly in favour of members' participation in party life and control of party officers by party activists, even if actual party operations do not always reflect these democratic principles.

Although Canadian parties tend to have similar formal structures, they show marked differences in the actual operation of their various organizations. To cite only one example, the biennial convention, always significant, is even defined as a party's highest authority; however, resolutions adopted in convention do not bind Liberal or Conservative top management. NDP activists, on the other hand, meet in convention to help define party policy, and the leader must comply, at least in a general way.

The views of officers of the three major Canadian parties on the actual operations of the various national organizations constitute the most important part of this report. Because only they can speak and act for their parties, and because the media have helped "nationalize" Canadian political life or, at the very least, concentrate it on Parliament Hill, each party's national organizations are integral to regular party operations and internal party life.

Similarly, as a consequence of the almost universal phenomena of personalization of power and concentration of power in the hands of very few, the party leader is easily identified as the person with the most power, the organization's "big boss." Around the leader, a few other influential figures or groups are also recognizable, in particular the Prime Minister's Office when the party is in power. This model of concentration of power is not as evident in the NDP, which still favours a democratic mode of participation by members, although the leader may sometimes wish to evade the control of activists.

It was acknowledged that although activists in the two major traditional parties must play a certain role in policy development by participating in conventions and various committees, the leader and the parliamentary wing represent the essential nucleus that defines the party's major policies. On the other hand, the NDP sets more value on participation by members, who are called on at national conventions to establish party policies or programs: this does not prevent the NDP from turning to a certain political "realism" when establishing its program.

These three issues (nationalization of structures, concentration of leadership and policy development) primarily concern internal party life, although they also influence the democratic process as a whole. We believe the Commission should not intervene directly with recommendations for obligations backed up by sanctions or rewards. At most, it should issue directives or suggest improvements, leaving the political parties to carry out reforms. Members and officers should improve their parties' internal democratic life under pressure exerted by activists, the influence of other parties, criticism by the media and intellectuals, and more generally, public opinion – without forgetting, of course, party officers' own determination to carry out these reforms.

The Commission could certainly recommend that parties improve policy development by encouraging participation by members, who could define not only major party orientations but also more specific programs. Nevertheless, officers of parties that have been in power could retort that once elected, a party is not there solely to implement its program (although the public usually expects it to); it must both respond to the electorate's demands and confront new situations not provided for in the party program. Above all, they would add, the party was elected by the public as a whole and not by party members only, so it is responsible to the entire electorate and not to the party alone.

The experience of the Parti québécois, in power from 1976 to 1985, is rather revealing. As we have pointed out elsewhere (Pelletier 1977), scarcely a month after its election, at the end of a meeting of the National Council, Premier Lévesque – also president of the party – declared that to strike a balance between the party and the state, it had, on the one hand, to prevent the parliamentary wing from devitalizing and engulfing the party, which would dry up its capacity for thought and make valid reflection impossible, and on the other hand, to prevent party activists from running the state. For activists' benefit he made the following recommendation: "The party must not mistake itself for the government and profess to dictate to it what the party wants."

What Lévesque then suggested was to ask activists to be watchdogs and critics of the government, but not to let party organizations such as the National Council and the Executive Committee assure them of absolute control over the people's elected representatives. The goal was thus to achieve a difficult balance between the parliamentary and activist wings, and this was to be done without unduly limiting members' participation in party life.

At most, the Commission should recommend or, better, suggest that parties strengthen member participation in policy development and set up mechanisms to allow activists to control party officers, along the lines of NDP practice. Again, members really have to want to participate; gradually, they will have to learn to use the existing participatory mechanisms. For the Liberal and Progressive Conservative parties, this is still far in the future.

The Commission could also recommend – more imperatively – increasing the age at which one can join a political party from 14 to 16. By setting both the required age for becoming a party member and the minimum age for exercising the right to vote at 16 years, the age for entry into both electoral processes could be made uniform.

As we have seen above, candidate selection provides the ideal opportunity for the party rank and file to express itself, so ideal that members remain deeply attached to the process. Intervention from the centre or top party management is usually frowned upon, although the validity of some directives coming from the centre may be acknowledged.

The firmly established practice of rank-and-file participation in candidate selection should be kept. It can, however, raise problems related to the Commission's terms of reference. First of all – although this is not directly within the Commission's terms of reference – we have a better understanding of the strong, general political opposition to changes in the current balloting system: people remain attached to "their" candidate, "their" MP and "their" riding, and this favours the single-candidate balloting system.

Second, the nomination meeting is significant in local party life. Although the Commission must regulate constituencies' election expenses strictly, we think it is problematic to include nomination meetings under election expenses because they are not all alike: some lead to keen struggles between candidates (which allows a higher media profile) and others do not; some are held after election writs are issued and others before; some attract many members and others very few. Here, the search for fairness could lead to unfairness. In other words, the inclusion of expenditure on nomination meetings held after the writ as election expenses should entail a counterbalancing arrangement in which this expenditure could be entered before the writ, for obvious reasons of fairness. How to compel the parties to accept such a policy? And on what grounds could the practice be justified?

The Commission could, however, recommend that parties issue instructions to select more female candidates or even to achieve gender parity, as the NDP has proposed. Over the last 12 years the number of female candidates coming forth has increased, so it would be a question of recommending the pursuit and even acceleration of this trend by setting a more clearly defined goal and a stricter deadline. Moreover, what we have just said about encouraging female candidates and members of Parliament could equally apply to members of various minority groups in society.

Now we come to the most critical problem of all, that of financing. The parties, as we have seen, rely on a variety of sources. However, they favour fund-raising dinners, direct-mail campaigns addressed to individuals, and political clubs. Membership sales are not a major source of revenue for the Progressive Conservatives or the Liberals; they are more significant to the NDP, but only on the provincial level. Similarly, the NDP receives contributions from trade unions, whereas the other two political parties collect more from businesses.

It is particularly important to keep in mind that *all* parties tend to broaden their sources of financing by increasing the emphasis on individuals' contributions, especially through direct-mail campaigns. The Commission should, therefore, continue on this path. First of all, we do not think it is necessary to pass a law as Draconian as the *Act to govern the financing of political parties* of Quebec which limits the right of political contribution to individuals or electors only. The right of "legal persons" such as corporations, companies, partnerships, trade or farm unions, employee associations and co-operatives to make political contributions could also be recognized, but their donations should be subject to stricter limitations. This would require setting limits neither low enough to suit individuals only, nor high enough to accommodate groups only.

Finally, as our respondents so often observed, the tax credit should be increased so parties can broaden their sources of financing still more. We propose the following formula for a tax credit that would apply to all types of contributors: 75 percent of the first $100 paid, 50 percent for amounts above $100 and up to $500, and 25 percent for amounts greater than $500 and up to $1 400. Such a policy would encourage more contributions from those who can make only modest donations.

These few proposals are designed only to improve the electoral process and, more broadly, the democratic process in Canadian society. In the same spirit, we might point out that although the overall structure of Canadian political parties is to encourage participation by members and democratic life in political parties, their actual operation does not always follow this ideal. The NDP probably comes closest to it, even if its actual operations do not always match its stated principles.

It might also be noted that it is usually easier for activists to participate when a party is in opposition than when it is in power. When the party is in power, it tends to concentrate everything around the prime minister, the PMO, the Cabinet and the caucus – in short, around the parliamentary wing at the expense of the activist wing. Moreover, all our respondents stressed the difficulty of keeping local and sometimes even national associations active between elections. At the same time, they observed that during election campaigns, when member participation is normally stronger, the candidate often surrounds himself or herself with a team of organizers that does not always include activists of long standing, which tends to erode rank-and-file participation.

All these facts combine to increase the power of the leader and his or her principal advisers. This strengthens the phenomena of the nationalization of structures and of the personalization and concentration of power at the expense of the activist rank and file; new techniques such as polls and advertising help to accentuate these characteristic features of Canadian political parties.

APPENDIX

Questionnaire: How Party Structures Operate

This questionnaire will help us understand the actual power attached to structures in political parties and the operation of their finances. It will also assess parties' degree of centralization or decentralization.

1. **What is the role of each of these structures in** *policy making*:

    a. the party leader?

    b. the parliamentary wing?

    c. the central organization of the party (for example, the national executive)?

    d. party activists and members of the party?

    e. party organizers?

    Who has the most important role? Why?

    Is it the same when the party is in *power*? In *opposition*?

2. **Who plays the most important role in an** *election campaign*:

    a. at the national level?

    b. at the provincial level?

    c. at the constituency (riding) level?

Who selects the *themes* (issues) of the election campaign:

a. at the national level?

b. at the provincial level?

c. at the level of the constituency (riding)?

Are the issues the same at all levels?

3. **In a constituency, how does the party select** *candidates*?

a. Does the leader intervene?

b. Does the executive intervene?

c. Is it the prerogative of party members and activists?

d. Do the election organizers intervene?

4. **For you, what is the function of** *constituency associations*?

Do they have the same functions when the party is in power? In opposition?

Do they have the same functions during an election campaign as between elections?

5. **How is your party** *financed* **now?**

a. Sale of membership cards?

b. Fund-raising campaigns? Who is approached?

c. Fund-raising dinners?

d. Direct-mail campaigns? Who is approached?

e. Political clubs with a fee?

f. Other means?

6. **Who plays the most** *important* **role in party financing?**

a. The central organizers of the party?

b. The national executive of the party?

c. The leader of the party?

d. The parliamentarians (MPs and Senators)?

e. Party activists or the grass roots?

Is the pattern the same whether or not the party is in power?

Is the pattern the same during and between elections?

7. **Who** *controls* **party finances?**

8. **How are those funds** *distributed* **within the party? And by whom?**

Is it done the same way whether or not there is an election campaign?

9. Who makes the main *decisions* concerning the party:

    a. The leader or the leader and principal advisers?

    b. The parliamentary wing (MPs and Senators)?

    c. The party president and national executive?

    d. The central organizers?

    e. Party activists meeting in convention?

    When the party is in power, is this different from when it is in opposition?

10. What are the functions of the party's *national executive*?

    What is its real *influence* in the party?

11. What are the functions of the party's national *conventions*?

    Do they have a role in defining party policies?

    Does the leader comply with the policies adopted by the convention, or does he retain full independence as far as policies are concerned?

12. Do you find that party *activists* or members play a more important role when there is an election campaign or between elections?

    Is that role more important when the party is in power or when it is in opposition?

13. When the party is in power, does the Prime Minister's Office play an important role in making decisions and approving policies?

    Is its role more important than that of:

    a. The national executive?

    b. The parliamentarians (MPs and Senators)?

    c. The convention?

    d. Party activists or members?

14. In your party, who has *more power*:

    a. The leader?

    b. The cabinet ministers (if the party is in power)?

    c. The parliamentarians as a group?

    d. The party president?

    e. The national executive?

    f. The national convention?

    g. The central organizers?

    h. Party activists or members?

15. **On the whole, do you consider your party as *controlled* mainly by:**

    a. The leader?

    b. The parliamentarians?

    c. A small group of leaders? (Please specify)

    d. Party activists or members, as a group?

    e. Others?

Thank you.

N.B.: In the case of the NDP, please interpret the questions relating to whether the party is in power or in the opposition thus: "If your party were in power, do you think this situation (or phenomenon) would be the same as it would if your party were in opposition?"

INTERVIEWS

Progressive Conservative Party of Canada

1. The national president, 11 December 1990.

2. The national secretary, 28 November 1990.

3. The national vice-president, Quebec section, 10 December 1990.

4. The chairman of the caucus, 6 December 1990.

Liberal Party of Canada

1. The president of the party, 12 December 1990.

2. The past president, 27 November 1990.

3. The vice-president, English speaking, 7 December 1990.

4. The vice-president, French speaking, 28 November 1990.

5. The vice-president, Ontario section, 3 December 1990.

New Democratic Party

1. The national president, 11 and 13 December 1990.

2. The associate president, 4 December 1990.

3. The federal secretary, 18 December 1990.

4. A member of the federal executive, 14 December 1990.

ABBREVIATIONS

c.   chapter

R.S.C.   Revised Statutes of Canada

R.S.Q.   Revised Statutes of Quebec

S.C.   Statutes of Canada

REFERENCES

In this study, quoted material that originated in French has been translated into English.

Amyot, Grant. 1986. "The New Politics." *Queen's Quarterly* 93:952–55.

Canada. *Canada Elections Act*, R.S.C. 1985, c. E–2.

—————. *Election Expenses Act*, S.C. 1973–74, c. 51.

Carty, R. Kenneth. 1988. "Three Canadian Party Systems: An Interpretation of the Development of National Politics." In *Party Democracy in Canada: The Politics of National Party Conventions*, ed. George Perlin. Scarborough: Prentice-Hall Canada.

Clarke, Harold D., Jane Jenson, Lawrence LeDuc and Jon H. Pammett. 1984. *Absent Mandate: The Politics of Discontent in Canada*. Toronto: Gage.

Edwards, Kevin. 1985. "Limits on Policy-Making by Social Democratic Parties." In *Party Politics in Canada*. 5th ed., ed. Hugh G. Thorburn. Scarborough: Prentice-Hall Canada.

Eldersveld, Samuel J. 1964. *Political Parties: A Behavioral Analysis*. Chicago: Rand McNally.

Etzioni, Amitai. 1960. "Two Approaches to Organizational Analysis: A Critique and a Suggestion." *Administrative Science Quarterly* 5:257–78.

Gibson, James L., Cornelius P. Cotter, John F. Bibby and Robert J. Huckshorn. 1983. "Assessing Party Organizational Strength." *American Journal of Political Science* 27:193–222.

Janda, Kenneth. 1980. *Political Parties: A Cross-National Survey*. New York: Free Press.

LaPalombara, Joseph, and Myron Weiner. 1966. *Political Parties and Political Development*. Princeton: Princeton University Press.

LaTerreur, Marc. 1973. *Les tribulations des conservateurs au Québec, de Bennett à Diefenbaker*. Quebec: Les Presses de l'Université Laval.

Lemieux, Vincent. 1985. *Systèmes partisans et partis politiques*. Sillery: Les Presses de l'Université du Québec.

Liberal Party of Canada. 1990. *Constitution*. Ottawa.

McAllister, James A. 1980. "The Fiscal Analysis of Policy Outputs." *Canadian Public Administration* 23:458–86.

Michels, Robert. 1971. *Les partis politiques: essai sur les tendances oligarchiques des démocraties*. Paris: Flammarion.

Morton, Desmond. 1986. *The New Democrats, 1961–1986: The Politics of Change*. Toronto: Copp Clark Pitman.

Murray, Vera. 1976. *Le Parti québécois: de la fondation à la prise de pouvoir*. Montreal: Hurtubise HMH.

New Democratic Party of Canada. 1989. *Constitution*. Ottawa.

Paltiel, Khayyam Z. 1989. "Political Marketing, Party Finance and the Decline of Canadian Parties." In *Canadian Parties in Transition*, ed. Alain G. Gagnon and A. Brian Tanguay. Scarborough: Nelson Canada.

Panebianco, Angelo. 1988. *Political Parties: Organization and Power*. Cambridge: Cambridge University Press.

Pelletier, Réjean. 1977. "Les relations entre le Parti québécois et le nouveau gouvernement." In *Premier mandat: une prospective à court terme du gouvernement péquiste*, ed. Daniel Latouche. Montreal: l'Aurore.

———. 1989. *Partis politiques et société québécoise: de Duplessis à Bourassa, 1944–1970*. Montreal: Québec/Amérique.

Perlin, George C. 1980. *The Tory Syndrome: Leadership Politics in the Progressive Conservative Party*. Montreal: McGill–Queen's University Press.

Progressive Conservative Association of Canada. 1989. *Constitution*. Ottawa.

Pross, A. Paul. 1986. *Group Politics and Public Policy*. Toronto: Oxford University Press.

Quebec. *An Act to govern the financing of political parties*, R.S.Q., c. F-2.

Ranney, Austin. 1981. "Candidate Selection." In *Democracy at the Polls: A Comparative Study of Competitive National Elections*, ed. D. Butler, H.R. Penniman and A. Ranney. Washington DC: American Enterprise Institute for Public Policy Research.

Sabato, Larry J. 1981. *The Rise of Political Consultants: New Ways of Winning Elections*. New York: Basic Books.

Sartori, Giovanni. 1976. *Parties and Party Systems: A Framework for Analysis*. Cambridge: Cambridge University Press.

Le Soleil. 1984. "L'autocritique du Parti libéral du Canada: un parti statique dominé par son chef." 8 February.

Sorauf, Frank J. 1964. *Political Parties in the American System*. Boston: Little, Brown.

———. 1968. *Party Politics in America*. Boston: Little, Brown.

Wearing, Joseph. 1981. *The L-Shaped Party: The Liberal Party of Canada, 1958–1980*. Toronto: McGraw-Hill Ryerson.

———. 1988. *Strained Relations: Canadian Parties and Voters*. Toronto: McClelland and Stewart.

———. 1989. "Can an Old Dog Teach Itself New Tricks? The Liberal Party Attempts Reform." In *Canadian Parties in Transition*, ed. Alain G. Gagnon and A. Brian Tanguay. Scarborough: Nelson Canada.

Whitaker, Reginald. 1977. *The Government Party: Organizing and Financing the Liberal Party of Canada, 1930–58*. Toronto: University of Toronto Press.

Wilson, James Q. 1973. *Political Organizations*. New York: Basic Books.

Young, Walter. 1969. *Anatomy of a Party: The National CCF, 1932–61*. Toronto: University of Toronto Press.

6

THE NEW DEMOCRATS, ORGANIZED LABOUR AND THE PROSPECTS OF ELECTORAL REFORM

Keith Archer

U NLIKE THE OTHER parties in Canada, the New Democratic Party is formally and structurally linked to an interest group. Representatives of organized labour can be found on most policy-making bodies of the party, and labour contributes a not insignificant amount to the party's revenues. In light of the mandate of the Royal Commission to advise the government on matters relating to the election of candidates and the financing of parties, the question arose whether labour's links with the NDP has consequences which violate the principle of equity among political parties, or whether the relationship affects, either positively or negatively, labour's ability to have its interests represented in the political system.

This study examines the causes and consequences of labour's relationship with the NDP. It begins with a brief historical background on the transformation of the Co-operative Commonwealth Federation (CCF) into the New Democratic Party, and the implication of that change for labour's involvement with the party. It then turns to a description of the costs and benefits to the labour movement of its link with the party, followed by an assessment of labour's role in NDP decision making. The analysis shifts to an examination of the union–party relationship in other advanced industrial democracies, and the union–NDP relationship is then placed in comparative context. Focusing back on Canada, leaders from the union movement and the NDP are asked to evaluate the union connection with the NDP from the unions' perspective. The study draws a number of conclusions and makes several recommendations.

THE HISTORICAL LEGACY

The organizational structure of the NDP differs from that of the Liberal and Conservative parties in at least two fundamental respects. Like the CCF before it, the NDP has a federated structure and is an amalgam of relatively independent groups, or sections, which link themselves to the party. This structure was introduced by the CCF, which was created to incorporate "the three major classes in the community whose interests are the same – industrial workers, farmers and the middle class," and which even attached the subtitle "Farmer-Labour-Socialist" to its name (Horowitz 1968; Young 1969). The CCF was federated in two ways: only groups, not individuals, could join the party; and groups could affiliate only to a provincial wing of the party. Thus, the CCF was an amalgam of provincial sections, which in turn consisted of affiliated organizations. The first part of this structure was carried forward to the NDP, such that individuals cannot join the federal party directly but must join through an organization that is linked to the party. The most important such organizations are the provincial sections of the federal party. This organizational structure vests considerable power in the party's provincial sections, as they have become the basis of organization.

The second unique characteristic is the NDP's relationship with organized labour. The creation of the NDP in 1961 was an attempt to integrate organized labour more fully into the party.[1] Two events led to this decision. From the unions' perspective, the relative harmony that was created from the merger of the Trades and Labour Congress (TLC) and the Canadian Congress of Labour (CCL) to create the Canadian Labour Congress (CLC) in 1956 provided an opportunity for labour to re-examine its political strategy. The CLC created a Political Education Committee at its founding convention, and at its following convention in 1958 it called for "a broadly based people's political movement, which embraces the CCF, the Labour Movement, farm organizations, professional people and other liberally minded persons," and it instructed its executive council to enter into discussion with those groups "to formulate a constitution and a program for such a political instrument" (Archer 1990, 22; see also Lewis 1981, 438).

From the CCF's perspective, the decision to establish a closer relationship with organized labour was born partly of necessity. After reaching the zenith of its electoral support in the mid-1940s, the national CCF's growth stalled and numbers began to decline. By the mid-1950s the CCF was obtaining, on average, approximately 11 percent of the vote. Its most devastating setback occurred in the Diefenbaker land-slide election of 1958, when the party was reduced to less than 10 per-cent of the vote and, more significantly, to only 8 seats in the 265-seat Commons. Worse still, the defeated candidates included the party's leader, M.J. Coldwell, and one of its leading figures, Stanley Knowles, in the riding of Winnipeg North Centre, which had been held by J.S. Woodsworth and then Knowles since 1921.

The 1958 election reinforced concerns that had surfaced over the preceding decade. The inability to make significant inroads in the industrial heartland of Ontario and Quebec and in the larger urban centres elsewhere in the country was particularly troublesome, espe-cially in light of the strong trends toward urbanization in Canada. As well, the party's chronic shortage of funds made it difficult to mount a concerted effort to compete with the Liberals and Conservatives in conducting national election campaigns. The party's organizing efforts lacked the personnel, resources and money to mobilize effectively in those areas in which it wished to expand. Although there had always been some support for a stronger role for labour, the 1958 election defeat served to confirm for some – and convert others to – a belief in the necessity of incorporating unions in the party (see, among others, Archer and Whitehorn 1990b; Archer 1990; Horowitz 1968; Lewis 1981; Morton 1986).

The discussions organized by a joint committee of the CCF and CLC led to the creation in 1961 of the NDP. Whereas the CCF had attempted to forge an alliance of "Farmer-Labour-Socialist," the NDP was a de facto alliance of organized labour and "liberally minded" Canadians. This alliance, although based loosely on the model of the British Labour Party, differed from it in two respects. The Trades Union Congress (TUC) founded the British Labour Party in 1899, but since 1906 the labour fed-eration has maintained an arm's-length relationship with the party (this is discussed more fully below). The TUC encouraged its affiliates to affil-iate with the Labour Party, and most of the large unions have done so. Thus, the unions are able to control party policy through bloc voting at conferences (Minkin 1978).

The CLC maintains an arm's-length relationship with the NDP but it too encourages its affiliates to affiliate with the party. However, whereas in Britain the national unions (some with more than one mil-lion members) affiliate with the Labour Party, in Canada affiliation with the NDP is based on local unions. Thus, the unions which affiliate in Canada are much smaller. Also, Canadian unions receive one conven-tion delegate for each 1 000 members they affiliate, and there is no bloc voting at NDP conventions. As a result, unions never wield as many as 35 percent of convention votes and typically have only 20 to 25 percent (Archer and Whitehorn 1990b, table 1). A majority of delegate votes, and usually a very large majority, are controlled by the constituency associations.

Thus, two important principles underlie the organization of the NDP. A federated structure ensures a continuing primacy of the provincial sections, and, within these, the centrality of constituency associations is maintained. There exists an overarching tendency toward equality in representing the various sections of the party in the NDP's governing bodies. The exception is at the party's convention, where representation is based on size rather than on the principle of equality. The second principle is that labour plays an important but not dominant role in the party. It does not control the convention, and, in allocating representation on the party's governing bodies, labour tends to be viewed as a section, equal to the other provincial sections. At times, labour is able to obtain somewhat greater representation than the provincial sections, but at other times, less so.

COSTS AND BENEFITS OF THE UNION–PARTY LINK

There are many ways in which one could attempt to calculate the costs and benefits of the union–NDP relationship. Some of the costs, such as affiliation fees, are straightforward and can be calculated precisely. Others, such as the direct or potential costs associated with choosing to forgo other relationships, are much more difficult to calculate and far more contentious in quantifying. Likewise, it is difficult to calculate the benefits received from a relationship. For example, one may believe that an outcome resulted from a particular cause, when in fact it would have happened in any event. Similarly, the perception of benefits, like beauty, often lies in the eye of the beholder. A benefit to one individual may be interpreted as a cost for others. With these caveats in mind, this section will attempt to estimate some of the costs and benefits of the union–party relationship from the perspective of organized labour.

The benefits of the unions' link with the NDP are found in its representation on party decision-making bodies and in the party's active pursuit of labour's political and legislative objectives. Representation at conventions was discussed above, and it was noted that labour delegates, both from central labour and from affiliated locals, usually comprise approximately 20 to 25 percent of total delegates. If the leadership of the labour movement was able to persuade labour delegates to vote as a bloc through the labour caucus, these delegates would constitute a powerful lobby within the party at conventions. Some have suggested that labour voted as a bloc in 1971 in order to guarantee the victory of David Lewis over Waffle candidate Jim Laxer, who was opposed to the party "establishment" and to labour's strong role in the NDP (Brodie 1985; Hackett 1979).

The greater the consensus among the labour leadership, the greater is the likelihood that the labour vote can significantly affect the outcome of the leadership race. But the opposite is also true. In the 1989 contest, labour leaders were divided in their support for the candidates and the labour vote split in many directions. On the final ballot, labour was more likely to support the losing candidacy of Barrett than to vote for McLaughlin (Archer 1991). Thus, although labour does not control the outcome of convention balloting, its participation in the NDP enables it to play an active part in the decision-making process.

This position characterizes labour's participation in the party more generally. However, unlike party conventions, where there is a rigorous formula for determining the size of the labour delegation, on other NDP bodies the number of labour representatives is decided more by custom, or unwritten understanding. For example, of the party's current contingent of 16 table officers, it is understood that labour's entitlement is 3. Of these, by tradition either the president or treasurer generally comes from labour. Of the 30 members of the party executive, labour is entitled to 6 positions, or 20 percent. It is not unusual for some of the other 24 executive members to be high-ranking union officials, so that as many as 25 to 30 percent of the executive may have a labour connection. Representation beyond that proportion, however, would be rare.

The union representation among the officers and executive tends to be from central labour or from the head offices of national or regional unions. Representation on the federal council, which numbers approximately 120 to 130, includes one member from each of the 12 largest unions affiliated to the party. However, there are 4 members from each of the provincial parties' table officers, and there are another 30 members selected from the provincial parties' conventions and 20 members selected from the federal convention. The provinces vary in the degree to which they have informal provisions for union representation from their delegates, depending on the strength of organized labour in the province and its commitment to the NDP. Labour representation on the nominating committee of the federal convention – where each province has one seat, as do organizations representing youth, women and labour – ensures that nominations from federal convention to council include labour representatives.

There are numerous other committees, both standing and ad hoc, in which labour representation is guaranteed. The Policy Review

Committee, the Platform Committee and the Convention Resolutions Committee are all based on the general formula used by the Nominating Committee, with one seat allocated to each section, and labour designated as a section. In other committees, such as the Finance Committee, the Convention Planning Committee and the Convention Resolution Appeals Committee, there is no requirement for a labour representative, although the fact that the treasurer often is from labour ensures that labour has a place on the Finance Committee. In general, when the party committee or task force touches on areas that are particularly important to labour, then labour will manage to gain representation. The greater labour's interest in the area, the larger is its contingent of representatives, although they never approach a majority.

A telling example of labour's role in the party can be seen in two committees that have recently gained considerable attention, both relating to the conduct of national elections. Following the 1988 federal election, several high-ranking union officials publicly expressed their dissatisfaction over the NDP's decision to downplay the Free Trade Agreement in the campaign and criticized the management of the campaign, particularly the perceived exclusion of labour from strategic decision making (Whitehorn 1989, 51–52). As a result, the party established an election review committee, which included three representatives from labour. The Committee's report described labour as "one of the most important constituencies of the party," and, among other things, recommended an increase in labour's representation on the key Strategy and Election Planning Committee (NDP 1989; for a discussion of the committee in the 1988 election, see Whitehorn 1989). In the 1990 Ontario election, the Ontario NDP's Election Planning Committee consisted of roughly equal representation from caucus, the party organization and labour (interview with Jill Marzetti, provincial secretary).

Labour representation on the party's councils also extends to a certain degree to relations with caucus. On the one hand, there is a strong expectation that the party leader will make himself or herself available for consultations and discussions with leaders from the labour movement, particularly with the CLC president. The party and the CLC have recently agreed to hold a series of retreats for individuals in key leadership positions in both organizations in order to establish stronger personal relations and to develop legislative priorities. In addition, the coordinator of the CLC's Political Action Department attends the weekly caucus meeting with voice but no vote and also attends the weekly meetings of the key Priorities and Planning Committee. Thus, across the full range of the NDP's organization, labour has gained representation but not control. By any measure, this is an important benefit for labour's link to the NDP.

The other major benefit for the unions is that their relationship with the NDP enables them to pursue directly their political and legislative goals. Time and again, in interviews with labour leaders, political and legislative action was described as one of the key components of the unions' representation of their members' interests. Labour's pursuit of its legislative and political goals takes place across a broad front of activities, a major component of which is through its support of the NDP. The winner-take-all nature of the Westminster model parliamentary system used in Canada places a premium on being associated with the party forming the government.

Labour leaders often point to two benefits that accrue from its relationship with the NDP. Most directly, they often list the major legislative accomplishments of CCF or NDP governments, or changes that were brought about through the NDP's ability to pressure a Liberal or Conservative government, typically when the latter had minority control of the legislature. For example, in the field of health care, CCF-NDP governments were the first to introduce universal hospital and medical insurance in Saskatchewan in 1947 and 1962, respectively, as well as pharmacare for seniors and dental care for children in Manitoba in 1973 and 1974. J.S. Woodsworth and the Ginger Group in the Commons, the forerunners of the CCF, forced the government to introduce pensions in the 1920s. In the 1960s, the minority Liberal government introduced universal pensions, a proposal made by the CCF in the 1940s. In the 1970s, a minority Liberal government was forced to index to inflation old-age security payments. In addition, the CCF-NDP are viewed as having adopted favourable labour legislation, forcing the adoption of pay equity in Ontario, adopting or forcing the adoption of rent controls and forcing the creation of Petro Canada and the Foreign Investment Review Agency. In short, the legislative initiatives introduced by CCF-NDP governments, or brought about through CCF-NDP pressure in the legislature, are often viewed as most consistent with the political and legislative goals of the labour movement, at least when compared to the policy orientation of the Liberal and Conservative parties.

The other benefit often discussed is the ability of labour unions to deliver the vote for the NDP. This claim, however, is somewhat more contentious. For example, union members are more likely than non-union members to vote NDP. About 10 to 12 percent of non-union members usually vote NDP federally, compared to 20 to 25 percent of union members. Furthermore, among those who belong to union locals affiliated with the NDP, the percentage supporting the party increases to between 30 and 40 percent (Archer 1990, 57–63). However, very few union members (less than 1 voter in 20) are affiliated with the NDP, and this decreases the overall effect of the union tie on election outcomes.

The costs to unions of their link to the party are of several types. The most obvious are the direct financial contributions. Unions contribute funds in two ways: through affiliation fees and through general contributions to the party. In 1990, the affiliated locals paid $607 639 in affiliation fees and unions gave $563 127 in other contributions. During election years, affiliation fees remain consistent and the unions' other contributions increase substantially to approximately $2 million.

The costs to unions of their contributions to the NDP can be interpreted meaningfully only in relation to the financial contributions that businesses give to the Liberal and Conservative parties. In 1990, whereas labour contributed a total of $1.2 million to the NDP, the Liberal party received $4.6 million from business organizations, outspending labour by a factor of almost 4 to 1. The Conservative party was even more effective in raising funds from business. In 1990, business contributed $6.3 million to the Conservatives, thereby outstripping labour's contribution to the NDP by a factor of almost 6 to 1 (computed from Canada, Elections Canada 1991). Therefore, by the standard of business contributions to the Liberals and Conservatives, the direct financial costs to labour in supporting the NDP are relatively modest.

An additional potential cost to labour, but one that is much more difficult to measure, is the effect its relationship with the NDP has on its ability to maintain a productive relationship with the Liberals and Conservatives, particularly since the latter two have always formed the government nationally. The attitudes of labour leaders toward the size and importance of this "cost" to labour are discussed in detail below. Leaving this discussion aside for the moment, it is important to note that a recognition of the continuing responsibilities of the labour movement to represent their members' interests, regardless of the party in power, was influential in the decision of the CLC and NDP to structure an arm's-length relationship. The CLC remains formally distinct from the NDP, and the major linkage is through the affiliation of union locals to the party. In those instances in which labour has a position on an NDP organ, it is never a controlling position. Thus, the CLC is able to pursue its legislative and political goals both inside and outside the party.

Do the benefits of affiliation outweigh the costs from the perspective of Canadian unions? Judging by rates of affiliation, one might be tempted to answer negatively. The membership of unions affiliated with the NDP peaked at almost 15 percent of the unionized workforce in the mid-1960s and has declined to less than 10 percent today (Archer 1990, 37). However, this measure may be misleading. The affiliation of union locals with the NDP has the characteristics of a collective action problem, in which the logic of decision making differs depending on whether one examines the cost–benefit ratio for the group as a whole (i.e., CLC-affiliated unions) or individual group members (the local union) (see Archer 1990, 41–55; Olson 1965). Simply put, the collective action problem implies that unions could agree that benefits outweigh costs for the labour movement as a whole but that their individual decision adds so little that there is no need for them to engage in collective action, which in this case is affiliating with the NDP.

On the other hand, it is difficult to escape the fact that many unions do choose to affiliate. In 1990, 684 unions affiliated a total of 290 000 members (NDP 1990). Unions continue to contribute from $1 to $2.5 million annually toward the financing of the party; and – as the report of the Election Review Committee suggests, and as the recent experience of the Election Planning Committee of the Ontario NDP confirms – in some areas, labour is strengthening its ties with and commitment to the party. These actions suggest that for a significant number of local union affiliates, as well as for the CLC and many of the provincial federations of labour, the perception remains that unions' relationship with the NDP is of benefit to those unions. This is a perception that is shared by many non-union party activists. When asked in 1987 whether the union link with the party had been beneficial, more than 80 percent of non-union delegates and more than 98 percent of union delegates believed it was. As well, more than 4 in 10 non-union delegates and 7 in 10 union delegates thought the relationship should be strengthened (Archer and Whitehorn 1990b).

LABOUR'S ROLE IN NDP DECISION MAKING

Unions have many points of entry into the decision-making organs of the party. Labour has a seat on most party committees and is provided access to caucus meetings. It is worth exploring whether labour's concerns are consistent with those of the party and the degree to which they are adequately represented in the party. This section explores labour's role in the decision-making process, but it does so under the following limitations. When speaking of labour's link to the NDP, it is important to recall that the relationship is limited to the CLC and its affiliated unions. It has always been the CLC, not "organized labour" as such, that has pursued political action through the NDP. In addition, the focus will be on those unions that have affiliated with the NDP. They are the ones that have formed an integral relationship with the party and would be most directly affected by any change in the party's structure. This section will examine labour's role in the party by focusing on delegates to the party's convention. It is here that large numbers of union members, both from the affiliates and from central labour, come together with other party members to debate and formulate party policy and to choose party leaders (for technical information on the 1987 and 1989 NDP convention surveys, see Archer and Whitehorn 1990b; Archer 1991).

Labour's representation in the NDP is heavily weighted with members from Ontario, a fact reflected in the allocation of convention delegates. More than 73 percent of the affiliated membership is from Ontario, and there is a corresponding percentage of Ontarians among labour delegates at conventions. Union delegates tend to be less highly educated than non-union delegates and are much more likely to be skilled blue-collar workers or union representatives, whereas non-union delegates tend to be professional or skilled white-collar employees. As well, to date, labour delegates have overwhelmingly been male, by a factor of about 5 to 1, compared to the overrepresentation of males among non-union delegates by a ratio of less than 2 to 1 (Archer and Whitehorn 1990b). The data in table 6.1 compare attitudes across a wide

Table 6.1
Attitudinal differences between parties and between union categories in the NDP
(mean scores)

	Delegate type			
	NDP			
Attitude scale (range)	Non-union	Union	Liberal	Conservative
Continentalism (0–4)	0.28	0.48	1.80	2.90
Hawkishness (0–6)	0.51	1.23	2.65	4.17
Social security (0–5)	3.29	3.21	2.63	1.67
Pro-bilingualism (0–2)	1.81	1.51	1.71	1.01
Moralism (0–3)	0.54	0.76	1.65	2.16
Against corporate power (0–3)	2.63	2.68	1.98	1.58
Privatization (0–6)	0.12	0.35	2.21	4.00
Civil liberties (0–3)	1.89	2.05	1.22	1.51

Source: Archer and Whitehorn (1990b).

Note: Data for Liberals and Conservatives are taken from Blake (1988, 40).

range of policy questions among delegates to Liberal, Conservative and New Democrat conventions (for technical information on index construction, see Archer and Whitehorn 1991). Data for the NDP are further broken down according to whether the delegates were union or non-union.

Overall, in looking at policy questions, the preferences of union delegates are very close to those of non-union delegates and are substantially different from those of Liberal and Conservative delegates. For example, the first item in the table is a four-point index measuring attitudes favourable to continentalism. It is based on questions about the integration of the Canadian and American economies. Those scoring high on this measure could be thought of as continentalists, whereas those scoring low could be described as economic nationalists. The delegates to the 1983 Conservative leadership convention scored 2.9, which is close to the continentalist end of the index, whereas non-union NDP delegates scored 0.28, very near the economic nationalist end. Note that labour delegates are very close to other New Democrats and are quite distant from both the Liberals and the Conservatives. With very few exceptions, this general trend is consistent across the various policy areas. Labour delegates are closer to non-union NDP delegates than they are to either Liberal or Conservative delegates on the indexes of hawkishness, the right to social security, moralism, opposition to corporate power, privatization and attitudes supportive of civil liberties. The one exception is the area of bilingualism; but even here, Liberals, non-union NDP and union NDP delegates all place themselves toward the pro-bilingualism end, although with the order somewhat changed.

This is not to deny that differences exist between the policy preferences of union and non-union New Democrats.[2] For example, union delegates have been more supportive than non-union delegates on defence spending and on maintaining military alliances, whereas non-union New Democrats give greater support to spending on foreign aid or on the arts. In addition, union delegates tend to take more liberal positions on labour relations issues than non-union delegates do. For example, union delegates give greater support to the views that an NDP government should never interfere with free collective bargaining, that strikers should be eligible for unemployment insurance payments and that the right to strike should never be restricted (Archer and Whitehorn 1990b). Nonetheless, when compared to the views of Liberals and Conservatives, labour finds its views most closely reflected in the views of non-union New Democrats. As such, one might describe the union–NDP relationship as a natural alliance.

THE UNION–PARTY LINK IN COMPARATIVE PERSPECTIVE

Perhaps the most common feature of the organizational structure of social democratic parties is their characteristic linkage to other working-class organizations, particularly to trade unions. With remarkably few exceptions, social democratic parties across the advanced industrial democracies maintain some kind of link with their corresponding trade unions. However, two other observations follow immediately. The first is that there is an unusually diverse array of linkages between unions and political parties, with each country adapting the general feature to its own particular circumstances. Beyond that, there is also variation across time, with some general patterns emerging with respect to the contemporary period. To gain a better understanding of the nature of the union–party relationship in Canada, it is useful to survey the relationship in a comparative context. In light of the importance of the British Labour Party model in defining the union–party relationship in Canada (see Lewis 1981), this section will begin by discussing the British case. It will then discuss the contrasting models used in Scandinavia and several other cases from continental Europe.

Great Britain

From its inception, the British Labour Party has been heavily dependent on the labour movement for money and organizational resources. The party was created in 1899 as the Labour Representation Committee of the Trades Union Congress, the major central body of the labour movement (Leys 1989, 214). By 1906, it had been reorganized as the Labour Party with direct union participation through the affiliation of national unions. Unions are provided with representation at the party's conferences by having one vote for each affiliated member, and these votes are cast as a bloc. Several of the affiliated unions are larger than the entire contingent of constituency delegates and wield as many conference votes. The result is that the unions control over 90 percent of the conference votes (Koelble 1987, 255).

The practice of union affiliation and the contribution of union dues to the Labour Party has generated controversy almost from the start. For example, in the Osborne judgement of 1909, the House of Lords ruled that trade unions could not use their funds for political purposes, a decision that greatly threatened the Labour Party (Minkin 1974). The decision was effectively reversed by the Liberal government four years later, through the passage of the *Trade Union Act* of 1913. The use of union funds for political purposes was once again permitted, provided the union balloted its members, created a separate political fund for political purposes and provided a mechanism whereby those disagreeing could opt out from the obligation to contribute to the fund (Ewing 1987).

The dispute then turned to whether union contributions would be based on the principle of objectors opting out or of supporters opting in. Those favouring the latter won their point in 1927 with the passage of the *Trade Disputes and Trade Unions Act*, at which time the opting-in formula was adopted. The percentage of TUC members paying the political levy dropped from 75 percent in 1925 to 48 percent in 1938 (Ewing 1987, 51). One of the first acts of the Labour government elected in 1945 was the restoration of the opting-out procedure for union affiliation.

The issue of individual union members opting in or out of affiliation appeared finally to be settled in the postwar era. Changes of government did not produce renewed action toward another reversal in the formula used – not until election of the Thatcher government in 1979. In an effort to weaken the ties between unions and the Labour Party, the Thatcher government passed the *Trade Union Act, 1984*. This legislation required the periodic review of unions' commitment to maintain a political fund by having them ballot their members every 10 years, at which time they were required to remind members that they could opt out of affiliation. Furthermore, the TUC was directed to establish appropriate rules for member balloting, and failure to do so would result in a reversion to the opting-in formula (TUC 1984, 24–31 and 84–85; see also Fatchett 1984, 30–34).

In addition, the Act stipulates that the political funds can only be financed by member contributions for that purpose. Therefore, a union cannot transfer funds from outside the political fund into the political fund, nor can it use outside funds for political purposes. Indeed, it cannot even borrow money to spend on political purposes, such as financing an election campaign, because the interest for such borrowing could not be paid through the political fund (Ewing 1987, 66). Furthermore, through the establishment of a broad definition of "political acts," the *Trade Union Act, 1984*, further constrains unions in their political spending (Towers 1989, 170; Ewing 1987, 68; the Act is printed in Ewing 1987, 216–25).

Despite these constraints, unions continue to provide the bulk of the financing for the Labour Party in Britain. During the non-election years of 1984–86, union contributions constituted approximately 75 percent of the party's revenue, almost all of which was through affiliation fees. In the election years of 1983 and 1987, union contributions increased to 87 percent of the party's revenues (calculated from Pinto-Duschinsky 1989, 200).

Despite the size of union contributions to the Labour Party, they still are outstripped by the corporate sponsorship of the Conservative Party. More generally, the very small quantity of public funding made available to British parties, and the importance of controlling the legislature in British government, have forced parties to solicit substantial funds from those groups and individuals that support them. The recent Labour Party data on funding suggest that the *Trade Union Act, 1984*, has not had an appreciable effect on the party's reliance on organized labour for the bulk of its funding. In large part, this is because of the success of the reballoting efforts. All of the unions affiliated with the Labour Party at the time the Act was implemented have reaffirmed their commitment to create a political fund and to affiliate.

Two other aspects of the unions' relationship with the Labour Party are particularly germane to the purposes of this research. Regarding the percentage of affiliation, it is common practice in Britain to affiliate fewer members than belong to the union and fewer than the proportion who opt out. This practice enables both the unions and the party to argue that they are not receiving substantial financial support from those who do not support their policies, and it also frees money in the political fund to be used for other political purposes. As well, in 1980 the party adjusted the weight of conference balloting for the selection of party leaders. Votes are now accorded on the formula of 40 percent to trade union delegates, 30 percent for constituency party delegates and 30 percent for parliamentary party delegates (Whiteley 1983, 4). As a result, the role of labour in leadership selection remains strong, but it is balanced with other key components of the party.

Scandinavia

The link between unions and the social democratic parties in the Scandinavian countries has been based on a model that is different from that used in Britain. Like the British case but unlike the experience elsewhere in Europe, Scandinavian unions tend to be linked to a single union federation (LO). However, in contrast to the British TUC's approach, the LO has not pursued large-scale direct affiliation with the social democratic parties in the three countries, and for the most part it has decreased its financial commitments to them. Nonetheless, in each instance, important links between unions and the party remain, with the unions and the social democratic parties described as two legs of a single movement (Einhorn and Logue 1988, 170).

When the LO was founded in Sweden in 1898, unions were required to join the party as a condition of membership in the labour federation. However, this arrangement proved unpopular and was short-lived;

within a decade the formal link between the LO and the Social Democratic party (SAP) was severed (Elvander 1974). Moreover, there was no link between national unions and the party, as there is in Britain. Instead, local unions were linked to the local party organization (Ewing 1987, 169; Einhorn and Logue 1988, 170). Local affiliation took place at a collective level; that is, when a trade union branch affiliated, all members of that union branch became full members of the party, with all the rights and privileges of individual party members. Because of its controversial nature, this provision was recently changed so that when a local union branch votes to affiliate, members of that branch become party members only upon application for membership (Ewing 1987, 172). The rules on affiliation have always been stricter than in Britain. Trade union branches that wish to be affiliated must vote on affiliation each year.

The unions' relationship with the party extends beyond the affiliation of union branches. It is typical to find senior union officials on the party's executive, and unions conduct considerable promotion of the party through the union-sponsored newspapers. In addition, although unions continue to provide financial support to the party, particularly around election time, Sweden has moved increasingly toward the public funding of parties. Since funding is based on a party's support at the polls and since the SAP has been the strongest party at the polls since the 1930s, its public support is considerable. Indeed, it often gets more than half of its funds from public subsidy (Ewing 1987, 162–63).

An important feature of the Swedish system of policy development is the close integration of major interest groups into the process, a system described as neocorporatism (Bornstein 1984, 56). Indeed, some have suggested that key groups such as labour wield a degree of decision-making authority that rivals that of Parliament itself and clearly exceeds that of the individual parties (Heckscher 1958, 170). Thus, the LO is able to pursue its policy preferences outside the confines of the Social Democratic party as an integral part of the political process in its own right (Smith 1980, 52).

The Danish variant of the Scandinavian model is based on several premises. On the one hand, the trade unions (LO), the cooperative movement and the Social Democrats (SD) have looked upon themselves as three branches of the same movement. Consequently, they are heavily represented on one another's executives, and union leaders are strongly Social Democratic. This close relationship has been superimposed on a political system whose major feature is cooperation and compromise, and one in which the parties engage in extensive bargaining in an effort to govern by consensus (Pedersen 1987). Furthermore, it has been assumed that the negotiations extend beyond the parties in the legislature and include representatives of the major interest organizations, of which labour remains of central importance.

The use of corporatist policy making and nonpartisan compromise has been so important as to decrease the overall utility of parties as organizations. Ironically, it has been the success of the social democratic parties in establishing the welfare state, produced by the achievements of corporatist policy making, which has led to an erosion of a separate working-class culture and of the party's electoral base (Einhorn and Logue 1988, 180). One measure of this is in the decline in party membership. Between 1961 and 1981, party members as a percentage of voters declined from 21 percent to 8 percent overall, and among Social Democrats it declined from 25 percent to 10 percent (Pedersen 1987, 35). In absolute terms, membership in the Social Democratic party fell from 300 000 in 1947 to 120 000 in 1988 (Einhorn and Logue 1988, 179).

In addition, there is little public funding of parties, and that which exists is limited to paying the costs of secretarial support and research support for the parliamentary party. Unions provide some funds to the party, but mainly for the running of elections and to cover the costs of the party newspaper. The relations between the unions and the party are being blurred because of their tendency to become involved in each other's affairs. The party has become heavily involved in setting wages, and the unions have taken policy positions independent of the Social Democrats, with some unions going so far as to provide funds for all working-class parties (Einhorn and Logue 1988, 181). Thus, whereas the relationship between Danish unions and the Social Democrats remains strong, there is greater instability and change than there was a decade ago.

As the third Scandinavian variant, Norway combines features of both the Swedish and Danish arrangements. The Norwegian labour party (DNA) and trade union federation (LO) are thought of as dual arms of a single labour movement but remain completely autonomous organizations. As in Denmark, the party and union are joined at the top, although the relationship goes further through the existence of a joint committee of the party and union which consists of key representatives of each, including their separate chairs (Martin 1974). More generally, there is strong representation of LO members on key party decision-making bodies, and most of the LO secretariat hold party memberships.

As in Scandinavia generally, the union representatives are influential in the party because of the party positions they hold, not because of the convention votes they wield. At the level of the LO, or the national union level, there is no collective affiliation with the party. As in Sweden, affiliation may take place between the local unions and the local party organization for which the unions are rewarded with seats on the local party's council (Einhorn and Logue 1988). Nonetheless, the linkages remain much stronger at the top than at the bottom of the party's structure.

Thus, the Scandinavian model of union linkages with social democratic parties has tended to develop a distinct character. High rates of unionization within a highly centralized union movement provide the framework for discussion and cooperation. In addition, lengthy periods of social democratic government, combined with corporatist policy making, have provided an outlet for the representation of union interests. Together, the unions and the social democratic parties have functioned as two legs of a single movement, and although their relationship has experienced increasing strain recently, they continue to operate in considerable harmony.

Austria

A significant degree of variation exists in the union–party relationship in continental Europe. Some countries, such as Austria and the Federal Republic of Germany, have developed union movements organized under a single federation. More typically, as seen in France, multiple union movements have arisen which have been divided along ideological lines (Windmuller 1975; Bornstein 1984). Furthermore, the divisions among the latter have not been between craft unions and industrial unionism as was the case in Canada and the United States from the mid-1930s to the mid-1950s. Instead, they have typically been between secular and confessional unions and between unions supporting democratic reforms and those seeking revolutionary change. Furthermore, their party systems have developed in light of (and often reflecting) this organizational fragmentation (Windmuller 1975). Some of the more notable differences in union–party relations will be examined by focusing on Austria, the Federal Republic of Germany and France.

The Austrian system of union–party relations shares many of the neocorporatist characteristics of the Scandinavian model (Bornstein 1984, 56). Interest representation is based on the premise of group cooperation and accommodation among political élites (Gerlich 1987) in a system known as the social partnership. The implication of the social partnership is that all interests are represented in the four large semipublic institutions; namely, the chambers of business, agriculture, and labour, and the Trade Union Federation. Membership in these organizations is compulsory. Consultation, cooperation and bargaining take place between these large groups, which set incomes and many prices, and which generally influence economic policy (ibid.). The interest groups are formally nonpartisan, and all parties have a role in their governing committees. Nonetheless, one of the parties always holds a very clear majority. By way of illustration, in 1979 the Social Democrats held 64 percent and 77 percent of the seats in the Chamber of Labour and the Trade Union Federation, respectively. The Christian Social party, on the other hand, held 86 percent and 85 percent of the seats in the Chamber of Commerce and the Chamber of Agriculture, respectively (ibid., 88).

The importance of the social partnership and of the effective removal of economic policy making from the partisan political agenda has strengthened organized interests while weakening parties – or at the least helping to transform them into catch-all parties. That is, although party membership is quite large (as many as 30 percent of voters are party members [Engelmann 1988, 89]), one should not evaluate party strength solely on the basis of membership. For the bulk of their funding, the Social Democrats rely on state subsidies and on a combination of individual membership dues and taxes on their deputies, with very little coming from unions (Gerlich 1987, 84–85). Thus, although there remains a close relationship between the unions and the party, it takes place through a system of interlocking personnel as well as through interest group consultation, with the parties often occupying the weaker position (Windmuller 1975). Consequently, policy making tends not to be centred within the party apparatus, though the parties and their members remain highly involved in the policy process (Gerlich 1987, 89).

Germany

The union–party relationship in Germany has been close, despite the fact that the major organizations remain formally independent (Markovits and Allen 1984, 101). The Social Democratic party (SPD) formally changed its electoral and economic strategy through adopting the Bad Godesburg Program in 1959, thereby rejecting large-scale nationalization in favour of a greater "catch-all" appeal (Dalton 1989, 110). It therefore shifted from an attempt to represent trade union interests solely toward adopting a strategy to appeal also to non-unionized and white-collar workers.

The party was able to change its electoral strategy without a major internal reorganization because its link with labour never had a strong institutionalized character. Although the workforce is organized in one major federation – the DGB, which consists of 16 affiliates representing approximately 85 percent of unionized workers (Markovits and Allen 1984, 95) – no unions are affiliated with the party (Smith 1980, 55). Instead, the ties have primarily been through overlapping personal memberships. For example, in the 1970s, it was typical for 90 percent of union officials to be SPD members and for 90 percent of SPD members of the Bundestag to be DGB members (Willey 1974). In addition, although as many as three-quarters of SPD convention delegates were union members, they did not represent the union at conventions and did not vote as a bloc (ibid., 45).

There has been little evidence of the DGB providing direct financial aid to the party. Nonetheless, its indirect aid has been important. The unions are heavily involved in candidate and party recruitment drives, and they make available to their members joint membership in the party. Union officials also provide valuable organizational and, at times, material resources in pursuing the ends of the party.

It would be a mistake, however, to interpret the absence of a strong organizational and financial link between the DGB and SPD as implying that labour is poorly represented in the party. The strong overlap in personnel has led to a mutual shaping of policy preferences. In addition, the strong contingent of union members on the party's policy-making bodies has ensured that labour's voice and its favoured position within the party cannot easily be challenged. For example, the left's challenge to the party's program and internal structure that arose in the 1970s was effectively forestalled and defeated through the combined efforts of the established party leadership and because of the strong representation of unionists at all levels of decision making (Koelble 1987). Thus, labour has managed to establish and maintain an important position within the party while not sacrificing its own autonomy or even providing many financial resources.

Although there have always been tensions between unions and social democratic parties, these tensions were heightened in Germany in the late 1980s. The dual challenges from "above" (through the state and business groups, to stake a greater reliance on market forces in determining the nature of social relations) and from "below" (through the emergence of new social movements, to challenge labour's monopoly as the representative of progressive social forces) strained the union–party relationship (Markovits and Allen 1989, 294). As a result, the 1980s witnessed attempts by some SPD leaders to move away from their traditional blue-collar supporters; there were also large-scale union defections from SPD voting in 1983, although most had returned by 1987 (ibid., 305–307). However, the union–SPD relationship of mutual self-interest continues to ensure a continuation of considerable agreement and cooperation. The logic of this relationship is well captured by Willey (1974): "The unions have nowhere else to go, and the party needs their services."

France

The union movement in France differs dramatically from those discussed above. With only 15 percent of the workforce organized in unions, France has among the lowest rate of unionization in Europe (Smith 1983, 60). In contrast to the single central federation of labour in many countries, there are three major union centrals in France – the CGT, FO and CFDT – each representing a unique perspective on the linkage between unions and parties.

The CGT represents a Marxist-Leninist approach in which strong ties are maintained with the Communist party. The party's role is to provide the movement with an intellectual vanguard and with policy and organizational leadership. The linkage between the two has remained strong, despite the poor electoral performance of the party. A Social Democratic model has characterized the relationship between FO and the Socialist party, with their relations being described as "discreet, reserved and cordial" (Reynaud 1975, 210). The third pattern, followed by CFDT, has been syndicalist, emphasizing the unions' independence from parties and their reliance on direct political action.

Two contradictory trends have characterized union–party relations in recent years. Beginning in the early 1970s, the Socialist party promoted the themes of environmentalism, worker self-management and regionalism, policies that were welcomed by both FO and CFDT. The adoption of this strategy has led to closer ties between the two unions and the Socialist party, particularly through overlapping memberships at the local level (LaGroye 1989, 371–72). The election of the Socialists to government in 1981 led many to expect a greater role for unions in the governmental process. However, these expectations were soon dashed. The divisions that existed within the union movement, the severity of the economic crisis and the unions' loss of membership prevented them from taking advantage of the opportunity that was provided by a Socialist government (Wilson 1988, 24–25; Bornstein 1984, 80).

Added to this has been the overarching yet contrary impulse of the Fifth Republic, which stresses the necessity of forging representational linkages at the executive rather than the legislative level. The logic and structure of the Fifth Republic are aimed unambiguously at limiting the power of interest intermediacy – of parties and interest groups alike

(Smith 1983, 62; Wilson 1988, 25). Thus, the general decoupling of union and party in France has been a response to the larger organizational imperatives produced by a decision-making structure that has moved away from the Assembly toward a "nonpolitical" form.

THE NDP IN COMPARATIVE CONTEXT

Labour in Canada is highly decentralized. The bulk of the power in the labour movement rests with national and regional union bodies, such as the Canadian Auto Workers, United Steelworkers and the Canadian Union of Public Employees. They conduct collective bargaining and coordinate most other union activities. To the extent that the national or regional union offices delegate authority, they tend to do so downward to their union local, rather than upward to the union federations.

The locals have developed as important and influential decision-making units. In establishing a link between unions and the party, the organizational structure of the unions pointed toward a direct link between the locals of the union and the party. From the party's side, a federal organizational structure, with each of the provincial parties joining the national party as a separate section, implied that labour also would be represented as a section. Thus, the union–party link is a combination of a local union to national party linkage, and an assumption that labour is one of the party's sections.

Defining labour as a section of the party has several implications for the role of unions in party decision making. On the one hand, it means that the NDP is not simply a labour party but is also one that responds to the interests of each of the sections. By implication, labour cannot dominate the party. As was shown above, the representation of unions at party conventions and the absence of bloc voting ensure that the unions' position is one of an important minority, with labour representatives occupying about one-quarter of delegate seats.

The linkage between unions and the party extends beyond delegate representation at conventions but is limited both on the part of labour and on the party's side. For labour, it is limited almost exclusively to the CLC and its affiliates, as well as the corresponding provincial federations of labour. It should be borne in mind that only 58.6 percent of unions are CLC affiliates, the remainder being affiliated with the CFL (5.2 percent), the Quebec-based CNTU (5.3 percent) and other central organizations (9.4 percent), or else having chosen to remain unaffiliated (21.7 percent) (Canada, Labour Canada 1990, XIII). A recent task force of the CLC on its links with the NDP and also the recent election review committee (ERC) of the NDP both affirmed the need to maintain and indeed strengthen labour's involvement with the party. But the recommendations of the ERC confirm the limited, and sectional, position of unions. For example, the report recommends increasing labour's representation on the Strategy and Election Planning Committee, the key committee responsible for conducting the campaign. Although the report does not specify the size of the labour contingent, the need to represent diverse regional interests and past practice both make it likely that labour will hold less than one-quarter of the positions. The committee also recommended that one person act to provide communication and coordination between labour and the party's parliamentary wing, that there be a single representative of labour in the party's federal office, and that labour receive representation on election-related and policy review committees. In each case, the role of labour is important, but it is also a distinct minority.

The comparative analysis suggested that the financial relationship between unions and parties is also strongly affected by the overall structure of interest representation in society. For example, countries that arrive at collective decision making through consultation and compromise among the major interests tend to have political parties that lack a firm financial commitment from unions. To the extent that interest groups, and especially labour unions, constitute an essential component of the national political decision-making structure and are required to work effectively with all governments, they have tended to be organizationally distinct from the social democratic parties. As well, direct state aid to political parties has had the effect of decreasing the reliance on union financial commitments. These trends have achieved their clearest expression in Scandinavia. In contrast, countries governed by an adversarial decision-making structure, in which the interests of labour are poorly articulated in government unless labour's party controls the reins of power, have favoured the establishment and maintenance of strong direct union–party ties. Where there also exists only limited public financial support for parties, it has fallen to the unions to provide the necessary funding. The combination of the winner-take-all character of the Westminster model and very modest public funding has acted to produce in the British Labour Party the classic case of a party reliant on trade union financial support.

Canada contains aspects of each of these models, and as a result there is a continual and substantial reliance on trade union funding. Indeed, the financial link lies at the very heart of the unions' relationship with the NDP. When the NDP was created from the remnants of the CCF, public financial support for parties had not yet been introduced. Throughout its almost 30-year history, the national CCF suffered from serious and continual financial difficulties (Lewis 1981). The widespread affiliation of unions to the new party, and the levying of annual affiliation fees, were explicit attempts to relieve this burden and to enable the party to introduce a national budgeting process. The party also raised funds through the sale of memberships, but given its federal structure, these were offered only at the provincial level, with a fraction of the funds transferred to the federal office. Thus, union financial contributions were crucial to the running of the party.

The situation has changed since the introduction of partial public funding for parties and the additional innovation of direct mail soliciting, which is strongly based on the system of tax credits to encourage public funding. Both measures have decreased the party's reliance on support from unions. Nonetheless, unions' financial support remains important and is especially important during elections. To understand this better, it is useful to examine the federal party's financial statements instead of the fiscal period returns. The latter are distorting because they present the party's revenues without taking account of the fact that much of the money is spent by the provincial sections. The party uses a general cost-sharing formula by which 85 cents of each dollar raised in a province remains in the province and 15 cents is transferred to the federal office. Thus, whereas the 1989 fiscal period return reports approximately $6 million in sectionally receipted income, the federal party budgeted $1.2 million from the sections in 1990. Likewise, a cost-sharing scheme exists for union affiliation fees, with 60 percent being retained by the federal party and 40 percent transferred to the province in which the local is affiliated.[3]

In 1990, union affiliation fees constituted approximately 11 percent of the federal party's budget. In contrast, the party budgeted $1.6 million, or 47 percent, of its funds from direct mail, and the unaudited financial statement indicates that 46 percent of funds came from direct mail (NDP 1991). Thus, individual party memberships and contributions account for well over 80 percent of the NDP's revenues in a non-election year. During election years, union contributions increase substantially to as much as $2 million, providing the federal party with less than half its revenues, but providing a very substantial sum nonetheless. However, as noted above, union contributions to the NDP in 1990 paled in comparison with corporate contributions to the Liberals ($4.6 million) and Conservatives ($6.3 million). As well, the NDP receives far more contributions from individual Canadians (89 000 individuals) than either the Liberals (20 000) or Conservatives (40 000) (Canada, Elections Canada 1990). Public funding has decreased but not eliminated the importance of union funding for the NDP.

UNION EVALUATIONS OF THE NDP CONNECTION

Evaluating the efficacy of the union connection with the NDP is a difficult task. As suggested previously, all social democratic parties in advanced industrial democracies are linked to their union movement in one way or another. However, there are as many variations on the theme as there are cases. Furthermore, each relationship has been developed in response to a set of conditions that vary across countries and across time. The relationship does not develop in a vacuum. In understanding the particular path that has been followed in a country, it is necessary to examine the way in which the union movement developed, the set of structures that exist outside Parliament for the representation of group interests, the nature of decision making within Parliament, the regime of election financing and other variables. It is only within such a broad context that one can understand and evaluate the union–party connection.

Three questions concerning the union–party relationship are of particular interest to the Royal Commission on Electoral Reform and Party Financing:

- Do union leaders see their relationship with the NDP as constraining their ability to deal more freely with government?
- How do union leaders justify using mandatory contributions of members who obviously do not support the NDP to support this party?
- How does the union–party relationship affect the "global" image of the NDP as a party that is beholden to a specific and exclusionary group?

Since these questions all concern the union–party relationship as it currently exists, it seemed they could best be answered by those most closely involved in maintaining the relationship. Consequently, interviews were conducted with key officials in the labour movement and the party in order to ascertain their views on these issues and to distil an overall assessment of the relationship, mainly from the unions' perspective. Interviews were conducted with senior officials in the Steelworkers and Auto Workers unions, with officers responsible for political action in the CLC and the Ontario Federation of Labour, and with key staff members of the NDP federal office and the provincial office of the Ontario New Democrats (see Interviews list).

There was a consensus among those interviewed that the relationship between unions and the NDP has, at most, a marginal effect on labour's relationship with a Liberal or Conservative government. This position was argued from one of several perspectives. Most respondents suggested that the major encumbrance to unions' relationship with the Liberals and Conservatives was the substantial and consistent differences in their positions on policy. It was further suggested that these differences in policy preferences led to labour's decision to lend greater organizational and financial support at the time of the NDP's creation. In other words, the period before the creation of the NDP, or preceding the development of the CCF, was not marked by the accommodation of labour's interests on the part of Liberal and Conservative governments. Similarly, one of the union leaders stated that the question was analogous to asking banks or business firms whether their contributions to the Liberals and Conservatives affected their relationship with an NDP government. This official suggested the answer would be negative – that any difficulty would arise from fundamental differences in philosophy, not from cash payments to political opponents. Furthermore, it was suggested that, when in power, it was up to the party to take into account divergent views, regardless of whether it receives funding from particular individuals, from businesses or from unions. Thus, there was an explicit recognition by several union leaders that although they consider the NDP to be the political arm of labour, it is incumbent upon the NDP government in Ontario to balance and reconcile competing interests. This same responsibility applies to other parties when they are in power.

All of the union and party leaders interviewed argued that the use of mandatory contributions for political purposes was both justified and essential in representing their members' interests. It should be noted, of course, that this issue is currently before the Supreme Court in the Lavigne case, with a decision expected soon (Beatty 1990, 187–214). Those interviewed provided remarkably similar justifications of their viewpoint. In its broadest form, it is based on the supposition that unions have an important role to play in the community. Beyond the representation of their members' interest in collective bargaining, this includes support for charitable organizations, involvement in the development of social policy alternatives based on social democratic principles, political education and the pursuit of legislative action. Thus, unions are involved in such agencies as the United Way, the Canadian Centre for Policy Alternatives and in leadership training seminars, as well as being involved in the pursuit of legislative action, lobbying efforts and the linkage with the NDP. The latter is therefore just one component of a larger commitment to participation in the affairs of the Canadian political community.

Despite the commitment to community involvement, there was general agreement and recognition that not all union members support union involvement outside collective bargaining, especially the donation of contributions to the NDP. However, it was noted that unlike some of the other areas of union involvement in the community (such as contributing to charitable organizations), the union links to the NDP are designed to be democratic and to recognize dissenting opinions. For example, union affiliation is not an administrative decision; it requires a vote of the union membership. Furthermore, that vote takes place at the local union level, where the efforts and actions of individuals and small groups can have a strong effect. In addition, any member of an affiliated local can choose to opt out of affiliation and thus does not have to pay the affiliation fee of 20 cents per month. As well, it is common practice for unions to affiliate less than their total membership, thereby ensuring that there are more members not affiliated than there are requests for affiliation. A rather extreme example occurred recently with CUPE 1000, a union of Ontario Hydro workers. When it first affiliated, it did so on the basis of 10 percent of its members, and it increased this to 50 percent after a trial period of affiliation. Several of those interviewed suggested that the openness of the affiliation decision, the ability to opt out and the affiliation of only a portion of members compare favourably with the process used when business organizations choose to give financial support to the Liberal or Conservative party.

The third question put to the labour and party leaders interviewed was whether the link with unions affects the "global image" of the party, suggesting that it is beholden to an exclusionary group. Three types of reply were received. Several respondents confirmed the general statement that the party was beholden to labour, but they viewed this as a virtue rather than a vice; that is, labour and the party were portrayed as two branches of a single movement, cooperating because they pursue similar ends, not because they are linked by other means. It follows from this perspective that the particular institutional configuration of labour–party links is less important than the intention of the party and labour to represent the interests of the working class and the socially disadvantaged.

A second view also affirmed the exclusionary image that followed from the union–party relationship but saw merit in the openness and honesty of the relationship. It was suggested that the "Quebec model," in which only individuals can contribute to a political party, encourages potential political donors to circumvent the rules by channelling organizational resources through individuals. This system was described as being easier to manipulate for businesses than for unions. The virtue of labour's links with the federal NDP is that the links are remarkably visible and that all financial contributions are reportable. Furthermore, it is the responsibility of the party, not the state, to be concerned about the party's image.

The third view took exception to the assumption that the party was beholden to labour. It was suggested that although the party's political opponents often try to portray it as being dominated by "union bosses," this is not supported by the evidence. The analysis presented in this study tends to confirm this assessment. The NDP receives the bulk of its funding from tax-creditable contributions from individual Canadians, and it obtains a far greater proportion of its money in this way than either the Liberals or Conservatives do. In addition, unions simply do not control the party's decision-making structure. Although it may well be true that Canadians view the NDP as being controlled by and beholden to organized labour, this perception fits poorly with the reality of the party's financing and decision making.

CONCLUSIONS AND RECOMMENDATIONS

Following the 1988 federal election, several high-profile union leaders were harshly and publicly critical of the NDP's campaign strategy and of labour's role within that strategy. The outbursts by Bob White of the Canadian Auto Workers and Gérard Docquier of the United Steelworkers of America took many Canadians by surprise. They were inconsistent with the popular perception that organized labour had a controlling influence in the NDP. Bob White and Gérard Docquier knew otherwise. The experience of 1988 led to a re-evaluation of the union–party relationship and to a reaffirmation of labour's commitment to the party. If anything, this commitment has grown in the intervening years, and yet remains based on the fundamental premises on which it has always been based – that the link will be mainly through the affiliation of union locals to the national party and that labour is an important section of the party. The review process has led to a modest increase in labour's representation on several of the party's organs, but everywhere it remains a distinct minority voice. The question for the Royal Commission is whether this constitutes an inappropriate relationship. The recommendations are as follows:

1. The NDP Should Not Be Treated Differently from Other Parties

One of the principles upon which democracies function is the ability of individuals and groups to organize for political purposes. This organization takes place both within and outside parties. However, there is no one type of organization that is superior to all others. Groups organize themselves differently, and therefore their involvement in political parties is often organized differently. As noted above, social democratic political parties tend to organize themselves with linkages to the labour movement, but even here the variation is substantial. The fact that the NDP provides labour organizations with a role within its organizational structure in exchange for financial and other support should not lead one to conclude that the relationship between the two should be regulated differently from the relationships affecting the Liberals and Conservatives. In fact, the data suggest that the latter parties are more heavily reliant on corporate sponsors than the NDP is on unions.

2. The Principle in Regulating Parties Should Be toward Making the Structure Visible and Open, Not Regulating the Outcome

It should be recognized that a vast array of institutional characteristics play a role in the development of political arrangements. For example, it was noted that the nature of executive-legislative relations, the degree of cooperation and compromise among competing interests, the centralization of the union movement, the degree of public funding of parties and other characteristics can all affect the relationship that develops between unions and a party. The relationship did not develop in a vacuum, and changes should not be proposed without taking into account the rationale for the existing relationship. Openness should be an overarching principle in the internal structure of parties. If the structures are open and visible, then the electorate can decide whether a relationship is appropriate.

3. Parties Should Be Funded as Much as Possible through Public Sources

The current system of partial public funding for parties rests on a strong foundation. In effect, parties compete for public funding, based on their public support and their capacity to mount effective fund-raising enterprises. However, all the major parties still go to outside sources, either businesses or unions, for a substantial amount of funds. The Liberals and Conservatives get approximately 50 percent of their funds from public sources, and the New Democrats get from 60 to 80 percent. The Commission should look into ways of increasing the proportion of public funding for all parties. One way is to extend the 75 percent tax-creditable threshold to a higher contributing level, such as $500.

4. One Should Not Be Too Concerned about Union Affiliation with the NDP

The courts will soon be deciding on the unions' use of their revenues for political purposes. However, it has been noted that no individual is required to contribute to a political fund as a result of his or her union's decision to affiliate. The decision on affiliation is itself taken according to democratic procedures. The Commission's interest in this area, if any, should be limited to ensuring that the procedures meet generally accepted norms of democracy. In particular, guidelines could be established for the nature of balloting and for the periodic review of affiliation decisions. Nonetheless, in general, the use of affiliation corresponds to a union's organization better than it does a business's organization, and a decision to preclude it could unfairly disadvantage unions.

ABBREVIATIONS

A.C.	Appeal Cases
c.	chapter
CFDT	Confédération française democratique du travail
CGT	Confédération générale du travail
FO	Force ouvrière
H.L.	House of Lords
LO	Landsorganisationen i Sverige (Sweden)
	Landsorganisation (Denmark)
	Landsorganisasjon (Norway)

NOTES

This study was completed in June 1991.

1. Organized labour's ties with the CCF tended to be more informal, although some unions did affiliate with the CCF, and from 1943 on, the CCL declared that the CCF was the "political arm of labour."

2. One should also bear in mind that the union delegates may not be representative of the attitudes of rank-and-file union members. They constitute a part of the union élite.

3. For a discussion of the complexity surrounding revenue transfers between the federal and provincial wings of the NDP, see Stanbury (1991).

INTERVIEWS

These interviews were conducted in February 1991.

Kerwin, Pat, political education director, Canadian Labour Congress, Ottawa.

Lewis, Michael, representative, United Steelworkers of America, Toronto.

Marzetti, Jill, provincial secretary, Ontario New Democratic Party, Toronto.

McKenzie, David, assistant to the national director, United Steelworkers of America, Toronto.

Nash, Peggy, assistant to the president, Canadian Auto Workers, Toronto.

Paré, Jim, director of organization, Ontario Federation of Labour, Toronto.

Proctor, Dick, federal secretary, New Democratic Party, Ottawa.

REFERENCES

Amalgamated Society of Railway Servants v. Osborne, [1910] A.C. 87 (H.L.).

Archer, Keith. 1990. *Political Choices and Electoral Consequences: A Study of Organized Labour and the New Democratic Party.* Montreal and Kingston: McGill-Queen's University Press.

———. 1991. "Leadership Selection in the New Democratic Party." In *Canadian Political Parties: Leaders, Candidates and Organization,* ed. Herman Bakvis. Vol. 13 of the research studies of the Royal Commission on Electoral Reform and Party Financing. Ottawa and Toronto: RCERPF/Dundurn.

Archer, Keith, and Alan Whitehorn. 1990a. "Opinion Structure among New Democratic Party Activists: A Comparison with Liberals and Conservatives." *Canadian Journal of Political Science* 23:101–13.

———. 1990b. "Organized Labour in the New Democratic Party." Paper presented at the annual meeting of the Canadian Political Science Association, University of Victoria, 27–29 May.

———. 1991. "Opinion Structure among Party Activists: A Comparison of New Democrats, Liberals and Conservatives." In *Party Politics in Canada.* 6th ed., ed. Hugh G. Thorburn. Scarborough: Prentice-Hall.

Beatty, David. 1990. *Talking Heads and the Supremes: The Canadian Production of Constitutional Review.* Toronto: Carswell.

Blake, Donald. 1988. "Division and Cohesion: The Major Parties." In *Party Democracy in Canada: The Politics of National Party Conventions,* ed. George Perlin. Scarborough: Prentice-Hall.

Bornstein, Stephen. 1984. "States and Unions from Postwar Settlement to Contemporary Stalemate." In *The State in Capitalist Europe: A Casebook,* ed. Stephen Bornstein, David Held and Joel Krieger. London: George Allen and Unwin.

Brodie, Janine. 1985. "From Waffles to Grits: A Decade in the Life of the New Democratic Party." In *Party Politics in Canada*. 5th ed., ed. Hugh G. Thorburn. Scarborough: Prentice-Hall.

Canada. Elections Canada. 1991. "Registered Political Parties Fiscal Period Returns, 1990." Ottawa: Minister of Supply and Services Canada.

Canada. Labour Canada. 1990. *Directory of Labour Organizations in Canada, 1990/91*. Ottawa: Minister of Supply and Services Canada.

Crouch, Colin. 1982. "The Peculiar Relationship: The Party and the Unions." In *The Politics of the Labour Party*, ed. Dennis Kavanagh. London: George Allen and Unwin.

Dalton, Russell J. 1989. "The German Voter." In *Developments in West German Politics*, ed. Gordon Smith, William E. Patterson and Peter H. Merkl. London: Macmillan.

Einhorn, Eric S., and John Logue. 1988. "Continuity and Change in the Scandinavian Party System." In *Parties and Party Systems in Liberal Democracies*, ed. Steven B. Wolinetz. London: Routledge.

Elvander, Nils. 1974. "In Search of New Relationships: Parties, Unions and Salaried Employees' Associations in Sweden." *Industrial and Labor Relations Review* 281:60–74.

Engelmann, Fredrick C. 1988. "The Austrian Party System: Continuity and Change." In *Parties and Party Systems in Liberal Democracies*, ed. Steven B. Wolinetz. London: Routledge.

Ewing, Keith. 1987. *The Funding of Political Parties in Britain*. Cambridge: Cambridge University Press.

Fatchett, Derek. 1984. "Trade Union Political Funds." *Industrial Relations Journal* 153:30–35.

Gerlich, Peter. 1987. "Consociationalism to Competition: The Austrian Party System since 1945." In *Party Systems in Denmark, Austria, Switzerland, The Netherlands and Belgium*, ed. Hans Daalder. London: Pinter.

Hackett, Robert A. 1979. "The Waffle Conflict in the NDP." In *Party Politics in Canada*. 4th ed., ed. Hugh G. Thorburn. Scarborough: Prentice-Hall.

Heckscher, D. 1958. "Sweden." In *Interest Groups on Four Continents*, ed. H.W. Ehrmann. Pittsburgh: University of Pittsburgh Press.

Horowitz, Gad. 1968. *Canadian Labour in Politics*. Toronto: University of Toronto Press.

Koelble, Thomas A. 1987. "Trade Unions, Party Activists, and Politicians: The Struggle for Power over Party Rules in the British Labour Party and the West German Social Democratic Party." *Comparative Politics* 9:253–66.

LaGroye, Jacques. 1989. "Change and Permanence in Political Parties." *Political Studies* 37:362–75.

Lewis, David. 1981. *The Good Fight: Political Memoirs, 1909–1958*. Toronto: Macmillan.

Leys, Colin. 1989. *Politics in Britain: From Labourism to Thatcherism*. Rev. ed. London: Verso.

Markovits, Andrei S., and Christopher S. Allen. 1984. "Trade Unions and the Economic Crisis: The West German Case." In *Unions and Economic Crisis: Britain, West Germany and Sweden*, ed. Peter Gourevitch, Andrew Martin, George Ross, Christopher Allen, Stephen Bornstein and Andrei Markovits. London: George Allen and Unwin.

———. 1989. "The Trade Unions." In *Developments in West German Politics*, ed. Gordon Smith, William E. Patterson and Peter H. Merkl. London: Macmillan.

Martin, Peggy Gill. 1974. "Strategic Opportunities and Limitations: The Norwegian Labour Party and the Trade Unions." *Industrial and Labor Relations Review* 281:75–88.

Minkin, Lewis. 1974. "The British Labour Party and the Trade Unions: Crisis and Compact." *Industrial and Labor Relations Review* 281:1–37.

———. 1978. *The Labour Party Conference: A Study in the Politics of Intra-Party Democracy*. London: Allen Lane.

Morton, Desmond. 1986. *The New Democrats, 1961–1986: The Politics of Change*. Toronto: Copp Clark Pitman.

New Democratic Party. 1989. *Report of the Election Review Committee*. Ottawa.

———. 1990. *Organizations Affiliated to the New Democratic Party*, for period ending 1 August 1990. Ottawa.

———. 1991. *Statement of Revenue (Unaudited)*, for period ending 31 December 1990. Ottawa.

Olson, Mancur. 1965. *The Logic of Collective Action: Public Goods and the Theory of Groups*. Cambridge: Harvard University Press.

Pedersen, Mogens N. 1987. "The Danish 'Working Multiparty System': Breakdown or Adaptation?" In *Party Systems in Denmark, Austria, Switzerland, The Netherlands and Belgium*, ed. Hans Daalder. London: Pinter.

Pinto-Duschinsky, Michael. 1989. "Trends in British Party Funding, 1983–1987." *Parliamentary Affairs* 422:197–212.

Reynaud, Jean-Daniel. 1975. "Trade Unions and Political Parties in France: Some Recent Trends." *Industrial and Labor Relations Review* 282:208–25.

Smith, Gordon. 1980. *Politics in Western Europe: A Comparative Analysis*. 3d ed. New York: Holmes and Meier.

———. 1983. *Politics in Western Europe: A Comparative Analysis*. 4th ed. Aldershot: Gower.

Stanbury, W.T. 1991. *Money in Politics: Financing Federal Parties and Candidates in Canada*. Vol. 1 of the research studies of the Royal Commission on Electoral Reform and Party Financing. Ottawa and Toronto: RCERPF/Dundurn.

Towers, Brian. 1989. "Running the Gauntlet: British Trade Unions under Thatcher, 1979–1988." *Industrial and Labor Relations Review* 422:163–80.

Trades Union Congress (Britain). 1984. *Report of Conference Proceedings, 1984*. London.

———. 1985. *Report of Conference Proceedings, 1985*. London.

United Kingdom. *Trade Disputes and Trade Unions Act, 1927*, 17 & 18 Geo. V, c. 22.

———. *Trade Union Act, 1913*, 2 & 3 Geo. V, c. 30.

———. *Trade Union Act, 1984*, 1984, c. 49.

Whitehorn, Alan. 1989. "The NDP Election Campaign: Dashed Hopes." In Alan Frizzell, Jon Pammett and Anthony Westell, *The Canadian General Election of 1988*. Ottawa: Carleton University Press.

Whiteley, Paul. 1983. *The Labour Party in Crisis*. London: Methuen.

Willey, Richard J. 1974. "Trade Unions and Political Parties in the Federal Republic of Germany." *Industrial and Labor Relations Review* 281:38–59.

Wilson, Frank L. 1988. "The French Party System in the 1980s." In *Parties and Party Systems in Liberal Democracies*, ed. Steven B. Wolinetz. London: Routledge.

Windmuller, John. 1975. "European Labor and Politics: A Symposium." *Industrial and Labor Relations Review* 282:203–208.

Young, Walter D. 1969. *The Anatomy of a Party: The National CCF 1932–1961*. Toronto: University of Toronto Press.

Contributors to Volume 13

Keith Archer	University of Calgary
R. K. Carty	University of British Columbia
William M. Chandler	McMaster University
Lynda Erickson	Simon Fraser University
Réjean Pelletier	Université Laval
George Perlin	Queen's University
Alan Siaroff	McMaster University

Acknowledgements

The Royal Commission on Electoral Reform and Party Financing and the publishers wish to acknowledge with gratitude the permission of the following to reprint and translate material:

Oxford University Press Canada; *Le Soleil.*

Care has been taken to trace the ownership of copyright material used in the text, including the tables and figures. The authors and publishers welcome any information enabling them to rectify any reference or credit in subsequent editions.

~

Consistent with the Commission's objective of promoting full participation in the electoral system by all segments of Canadian society, gender neutrality has been used wherever possible in the editing of the research studies.

THE COLLECTED RESEARCH STUDIES*

---

* The titles of studies may not be final in all cases.

ROBERT A. HACKETT,
WITH THE ASSISTANCE OF
JAMES MACKINTOSH,
DAVID ROBINSON AND
ARLENE SHWETZ

Smaller Voices: Minor Parties,
Campaign Communication and
the News Media

EILEEN SAUNDERS

Mass Media and the Reproduction
of Marginalization

VOLUME 23
Canadian Political Parties in the Constituencies:
A Local Perspective

R.K. CARTY

Canadian Political Parties in the
Constituencies: A Local Perspective

COMMISSION ORGANIZATION

CHAIRMAN
Pierre Lortie

COMMISSIONERS
Pierre Fortier
Robert Gabor
William Knight
Lucie Pépin

SENIOR OFFICERS

Executive Director
Guy Goulard

Director of Research
Peter Aucoin

Special Adviser to the Chairman
Jean-Marc Hamel

Research
F. Leslie Seidle,
  Senior Research Coordinator

Legislation
Jules Brière, Senior Adviser
Gérard Bertrand
Patrick Orr

Coordinators
Herman Bakvis
Michael Cassidy
Frederick J. Fletcher
Janet Hiebert
Kathy Megyery
Robert A. Milen
David Small

Communications and Publishing
Richard Rochefort, Director
Hélène Papineau, Assistant
  Director
Paul Morisset, Editor
Kathryn Randle, Editor

Assistant Coordinators
David Mac Donald
Cheryl D. Mitchell

Finance and Administration
Maurice R. Lacasse, Director

Contracts and Personnel
Thérèse Lacasse, Chief

EDITORIAL, DESIGN AND PRODUCTION SERVICES

DUNDURN PRESS

J. Kirk Howard, *President*
Ian Low, *Comptroller*
Jeanne MacDonald, *Project Coordinator*

Avivah Wargon, *Managing and Production Editor*
Beth Ediger, *Managing Editor*
John St. James, *Managing Editor*
Karen Heese, *Special Project Assistant*

Ruth Chernia, *Tables Editor*
Victoria Grant, *Legal Editor*
Michèle Breton, *Special Editorial Assistant*

Editorial Staff   Elliott Chapin, Peggy Foy, Lily Hobel, Marilyn Hryciuk, Madeline Koch, Elizabeth Mitchell, John Shoesmith, Nadine Stoikoff, Shawn Syms, Anne Vespry.

Copy Editors   Carol Anderson, Elizabeth d'Anjou, Jane Becker, Diane Brassolotto, Elizabeth Driver, Curtis Fahey, Tony Fairfield, Freya Godard, Frances Hanna, Kathleen Harris, Andria Hourwich, Greg Ioannou, Carlotta Lemieux, Elsha Leventis, David McCorquodale, Virginia Smith, Gail Thorson, Louise Wood.

Formatting   Green Graphics; Joanne Green, *Formatting Coordinator*; *Formatters*   Linda Carroll, Mary Ann Cattral, Gail Nina, Eva Payne, Jacqueline Hope Raynor, Andy Tong, Carla Vonn Worden, Laura Wilkins.